Bloody Zion

Refuting the Jewish Fables That Sustain Israel's War Against God and Man

Edward Hendrie

"They build up Zion with blood, and Jerusalem with iniquity." Micah 3:10.

"This witness is true. Wherefore rebuke them sharply, that they may be sound in the faith; Not giving heed to Jewish fables, and commandments of men, that turn from the truth." Titus 1:13-14.

Copyright © 2012 by Edward Hendrie
All rights reserved.

ISBN-13: 978-0-9832627-6-3
ISBN-10: 0983262764

Other books by Edward Hendrie:

- 9/11-Enemies Foreign and Domestic
- Solving the Mystery of BABYLON THE GREAT
- The Anti-Gospel
- What Shall I Do to Inherit Eternal Life?
- Murder, Rape, and Torture in a Catholic Nunnery
- Antichrist: The Beast Revealed
- The Greatest Lie on Earth
- The Greatest Lie on Earth (Expanded Edition)
- The Sphere of Influence
- The Damnable Heresy of Salvation by Dead Faith

EdwardHendrie@gmail.com

Edward Hendrie rests on the authority of the Holy Bible alone for doctrine. He considers the Holy Bible to be the inspired and inerrant word of God. Favorable citation by Edward Hendrie to an authority outside the Holy Bible on a particular issue should not be interpreted to mean that he agrees with all of the doctrines and beliefs of the cited authority.

All Scripture references are to the Authorized (King James) Version of the Holy Bible, unless otherwise indicated.

"Finally, my brethren, be strong in the Lord, and in the power of his might. Put on the whole armour of God, that ye may be able to stand against the wiles of the devil. For we wrestle not against flesh and blood, but against principalities, against powers, against the rulers of the darkness of this world, against spiritual wickedness in high places." Ephesians 6:10-12.

Table of Contents

Introduction.................................... 1

1 Stripping Sheep's Clothing From a Wolf 8

2 Salvation Without Jesus Christ 14

3 Who is Abraham's Seed?.................... 23

4 The True Israel of God...................... 36

5 The Ingrafting of the Natural Branches 56

6 Dispensational Zionism 89

7 Tim LaHaye Left Jesus Behind 113

8 The Fifth Column.......................... 126

9 Treasonous *Provocateurs*................... 142

10 Protocols of the Learned Elders of Zion 155

11 Billy Graham: Zionist Shill 162

12 Freemasonry: Judaism For Gentiles........... 170

13 Proofs of a Conspiracy..................... 196

14 The Love of Money is the Root of All Evil..... 208

15 Zionism is Communism.................... 214

16 The Dark Secret of Judaism................. 224

17	Catholic Judaism	261
18	The Occult Catholic Liturgy	304
19	Censoring the Gospel	316
20	Zionist Nazis	325
21	Carroll Quigley's Limited Hangout	350
22	The Tyranny of Zionism	366
23	License to Kill	386
24	Teaching Religious Myths as Science	390
25	Jewish Media Control	405
26	The Real Reason Politicians Support Israel	415
Conclusion		433
Endnotes		445

Bloody Zion Banned

Lulu Press was a printer and distributor used by this author. Lulu Press terminated this author's account without informing me they had done so. I found out my account had been shut down on August 25, 2022, when I could not log in to it and sought support from the technical staff. Lulu Press responded to my support request by informing me that my account had been terminated because my book, *Bloody Zion*, violated its membership agreement. Lulu Press did not simply refuse to print the book; it deleted my entire account, which contained more than ten books published in hard copy and ebook formats. *Bloody Zion* had been printed by Lulu Press and listed on its bookstore since 2012.

In their August 25, 2022 email, the Lulu Press Questionable Content Team gave several alternative reasons for deleting my account, ranging from invasion of privacy to defamation. They did not specify which was the actual reason. And none of the enumerated reasons applied to *Bloody Zion*. But they had a nebulous catch-all standard that allowed them to arbitrarily and capriciously delete an account for almost any reason. They stated in the email notice that an alternative reason for deleting my account could be if my book contained material that was "otherwise questionable and/or determined by us in our sole discretion to violate our Membership Agreement." Lulu Press deleted my account with a perfunctory statement: "As a result, we must remove your Content from availability and terminate your Lulu Account."

Lulu Press did not specify what part of the membership agreement the book violated, and when I emailed them asking how my book violated that agreement, they refused to respond. Lulu Press certainly was not going to admit the real reason for deleting my account. It did so to stop the circulation of *Bloody Zion* because it accurately portrayed the hegemony of the worldwide Zionist conspiracy against God and man.

The Lulu Press's termination of this author's account was followed on December 2, 2022, by Amazon removing the hard copy of *Bloody Zion* from Amazon's website. The hard copy of *Bloody Zion* had been listed on Amazon since approximately 2012. Amazon also suspended this author's Kindle Direct Publishing (KDP) account, containing eight of my ebooks, including *Bloody Zion*, published for Kindle.

When this author asked Amazon why they suspended my KDP account, they informed me that *Bloody Zion* contained content they "considered offensive" in violation of their content guidelines. Undoubtedly, Amazon removed the hard copy of *Bloody Zion* for the same reason they shut down my KDP account.

As a condition to lifting the KDP account suspension, Amazon demanded I declare in writing that "I will remove any previously published titles that do not meet these guidelines." Such a declaration would amount to an implied admission that *Bloody Zion* contained offensive content as defined by Amazon, which I would not do. I contested Amazon's December 12, 2022, KDP shutdown; I asked Amazon in an email to point to a passage they deemed offensive in my book. Amazon responded to my question by falsely claiming that they had not received a reply from me. It seems that Amazon will only accept capitulation, and because I would not admit the violation, they ignored my response. In that same email, Amazon told me, "[w]e are terminating your account immediately." Amazon explained that "[a]s part of the termination process: We will close your account; You'll receive any unpaid royalties you have earned; You'll no longer have access to your accounts; This includes, editing your titles, viewing your reports and accessing any other information within your account; All of your published titles will be removed from sale on Amazon; Additionally, as per our Terms and Conditions, you aren't allowed to open any new KDP accounts."

Lulu Press and Amazon's account terminations testify to the power and influence of the Jewish world oligarchy. Just as when Jesus Christ walked the earth, so is it today; governments, corporations, and individuals are all imbued with "fear of the Jews." *See* John 7:13.

The actions of shutting down my accounts and banning *Bloody Zion* bear witness to the validity of the book's evidence about the worldwide Zionist conspiracy against God and man. If the information in the book were false, then the Zionist cabal would want the book to remain in circulation so that they could hold it up, refute its claims, and prove their innocence. But the information in the book is verifiably accurate; they cannot refute it, so the Zionist Jews must use their power to suppress the book. The censoring of the book authenticates its contents.

There is no doubt that this is just the beginning of the censorship of this book. It presently remains for sale in other venues. But the Jewish influence is broad, and the noose is tightening. Please share this crucial information with others while the book is still available. God commands us to get wisdom and understanding. "Wisdom is the principal thing; therefore get wisdom: and with all thy getting get understanding." Proverbs 4:7. Ruin awaits those who violate God's command and willfully remain ignorant. "My people perish from a lack of knowledge." Hosea 4:6. Above all, pray to the Lord Jesus Christ. "The effectual fervent prayer of a righteous man availeth much." James 5:16.

Edward Hendrie
December 18, 2022

Introduction

During the Babylonian captivity, an occult society of Jews replaced God's commands with Babylonian dogma. Their new religion became Judaism. Jesus explained the corruption of the Judaic religion: "Howbeit in vain do they worship me, teaching for doctrines the commandments of men." (Mark 7:7) Jesus revealed the satanic origin of Judaism when he stated: "Ye are of your father the devil, and the lusts of your father ye will do." John 8:44.

The Old Testament documents the long history of Jewish rebellion against God. The rebellion by the Jews against God is defined by the crucifixion of Jesus Christ, the Lord of Lords and King of Kings. Revelation 17:14. The Jews are in a spiritual war against God and a bloody war against man. Micah 3:10 is as applicable today as it was when it was written thousands of years ago: "They build up Zion with blood, and Jerusalem with iniquity." Micah 3:10.

The Jews are in a Babylonian inspired conspiracy against God and man. Conspiracy is a concept that has been propagandized into disfavor, much to the delight of Satan and his minions, who are only too happy to push the idea that if one believes there is a world conspiracy against Jesus Christ and his followers, he must be a radical on the fringe of society or worse. Most people are afraid of being marginalized and thus avoid speaking of conspiracies, especially when it is a Jewish conspiracy. People instead try to construe events as coincidental, when in fact they can only be adequately explained as the product of prior agreements of conspirators who have combined in coordinated actions.

The bible explains that many evil events are brought about by conspiratorial agreements. For example, we read in the following passage, how the Jewish religious leaders conspired to kill Jesus.

> Then assembled together the chief priests, and the scribes, and the elders of the people, unto the palace of the high priest, who was called Caiaphas, And consulted that they might take Jesus by subtilty, and kill him. (Matthew 26:3-4)

The religious leaders stirred up the people, who then persuaded the Roman governor, Pontius Pilate, to crucify Jesus. "[T]he chief priests and elders persuaded the multitude that they should ask Barabbas, and destroy Jesus." (Matthew 27:20) The methods used by God's adversaries have not changed. Today, the Jews control the mass media, which they use to propagandize the people into pushing the politicians into doing their bidding against God and his anointed.

This conspiracy against the LORD and his anointed has been festering since the fall of man in the garden of Eden and involves the kings and rulers of the earth.

> Why do the heathen rage, and the people imagine a vain thing? **The kings of the earth set themselves, and the rulers take counsel together, against the LORD, and against his anointed, saying, Let us break their bands asunder, and cast away their cords from us.**

He that sitteth in the heavens shall laugh: the Lord shall have them in derision. (Psalms 2:1-4)

This monstrous conspiracy, while it involves men, it is not headed by a man. "For we wrestle not against flesh and blood, but against principalities, against powers, against the rulers of the darkness of this world, against spiritual wickedness in high places." (Ephesians 6:12) The kingpin of this diabolical conspiracy is that terrible dragon, Satan. He is the adversary of Almighty God. He is also an adversary to all of God's creation.

Notice in Ezekiel 22 that God has identified those in the conspiracy against him as the Jewish prophets and priests who violated his laws and were as ravening wolves shedding blood and destroying souls. We see that same conduct among the Jewish hierarchy today.

> **There is a conspiracy** of her prophets in the midst thereof, like a roaring lion ravening the prey; they have devoured souls; they have taken the treasure and precious things; they have made her many widows in the midst thereof. Her priests have violated my law, and have profaned mine holy things: they have put no difference between the holy and profane, neither have they shewed difference between the unclean and the clean, and have hid their eyes from my sabbaths, and I am profaned among them. Her princes in the midst thereof are like wolves ravening the prey, to shed blood, and to destroy souls, to get dishonest gain. And her prophets have daubed them with untempered morter, seeing vanity, and divining lies unto them, saying, Thus saith the Lord GOD, when the LORD hath not spoken.

(Ezekiel 22:25-28)

God explains that the inhabitants of earthly Jerusalem had refused to hear God's words (i.e., his gospel). Incidently, gospel literally means God spell (that is God's word). The Jews went after and served other gods. That is just as it is today in Jerusalem.

And the LORD said unto me, A conspiracy is found among the men of Judah, and among the inhabitants of Jerusalem. They are turned back to the iniquities of their forefathers, which refused to hear my words; and they went after other gods to serve them: the house of Israel and the house of Judah have broken my covenant which I made with their fathers. (Jeremiah 11:9-10)

Jews today call earthly Jerusalem the "holy land." However, the spiritual state of earthly Jerusalem is so corrupt that God calls it "Sodom and Egypt." Revelation 11:8.

Jesus told Pontius Pilate: "My kingdom is not of this world." John 18:36. God has a spiritual Zion that is in a heavenly Jerusalem. Hebrews 12:22; Revelation 21:10. Jesus Christ is the chief corner stone laid by God in Zion. 1 Peter 2:6. Those who believe in Jesus Christ are living stones in the spiritual house of God. 1 Peter 2:5; Ephesians 2:20-22. Believers are in Jesus and Jesus is in believers. John 14:20; 17:20-23. All who are elected by God to believe in Jesus Christ are part of the heavenly Zion, without regard to whether they are Jews or Gentiles. Romans 10:12.

All Christians are the body of Christ, without regard to their ethnic background. "Now ye are the body of Christ, and members in particular." 1 Corinthians 12:27. There is one spiritual body of Christ, with Jesus the head. Colossians 1:18.

Satan is a great adversary of God, who has created his own devilish religions. Satan's religions are antithetical to God's pure religion. Satan has created many counterfeit "Christian" denominations. Satan also has a counterfeit earthly Zion. Indeed, Satan's Zion must be earthly; Satan has no choice, since he has been cast out of heaven. "Christian" Zionism not only has an imitation earthly Zion, it also has an imitation earthly people to take the place of the spiritual church of Jesus Christ. The ministers of the counterfeit "Christianity" mixed with counterfeit Zionism appear as gentle lambs of mercy, but spiritually they are ravening wolves. Jesus warned of such:

> **Beware of false prophets, which come to you in sheep's clothing, but inwardly they are ravening wolves**. Ye shall know them by their fruits. Do men gather grapes of thorns, or figs of thistles? Even so every good tree bringeth forth good fruit; but a corrupt tree bringeth forth evil fruit. A good tree cannot bring forth evil fruit, neither *can* a corrupt tree bring forth good fruit. Every tree that bringeth not forth good fruit is hewn down, and cast into the fire. Wherefore **by their fruits ye shall know them**. (Matthew 7:15-20)

In 2 Corinthians 11, we read this warning about false brethren who would appear as ministers of righteousness:

> For such are false apostles, deceitful workers, transforming themselves into the apostles of Christ. And no marvel; for Satan himself is transformed into an angel of light. Therefore it is no great thing if his ministers also be transformed as the ministers of righteousness; whose end shall be according to their works. (2 Corinthians 11:13-15)

There is a leaked document that reveals a plan for an earthly Zion, which is intended to be the headquarters of a world government under Jewish communist rule. "Christian" Zionists are a crucial part of the Zionist plans to bring about their world kingdom headquartered in Israel. Not all "Christian" Zionists are knowing participants in a conspiracy against God. Some of them are ignorant and have been duped by the clever sophistry of Satan's minions. Many other "Christian" Zionists are knowing participants in the satanic plan for world domination. One thing that Jewish Zionists do not want "Christian" Zionists to know is that the Jews consider their Gentile cohorts "useful idiots" to be disposed of once they attain their satanic kingdom.

Throughout this book "Christian" Zionism will be described with quotation marks around the word "Christian." That is because "Christian" Zionism is not Christian at all. Indeed, "Christian" Zionism is not truly Zionism in the biblical sense either. This book exposes "Christian" Zionism as a Judaic/Babylonian religion that is being used to promote Satan's war against God and man. In a very real sense, "Christian" Zionist churches are more akin in their theology to Jewish Synagogues than to Christian churches.

This book is written to open the eyes of those who have been chosen for salvation but have been temporarily seduced by the doctrines of "Christian" Zionism, Judaism, Roman Catholicism, and other worldly religions, and to reveal to the Christian world the ravenous religious wolves in sheep's clothing who are prowling in their midst. These religious charlatans have taken on a form of godliness, but inwardly they are hypocrites, speaking lies. This book pulls back the veil and takes the reader inside the spiritual conspiracy to see the dark secrets of Satan's religions.

The Holy Spirit predicted that many would depart from the faith of Jesus Christ, being seduced by doctrines of devils:

Now the Spirit speaketh expressly, that in the latter times some shall depart from the faith, giving heed to seducing spirits, and doctrines of devils; Speaking lies in hypocrisy; having their conscience seared with a hot iron. (1 Timothy 4:1-2)

Jewish scholar Henry Makow, Ph.D., succinctly describes the dangers of the Jewish fables that sustain Zionism:

> Mightier than the nuclear bomb, the lie is Satan's most powerful weapon. The bomb merely devastates. The lie steals souls. It enlists millions of naive people to Satan's cause.[1]

1 Stripping Sheep's Clothing From a Wolf

Isaiah told the people of Jerusalem: "O my people, they which lead thee cause thee to err." Isaiah 3:12. John Hagee is a modern day false prophet who is leading God's people astray. John Hagee is the senior pastor of Cornerstone Church in San Antonio, Texas.[2] Cornerstone Church of San Antonio is ranked by Outreach Magazine as the 65th largest non-Catholic church in the United States, with more than 19,000 active members and an average service attendance of more than 8,000.[3]

Cornerstone Church and Hagee Ministries state the following as part of their doctrinal beliefs: "We believe in the scripture as the inspired Word of God and that it is the complete revelation of God's will for mankind. We believe in the absolute authority of the scripture to govern the affairs of men."[4] It seems, however, that Hagee is only paying lip service to his belief in the authority of scripture. If Hagee truly believed in the divine authority of the bible, he would immediately step down as senior pastor of Cornerstone Church, because he does not meet the foundational qualifications for a pastor as set forth in the bible.

Hagee has had two wives. The bible requires that a church overseer "must be blameless, the husband of one wife." 1 Timothy 3:2. Hagee had two children with his first wife, Martha, whom he divorced in 1975. In 1976, he married his second wife, the former Diana Castro, with whom he had three children. Hagee's divorce and remarriage disqualify him from being a Christian pastor.

Another qualification of a church overseer is that he must be "blameless" and "of good behaviour." 1 Timothy 3:2. Hagee is not blameless and is not of good behavior. G. Richard Fisher reveals that contemporaneously with Hagee's 1975 divorce: "[i]n a letter to the church, Hagee admitted immorality, which later became part of the court records in the custody battle."[5]

Hagee is the President and CEO of John Hagee Ministries.[6] He oversees an empire that includes a national radio and television ministry that broadcasts in the United States on 160 TV stations, 50 radio stations, including shows on the Trinity Broadcasting Network (TBN) and The Inspiration Network (INSP).

Hagee is an ardent Zionist who believes that the bible commands all Christians to support the state of Israel. He believes that "Jerusalem is the spiritual home for millions of Jews and Christians in America."[7] Hagee's theology is carnal and temporal, wherein he views Jerusalem as a "holy city" where the very ground is sacred. In reference to Jerusalem, he stated during an interview that "[t]he very dust in the street is sacred in this holy city."[8] God, disagrees with Hagee and states that Jerusalem is not a holy city, but rather "spiritually is called Sodom and Egypt." Revelation 11:8.

Hagee is the founder and National Chairman of Christians United for Israel.[9] Hagee has traveled to Israel more than 20 times and has met with every Israeli prime minister since Menechim Begin.[10] John Hagee Ministries has spent millions of dollars to bring Soviet Jews to Israel.[11] The San Antonio *B'nai B'rith* Council gave Hagee its Humanitarian of the Year Award.[12] That award had never before been given to a Gentile. Hagee was also given the Zionist Organization of America's Israel Award by the Jewish Community of Dallas, Texas.

Hagee has been characterized as the Dr. Strangelove of "Christian" pastors for his bloodthirsty call for the United States to join with Israel in a preemptive military strike against Iran.[13] Max Blumenthal of *The Nation* states: "The only way to defeat the Iranian evildoers, he [Hagee] says, is a full-scale military assault."[14] Hagee seems to relish the idea of a preemptive military strike against Iran. As one defense analyst puts it: "Apparently, the bigger and bloodier the war, the closer the day of Armageddon looms. And the end of the world is what he seeks."[15]

Hagee's war drum for a preemptive attack on Iran can only be described as an attempt to incite a war crime and is inconsistent with the gospel of Christ. His strange theology has hardened his heart. He is hell-bent on fulfilling what he believes is God's plan for Israel; he apparently has a desire to hasten Armageddon.[16]

Thomas L. McFadden of the American Free Press explains the bloody mission of John Hagee:

> John Hagee, the megachurch televangelist, is approaching the Washington, D.C. area again, ready to land in his private jet on July 20. An army of politicians and wide-eyed believers will follow this professed "man of God" who outdoes, in a sinister way, televangelists Pat Robertson and the late Jerry Falwell combined. Although Falwell did receive a Lear jet from

the Israeli government in 1979, he never had an 8,000-acre luxury ranch loaded with mansions, hotels, barns and a private landing strip. But Hagee, the "corpulent con man," as he is popularly known, does.

This Texas pirate is running a large number of organizations all geared toward spreading the word of the coming rapture and promoting war for Israel.

Cornerstone Church in San Antonio and John Hagee Ministries telecast his national radio and television ministry, carried in America on 160 TV stations, 50 radio stations and eight networks and are heard or seen weekly in 99 million homes. He is the founder of Christians United for Israel (CUFI).

Hagee spreads misery, destruction and greed wherever his Lear jet lands. He is pumping part of the cash he fleeces from the flock into the illegal settlements in the counterfeit state of Israel, while the child murderers there are aiming to dispose of the remainder of the Christians and Muslims in Palestinian villages with phosphorous bombs received free from America.

Regardless, just like for food, obese Hagee has a bottomless appetite for dead American kids as well, endlessly pushing for a war on Iran to satisfy his Zionist masters and strange followers who jump up and down like so many steroid-loaded basketball players waving their Israeli flags while the cash is collected. He is burning both ends of the candle manufacturing "moral support" for the endless flow of limbless and lifeless bodies that are flown and wheeled back to America to their parents from Iraq and Afghanistan.

But this is not enough for Hagee. At the last Washington conference he said: "[I]t is time for America to embrace the words of Sen. Joseph Lieberman and consider a military pre-emptive strike against Iran to prevent a nuclear holocaust in Israel." Actually jetsetter Hagee and his gang were lobbying Congress for the territorial expansion of Israel and a genocidal American nuclear strike on Iran. These well-financed people seem to be living from holocaust to holocaust just for the excitement of it.

* * *

Hagee is also a frequent guest of Israel. He met Prime Minister Binyamin Netanyahu just recently, a day before Vice President Joe Biden arrived and was humiliated by the Israeli leader.

Hagee also receives extraordinary coverage from the U.S. media, publicity that could not be purchased for tens of millions of dollars. He even appeared as a guest writer for The Washington Post in January 2009 under the title: "My Hopes and Concerns for Obama."

This is a major PR drive to extend the useful life of the "Holocaust" and to serve the Zionist agenda in the United States. There are hundreds of millions of dollars donated by these Israel-worshippers.¹⁷

2 Salvation Without Jesus Christ

Hagee has won the trust of the Jewish Hierarchy. He has even agreed not to evangelize Jews. Hagee's refusal to preach the Christian gospel to the Jews is hard to reconcile with his position as a church pastor. G. Richard Fisher states:

> Hagee's website tells us that his 'vision is for world evangelism. The burning passion of his heart is to win the lost to Jesus Christ in America and around the world.' That statement is not altogether true since he will not evangelize Jews and teaches salvation on another basis than the Gospel for the Jewish people.[18]

Fisher further explains that "Hagee reported to the *Houston Chronicle* that he believes that Jews already have a covenant with God and a relationship to God and do not need to come to the cross. Hearing this is startling."[19]

Hagee told the *Houston Chronicle* newspaper: "I'm not trying to convert the Jewish people to the Christian faith."[20] Hagee elaborated during the interview:

In fact, trying to convert Jews is a 'waste of time,' he said. 'The Jewish person who has his roots in Judaism is not going to convert to Christianity. There is no form of Christian evangelism that has failed so miserably as evangelizing the Jewish people. They (already) have a faith structure.' Everyone else, whether Buddhist or Baha'i, needs to believe in Jesus, he says. But not Jews. Jews already have a covenant with God that has never been replaced by Christianity, he says.[21]

Hagee's Zionist theology is diametrically opposed to the true Christian gospel. Under the true gospel, there is no salvation for Jew or Gentile aside from Jesus. "Jesus saith unto him, I am the way, the truth, and the life: no man cometh unto the Father, but by me." John 14:6. There is only one way to salvation, and that is by the grace of God through faith in Jesus Christ. Ephesians 2:8. "He that hath the Son hath life; and he that hath not the Son of God hath not life." 1 John 5:12.

There is not a separate means of salvation for the Jew and another for the Gentile. There is only one means of salvation for both. "There is neither Jew nor Greek, there is neither bond nor free, there is neither male nor female: for ye are all one in Christ Jesus." Galatians 3:28. All who are saved by grace through faith are Abraham's spiritual seed (i.e., Christians). "And if ye be Christ's, then are ye Abraham's seed, and heirs according to the promise." Galatians 3:29.

To refuse to evangelize the Jews is a sin, as it is disobeying a direct command from God to "[g]o ye into all the world, and preach the gospel to every creature." Mark 16:15. Jesus did not say to preach only to Gentiles; he commanded that the gospel be preached to "every creature;" that includes Jews.

Preaching of the gospel is the means God uses to save. Without preaching the word of God, there is no salvation. The preaching must be to both the Jew and Gentile. Jesus is the Lord over all men:

> **For there is no difference between the Jew and the Greek: for the same Lord over all is rich unto all that call upon him. For whosoever shall call upon the name of the Lord shall be saved.** How then shall they call on him in whom they have not believed? and how shall they believe in him of whom they have not heard? and how shall they hear without a preacher? And how shall they preach, except they be sent? as it is written, How beautiful are the feet of them that preach the gospel of peace, and bring glad tidings of good things! But they have not all obeyed the gospel. For Esaias saith, Lord, who hath believed our report? So then **faith cometh by hearing, and hearing by the word of God.** Romans 10:11-17.

G. Richard Fisher succinctly explains the implications of Hagee's Zionist theology:

> If the early Church had taken this view that Jews are saved just by being Jews there would have been no Christians in Jerusalem, Judea or Samaria. When Paul was converted, God would have violated His own plan. Under this view Jesus would not have had Apostles and there would not be a Church today. These logical results seem to escape the purveyors of this form of Christian Zionism, which is neither Christian or Zionist.[22]

Hagee's false gospel is the same fallacious Jewish doctrine that God repudiated in the true gospel. Jesus told the

Jews that if they truly followed the teachings of Moses, they would accept him as their Messiah, because Moses wrote of him. *See* John 5:39, 46-47. Jesus further told the Jews that "if ye believe not that I am he [Christ], ye shall die in your sins." John 8:24. Peter told the Jews that salvation only comes through Jesus Christ: "Neither is there salvation in any other: for there is none other name under heaven given among men, whereby we must be saved." Acts 4:12.

John Hagee says the following in his book *In Defense of Israel*: "There is not one verse of Scripture in the New Testament that says Jesus came to be the Messiah"[23] In a promotional video, Hagee states this about the book: "It will also prove that Jesus did not come to earth to be the Messiah. . . . Since Jesus refused by word and deed to claim to be the Messiah, how can the Jews be blamed for rejecting what was never offered?"[24]

> The bible refutes the false claims of John Hagee.

> The woman saith unto him, I know that Messias cometh, which is called Christ: when he is come, he will tell us all things. Jesus saith unto her, I that speak unto thee am he. John 4:25-26.

> Therefore let all the house of Israel know assuredly, that God hath made that same Jesus, whom ye have crucified, both Lord and Christ. Acts 2:36.

By making the claim that Jesus did not come to be the Messiah (Christ), John Hagee has exposed himself as a liar and antichrist. Anyone who denies that Jesus is the Christ (Messiah) is antichrist. "Who is a liar but he that denieth that Jesus is the Christ? He is antichrist, that denieth the Father and the Son." 1 John 2:22. That does not mean that Hagee is the beast of Revelation, however, it does mean that he is one of many enemies of Christ who are in a spiritual war against God and man.

Hagee is making the same claim for the Jews that Jesus refuted in the gospel of John. Jesus started out by telling the Jews that if they were his disciples they would know the truth and be set free from sin. John 8:31-32. The Jews objected and argued that they were not in bondage and had no need to be set free because they were Abraham's seed. John 8:33. They argued that by virtue of their status as the physical descendants of Abraham they were in no need of a savior. They claimed that God was their Father by virtue of their physical lineage from Abraham. John 8:39-41. John the Baptist told the Jews from the beginning that their lineage from Abraham would not help them. "And think not to say within yourselves, We have Abraham to our father: for I say unto you, that God is able of these stones to raise up children unto Abraham." Matthew 3:9.

Jesus made clear to the Jews that their father was the devil and that if God were truly their Father, they would love him. John 8:42. Those without the Son are also without the Father. The claim by Hagee that the Jews have redemption other than by the grace of God through faith in Jesus Christ is impeached by scripture. The Jews deny Jesus is the Christ, and therefore they do not have the Father and are by definition antichrist.

> Who is a liar but he that denieth that Jesus is the Christ? He is antichrist, that denieth the Father and the Son. Whosoever denieth the Son, the same hath not the Father: he that acknowledgeth the Son hath the Father also. 1 John 2:23-24.

Hagee's dual-covenant theology serves to kill any mission by "Christian" Zionists to spread the gospel to the

Jews.[25] Why would Jews come to Christ, if they are told by the "Christian" Zionists that their conversion is irrelevant to their salvation? If they are nationally saved without Jesus Christ anyway, what is the point of believing in Jesus Christ?

Hagee is not alone in this devilish subterfuge. Steven Paas revealed in his book, *Christian Zionism Examined,* that some "Christian" Zionist missionary groups do not consider their activities in Israel as a mission but simply as "meeting with Israel."[26] They do not see the conversion of Jews to Christ as part of their mission. Paas concluded the following about the missionary activities of the "Christian" Zionist *Center for Israel Studies* (CIS): "Their first priority is not leading Jews to Christ, but listening to and learning from Jews and Judaism."[27]

What are the teachings of the Jews and Judaism to which Paas refers? The Jewish teachings followed by "Christian" Zionists are found in the Talmud, which in *Sanhedrin Folio* 90a provides that all Jews ("Israel") are guaranteed a portion in the world to come.[28] According to the "Christian" Zionist thought, there is no point in evangelizing the Jews, since they are already guaranteed entrance into heaven without Christ; so say the authoritative Jewish doctrines found in the Talmud.

Jews view "Christian Zionists as "useful idiots," which is a pejorative phrase used by communists to describe Gentile communist propagandists who do not understand the Jewish goals behind communism. Jews have a secret that they keep from the "Christian" Zionists. According to the previously mentioned tractate in the Talmud (*Sanhedrin Folio* 90a), Christians, who are described as those who read the New Testament ("uncanonical books"), have no portion in the world to come.[29] In fact, Jews have a particular hatred for Christians. The hatred by Jews against Christians is so intense that Jews are taught to utter a curse when passing a Christian Church, calling on their heathen god (Hashem) to "destroy this house of the proud."[30]

Elizabeth Dilling explains: "The 'religious' Orthodox Jew recites the 'Eighteen Benedictions,' or 'Shemoneh Esreh,' three times week days, four times on holidays and Sabbaths, the 7th and 12th of which curse the Christians and non-Jews to hell and perdition. Thus, the 'good Orthodox Jew' gives us Christians 6 cursings on ordinary days, 8 on 'specials.'"[31]

The halacha (Jewish religious law) is that it is forbidden for a Jew to engage in any of the religious practices of Christians. The Jews sit smugly meeting with "Christian" Zionists firm in their belief that the Christians are damned to hell, while they are guaranteed entrance into heaven without believing in Jesus Christ. By not evangelizing the Jews, "Christian" Zionists are unwittingly acceding to the laws of the Jews and lending a degree of authenticity to the antichrist Jewish teachings.

The point of a church missionary activity should be to spread the gospel of Jesus Christ. However, the "Christian" Zionists go out their way to avoid doing that very thing. Paas concludes: "Western Christian organisations in Israel often limit themselves to activities of dialogue, study, representation, or support."[32]

The "Christian" Zionists deliberately violate Jesus' command to "go ye into all the world, and preach the gospel to every creature." Mark 16:15. The "Christian" Zionists are the very instrument being used by Satan to keep the Jews in spiritual bondage by convincing them that they are part of a unique plan by God simply by virtue of their status as Jews. Despite their claims to love the Jews, Paas concludes that "[f]ailing to communicate Christ-given insights to the Jews is lacking love for them."[33]

Paas has found that in countries where "Christian"

Zionism has a stronghold, the presence of Christian churches is decreasing rapidly.[34] In some cases this is due to the fact, as Paas explains, "that teaching people that God's covenant in light of the New Testament is still principally with Israel, puts Africans and Asians off. In their ears this sounds as if God's special love is limited to an ethnic group, not being their own group."[35]

Paas opines that "Christian" Zionism represents "the deep-seated human desire to attach religious or spiritual hopes to tangible physical things. The dream of Zion, distorting the meaning of Israel's people, land and religion, tends to become an obsession, and ultimately an idol."[36] Paas's study of "Christian" Zionism leads him to the following conclusion:

> In the question of Christian Zionism, either in its negative or in its positive aspect, the nucleus of the Christian faith is at stake. Those who are unbiblically fascinated by Israel, either in hatred or in love, have decentralised Christ or even pushed him out of their sight. This immediately affects the relationship with God. Confession of sins, repentance, forgiveness, the gift of righteousness, rebirth, the gift of a new life cannot be realities when Israel-fascinations have taken centre stage of man's heart and mind.[37]

Paas correctly states that "[t]he reality of future consummate Jerusalem is not anchored in present Jerusalem, but in Christ."[38] The "Christian" Zionists, reject that truth. They overlook the heavenly Jerusalem found in Revelation 21:10 that is based upon the spiritual seed of Abraham as the fulfillment of Christ's promise. They are, instead, fixated upon the earthbound Jerusalem, containing the fleshly seed of Abraham. "Christian" Zionism is neither Christian nor Zionist in the biblical sense. "Christian" Zionism is a satanic deception, plain and simple. "Christian" Zionist churches provide aid and comfort to the Jews in their rejection of Jesus Christ. They act very much like auxiliary Jewish Synagogues.

3 Who is Abraham's Seed?

Zionist theology in the nominal Christian churches acts to anesthesize the Christian community against a formidable spiritual enemy. The Zionist pastors have taken bible passages out of context and twisted them beyond recognition. Let us look at the bible passages that "Christian" Zionists take out of context to support their heathen theology. The John Hagee Ministries website states:

> Our Commitment to Israel
>
> We believe in the promise of Genesis 12:3 regarding the Jewish people and the nation of Israel. We believe that this is an eternal covenant between God and the seed of Abraham to which God is faithful.[39]

Hagee further states:

> We support Israel because all other nations were created by an act of men, but Israel was created by an act of God! The Royal Land Grant that was given to Abraham and his seed through Isaac and Jacob with an everlasting

and unconditional covenant. (Genesis 12:1-3, 13:14-18, 15:1-21, 17:4-8, 22:15-18, 26:1-5 and Psalm 89:28-37.)[40]

Let us look at a couple of passages that Hagee cites:

I will bless them that bless thee, and curse him that curseth thee: and in thee shall all families of the earth be blessed. Genesis 12:3

And I will make thee exceeding fruitful, and I will make nations of thee, and kings shall come out of thee. And I will establish my covenant between me and thee and thy **seed** after thee in their generations for an everlasting covenant, to be a God unto thee, and to thy **seed** after thee. And I will give unto thee, and to thy **seed** after thee. Genesis 17:6-8 (emphasis added).

And in thy **seed** shall all the nations of the earth be blessed. Genesis 22:18 (emphasis added).

I will make thy **seed** to multiply as the stars of heaven, and will give unto thy **seed** all these countries; and in thy **seed** shall all the nations of the earth be blessed. Genesis 26:4 (emphasis added).

In the above bible passages we find God stating to Abraham that his seed will not only be the recipient of God's blessing, but also the source of that blessing. How can it be that the seed is both the source and the recipient of the blessing? Hagee and his ilk conceal the answer to that question by avoiding the truth of the gospel found in Galatians 3:16: "Now to Abraham and his **seed** were the promises made. He saith not,

And to seeds, as of many; but as of one, **And to thy seed, which is Christ**." Jesus Christ is the seed that is the source of the blessing. All who believe in Jesus Christ, are the recipients of the promises as the spiritual children of God. All who believe in Jesus Christ are Abraham's spiritual seed, and heirs according to the promise of the coming Christ given to Abraham. "And if ye be Christ's, then are ye Abraham's seed, and heirs according to the promise." Galatians 3:29.

Steve Van Nattan is a "Christian" Zionist who follows the Jewish fables instead of God's word and clings to the myth that the promised "seed" is not Christ but are the fleshly Jews. Van Nattan misinterprets Isaiah 59:20-21 to conform to his Zionist view:

> The point here is that the Jews of today, who are descended from Jacob, are "seed" children (vs. 21), not a mixed multitude, like the crowd of wana be Kenites who followed the Jews out of Egypt. God never stopped referring to them as the "mixed multitude." The covenant here is to blood line Jews, "seed" Jews.[41]

That interpretation of Isaiah is simply wrong. Jacob was the son of Isaac, who was the son of Abraham. God made his promise of blessings first to Abraham. God's promised blessings, however, were not intended to flow through the blood line of Abraham; God's promised blessings were to flow to those who have the faith of Abraham. The "seed" of Abraham who inherit the blessings from God are those that have the faith of Abraham, not those that have the flesh of Abraham. (Galatians 3:16, 26, 29)

> Not as though the word of God hath taken none effect. For they are not all Israel, which are of Israel: Neither, because they are the seed of Abraham, are they all children: but, In

Isaac shall thy seed be called. **That is, They which are the children of the flesh, these are not the children of God: but the children of the promise are counted for the seed.** (Romans 9:6-8)

Christ has broken down forever any distinction between Jew and Gentile in his kingdom.

For the scripture saith, Whosoever believeth on him shall not be ashamed. **For there is no difference between the Jew and the Greek: for the same Lord over all is rich unto all that call upon him.** For whosoever shall call upon the name of the Lord shall be saved. (Romans 10:11-13)

The children of the flesh are not the elect of God; God's elect are the children of the promised Christ; they are spiritual children. Romans 9:6-8. "For ye are all the children of God by faith in Christ Jesus." (Galatians 3:26) The promises to Abraham were to be fulfilled on behalf of spiritual Israel, which is the church.

Abraham was the father of Isaac, who in turn was the father of Jacob; Jacob (also known as Israel) had 12 sons that were the progenitors of the 12 tribes of Israel. Abraham was also the father of Ishmael, but because Ishmael was the son of Abraham's bondwoman, the bondwoman and Ishmael were cast out. Genesis 21:10-14. Through Isaac, who was the son of Abraham's wife, Sarah, were to flow the promises of God to Abraham. Genesis 21:12. However, Isaac had two sons, Jacob and Esau. The promise given to Abraham flowed not to Esau, but to Jacob. In fact, God states in Romans 9:13: "As it is written, Jacob have I loved, but Esau have I hated." *See also* Malachi 1:1-3. God elected Jacob (Israel) as the person through whom his promises would flow.

In each of Abraham's generations the blessing to Abraham flowed according to the election of God. No blessing was obtained that was sought through blood or effort. For example, the bondwoman (Hagar) conceived and gave birth to Abram's first son (Ishmael). God later renamed Abram, Abraham. Genesis 17:5. However, Ishmael was not the seed through which the promises would flow. Ishmael was born because Abraham's wife, Sarai, decided that she would help God with his promise that Abram (Abraham) would be the father of many. Sarai was later renamed Sarah by God. Genesis 17:15. Sarai arranged for Hagar to conceive a child by Abram (Abraham). Genesis 16:1-4. However, Ishmael was not a child of the promise. God worked a miracle and had Sarah bear a child of Abraham, even though she was at that time beyond child bearing age (Sarah was 90 years old and Abraham was 100 years old). Genesis 17:17. That child born of the promise was Isaac. It was the bloodline of Isaac through which the promised seed, who is Christ, would be born. Genesis 17:19-21, 21:3; Hebrews 11:18; Galatians 4:28.

God told Abraham:

And God said, Sarah thy wife shall bear thee a son indeed; and thou shalt call his name Isaac: and I will establish my covenant with him for an everlasting covenant, and with his **seed** after him. Genesis 17:19.

God reveals the spiritual truth of Geneis 17:19 in Galatians 4:28, where Paul states: "Now we, brethren, as Isaac was, are the children of promise." As Isaac was Abraham's physical seed, so also Christians are the spiritual seed of Abraham, through whom the everlasting covenant flowed. Isaac's miraculous physical birth is an allegory for the miraculous spiritual birth of those who are of the faith of Abraham. Christians are miraculously born again by the grace of God through faith in Jesus Christ. John 3:3. "Even as

Abraham believed God, and it was accounted to him for righteousness. Know ye therefore that they which are of faith, the same are the children of Abraham." Galatians 3:6-7. The physical seed of Abraham are not the objects of the promise, it is only the spiritual seed that is born by the Grace of God through faith in Jesus Christ. "That which is born of the flesh is flesh; and that which is born of the Spirit is spirit." John 3:6.

Fleshly Israel rebelled against God and therefore has been cut off from the tree of life. God has saved a remnant of fleshly Israel to be grafted back into the tree of life, but their ingrafting is upon the same grounds as everyone else, by the grace of God through faith in Jesus Christ.

John Hagee cites Romans chapter 11 as authority for his view that the Jews are to be blessed and renewed outside the church. Hagee believes that Jews are saved apart from faith in Jesus Christ. While Hagee pays lip service to the grace of God, he gives it an unbiblical meaning. He believes that Jews are saved through God's grace without faith in Jesus Christ. He has decoupled grace from faith. Hagee believes fleshly Jews are saved by the simple fact of their status as fleshly Jews.[42]

G. Richard Fisher concludes: "In short, Hagee believes that some Jews are not saved by the cross of Christ but by prior election and their pedigree in Abraham. There is a way of salvation in Christ and an election of grace for the Jew apart from Christ. No matter how you nuance it or define it, this is 'Two Covenant' theology."[43]

Not all "Christian" Zionists adhere to the two-covenant theology, but it is a growing and powerful influence in the "Christian" Zionist community. Even those among "Christian" Zionists who do not totally accept the dual-covenant theology in every respect, have so compromised their stance for Christ that they have a theology that is not at all Christian. Their compromised theology states the Jews who believe in Jesus "do not need to change their religion."[44] The difference between that hybrid Zionist theology and the dual-covenant theology is one of degree rather than kind. It is in essence dual-covenant theology in all but name, with a false Jesus added to Judaism as a theological bauble.

Jesus told the Jews that they were "[m]aking the word of God of none effect through your tradition." (Mark 7:13) Yet, along come the "Christian" Zionists to contradict Jesus and tell the Jews that they can keep their traditions. Telling a Jew that he can continue his heathen practices of Judaism after accepting Christ is to preach a false Christianity without regeneration. Saying that Jews can remain adherents to Judaism while being Christians would be like telling witches that they can continue to practice witchcraft and be Christians at the same time. "Christian" Zionism undermines true Christian theology.

Jesus is the Word that became flesh. John 1:1. To contradict the words of Jesus and present it as Jesus's gospel is to preach a false gospel with a false Jesus.

> For if he that cometh preacheth **another Jesus**, whom we have not preached, or if ye receive another spirit, which ye have not received, or another gospel, which ye have not accepted, ye might well bear with him. (2 Corinthians 11:4)

"Christian" Zionists contradict Jesus and are therefore in opposition to Jesus. "He that is not with me is against me; and he that gathereth not with me scattereth abroad." Matthew 12:30. To preach that Jews are saved by virtue of being Jewish is a false gospel. It is also a false gospel to teach that once a Jew is saved he may continue practicing his antichrist Judaism. Salvation is by the grace of God through faith in Jesus Christ without regard to someone's status as a Jew or Gentile.

> But as many as received him, to them gave he power to become the sons of God, even to them that believe on his name: Which were born, not of blood, nor of the will of the flesh, nor of the will of man, but of God. (John 1:12-13)

Salvation is by the grace of God alone through faith in Jesus Christ alone:

> For by grace are ye saved through faith; and that not of yourselves: it is the gift of God: Not of works, lest any man should boast. (Ephesians 2:8-9)

The "Christian" Zionists that contradict the bible theme of salvation by grace alone through faith alone and instead preach a false gospel, whereby there is special treatment for Jews are under a curse from God.

> I marvel that ye are so soon removed from him that called you into the grace of Christ unto another gospel: Which is not another; but there be some that trouble you, and would pervert the gospel of Christ. But though we, or an angel from heaven, preach any other gospel unto you than that which we have preached unto you, let him be accursed. As we said before, so say I now again, If any man preach any other gospel unto you than that ye have received, let him be accursed. (Galatians 1:6-9)

A Jew who is truly saved and believes in the Jesus of the bible will not go back and follow his heathen Judaic superstitions. "And a stranger will they not follow, but will flee from him: for they know not the voice of strangers." John 10:5.

The dual-covenant theology is endemic in the ersatz "Christian" community. Dr. William Varner is typical of the modern theologians who have subtly twisted scripture to give fleshly Israel a special status in God's plan. Dr. Varner claims that God's promises to fleshly Israel are to be certainly fulfilled in the future:

> The Apostle Paul is clear on the great privileges that God has granted Israel. He wrote in Romans 9:4: "who are Israelites, to whom pertain the adoption, the glory, the covenants, the giving of the law, the service of God, and the **promises**." Paul nowhere intimates that these great privileges have been annulled, forfeited, or cancelled. As a matter of fact the three chapters of which this verse is a part (Romans 9-11) have as one of their purposes to emphasize that God has **not** cancelled His promises to Israel or transferred them to some other people! What says Paul in Romans 11:1? "I say then, has God cast away His people? Certainly not! For I also am an Israelite, of the seed of Abraham, of the tribe of Benjamin. God has not cast away His people whom He foreknew."
>
> Specifically, what are those promises to Israel? Well, they ultimately are derived from those to "Father Abraham" in Genesis 12:1-3. To sum them up, they are basically the promises of a **people**, a **land** and a **blessing**.[45] (emphasis in original).

Dr. Varner cites Romans 11:1 to support his claim. However, he only cites the first verse. He takes the verse out of context. When the verse is read in context, we see that it does not support Varner's claim at all.

I say then, Hath God cast away his people? God forbid. For I also am an Israelite, of the seed of Abraham, of the tribe of Benjamin. God hath not cast away his people which he foreknew. Wot ye not what the scripture saith of Elias? how he maketh intercession to God against Israel, saying, Lord, they have killed thy prophets, and digged down thine altars; and I am left alone, and they seek my life. But what saith the answer of God unto him? I have reserved to myself seven thousand men, who have not bowed the knee to the image of Baal. **Even so then at this present time also there is a remnant according to the election of grace.** And if by grace, then is it no more of works: otherwise grace is no more grace. But if it be of works, then is it no more grace: otherwise work is no more work. What then? **Israel hath not obtained that which he seeketh for; but the election hath obtained it, and the rest were blinded (According as it is written, God hath given them the spirit of slumber, eyes that they should not see, and ears that they should not hear;) unto this day.** And David saith, Let their table be made a snare, and a trap, and a stumblingblock, and a recompence unto them: Let their eyes be darkened, that they may not see, and bow down their back alway. Romans 11:1-10 (emphasis added).

It is clear when Romans 11:1 is read in context that God has not elected all Jews as objects of his promises; he has only elected certain Jews for salvation, according to his grace.

Furthermore, the salvation of Jews is not by virtue of their status as Jews, but rather the salvation of Jews, as with the salvation of Gentiles, is totally based upon God's election by his sovereign grace through faith in Jesus alone.

Dr. Varner further quotes Romans 9:4 out of context and claims that the entirety of Romans chapters 9-11 support his claim that fleshly Jews are set apart for unique blessings according to God's eternal plan. When we read Romans 9:3-4, we see that Paul is in fact speaking of fleshly Jews, for he says he is talking about "my kinsmen according to the flesh."

> For I could wish that myself were accursed from Christ for my brethren, **my kinsmen according to the flesh**: Who are Israelites; to whom pertaineth the adoption, and the glory, and the covenants, and the giving of the law, and the service of God, and the promises. Romans 9:3-4.

Paul later makes it clear that his desire for his kinsmen according to the flesh is not that all fleshly Israel are a part of God's plan for the Jews. Paul reveals that the seed of Abraham referenced in the bible is not a reference to the flesh of Abraham; the biblical seed of Abraham are those who have the promised faith of Abraham. They are a unique people made up of both Jews and Gentiles. Paul explains that point a few verses later in Romans 9:6-8:

> Not as though the word of God hath taken none effect. **For they are not all Israel, which are of Israel: Neither, because they are the seed of Abraham, are they all children**: but, In Isaac shall thy seed be called. That is, **They which are the children of the flesh, these are not the children of God**: but the children of the promise are counted for the seed. Romans 9:6-8 (emphasis added).

Paul emphatically states that the children of the flesh of Abraham "are not the children of God." It could not be clearer. The Jews of the flesh are not the seed of Abraham to whom the promises flow. The promises flow to the Jews and Gentiles who are elected by God for salvation.

> And that he might make known the riches of his glory on the vessels of mercy, which he had afore prepared unto glory, Even us, whom he hath called, **not of the Jews only, but also of the Gentiles?** As he saith also in Osee, I will call them my people, which were not my people; and her beloved, which was not beloved. And it shall come to pass, that in the place where it was said unto them, Ye are not my people; there shall they be called the children of the living God. Romans 9:23-26.

Paul makes the point in Romans 10:1-4 that although his desire is that fleshly Israel be saved, he knows that the zeal of fleshly Jews for God is without knowledge. Fleshly Israel has refused to believe in Jesus Christ. They cannot hope to enter the kingdom of heaven without the perfect righteousness that can only be imputed through faith in Jesus Christ.

> Brethren, my heart's desire and prayer to God for Israel is, that they might be saved. For I bear them record that they have a zeal of God, but not according to knowledge. For they being ignorant of God's righteousness, and going about to establish their own righteousness, have not submitted themselves unto the righteousness of God. For Christ is the end of the law for righteousness to every one that believeth. Romans 10:1-4.

The New Testament is a codicil to the Old Testament.

The codicil gives further revelation about God's plan for his people. God's people are his elect who are made up of both Jew and Gentile.

> For the scripture saith, Whosoever believeth on him shall not be ashamed. For **there is no difference between the Jew and the Greek**: for the same Lord over all is rich unto all that call upon him. Romans 10:11-12.

4 The True Israel of God

In Christ there is neither Jew nor Gentile, we are all one by faith in Christ. He is not going to divide us once again into Jew and Gentile. His church is his body which cannot be divided. 1 Corinthians 1:13. For a kingdom divided against itself cannot stand. Mark 3:24. The seed of the promises to Abraham is Christ and those who have the faith of Christ, his church, not fleshly Israel.

> But before faith came, we were kept under the law, shut up unto the faith which should afterwards be revealed. Wherefore the law was our schoolmaster to bring us unto Christ, that we might be justified by faith. **But after that faith is come, we are no longer under a schoolmaster.** For ye are all the children of God by faith in Christ Jesus. For as many of you as have been baptized into Christ have put on Christ. **There is neither Jew nor Greek, there is neither bond nor free, there is neither male nor female: for ye are all one in Christ Jesus. And if ye be Christ's, then are ye Abraham's seed, and heirs according**

to the promise. Galatians 3:23-29.

A Jew who believes in Jesus as Christ becomes a new creation. He is no longer a fleshly Jew. He becomes a spiritual Jew, a Christian. "For in Christ Jesus neither circumcision availeth any thing, nor uncircumcision, but a new creature." Galatians 6:15.

The bible makes clear that the old covenant made to fleshly Israel has vanished away, being replaced by the new covenant of faith in Jesus Christ. "In that he saith, A new covenant, he hath made the first old. Now that which decayeth and waxeth old is ready to vanish away." (Hebrews 8:13) Why would God reinstate something in which he has said would vanish away and in which he has had no pleasure? "In burnt offerings and sacrifices for sin thou hast had no pleasure." Hebrews 10:6.

Fleshly Israel is symbolized by the fig tree. That fig tree will never again bear fruit.

> And seeing a fig tree afar off having leaves, he came, if haply he might find any thing thereon: and when he came to it, he found nothing but leaves; for the time of figs was not yet. And Jesus answered and said unto it, **No man eat fruit of thee hereafter for ever.** And his disciples heard it. . . . And in the morning, as they passed by, they saw the fig tree dried up from the roots. And Peter calling to remembrance saith unto him, Master, behold, the fig tree which thou cursedst is withered away. Mark 11:13-14, 20-21.

Spiritual Israel is symbolized by the olive tree. "Can the fig tree, my brethren, bear olive berries? either a vine, figs? so can no fountain both yield salt water and fresh." James 3:12.

The answer is no! Fleshly Israel will never ever bear spiritual fruit for God. The spiritual fruit only comes from the spiritual olive plant, the church.

As we have already seen, the blessings of God do not flow to the physical seed of Abraham but rather to his spiritual seed. We know that Jesus is the seed of Abraham. Galatians 3:16. All who believe in Jesus are heirs of the promise given to Abraham. Galatians 3:23-29. Obedience to God is the result of salvation, not the cause of it. Ephesians 2:8-10. Just as with Abraham, who believed God and it was accounted to him as righteousness, so too for all others who believe God it is also accounted unto them as righteousness. Galatians 3:6-9.

A true Jew is the spiritual seed of Abraham, not the physical seed. "For he is not a Jew, which is one outwardly; neither is that circumcision, which is outward in the flesh: But he is a Jew, which is one inwardly; and circumcision is that of the heart, in the spirit, and not in the letter; whose praise is not of men, but of God." Romans 2:28-29. "Not as though the word of God hath taken none effect. For they are not all Israel, which are of Israel: Neither, because they are the seed of Abraham, are they all children: but, In Isaac shall thy seed be called. That is, They which are the children of the flesh, these are not the children of God: but the children of the promise are counted for the seed." Romans 9:6-8.

The eternal blessings of Abraham flow to all who believe in Jesus Christ. God's kingdom is a spiritual kingdom, not an earthly kingdom. His children are spiritual children, not earthly children. In God's kingdom there are no distinctions between Jew or Gentile. "There is neither Jew nor Greek, there is neither bond nor free, there is neither male nor female: for ye are all one in Christ Jesus. And if ye be Christ's, then are ye Abraham's seed, and heirs according to the promise." Galatians 3:28-29.

Fleshly Israel of the Old Testament is a temporal type of the spiritual Israel of the New Testament, which is the church.

> But with many of them God was not well pleased: for they were overthrown in the wilderness. **Now these things were our examples, to the intent we should not lust after evil things, as they also lusted.** 1 Corinthians 10:5-6.
>
> **Now all these things happened unto them for ensamples: and they are written for our admonition, upon whom the ends of the world are come.** 1 Corinthians 10:11.

Thus, the prophecies regarding Israel had both temporal and spiritual fulfillments. The distinction between the temporal Israel and the eternal Israel is explained clearly in R. B. Yerby's book *The Once and Future Israel*. First there is the temporal earthly fulfillment and then there is the spiritual fulfillment. 1 Corinthians 15:46.

> The scriptures teach us that in all of God's dealings with mankind, from the time of Adam, we may discern the same divine principle at work, namely, "first the natural, then the spiritual." (1 Cor 15:45-46) God has progressively revealed his purpose through, first, his dealings with the natural Israel and, second and finally, his dealings with spiritual Israel. (There is no scriptural basis for the regressive idea that God's dealings will again be centered exclusively on natural Israel at some future date.)
>
> Because God's dealings follow the sequence of

first the natural, then the spiritual, it is easy to see and understand that the same progression applied to his people and his promises. The natural people of Old Testament Israel enjoyed the natural fulfillment of the promises made to them, and saw the promises invalidated through sin and unbelief. Likewise, the spiritual people of New Testament Israel, the followers of Jesus Christ, have received, are receiving and will receive all spiritual fulfillments of the promises.

* * *

[In Galatians 4:21-31] as in many other New Testament passages, Paul skillfully defeated his adversaries with their own ammunition. He took the "foolish Galatians" who desired to be under the law (Gal 4:21) right into the thick of Old Testament Law, into Genesis, the first book of Moses, to prove a spiritual truth with natural types. The early church recognized the need for spiritual authority to support their doctrines (for them, of course, the scriptures were the writings we today call the Old Testament) and therefore, under the inspiration of the Holy Spirit, they quoted freely from the Old Testament.

In the fourth chapter of Galatians, as elsewhere, Paul proved his point through the superior understanding God gave him of the true meaning of the Old Testament scriptures. He said that the story of the two sons of Abraham was more than just a prominent part of the history of the Jewish people. It was, he said, an allegory (Gal. 4:24), that is, a story in which the people and events were symbols or types standing for some greater truth (Gal. 4:24).

The allegory speaks of two women and their two sons who were fathered by Abraham. Hagar, the bondwoman and the mother of Ishmael who was "born after the flesh" (Gal 4:23), typifies natural Jerusalem. Sarah, the freewoman and the mother of Isaac, the child of promise (Gal 4:23, 28), typifies the church which is spiritual Jerusalem. The children of natural Jerusalem are in bondage (Gal. 4:25), as are all who are unsaved, but the children of the church, the heavenly Jerusalem, are free (Gal. 4:26). Those who are in bondage, who are not born again are only "born after the flesh" (Gal. 4:29) cannot possibly be God's people. Therefore, the scriptures "cast out"(Gal 4:30) the natural Jerusalem and her children after the flesh, and identify the heirs as the believers in Christ who are the children of promise (Gal 4:30).

* * *

Paul was constantly in trouble with the Jews because his spiritual interpretations of the Old Testament scriptures warred with their natural interpretation. Our onetime Pharisee had come to see clearly that "the things that are seen are temporal, but the things which are not seen are eternal" (2 Cor 4:18) but his former colleagues could not believe that their highly vaunted institutions were ready to "vanish away" (Heb 8:13).

* * *

> Because the Lord Jesus "endured the cross, despising the shame" (Heb 12:2) spiritual Israel hears a better voice than the voices heard by natural Israel (Heb. 1:1, 2), and we have, among other things, a better Priest (Heb. 4:15), a better priesthood (Heb. 5:6), a better hope (Heb. 7:19), a better covenant (Heb. 8:10), a better Tabernacle (Heb. 9:11), a better altar (Heb. 13:10), a better sacrifice (Heb. 9:14), a better country (Heb. 11:16), and a better city (Heb. 12:22).[46]

Many believe that some of the prophecies in the Old Testament regarding natural Israel have not been fulfilled and therefore there must be a post-Christian period during which they will be fulfilled. Let us examine these Old Testament prophecies. In Genesis 12:2 God told Abraham: "And I will make of thee a great nation, and I will bless thee, and make thy name great; and thou shalt be a blessing." Abraham did not see the fulfillment of that prophecy. That promise was fulfilled in part by fleshly Israel. "And God spake unto Israel in the visions of the night, and said, Jacob, Jacob. And he said, Here am I. And he said, I am God, the God of thy father: fear not to go down into Egypt; for **I will there make of thee a great nation**" Gee3w2nesis 46:2-3. After 400 years of captivity, God raised up Moses who brought Israel out of Egyptian bondage and it became a great nation, just as promised by God. See Joshua 8-12; 1 Chronicles 17:21.

> Keep therefore and do them; for this is your wisdom and your understanding in the sight of the nations, which shall hear all these statutes, and say, **Surely this great nation is a wise and understanding people. For what nation is there so great, who hath God so nigh unto**

> **them, as the LORD our God is in all things that we call upon him for? And what nation is there so great, that hath statutes and judgments so righteous as all this law, which I set before you this day?** (Deuteronomy 4:6-8)

There was yet to be a spiritual fulfillment of the promise that from Abraham would spring a great nation. The church was the spiritual fulfillment of the promise given to Abraham.

> **But ye are a chosen generation, a royal priesthood, an holy nation, a peculiar people**; that ye should shew forth the praises of him who hath called you out of darkness into his marvellous light: Which in time past were not a people, but are now the people of God: which had not obtained mercy, but now have obtained mercy. 1 Peter 2:9-10.

On three different occasions God promised that Abraham's descendants would be too numerous to count.

> And I will make thy seed as the dust of the earth: so that if a man can number the dust of the earth, then shall thy seed also be numbered. Genesis 13:16.

> And he brought him forth abroad, and said, Look now toward heaven, and tell the stars, if thou be able to number them: and he said unto him, So shall thy seed be. Genesis 15:5.

> That in blessing I will bless thee, and in multiplying I will multiply thy seed as the stars of the heaven, and as the sand which is upon

the sea shore; and thy seed shall possess the gate of his enemies; Genesis 22:17.

Was that promise fulfilled in part by temporal Israel? Yes! We have the proof of the God inspired testimony of Moses, Solomon, and the author of Hebrews.

Now, O LORD God, let thy promise unto David my father be established: for **thou hast made me king over a people like the dust of the earth in multitude.** 2 Chronicles 1:9.

The LORD your God hath multiplied you, and, behold, ye are this day as the stars of heaven for multitude. Deuteronomy 1:10.

Therefore sprang there even of one, and him as good as dead, so many as the stars of the sky in multitude, and as the sand which is by the sea shore innumerable. Hebrews 11:12.

Judah and Israel were many, as the sand which is by the sea in multitude, eating and drinking, and making merry. 1 Kings 4:20.

There was to be a future spiritual fulfillment of that promise through the church. The seed of Abraham is a spiritual seed. The nation that would spring from him would be a nation built not on fleshly Israel only. There would be a better fulfillment of the promise through faith.

Therefore it is of faith, that it might be by grace; to the end the promise might be sure to all the seed; not to that only which is of the law, but to that also which is of **the faith of Abraham; who is the father of us all**.

Romans 4:16.

In Genesis 17:5, God told Abraham he would be a father of many nations.

> (As it is written, **I have made thee a father of many nations**,) before him whom he believed, even God, who quickeneth the dead, and calleth those things which be not as though they were. Romans 4:17.

As Abraham believed the promises of God and God counted it as righteousness, so too is it with those who have the faith of Abraham; they are the spiritual seed of Abraham. The church of God is the promised spiritual great nation.

> Who against hope believed in hope, that he might become the father of many nations, according to that which was spoken, **So shall thy seed be.** Romans 4:18.

Those that believe in Christ are Abraham's seed and the innumerable children that God promised Abraham. Galatians 3:29. First came the temporal earthly fulfillment of the promise through natural Israel, then came the spiritual eternal fulfillment through the church of Christ.

On no fewer than four different occasions God promised to Abraham and his descendants the land of Canaan. Genesis 12:7; 13:14-15; 15:7,18; 17:8. Many say that the promise of the land was not fulfilled. That is not true. God has stated clearly that all the land that he promised to fleshly Israel was given to them.

> **And the LORD gave unto Israel all the land which he sware to give unto their fathers; and they possessed it, and dwelt therein.**

And the LORD gave them rest round about, according to all that he sware unto their fathers: and there stood not a man of all their enemies before them; the LORD delivered all their enemies into their hand. **There failed not ought of any good thing which the LORD had spoken unto the house of Israel; all came to pass.** Joshua 21:43-45.

Some claim that the land that Israel occupied did not reach all the way from Egypt to the river Euphrates, as promised by God in Genesis 15:18, and therefore there is to be a future fulfillment of the promise. That claim is simply not true. Solomon, King of Israel, ruled from the river Euphrates to Egypt. "And Solomon reigned over all kingdoms from **the river unto the land of the Philistines, and unto the border of Egypt:** they brought presents, and served Solomon all the days of his life." 1 Kings 4:21. Is the river mentioned in verse 21 the Euphrates? Yes it is! In verse 24 we read that Solomon had dominion over Tipsah. Tipsah was located on the Euphrates in Mesopotamia. "For he had dominion over all the region on this side the river, from Tiphsah even to Azzah, over all the kings on this side the river: and he had peace on all sides round about him." 1 Kings 4:24.

Some have tried to beguile the children of God by stating that because Genesis 17:7-9 states that the land of Canaan was to be an everlasting possession of Israel, it is God's plan that natural Israel regain possession of that land. Let us look at that passage.

> **And I will establish my covenant between me and thee and thy seed after thee in their generations for an everlasting covenant, to be a God unto thee, and to thy seed after thee. And I will give unto thee, and to thy seed after thee, the land wherein thou art a**

stranger, all the land of Canaan, for an everlasting possession; and I will be their God. And God said unto Abraham, Thou shalt keep my covenant therefore, thou, and thy seed after thee in their generations. (Genesis 17:7-9)

The key passage is found in Genesis 17:9. It states: "And God said unto Abraham, Thou shalt keep my covenant therefore, thou, and thy seed after thee in their generations." A covenant is a mutual agreement. Each party has promised to do something. What many miss is that God has set forth both his promise and Abraham's promise. In Genesis 17:1 God tells Abraham "walk before me, and be thou perfect." Genesis 17:1. In return God promises to "be a God unto thee, and thy seed after thee." Genesis 17:7. How could Abraham be perfect? God provided a way for Abraham to keep his end of the bargain.

God supplied Abraham with faith. That faith was counted as perfect righteousness for Abraham. "Abraham believed God, and it was counted unto him for righteousness." (Romans 4:3) Abraham did not have the capacity to believe God (Ephesians 2:1), so God supplied the faith. The faith of Abraham was a gift from God. Ephesians 2:8. Jesus is the "author and finisher" of Abraham's faith and indeed the faith of all of the elect of God. Hebrews 2:2.

God fulfilled the requirements of both sides of the covenant he made with Abraham. That is what God meant when he said in Genesis 17:9: "And God said unto Abraham, **Thou shalt keep my covenant** therefore, thou, and thy seed after thee in their generations." God ensured that Abraham would keep his end of the agreement and "be perfect" by supplying Abraham's faith that was accounted unto him for perfect righteousness. God stated that Abraham's seed after him would keep the covenant. God ensures the perfection of his seed by supplying the faith that is accounted unto them for righteousness. John 6:37, 65; 17:2.

Salvation is not based upon anything intrinsically good in Abraham, it is based upon the intrinsic goodness and grace of God. Faith in Jesus Christ is accounted for righteousness. That faith is a gift of God (Romans 4) according to his sovereign will (Ephesians 1-2) without regard to the lineage or merit of his chosen (John 1:12-13).

The passage in Genesis 17:1-9 refers to an everlasting covenant. That everlasting covenant is the New Covenant of Christ, which is fulfilled in Christ. It is a spiritual covenant. The land promised is a heavenly land that will be "everlasting." God himself has revealed that truth to those who have ears to hear and eyes to see.

> By faith Abraham, when he was called to go out into a place which he should after receive for an inheritance, obeyed; and he went out, not knowing whither he went. By faith he sojourned in the land of promise, as in a strange country, dwelling in tabernacles with Isaac and Jacob, the heirs with him of the same promise: **For he looked for a city which hath foundations, whose builder and maker is God.** Through faith also Sara herself received strength to conceive seed, and was delivered of a child when she was past age, because she judged him faithful who had promised. Therefore sprang there even of one, and him as good as dead, so many as the stars of the sky in multitude, and as the sand which is by the sea shore innumerable. **These all died in faith, not having received the promises**, but having seen them afar off, and were persuaded of them, and embraced them,

and confessed that they were strangers and pilgrims on the earth. For they that say such things declare plainly that they seek a country. And truly, if they had been mindful of that country from whence they came out, they might have had opportunity to have returned. **But now they desire a better country, that is, an heavenly:** wherefore God is not ashamed to be called their God: for he hath prepared for them a city. (Hebrews 11:8-16)

Notice that those pilgrims of God died in faith not having received the promises on earth. The everlasting covenant of God is spiritual, the land is eternal in heaven, not temporal on earth. For the earthly land of Canaan could not possibly be an everlasting possession of fleshly Israel, because the earth will one day be destroyed and replaced by a new heaven and a new earth. "Looking for and hasting unto the coming of the day of God, wherein the heavens being on fire shall be dissolved, and the elements shall melt with fervent heat? Nevertheless we, according to his promise, look for new heavens and a new earth, wherein dwelleth righteousness." (2 Peter 3:12-13) "And I saw a new heaven and a new earth: for the first heaven and the first earth were passed away; and there was no more sea." (Revelation 21:1)

God made a conditional covenant with Israel that is referred to as the Mosaic covenant. The blessings were conditioned on the obedience of Israel. Israel violated that covenant and therefore the blessings did not flow to fleshly Israel.

> Now therefore, if ye will obey my voice indeed, and keep my covenant, then ye shall be a peculiar treasure unto me above all people: for all the earth is mine: And ye shall be unto me a kingdom of priests, and an holy nation.

> These are the words which thou shalt speak unto the children of Israel. And Moses came and called for the elders of the people, and laid before their faces all these words which the LORD commanded him. And all the people answered together, and said, All that the LORD hath spoken we will do. And Moses returned the words of the people unto the LORD. (Exodus 19:5-8)

Notice that "all the people answered together, and said, All that the LORD hath spoken we will do." Exodus 19:8. In this covenant the Jews agreed to fulfill the requirements of the covenant by their own effort. Further, notice that God did not say that they "shalt keep my covenant" as he said to Abraham in Genesis 17:9. God promised that Abraham would keep the covenant. In Exodus 19:8, however, the Jews promised to keep the covenant. God is showing us in these two different covenants, the difference between the futility of attempted salvation by the works of man and the solidity of salvation by the grace of God. No sooner did the Jews agree to obey God in Exodus 19:8 than they immediately fell into idolatry.

> Saying unto Aaron, Make us gods to go before us: for as for this Moses, which brought us out of the land of Egypt, we wot not what is become of him. And they made a calf in those days, and offered sacrifice unto the idol, and rejoiced in the works of their own hands. Then God turned, and gave them up to worship the host of heaven; as it is written in the book of the prophets, O ye house of Israel, have ye offered to me slain beasts and sacrifices by the space of forty years in the wilderness? Yea, ye took up the tabernacle of Moloch, and the star of your god Remphan, figures which ye made to worship them: and I will carry you away

beyond Babylon. (Acts 7:40-43)

The history of natural Israel is one of continual sin intermixed with periods of repentance, until God finally finished with them according to his foreordained plan. There is a spiritual Israel, the church, to whom the blessings flow. God's true Israel is and always was the church. The church contains the children of the promise. "Now we, brethren, as Isaac was, are the children of promise." (Galatians 4:28) The church is the Israel of God. "For in Christ Jesus neither circumcision availeth any thing, nor uncircumcision, but a new creature. And as many as walk according to this rule, peace be on them, and mercy, and upon the **Israel of God.**" (Galatians 6:15-16) The church is the temple of God. "Know ye not that ye are **the temple of God**, and that the Spirit of God dwelleth in you?" (1 Corinthians 3:16) The church is God's holy nation inheriting the promises made by God in Exodus 19:5-8. **"But ye are a chosen generation, a royal priesthood, an holy nation, a peculiar people**; that ye should shew forth the praises of him who hath called you out of darkness into his marvellous light." (1 Peter 2:9)

God does not have a plan of salvation for fleshly Israel that is any different from the plan of salvation he has for Gentiles. Salvation is by grace through faith in Jesus Christ for all. There is one body of Christ, his spiritual Israel, made up of Gentiles and the remnant of fleshly Israel.

> Even when we were dead in sins, hath quickened us together with Christ, (by grace ye are saved;) And hath raised us up together, and made us sit together in heavenly places in Christ Jesus: That in the ages to come he might shew the exceeding riches of his grace in his kindness toward us through Christ Jesus. For by grace are ye saved through faith; and that not of yourselves: it is the gift of God:

Not of works, lest any man should boast. For we are his workmanship, created in Christ Jesus unto good works, which God hath before ordained that we should walk in them. Wherefore remember, that ye being in time past Gentiles in the flesh, who are called Uncircumcision by that which is called the Circumcision in the flesh made by hands; That at that time ye were without Christ, being aliens from the commonwealth of Israel, and strangers from the covenants of promise, having no hope, and without God in the world: But now in Christ Jesus ye who sometimes were far off are made nigh by the blood of Christ. **For he is our peace, who hath made both one, and hath broken down the middle wall of partition between us; Having abolished in his flesh the enmity, even the law of commandments contained in ordinances; for to make in himself of twain one new man, so making peace; And that he might reconcile both unto God in one body by the cross, having slain the enmity thereby: And came and preached peace to you which were afar off, and to them that were nigh.** For through him we both have access by one Spirit unto the Father. Now therefore ye are no more strangers and foreigners, but fellowcitizens with the saints, and of the household of God; And are built upon the foundation of the apostles and prophets, Jesus Christ himself being the chief corner stone; In whom all the building fitly framed together groweth unto an holy temple in the Lord: In whom ye also are builded together for an habitation of God through the Spirit. (Ephesians 2:5-22)

Christ did not in any way provide some exclusive plan for the Jews. He stated that the gospel was to be preached to "all nations." Luke 24:47. The only difference for the Jews was that the preaching of the gospel should start at Jerusalem. Romans 1:16; Acts 18:5-6. It was to start with the Jews, but that does not mean it is to end with the Jews in some post-Christian era. The Old Testament has prophecies of the church of God consisting of both believing Jews and Gentiles. Amos 9:11-12; Hosea 1:10; 2:23. The Old Testament prophecies regarding salvation to both the Jews and Gentiles together are explained in Acts 15:13-17; 26:22-23; Romans 9:23-26; and 1 Peter 2:10.

The New Testament writers, being inspired by God, clearly understood that the church is the Israel of God and is the object of the promises made to Israel by God in the Old Testament.[47]

Paul said that believers are:

"The children of God" (Romans 8:16).
"The Household of God" (Ephesians 2:19).
"The children of Abraham" (Colossians 3:7).
"Abraham's seed" (Galatians 3:29).
"The Children of promise" (Rom. 9:8, Galatians 4:28).
"A peculiar people" (Titus 2:14).
"The elect of God" (Colossians 3:12).
"Heirs of God"(Rom. 8:17).
"Heirs according to the promise" (Galatians 3:29).
"The temple of God" (1 Cor 3:16).
"The circumcision" (Philippians 3:3).
"The Israel of God" (Galatians 6:16).

Peter said that believers are:

"A chosen generation" (1 Peter 2:9).
"A royal priesthood" (1 Peter 2:9).
"A holy nation" (1 Peter 2:9).

"A peculiar people" (1 Peter 2:9).

James said that believers are:

"Heirs of the kingdom" (James 2:5).

John said that believers are:

"The sons of God" (John 1:12).
"Kings and priests unto God" (Revelation 1:6).
"The new Jerusalem" (Revelation 3:12).
"The Holy city (Revelation 21:2).

The letter to the Hebrews said that believers are:

"The people of God" (Hebrews 4:9).
"Mount Sion" (Hebrews 12:22).
"The city of the living God" (Hebrews 12:22).
"The heavenly Jerusalem" (Hebrews 12:22).

The Jews are our enemies, because they are antichrist. Romans 11:28. Jews hate Christ and Christians. Those that are born after the flesh will always persecute those born after the spirit. Galatians 4:29. The spiritual children of God, however, are to love them and pray for them. "But I say unto you which hear, Love your enemies, do good to them which hate you, Bless them that curse you, and pray for them which despitefully use you." (Luke 6:27-28) God has chosen a remnant of Jews for salvation. We should preach the gospel to the lost world, including the Jews. We, however, should not think that a Jew is any different in God's plan than a Catholic, a Muslim, a Hindu, a Buddhist, a Satanist or any other follower of one of Satan's heathen religions.

Salvation for all, is by the grace of God through faith in Jesus Christ. If a Jew repents of his antichrist religion and believes in Jesus, then he is saved. Once saved, a Jew will not continue in his Talmudic practices any more than a Catholic will continue his Catholic practices or a Satanist will continue his satanic practices once they are saved. All believers in Christ become spiritual Jews, which are Christians. Romans 2:28-29.

Loving our enemies does not mean that we should condone the pagan practices of the Jews, Catholics, Muslims, or other heathens. Rather, we are called by God to reprove them. "And have no fellowship with the unfruitful works of darkness, but rather reprove them." (Ephesians 5:11)

5 The Ingrafting of the Natural Branches

Many Zionists cite to the passage in Romans 11, which mentions that God is able to graft the natural branches back into his vine of salvation. The Zionists interpret that passage to mean that fleshly Israel is central to God's plan of salvation. That is reading into the passage what is not there (eisegesis). Let us look at the operative passage in context and read it for what it says (exegesis):

> And if some of the branches be broken off, and thou, being a wild olive tree, wert graffed in among them, and with them partakest of the root and fatness of the olive tree; Boast not against the branches. But if thou boast, thou bearest not the root, but the root thee. Thou wilt say then, The branches were broken off, that I might be graffed in. Well; because of unbelief they were broken off, and thou standest by faith. Be not highminded, but fear: For if God spared not the natural branches, take heed lest he also spare not thee. Behold

therefore the goodness and severity of God: on them which fell, severity; but toward thee, goodness, if thou continue in his goodness: otherwise thou also shalt be cut off. **And they also, if they abide not still in unbelief, shall be graffed in: for God is able to graff them in again.** For if thou wert cut out of the olive tree which is wild by nature, and wert graffed contrary to nature into a good olive tree: how much more shall these, which be the natural branches, be graffed into their own olive tree? For I would not, brethren, that ye should be ignorant of this mystery, lest ye should be wise in your own conceits; that blindness in part is happened to Israel, until the fulness of the Gentiles be come in. And so all Israel shall be saved: as it is written, There shall come out of Sion the Deliverer, and shall turn away ungodliness from Jacob: For this is my covenant unto them, when I shall take away their sins. As concerning the gospel, they are enemies for your sakes: but as touching the election, they are beloved for the fathers' sakes. For the gifts and calling of God are without repentance. **For as ye in times past have not believed God, yet have now obtained mercy through their unbelief: Even so have these also now not believed, that through your mercy they also may obtain mercy. For God hath concluded them all in unbelief, that he might have mercy upon all.** O the depth of the riches both of the wisdom and knowledge of God! how unsearchable are his judgments, and his ways past finding out! Romans 11:17-33.

Romans 11 says nothing about the regeneration of

fleshly Israel aside from the grace of God through faith in Jesus Christ. The passage simply states that salvation comes only through being grafted into the olive tree of life through faith in Jesus, and that a remnant of fleshly Israel has been chosen by God for salvation. It does not say, as claimed by "Christian" Zionists that there is salvation for fleshly Jews by virtue of their status as Jews, without regard to their faith in Jesus Christ. Romans 11 makes clear that the grafting in of Jews is based entirely on their belief in Jesus Christ. Only those Jews who "abide not still in unbelief, shall be graffed in: for God is able to graff them in again." Romans 11:23.

Some take the position that fleshly Israel as a nation will be grafted back into the olive tree as fleshly Israel to remain fleshly Israel and be saved as such apart and distinct from the Christian church.[48] There is no biblical authority for such a theology. God's kingdom is not of the flesh, but of the spirit. Once a Jew is grafted into Christ he becomes a part of spiritual Israel, the church.

> Not as though the word of God hath taken none effect. For they are not all Israel, which are of Israel: Neither, because they are the seed of Abraham, are they all children: but, In Isaac shall thy seed be called. That is, **They which are the children of the flesh, these are not the children of God: but the children of the promise are counted for the seed.** Romans 9:6-8.

There is no more distinction between Jew or Gentile; all are one in Christ. Romans 10:12; Colossians 3:11, 28. Some state that the passage in Romans 11 "that blindness in part is happened to Israel, until the fulness of the Gentiles be come in" indicates that there will be a Jewish dispensation sometime in the future, at which time the Christian dispensation will end. Stephen Sizer explains the error of dispensational

Zionist theology.

> Based on this interpretative principle, dispensationalists hold that the promises made to Abraham and through him to the Jews, although postponed during this present Church age, are nevertheless eternal and unconditional and therefore await future realisation since they have never yet been literally fulfilled. So, for example, it is an article of normative dispensational belief that the boundaries of the land promised to Abraham and his descendants from the Nile to the Euphrates will be literally instituted and that Jesus Christ will return to a literal and theocratic Jewish kingdom centered on a rebuilt temple in Jerusalem. In such a scheme the Church on earth is relegated to the status of a parenthesis,[49] a 'Plan B',[50] and 'a sort of footnote or sidetrack in contrast to God's main mission to save ethnic, national Israel.'[51] (ellipses deleted).

Lewis Sperry Chafer, the founder of Dallas Theological Seminary (and follower of C.I Scofield), stated:

> The dispensationalist believes that throughout the ages God is pursuing two distinct purposes: one related to the earth with earthly people and earthly objectives involved which is Judaism; while the other is related to heaven with heavenly people and heavenly objectives involved, which is Christianity.[52]

The dispensational Zionism would not be possible without a systematic principle that allowed for a fundamental reinterpretation of bible passages. Stephen Sizer explains the devilishly subtle principle of bible interpretation that is at the core of dispensational Zionism:

> Dispensationalism is based on the hermeneutical principle that Scripture is always to be interpreted literally. Darby's approach might be summarized in one sentence in which he admitted, 'I prefer quoting many passages than enlarging upon them.'[53] Scofield, who popularized and synthesized Darby's theology explains further,

> "Not one instance exists of a 'spiritual' or figurative fulfilment of prophecy . . . Jerusalem is always Jerusalem, Israel is always Israel, Zion is always Zion. . . . Prophecies may never be spiritualized, but are always literal."[54]

Ryrie similarly asserts:

> "To be sure, literal/historical/grammatical interpretation is not the sole possession or practice of dispensationalists, but the consistent use of it in all areas of biblical interpretation is."[55]

The logical deduction of a literalist dispensational hermeneutic is, according to Dwight Pentecost, another former member of the Dallas faculty, that:

> "Scripture is unintelligible until one can distinguish clearly between God's program for his earthly people Israel and that for the Church."[56]

The Zionist theology of dispensationalism has gained

almost total primacy within the nominal "Christian" community. Sizer explains the origins and the popularity of dispensationalism:

> Dispensationalism is one of the most influential theological systems within the universal church today. Largely unrecognised and subliminal, it has increasingly shaped the presuppositions of fundamentalist, evangelical, Pentecostal and charismatic thinking concerning Israel and Palestine over the past one hundred and fifty years.
>
> John Nelson Darby is regarded as the father of dispensationalism and its prodigy, Christian Zionism. It was Cyrus. I. Scofield and D. L. Moody, however, who brought Darby's sectarian theology into mainstream evangelical circles. R. C. Sproul concedes that dispensationalism is now 'a theological system that in all probability is the majority report among current American evangelicals.'[57]
>
> Most of the early popular American radio preachers such as Donald Grey Barnhouse, Charles E. Fuller, and M. R. DeHaan were dispensationalists. Today, virtually all the 'televangelists' such as Jerry Falwell, Jim Bakker, Paul Crouch, Pat Robertson, Jimmy Swaggart and Billy Graham are also dispensationalists.
>
> Other leading dispensationalist writers include Charles Ryrie, Dwight Pentecost, John Walvoord, Eric Sauer, Charles Dyer, Tim LaHaye, Grant Jeffrey and Hal Lindsey. Notable political proponents include Jimmie

Carter and Ronald Reagan. Probably the most significant Christian organisations to espouse dispensationalism have been the Moody Bible Institute, Dallas Theological Seminary and the International Christian Embassy, Jerusalem.[58] (ellipse deleted).

Sizer explains that Darby was the most important dispensational Zionist missionary in history:

> Darby was a charismatic figure and dominant personality, a persuasive speaker and zealous missionary for his dispensationalist beliefs. He personally founded Brethren churches in Germany, Switzerland, France and the United States, which in turn sent missionaries to Africa, the West Indies, Australia and New Zealand. By the time of his death in 1885, around 1500 separatist Brethren churches had been founded world-wide. Don Wagner makes the point that:

> "During his lifetime, Darby wrote more hymns than the Wesleys, travelled further than the Apostle Paul, and was a Greek and Hebrew scholar. His writings filled forty volumes. . . . If Brightman was the father of Christian Zionism, then Darby was its greatest apostle and missionary."[59]

James Barr averred that the general theology of dispensationalism was an invention of J. N. Darby and "concocted in complete contradiction to all main Christian traditions."[60] Barr is correct insofar as he describes dispensationalism as unchristian and Darby as being responsible for popularizing it within the Protestant community. However, the origins of dispensationalism go back to the writings of a Jesuit priest, Emanuel De Lacunza (a/k/a Rabbi Juan Josaphat Ben Ezra). The Spanish edition of Lacunza's book, *The Coming of the Messiah in Glory and Majesty*, which was first published in 1812, became so popular in England that an English version was published. The job of translating the English version was performed by Edward Irving.[61] He completed the translation in 1826, but the book was not published until 1827.[62] Darby was very familiar with Lacunza's book and wrote about it in 1829, just two years after the publication of Lacunza'a book in English.[63]

Stephen Sizer explains that "Darby was convinced that the visible Church of his day was apostate. This assumption appears to have shaped his emerging belief that the Church era was therefore merely a 'parenthesis' to the Last Days. Darby regarded the Church as simply one more dispensation that had failed and was under God's judgement. Just as Israel had been cut off, so the Church would be."[64]

Sizer further explains that "Darby believed that the covenantal relationship between God and Abraham was binding forever and that the promises pertaining to the nation of Israel, as yet unfulfilled, would find their consummation in the reign of Jesus Christ on earth during the millennium."[65]

Clarence Bass explains that traditional Christian theology "always viewed the church as a continuation of God's single program of redemption begun in Israel."[66] Bass states that the Zionism that was popularized by Darby changed the traditional Christian view and was the foundation that ultimately created a theology of primacy of Israel over the church in God's plan for redemption:

> It is dispensationalism's rigid insistence on a distinct cleavage between Israel and the church, and its belief in a later unconditional fulfilment of the Abrahamic covenant, that sets

it off from the historic faith of the church.[67]

Charlie Samples in his book, *The Greatest Hoax,* stated that the undermining of the churches with the Judaic contagion of Zionism was long planned by the Jews. Samples cites to Jonathan Williams' 1781 book, *Legions of Satan*, wherein Williams avers that General Cornwallis revealed to General Washington during the surrender at Yorktown that in the future the churches in the United states would be infiltrated and "teach the Jews' religion." The churches would become auxiliary masonic temples, but that fact would be kept secret from the church members. The masonic churches would be working toward a world government.[68]

This author has been unable to verify the authenticity of the quote from Williams. This author personally travelled to the United States Library of Congress to search for William's book. The research librarians at the Library of Congress could not find the book in the Library of Congress, nor could they find it in a search of a database that spans over 100 university libraries. Furthermore, the librarians could not even determine if the book ever existed. Either the book never existed or someone went to extreme efforts to erase all trace of the book.

This author was able to determine that Jonathan Williams was a Colonel in the U.S. Army. Colonel Williams was the chief engineer and first Superintendent of West Point. Colonel Williams was a contemporary of George Washington and would have been in a position to know about the statement by Cornwallis.

Cornwallis did not personally surrender to Washington during the surrender ceremony at Yorktown, and there is no public record confirming William's account of Cornwallis speaking to Washington. That does not mean that such a conversation did not take place. Indeed, the nature of the alleged conversation suggests that Cornwallis was revealing a secret that would not ordinarily be discussed during a surrender ceremony but rather during a more informal and confidential conversation. Cornwallis was Washington's prisoner after all, and Washington would have had a desire and ample opportunity to converse with Cornwallis. Indeed, it would be unusual if the two did not converse. The fact that Cornwallis refused to take part in the surrender ceremony adds a degree of authenticity to the statements attributed to him. It would be just like Cornwallis, to spite Washington by first refusing to personally surrender to him and then revealing to him that Washington may have won the battle but his countrymen, for whom he and his army had sacrificed so much, would in the end be put in spiritual bondage.

Senator Joseph McCarthy (1908-1957) viewed Williams' account of General Cornwallis' statement to General Washington as authentic. Senator McCarthy was intimately aware of the communist threat to the United States. McCarthy died on May 2, 1957, at the age of forty-eight. He was hospitalized at Bethesda Naval Hospital purportedly for hepatitis, which is a disease that normally has a low fatality rate. He was hospitalized for four days. On the fourth day, McCarthy's health suddenly and unexpectedly took a turn for the worse and he died within an hour. Bethesda Naval Hospital is the same hospital from which another anti-communist, Secretary of Defense James V. Forrestal (1892-1949), fell out of a 16th floor window to his death.

Forrestal was found with a bathrobe sash knotted tightly around his neck, which is evidence indicating that he was murdered. He was killed on the day that he was to be released from the hospital. Forrestal's death was officially ruled a suicide, however, that finding has been criticized, since that conclusion ignores, and does not seek to explain, the clear evidence of foul-play, including evidence of a struggle indicating that Forrestal was thrown from the window.

Senator McCarthy was convinced that Forrestal was murdered. McCarthy stated: "The communists hounded Forrestal to his death."[69] McCarthy explained: "They killed him just as definitely as if they had thrown him from that sixteenth-story window in Bethesda Naval Hospital." McCarthy decided to begin his public fight against the communist threat on the day he heard of Forrestal's murder (May 22, 1949). "[W]hile I am not a sentimental man, I was touched deeply and left numb by the news of Forrestal's murder. But I was affected much more deeply when I heard of the communist celebration when they heard of Forrestal's murder. On that night, I dedicated part of this fight to Jim Forrestal."[70]

Forrestal was an anti-Zionist; McCarthy was an anti-communist. The differentiation between communism and Zionism is a distinction without a difference; they are one and the same. It was Forrestal who first brought the information of communist infiltration of the U.S. Government to Senator McCarthy's attention. The Zionist/communist infiltrators had to stop both Forrestal and McCarthy. Both of them entered Bethesda Naval Hospital without life-threatening illnesses; both died suspicious deaths. McCarthy was becoming aware of the Judaic core of communism. The Zionists/communists could not allow a sitting Senator to reveal that truth. He, like Forrestal before him, had to go. Medford Evans investigated the death of Senator McCarthy and was convinced that he was assassinated. He wrote a book about his findings titled *Assassination of Joe McCarthy*.[71]

The Zionists weren't satisfied with physically assassinating McCarthy, they had to make an example of him to keep anyone else from ever trying to expose them. The Zionists used their control of the corporate media to assassinate his character. The Jewish media coined the pejorative "McCarthyism"as a by-word to describe false accusations of disloyalty and subversion.

In fact, history has shown that McCarthy was absolutely correct in his accusations. M. Stanton Evans (son of Medford Evans) in his book *Blacklisted by History: The Untold Story of Senator Joe McCarthy and His Fight Against America's Enemies*, proves that McCarthy was correct and that his detractors were either dupes or communist sympathizers.[72]

Conservative political commentator Glenn Beck believed the historical propaganda about McCarthy. When he began reading Evans' book he told Evans "I don't want to believe this." Beck further stated: "I put it down and I went 'I'm not ready to hear that. I can't handle that.'" Beck later finished reading the book anyway; after doing so he was convinced that McCarthy was correct and has been falsely maligned. Beck told his audience, "Okay. Please, America, read this book."[73]

A year before Senator Joseph McCarthy died, he gave a speech in which he explained the subtle corruption of the nominal Christian churches with Judaic/Babylonian religious superstitions. Prior to that speech, Senator McCarthy stayed away from any public statement regarding Jewish influence in the communist infiltration in government. Many understood that the communist subversion was controlled by the Jews. For political reasons, McCarthy wanted to avoid the Jewish issue.

Scott Speidel explains: "His investigations into Communist subversion were turning up a vastly disproportionate number of Jewish Communists, and he was afraid that the Jews would believe he was hunting Jews rather than Communists."[74] Just as McCarthy feared, as soon as McCarthy began his public campaign against communist infiltration, the Jewish controlled corporate media began labeling McCarthy an antisemite. In order to curry favor with the Jewish controlled media and demonstrate that he was not an antisemite, McCarthy hired Jewish Lawyer, Roy Cohen, as his chief counsel for his Senate subcommittee investigation of communist subversion.

The historical evidence suggests that Cohen worked in subtle ways to undermine McCarthy's Senate investigation of communism. Roy Cohn, was not an anti-communist political conservative. Cohen in fact was a sodomite member of the political far left, whose lifestyle ultimately caused him to die of AIDS. Prior to his appointment as chief counsel by McCarthy, Cohen claimed a miraculous conversion to the anti-communist right wing. Scott Speidel states that Cohen's political conversion was only a ruse and that "as late as 1949 he was openly calling anti-Communism a 'witch-hunt' and said that Alger Hiss was a victim of a 'right-wing conspiracy.'"[75]

With Cohen as their secret agent in McCarthy's camp, the communist Jews knew McCarthy's strategy and were able to plan for it in advance. The double-cross of Senator McCarthy was abetted by the Jewish controlled media, which spun the Senate Committee hearings to make McCarthy appear as a heartless tyrant using his government power to harass poor innocent liberals.

Another false anti-communist working to undermine McCarthy was right-wing Jewish columnist for the Hearst newspapers, George Sokolsky. Sokolsky recommended Cohen to McCarthy. Cohen called Sokolsky his "rabbi."[76] At the age of 24 Sokolsky had gone to Russia with a large number of other Jews, to help the Bolshevik revolution. He was the editor of the English-language Communist newspaper Daily News in Petrograd.[77] After that, he left for China as a journalist on behalf of the communist revolutionary leader Sun Yat-sen.[78] Sokolsky claimed that his communist activities were all youthful mistakes, and since moving to the United States he had become an ardent anti-communist.

However, Sokolsky seems to have acted to undermine any effort to accurately reveal the communist threat. Scott Speidel states that Sokolsky was effective in "misdirecting the anti-Communist movement into blind alleys, false hopes, and confusion - and away from the truth."[79] Speidel states: "Considering these facts, are we justified in believing his claim that he had completely changed his ideals and in the 1950s was fervently against what he had been fervently for earlier in Russia and China?"[80]

The Jews were determined to destroy McCarthy and make an example of him, so that nobody would ever again dare try to root out communism in the government. It seems that they succeeded. McCarthyism is today a byword for tyrannical government witch hunts. Scott Speidel summarizes the end of McCarthy's political career:

> By September many of his supporters in the Congress, ever sensitive to the direction of the political wind, had thrown in the towel. McCarthy's Senate colleagues stripped him of his committee chair in November. On December 2, 1954, the Senate voted 67-22 to condemn him for "conduct contrary to Senatorial traditions." The condemnation permanently ended his effectiveness as a legislator.[81]

It is likely that once McCarthy realized that Cohen was behind the sabotage of his investigation, he fully understood the Jewish nature of communism and just how deep its tentacles had reached. McCarthy's speech referencing Cornwallis' statement to Washington about Jewish subversion is something that was so contrary to McCarthy's previous public position, he would never have said it unless he was convinced it was the key to understanding the true nature of the communist subversion. Below is an excerpt from Senator McCarthy's 1956 speech.

> The confession of General Cornwallis to General Washington at Yorktown (Oct. 17, 1781) has been well hidden by historians.

History books and text books have taught for years that when Cornwallis surrendered his army to General Washington that American independence came, and we lived happily ever after until the tribulations of the twentieth century.

Jonathan Williams recorded in his *Legions of Satan*, 1781, that Cornwallis revealed to Washington that "a holy war will now begin on America, and when it is ended America will be supposedly the citadel of freedom, but her millions will unknowingly be loyal subjects to the Crown."

Cornwallis went on to explain what would seem a contradiction:

"Your churches will be used to teach the Jew's religion and in less than two hundred years the whole nation will be working for divine world government. That government that they believe to be divine will be the British Empire. All religions will be permeated with Judaism without even being noticed by the masses, and they will all be under the invisible all-seeing eye of the Grand Architect of Freemasonry."

And indeed George Washington himself was a Mason, and he gave back through a false religion what he had won with his army.

Cornwallis well knew that his military defeat was only the beginning of world catastrophe that would be universal and that unrest would continue until mind control could be accomplished through a false religion. What he predicted has come to pass. A brief sketch of American religious history and we have seen Masonry infused into every church in America with their veiled Phallic religion.

Darby and the Plymouth Brethren brought a Jewish Christianity to America. Masons Rutherford and Russell started Jehovah Witnesses' Judaism which is now worldwide with their message of the divine kingdom. Mason Joseph Smith started Mormon Judaism with its Jewish teaching of millennialism.

At the turn of the twentieth century there appeared the Scofield Bible with a Jewish interpretation of the prophecies. With wide use of this "helpful" aid, all the American churches have silently become synagogues. We now have Baptist Jews, Methodist Jews, Church of God Jews, apostate Catholic Jews, and many Protestant Jews throughout America. We are aliens in our own country because of false religion. All are praying for divine deliverance into that "Divine Government" which Cornwallis knew to be the British Empire.

A false religion has been used to deceive us into allegiance to our enemies of Yorktown and Bunker Hill. No! Not a gun has been fired but the invisible and malignant process of conquering America with the Jew's religion has gone on unabated.

The Union Jack has been planted in our hearts with religious deception. All has happened "legally," "constitutionally," "freely" and completely within our most sacred trust -- our churches. Religious deception is painless inoculation against truth. It cannot be removed from the conscience with surgery, yet it is the motivator of our actions and directly controls our lives.

Once man gives over to false religion, he is no longer rational because he originates no thought. His life is controlled by whomever controls his religion.

The veil of false religion is the sword of Damocles and its power to control humanity defies even the imagination of tyrants who use it.

This is not to say that George Washington was a traitor willingly, or knowingly. He was beguiled into a Satanic religious order that insidiously controls men's minds. So have American statesmen and military leaders down through the years given aid and allegiance to the enemies of the United States because they did not have knowledge of the invisible subterfuge that stalks this land. My eyes were opened the day my colleague from Ohio handed me Wagner's *Freemasonry: An Interpretation*. If every American would read it, they would no longer ask why and how it has happened.[82]

The historical record of how the Judaic/Babylonian theology has been injected into the nominal Christian denominations testifies to the truth of General Cornwallis' statements and Senator McCarthy's explanation. Indeed, the prediction attributed to Cornwallis is coming to fruition before our very eyes. Judaism has permeated the nominal "Christian" churches through the doctrines of "Christian" Zionism. Those Judaic doctrines have been purposely injected into the churches by agents of the Judaic hierarchy. One of the principal agents of change was C.I. Scofield (1843-1921).

It was C.I. Scofield who injected the dispensational Zionism into the fundamental Christian churches, beginning in 1909 through the publication of his Scofield Reference Bible, which contained dispensational notes that relied heavily on Darby's writings. Bass states that "the Scofield Reference Bible became the leading Bible used by American Evangelicals and Fundamentalists for the next sixty years."[83]

Darby toured the United States seven times between 1862 and 1877.[84] During his travels to the United States he promoted his system of prophetic interpretation. Cyrus Ingerson Scofield wholeheartedly embraced Darby's doctrine. Scofield learned Darby's teachings from Dr. James H. Brookes, who was the pastor of the Compton Avenue Presbyterian Church in St. Louis and a follower of Darby's teachings.[85] Scofield put explanatory notes, which included Darby's dispensational system, in his famous Scofield Reference Bible.[86] The Scofield Reference Bible was published in 1909 and has since then sold more than three million copies. Including explanatory notes in the Holy Bible was unusual for the time and contrary to the practice of the Bible societies whose motto was "without note or comment."

Craig Blaising, professor of Systematic Theology at Dallas Theological Seminary, explains the influence of the Scofield Reference Bible on modern "Christian" theology. Blaising states that Scofield's bible "became the Bible of fundamentalism, and the theology of the notes approached confessional status in many Bible schools, institutes and seminaries established in the early decades of this century."[87]

The Scofield bible was funded and nurtured by World

Zionist leaders who saw the Christian churches in America as an obstacle to their plan for the establishment of a Jewish homeland in Palestine. These Zionists initiated a program to infiltrate and change the Christian doctrines of those churches. Two of the tools used to accomplish this goal were: 1) Cyrus I. Scofield and 2) a venerable, world respected European book publisher: The Oxford University Press.[88]

The scheme was to alter the Christian gospel and corrupt the church with a pro-Zionist subculture. "Scofield's role was to re-write the King James Version of the Bible by inserting Zionist-friendly notes in the margins, between verses and chapters, and on the bottoms of the pages."[89]

Charles Carlson cites the example of the notes at John 18:36 to show how the Scofield Reference Bible interspersed its reference notes to further the Zionist theology and contradict the plain meaning of the bible text.

> Jesus is being privately tried by Pilate, who tells Jesus, "Thine own nation and the chief priest have delivered thee unto me, What hast thou done?" "Jesus answered, My kingdom is not of this world . . ."
>
> But the Scofield footnote to verse 36 nullifies Jesus' spoken words by stating: "the verse is erroneously taken to mean Christ was disavowing that His kingdom would be establish[ed] on earth. Apart from the incompatibility of such a view with the entire testimony of Scripture . . ."
>
> We do not need to read further. The Zionist answer to words spoken by Jesus himself are that Jesus could not have meant what he said. The Scofield note says Jesus' words have to be

wrong because they are "incompatible" with the interpretation of those who wrote the notes to the Scofield Reference Bible.[90]

In 1909, the Oxford University Press published and implemented a large advertising budget to promote the Scofield Reference Bible. The Scofield Reference Bible was a subterfuge designed to create a subculture around a new worship icon, the modern State of Israel. The new state of Israel did not yet exist, but the well-funded Zionists already had it on their drawing boards.[91]

Carlson states: "Since the death of its original author and namesake, The Scofield Reference Bible has gone through several editions. Massive pro-Zionist notes were added to the 1967 edition, and some of Scofield's most significant notes from the original editions were removed where they apparently failed to further Zionist aims fast enough. Yet this edition retains the title, 'The New Scofield Reference Bible, Holy Bible, Editor C.I. Scofield.'"[92] It's anti-Arab, Zionist "Christian" subculture theology has fostered unyielding "Christian" support for the State of Israel and its barbaric subjugation of the native Palestinians.

Who was C.I. Scofield? Scofield was a young con-artist who engaged in a continual pattern of fraud and deception both before and after his alleged 1879 conversion. Scofield was a partner with John J. Ingalls, a Jewish lawyer, in a railroad scam which led to Scofield being sentenced to prison for criminal forgery.[93]

"Upon his release from prison, Scofield deserted his first wife, Leontine Carry Scofield, and his two daughters Abigail and Helen, and he took as his mistress a young girl from the St. Louis Flower Mission. He later abandoned her for Helen van Ward, whom he eventually married."[94]

Scofield had developed connections with a subgroup of the Illuminati, known as the Secret Six.[95] He was taken under the wing of Samuel Untermeyer (also spelled Untermyer) (1858-1940), an ardent Zionist who later became Chairman of the American Jewish Committee and President of the American League of Jewish Patriots.[96] Untermeyer was the powerful Zionist in charge of controlling and steering the policies of President Woodrow Wilson. "Untermeyer introduced Scofield to numerous Zionist and socialist leaders, including Samuel Gompers, Fiorello LaGuardia, Abraham Straus, Bernard Baruch and Jacob Schiff."[97] These powerful figures financed Scofield's research trips to Oxford and arranged the publication and distribution of his reference bible. He who pays the piper calls the tune.

In 1892 Scofield fraudulently claimed to have a Doctorate of Divinity and began calling himself "Doctor Scofield."[98] In fact, Scofield did not have a doctorate degree from any Seminary or University or for that matter any degree of any kind from any college. Below is an excerpt from an article titled "Cyrus I. Scofield in the Role of a Congregational Minister" which appeared on August 27, 1881 in the Topeka newspaper, The Daily Capital:

> The last personal knowledge that Kansans have had of this peer among scalawags, was when about four years ago, after a series of forgeries and confidence games he left the state and a destitute family and took refuge in Canada.
>
> For a time he kept undercover, nothing being heard of him until within the past two years when he turned up in St. Louis, where he had a wealthy widowed sister living who has generally come to the front and squared up Cyrus' little follies and foibles by paying good

round sums of money.

Within the past year, however, Cyrus committed a series of St. Louis forgeries that could not be settled so easily, and the erratic young gentleman was compelled to linger in the St. Louis jail for a period of six months.

Among the many malicious acts that characterized his career, was one peculiarly atrocious, that has come under our personal notice. Shortly after he left Kansas, leaving his wife and two children dependent upon the bounty of his wife's mother, he wrote his wife that he could invest some $1,300 of her mother's money, all she had, in a manner that would return big interest.

After some correspondence he forwarded them a mortgage, signed and executed by one Chas. Best, purporting to convey valuable property in St. Louis. Upon this, the money was sent to him. Afterwards the mortgages were found to be base forgeries, no such person as Charles Best being in existence, and the property conveyed in the mortgage fictitious.[99]

Scofield abandoned his wife and children and refused to support them. At that time it was difficult for a woman to work and support herself and her children. 1 Timothy 5:8 states: "But if any provide not for his own, and specially for those of his own house, he hath denied the faith, and is worse than an infidel."

When his first wife, Leontine, originally filed for divorce in July 1881, she listed the following reasons: "(he had) ... absented himself from his said wife and children, and had not been with them but abandoned them with the intention of not returning to them again . . . has been guilty of gross neglect of duty and has failed to support this plaintiff or her said children, or to contribute thereto, and has made no provision for them for food, clothing or a home, or in any manner performed his duty in the support of said family although he was able to do so."[100] At that time Scofield was the pastor of Hyde Park Congregational Church in St. Louis.[101] The divorce decree was granted in 1883, with the court finding that Scofield "was not a fit person to have custody of the children."[102]

Scofield's life was marked at every turn by duplicity. J.M. Canfield revealed that Scofield as a pastor concealed his abandonment of his family by telling the congregation prior to his divorce that he was single. In 1912, Scofield sent false biographical information to a publisher for an entry in *Who's Who in America*. Among the many lies and fabrications, Scofield falsely claimed that he was decorated for valor during the civil war. D. Jean Rushing discovered that in fact Scofield was a Confederate deserter. Having been married twice and being a demonstrably covetous and greedy con artist, Scofield did not qualify to be a church leader, let alone a respected commentator of God's word. "A bishop then must be blameless, the husband of one wife, vigilant, sober, of good behaviour, given to hospitality, apt to teach; Not given to wine, no striker, not greedy of filthy lucre; but patient, not a brawler, not covetous; One that ruleth well his own house, having his children in subjection with all gravity." (1 Timothy 3:2-4)

The Zionists who funded and directed the Scofield bible knew exactly what they were doing. Their strategy has born the sour fruit today whereby the ersatz "Christian" churches not only offer no resistance to Zionist aims, but they in fact promote Zionism. The satanic Zionist conspiracy against Christ and Christians is actually a cornerstone of many ersatz "Christian" churches. One example is Calvary Chapel founded by Chuck Smith.

Calvary Chapel has become one of the largest and most influential religious organizations in the world. Calvary Chapel of Costa Mesa, California, where Smith is senior pastor, is a mega-church with a membership of approximately 20,000 people.[103] According to a 2003 article in Forbes magazine, Calvary Chapel, Costa Mesa is the third largest non-Catholic church in the United States.[104] In addition, he has a regular radio program, "The Word for Today," which includes edited messages from Smith's sermons at Calvary Chapel, Costa Mesa. The television version of The Word for Today is seen nationwide on the blasphemous Trinity Broadcasting Network.

Calvary Chapel also owns and operates their radio station (KWVE). Calvary Chapel has a Bible College offering an Associate's Degree in Theology, and a Bachelor's degree in Biblical Studies. They own a 47-acre campus in Murietta Hot Springs, California. They also own a castle in Austria. In addition, Calvary Chapel ministries include: Calvary Chapel Music, Calvary Chapel Satellite Network International, Calvary Chapel Conference Center, Calvary Chapel Christian Camp, Maranatha Christian Academy, and Calvary Chapel High School. There are over 850 affiliated Calvary Chapels all over the globe, including approximately 700 in the United States. Some of the affiliated Calvary Chapels in the United States are mega-churches in their own right with memberships of more than 5,000 people.[105] Forbes magazine lists Calvary Chapel of Fort Lauderdale, Florida, an affiliate of Calvary Chapel, as the ninth largest non-Catholic church in the United States, with an average attendance of 17,000.[106]

In this author's previous book titled, *The Anti-Gospel*, I revealed that the initial funding for Calvary Chapel came from the Illuminati.[107] The Illuminati is a powerful Jewish secret society. We see the same Zionist forces behind Smith as were behind Scofield. Smith and his "ministry"are part of a conspiracy for Zionist conquest of Palestine and indeed the world. Smith's Zionist plans parallel the Zionist plans of the

Illuminati, which is not surprising in light of the Illuminati funding for Smith.

An investigative team from The Executive Intelligence Review discovered a group called the "American Jerusalem Temple Foundation," which was an early source of "massive amounts of money from American-based Darbyite Christian fundamentalists"[108] that were poured into "Jerusalem operations, aimed, ultimately, at blowing up the Muslim holy sites at the Temple Mount, and building the Third Temple."[109]

In the middle of this planned bloodfest we find Chuck Smith, pastor of Calvary Chapel. The Executive Intelligence Review discovered the following:

> At the core of the Gnostic "dispensational premillennarianism," advocated by Nineteenth-Century Anglican clergyman John Nelson Darby, is the belief that the extermination of the Jews, in a final battle of Armageddon, brought on by the rebuilding of Solomon's Temple, is the Biblical precondition for the second coming of the Messiah and the Rapture. **Pastor Chuck Smith, Dolphin's mentor at the Calvary Baptist Church, when asked by EIR whether he had any compunctions about unleashing a holy war that would lead to the possible extermination of millions of Jews and Muslims, replied, "Frankly, no, because it is all part of Biblical prophesy."**[110]
>
> **Smith was also full of praise for the Jewish zealots of the Temple Mount Faithful, and their founder, Goldfoot: "Do you want a real radical?" he asked. "Try Stanley Goldfoot. He's a wonder. His plan for the**

> **Temple Mount is to take sticks of dynamite and some M-16s and blow the Dome of the Rock and Al-Aqsa Mosques and just lay claim to the site."**[111]

Who is Stanley Goldfoot, upon whom Chuck Smith heaps such praise? He is a psychopathic mass murderer and internationally recognized terrorist! He has admitted he helped plan the 1946 dynamite bombing of the King David Hotel that killed approximately 100 Christian, Jewish, and Muslim civilians.[112] Goldfoot has also admitted that he planned and directed the execution of the United Nations mediator, Count Folke Bernadotte, in Jerusalem, in the fall of 1948.[113]

Chuck Smith is so impressed with Goldfoot that he invited that killer to lecture in his Calvary Chapel![114] Smith has also financed Goldfoot's Zionist activities! The Hebrew University of Jerusalem explains:

> Chuck Smith, a noted minister and evangelist whose Calvary Chapel in Costa Mesa, California, has been one of the largest and most dynamic Charismatic churches in America, invited Goldfoot to lecture in his church, and his followers helped to finance Goldfoot's activity.[115]
>
> Smith secured financial support for exploration of the exact site of the Temple. An associate of Smith, Lambert Dolphin, a California physicist and archeologist and leader of the "Science and Archeology Team," took it upon himself to explore the Temple Mount. An ardent premillennialist who believed that the building of the Temple was essential to the realization of messianic hopes.[116]

Can we regard Chuck Smith as a true minister of the Gospel when he praises and financially supports a terrorist killer? Why would he do such a thing? Because both he and Goldfoot are Zionists, who want to bring Palestine under the complete control of Israel. One of the key goals of the Zionist Illuminati is to rule the world. Jewish control of Palestine is one step toward that Zionist goal.

Another Zionist shill was Jerry Falwell. In 1979, Israel gave Falwell a gift of a Learjet.[117] Falwell put the Learjet to good use spreading the dispensational theology that includes a requirement of the Jews to return to Israel as part of God's plan for Christ to return.[118] His purpose was to influence the American Christian audience to favor Israel. Sean McBride explains how it worked:

> When Israel bombed Iraq's Osirak nuclear reactor in 1981, Begin made his first telephone call to Falwell, asking him to explain to the Christian public the reasons for the bombing. Only later did he call [President] Reagan.[119]

Notice that Israeli Prime Minister Menachem Begin called Falwell before calling the President of the United States. That should give the reader some idea of the political importance of the "Christian" Zionist movement to Israel. Falwell is now dead, but Israel has many arrows in its Zionist quiver. There are scores of American preachers under Israel's control, who have used their considerable influence to keep the American public pro-Zionist. Past and present "Christian" Zionists include, but are not limited to: Chuck Smith, Pat Robertson, Oral Roberts, Hal Lindsey, Michael David Evans, Tim LaHaye, Kenneth Copeland, Paul Crouch, Ed McAteer, Jim Bakker, Chuck Missler, and Jimmy Swaggart.[120]

In addition to individual Zionist hucksters, there is also an alphabet soup of influential "Christian" Zionist organizations that have been established to support Israel. They include, but are not limited to, the International Christian Embassy, Jerusalem (ICEJ), Bridges for Peace (BFP), Christian Friends of Israel (CFI), Christians United for Israel (CUFI) Unity Coalition for Israel (UCI), Prayer Friends of Israel (PFI), Bridges for Peace (BFP), The American Messianic Fellowship (AMF), The Messianic Jewish Alliance of America (MJAA), Jews for Jesus (JFJ), and the Council of Christians and Jews (CCJ).[121] These organizations comprise a broad coalition that furthers the Zionist agenda, including influencing the United States foreign policy in the Middle East.

Hal Lindsey is one of the most influential dispensational Zionists. He has been described by Time magazine as "The Jeremiah for this Generation," and by the New York Times as "the best selling author of the decade."[122] Lindsey is the author of over twenty books, one of which (*The Late Great Planet Earth*) has been described by the New York Times as the "#1 Non-fiction Bestseller of the Decade."[123] The Late Great Planet Earth has sold more than 18 million copies in English, and an additional 18-20 million copies in 54 foreign language editions.[124]

Sizer reveals that in Lindsey's book, Road to Holocaust, Lindsey "accuses those who refuse to accept dispensationalism's distinction between the Church and Israel of encouraging anti-Semitism since they apparently deny any future role for the State of Israel within the purposes of God."[125] Sizer further states:

> Through his many books, his International Intelligence Briefing,[126] a monthly Middle East political journal, together with weekly television Prophecy Watch programs, Lindsey has encouraged evangelicals and fundamentalists to support Israel's right-wing Zionist agenda. Yet there is great irony here

for Lindsey claims to support Israel and to refute anti-Semitism yet his "Armageddon' style theology'[127] may actually be a self-fulfilling prophecy - leading to the very holocaust which he abhors yet repeatedly predicts.[128]

The dispensational Zionists twist the scriptures and then try to orchestrate events to hasten Armegeddon and their idea of the millennial reign of Christ in earthly Jerusalem. They use Christ's name but act as though God does not exist and think it is necessary to orchestrate events to bring about Armageddon. Dr. Stan Moody coined the oxymoron "Christian Atheism" to describe the schizophrenic theology of the dispensational Zionists.

> Christian Atheism is a Christianity that seeks converts rather than makes disciples – that tires of waiting for God to act in human history and decides to take matters into its own hands. Christian Atheism is a belief system that prefers dogma over doctrine, power over weakness, works over faith, law over grace and ease over suffering. Christian Atheism is the product of sloppy theology that rears its ugly head when the people of God become too comfortable and too proud. In a word, Why waste time trying to discover the truth when you can so easily create it?[129]

Moody calls the Christian Atheists "narcissistic con artists, whose faith runs no deeper than a platform for self-protection and self advancement."[130] He states that their Zionist theology requires that "belief becomes secondary to the language of belief."[131] Moody makes a scary observation about their dispensational Zionism:

> Tired of waiting for God to lead His people to triumph and success, it becomes the mission of the Christian Zionist to create such chaos in the Middle East that Jesus will have no other option than to return. . . . Such policies as nuclear war with Iran and pushing the Palestinian people into Saudi Arabia, Egypt, the Jordan River and the Mediterranean Sea is a strategy of impatiently backing God into a corner.[132]

The following is the position of the dispensational Zionists toward Israel as presented in the official proclamation of the Fourth International Christian Congress on Biblical Zionism, which was a conclave, with wide representation of "Christian" Zionist, held in Jerusalem in February, 2001:

> Biblical Zionism is the firm belief that God chose the Jewish people and bequeathed to them as an everlasting possession the Land of Canaan. Christians must take courageous action to support the return of the Jewish people to the Land of Israel in all its parts.[133]

What about the Palestinians who occupy that land? The "Christian" Zionists don't much care about them. John Hubers explains that the "Christian" Zionists have adopted the extreme view of the militant settler movement in Israel:

> God gave all of the land to the Jews as an eternal possession, which means that they have the right to settle anywhere they choose, no matter what the UN or the United States or even their own government says. If it means forcibly removing Palestinians from lands they and their families have cultivated for generations, so be it. It's all theirs. To say

> otherwise is to argue with God.[134]

Hubers reveals that the "Christian" Zionists act to incite the Jewish populace to pressure their government not to compromise on territorial issues with the Palestinians.

> In an astonishing meeting held in Jerusalem several years back, one-time Republican presidential hopeful and Christian TV talk show host, Pat Robertson, showed how extreme Christian Zionists can be in asserting their convictions on this issue. Robertson used the occasion to urge a Jewish audience to put pressure on their government not [to] make any territorial compromises with the Palestinians, as to do so would be to set themselves in opposition to God's will for their country.[135]

In view of the unchristian attitude of the "Christian" Zionists, it is no surprise that their official position announced at the Fourth International Christian Congress on Biblical Zionism is that a Palestinian state is out of the question:

> The Bible puts its full weight behind the Return of the Jewish exiles to Eretz Israel. Therefore Christians have no biblical grounds upon which to base support for Palestinian nationalism.[136]

The International Christian Embassy, Jerusalem (ICEJ) was founded in 1980, with its purpose being to facilitate the restoration of the Jews to Israel.[137] The ICEJ has representatives in more than 80 countries. The ICEJ has a strident dispensational Zionist theology. The ICEJ sponsors an annual Feast of Tabernacles celebration, which typically attracts approximately 5,000 "Christian" Zionists from more than 70 nations. The ICEJ is politically influential. Since 1980, every sitting Israeli Prime Minister has attended and addressed the ICEJ Feast of Tabernacles conclave.[138]

The ICEJ is a "Christian" front that serves the political aims of Zionist Jews. That seems to be the case with all dispensational Zionist organizations and churches. The ICEJ unconditionally supports the position of the Likud party in Israel. The Likud party is an ultra-right wing party that was established by the notorious terrorist Menachem Begin in 1973. The Likud party was formed by merging several political groups with Begin's former terrorist comrades from the Irgun militia, which orchestrated the bloody terrorist bombing of the King David Hotel in Jerusalem in 1946.

The Likud party flatly rejects the establishment of a Palestinian state west of the Jordan river. Furthermore, the Likud party, which presently controls Israel, demands that Palestinian factions recognize Israel as a Jewish state. Agreeing to such a demand would be tantamount to national suicide for Palestinians, because they will have no right to a Palestinian state of their own and therefore they would have no rights whatsoever in a Jewish state of Israel. Under the Likud plan, the Palestinians will never be allowed to live free of Israeli military occupation. Under the Likud platform, it is impossible for there ever to be any territorial compromise with the Palestinians for peace.

The ICEJ misuses the bible by taking passages out of context to defend Israel's military settlement and colonization of Syria's Golan Heights and the Occupied Territories, despite international protests. The ICEJ is also implacably opposed to the political autonomy of the Palestinian people, a shared Jerusalem, or the right of return for refugees who have lost their property and land through war or confiscation. The ICEJ, which is supposed to be a Christian organization, has repudiated the indigenous Christian Palestinian community.[139]

The ICEJ, as is the case with almost all dispensational Zionist organizations, gives ethnic Jews primacy over Christians in God's eternal plan. Even though the Jews reject Jesus Christ, the ICEJ gives them status superior to believing Christians.[140] Stephen Sizer quotes from ICEJ publications that set forth the ICEJ theology of Jewish primacy.

> Whereas the New Testament emphasises in Ephesians 2:14 that Jesus Christ has "made the two one" so that, according to Galatians 3:28, in Christ there is now "neither Jew nor Greek," the ICEJ insist on maintaining a distinction and superior status for those of Jewish ethnic descent who remain, even apart from faith in Jesus Christ, the chosen people, "His Jewish sons and daughters."[141]

The theme of the Gospel is that there will be no end to Christ's kingdom, or his people, the church. 2 Peter 1:11. When the fullness of the Gentiles come in, then will be the end of the world. 1 Corinthians 15:23-24. God did not state that the Jews will be saved *en masse* after the fullness of the Gentiles comes in. He simply stated that the Jews will be blind in part until the world ends. God has chosen a remnant of Jews to save from every generation, not just one generation during some post-Christian era.

God's plan is to establish the earthly then the spiritual. "Howbeit that was not first which is spiritual, but that which is natural; and afterward that which is spiritual." 1 Corinthians 15:46. God will not reverse course and reestablish the earthly kingdom of Israel in place of his spiritual kingdom of Israel. That is contrary to his revealed plan. Fleshly Israel was intended by God for an example to us, his church. 1 Corinthians 10:6. It is not the circumcision of the flesh that counts but the circumcision of the heart. Colossians 2:11.

6 Dispensational Zionism

Dipsensational Zionism is based upon a myth that God has two separate plans for redemption; one redemptive plan for earthly Israel and another separate plan for the church. Dispensational Zionists created a false gospel wherein their false god's focus is on earthly Israel, with the church only being a parenthetical interlude in his plan for Israel. John Hubers explains the theology behind this alternative Zionist gospel:

> Dispensationalist Christian Zionists posit two redemptive streams in God's economy of salvation: 1) that which God purposes in, through and for the Jewish people, which finds its fullest expression in their restoration to the land which God gave them as an "eternal inheritance;" and 2) that which God purposes in and through His Son, Jesus Christ. The second stream has always been the predominant theme of Christian teaching and preaching, the central motif of a unique Christian witness. Yet in Christian Zionist literature and teaching, what predominates is the first stream.[142]

The very idea of two redemptive plans is not only contrary to the words of the bible, it is antichrist. The cornerstone of God's redemptive plan is Jesus Christ, who came to break down the barrier between Jew and Gentile, making out of the two one spiritual structure, his church. Redemption comes to the Jew and Gentile only by the grace of God through faith in Jesus Christ. Ephesians 2:8. There is no other separate redemptive plan for Israel. The myth of a dual redemptive plan is inspired by Satan and promoted by his minions. These minions appear as gentle lambs of mercy, but spiritually they are ravening wolves. Jesus warned of such: "Beware of false prophets, which come to you in sheep's clothing, but inwardly they are ravening wolves." Matthew 7:15. Only the most reprobate mind could interpret God's word to contain a dual redemptive plan.

> Wherefore remember, that ye being in time past Gentiles in the flesh, who are called Uncircumcision by that which is called the Circumcision in the flesh made by hands; That at that time ye were without Christ, being aliens from the commonwealth of Israel, and strangers from the covenants of promise, having no hope, and without God in the world: But now in Christ Jesus ye who sometimes were far off are made nigh by the blood of Christ. **For he is our peace, who hath made both one, and hath broken down the middle wall of partition between us; Having abolished in his flesh the enmity, even the law of commandments contained in ordinances; for to make in himself of twain one new man, so making peace; And that he might reconcile both unto God in one body by the cross, having slain the enmity thereby: And came and preached peace to you which were afar off, and to them that**

> were nigh. **For through him we both have access by one Spirit unto the Father**. Now therefore ye are no more strangers and foreigners, but fellowcitizens with the saints, and of the household of God; And are built upon the foundation of the apostles and prophets, Jesus Christ himself being the chief corner stone; In whom all the building fitly framed together groweth unto an holy temple in the Lord: In whom ye also are builded together for an habitation of God through the Spirit. Epesians 2:11-22 (emphasis added).

The phony redemptive plan for Jews that is based upon their status as Jews alone is impeached by the very words of the gospel. God has made it clear that the Jews rejected Christ and that salvation was not according to the flesh or blood but by God's sovereign election alone by faith in Jesus Christ alone.

> He came unto his own, and **his own received him not**. But as many as received him, to them gave he power to become the sons of God, even **to them that believe on his name**: Which were born, **not of blood, nor of the will of the flesh**, nor of the will of man, but of God. John 1:11-13.

Part and parcel of "Christian" Zionism is the theory that Jesus will return to rule on earth for 1,000 years from a Jewish temple in Jerusalem. This theological construct is commonly referred to as dispensational premillennialism (DP). Sam Storms explains how DP has become the predominate theology of TV preachers:

> Virtually all well-known TV preachers (all those who appear on TBN and most on the 700

Club) and radio teachers espouse the DP view of biblical prophecy. Prominent dispensationalists who utilize the media to communicate their views include W. A. Criswell, M. R. and Richard DeHaan (the Radio Bible Class), Warren Wiersbe, Charles Stanley, Adrian Rogers, Jack Van Impe, Chuck Swindoll, Billy Graham, Luis Palau, Bill Bright, James Dobson, Jerry Falwell, John Hagee, etc. I struggle to think of a single TV evangelist or minister of a mega-church that regularly broadcasts in America who isn't a DP.[143]

Steve Van Nattan is an example of a Dispensational Premillennialist who believes that the Jews will regain their prominence once again in God's plan:

I believe that the "dry bones" (Jews) of Israel and Judah are scattered all over the world today, and shortly Messiah Jesus Christ will gather those Jews again to initiate His literal 1000 year reign in the Middle East. Those wimps who will not take these promises literally are treacherous scoundrels, right to the pinnacle of their PhD (Piled Higher and Deeper) pilum lapidus in Calvin Seminary.[144]

Van Nattan has stated: "I believe that the kingdom promised to Israel is very real, and it is all in the future as promised by the prophets."[145] Van Nattan has further stated: "I believe Jesus Christ will return literally and restore Israel to glory and give those real Jews 1000 years of joy and Covenant blessing." [146]

Dispensational premillennialists are looking at the promised kingdom through carnal eyes. They are making the same error as the Jews at the time of Christ's appearance in Jerusalem. Dillard Thurman explains the parallel error of the dispensational premillennialists of today and carnal Jews of Christ's time:

> The matter of the kingdom was misunderstood by all. "When he was demanded of the Pharisees, when the kingdom of God should come, he answered them and said, The kingdom of God cometh not with observation . . . behold, the kingdom of God is within you" (Luke 17:20-21). His kingdom was to have its place in the hearts of men - but they misunderstood. Materialistic people could not visualize a spiritual kingdom with their Messiah (Christ) sitting on the throne of David! Materialistic folk still have the same problem.
>
> John the Baptizer, Jesus Christ and all of His apostles taught: "The kingdom of heaven is at hand" (Matt. 3:2; 4:17; 10:7; etc.). The imminence of kingdom was shown as Jesus taught: "Verily I say unto you, There are some here of them that stand by, who shall in no wise taste of death, till they see the kingdom of God come with power" (Mark. 9:1). Now, have any of these pre-millennialists seen any 2000-year-olds running around lately? Surely, then, that kingdom came over 1900 years ago, as Jesus promised.[147]

Jesus made it clear that God's kingdom is spiritual. Jesus did not mince words; he told the Pharisees that the kingdom of God, and hence the promises to Abraham are fulfilled in him, and his kingdom is a spiritual kingdom that "cometh not with observation." The kingdom of God is within the believer, by virtue of being born again of the Holy Spirit. *See* Luke 17:20.

The dispensational Zionism that has spread through the churches includes within its theological construct a reestablishment of animal sacrifices, once the new Jewish temple expected by the Zionists is rebuilt at Jerusalem. God, however, would not have us return to the weak and beggarly elements of the Old Testament law under fleshly Israel. See Galatians 4:9-11. To teach such a thing is to blasphemously state that Christ's sacrifice was imperfect and insufficient, and that therefore there is a need to reinstate the animal sacrifices. The Old Testament law was to act as a schoolmaster until the promise of Christ. Galatians 3:24-25. God would have no reason to reinstate something that was intended to be in place only until he came to offer his own body as a perfect sacrifice.

In the 1800's Zionist Jews needed a financial backing from the United States or their plan for a new Israel would fail. At that time, the United States was a predominately Christian Country. Any attempt to subjugate Palestine and reestablish Israel as a state in that region would be met with resistence from the then politically influential Christian quarter in the U.S. The Christians in the U.S. posed a political roadblock to funding the new state of Israel. The Zionists knew that they had to nullify the anticipated Christian resistance to their Zionist plan. They decided that the Christian theology in the Protestant churches must be changed to favor an Israeli state. They had ready theologians to perform this duty in their Jesuit auxiliary.

The Jesuits decided on a plan to inject a theology into the Protestant churches whereby the Jews would be restored to their lost prominence via the rebuilding of the Jewish temple in Jerusalem. There would be a reinstatement of animal sacrifices and the ordinances of the Old Testament law. Christ would return and rule from the temple during a millennial reign. Thus, the Christians would look upon the reestablishment of the Jewish state of Israel in Palestine as a fulfillment of the prophecy. They, consequently, would not offer any political resistance but rather be encouraged to support Israel.

As previously mentioned, Jesuit Emanuel De Lacunza's book, *The Coming of the Messiah in Glory and Majesty,* was published in 1812, 11 years after he died.[148] William Kimball in his book Rapture, *A Question of Timing,* reveals that De Lacunza wrote the book under the pen name of Rabbi Juan Josaphat Ben Ezra.[149] Kimball attributes the pen name to a motive to conceal his identity, thus taking the heat off of Rome, and making his writings more palatable to the Protestant readers.[150] It is as likely that in fact the pen name reveals something about Lacunza, and that is perhaps he was a Jewish Rabbi. It is possible that Lacunza was a crypto-Jew, who wrote the book under his true identity as a rabbi. He must have had the learning of a Rabbi in order to write a book that contains knowledge of Judaism expected of a Rabbi.

Lacunza's status as a rabbi is all the more believable when one considers the fact that he was a Jesuit and the first Jesuits were crypto-Jews.[151] For example, Ignatius Loyola, the founder of the Jesuit order, was a crypto-Jew of the Occult Kabbalah. Jews were attracted to the Jesuit order and joined in large numbers.[152] Francisco Ribera,[153] who was another early Jesuit purveyor of the futurist eschatology, was a crypto-Jew. Lacunza would not be out of place as a Jewish Jesuit. Lacunza and Ribera being Jews would explain why they introduced the eschatological teaching of a return to the Jewish animal sacrifices. That doctrine gives the Jews primacy in God's plan and relegates Christians to a prophetic parenthetical to be supplanted by the Jews during the supposed thousand-year earthly reign of Christ.

Lacunza wrote that during a millennium after a period of terrible tribulation the Jewish animal sacrifices would be reinstated along with the Eucharist (the mass) of the Catholic Church.[154] Lacunza has followed after Jewish fables and replaced the commandments of God with the commandments of men. See Titus 1:13. "They profess that they know God; but in works they deny him, being abominable, and disobedient, and unto every good work reprobate." Titus 1:16

While researchers have traced the origins of dispensational Zionism to Lacunza, Marshal Hall has traced its origins back even further than Lacunza. Hall attributes the erroneous eschatology to a 13th century rabbi, Moses ben Nahman Gerondi. Rabbi ben Nahman (a/k/a ben Nachman) is described by the Jewish Encyclopedia as a "Spanish Talmudist, exegete, and physician; born at Gerona."[155] The Jewish Encyclopedia even alludes to some of the dispensational writings of ben Nahman.

> The characteristic features of Moses' [ben Nahman's] commentary are the lessons which he draws from the various Biblical narratives, in which he sees adumbrations [foreshadowings] of the history of man. Thus the account of the six days of Creation constitutes a prophecy of the events of the following six thousand years, and the seventh day is typical of the Messianic millennium.[156]

The "Messianic millennium" referred to by ben Nahman is a millennium without Jesus as the Messiah. The defining characteristic of Jews is their rejection of Jesus as the Messiah, and ben Nahman is no different. Ben Nahman is on record as stating that he believed that Jesus could not have been the Messiah, because ben Nahman reckoned that the Messiah was supposed to be "a man of flesh and blood, and not as a divinity"[157] as is the claim of Jesus. Further, ben Nahman stated that the promised "reign of universal peace and justice had not yet been fulfilled."[158] Ben Nahman states: "On the contrary, since the appearance of Jesus, the world had been filled with violence and injustice, and among all denominations the Christians were the most warlike."[159] If only Zionist "Christians" knew that their dispensational Zionism is based upon Jewish eisegesis that is founded upon a rejection of Jesus as Christ.

The rabbinical origins of dispensational Zionism explains why John Hagee and others who espouse that doctrine have the opinion that the Jews are saved simply because they are Jews, and therefore there is no need to evangelize them. Hagee and his ilk do not think that the Jews need to believe in Jesus Christ to get to heaven. Hagee is simply spouting the rabbinical party line established through the centuries.

We read in the Jews' Babylonian Talmud at Tractate Sanhedrin, verse one of Chapter 11: **"All Israel have a portion in the world to come."**[160] The next clause in Sanhedrin Chapter 11 states: **"For it is written, thy people are all righteous; they shall inherit the land for ever."**[161] Jews are taught that they are righteous and will go to heaven, simply by virtue of being a Jew. That message is reinforced by phony Christian pastors. Dispensational Zionists are doing the devil's work in hardening the hearts of the Jews to the gospel of Jesus Christ.

God explains: "Now the Spirit speaks expressly, that in the latter times some shall depart from the faith, giving heed to seducing spirits, and doctrines of devils." 1 Timothy 4:1. Dispensational Zionism is a doctrine of devils. Marshal Hall succinctly explains the problem with Christians adopting devilish religious doctrines from Christ hating Jews:

> "IF" is the biggest word in the Bible relating to those Old Testament promises to the Hebrews, later called Jews. God made it all conditional. They didn't meet the conditions. The New

> Testament makes that plain a hundred times. That is why the New Testament is hated so fiercely and has been publicly burned in Jerusalem by the Zionists. Christians are supposed to be following the teachings of Jesus and His apostles in God's New Contract with a new people ("whosoever will . . . no respecter of persons . . . neither Jew nor Greek . . . wall of partition broken down, etc., etc.). Christians are not supposed to be following the teaching of Rabbis from any century, who get their doctrines from the Christ hating, New Testament destroying Talmud/Kabbala teachings. The fact of the matter is, however, that the most influential wing of supposedly fundamentalist New Testament Christianity has been deceived into promoting the Rabbinic agenda, an agenda which is totally dedicated to the destruction of the teachings of Jesus in the New Testament![162]

The truth of Hall's statement is self-evident. How did this devilish doctrine make its way into the churches? God explains that "we wrestle not against flesh and blood, but against principalities, against powers, against the rulers of the darkness of this world, against spiritual wickedness in high places." Ephesians 6:12. The spiritual wickedness is manifested in the false ministers, who have popularized the Zionist error into the churches.

> For such are false apostles, deceitful workers, transforming themselves into the apostles of Christ, And no marvel; for Satan himself is transformed into an angel of light. Therefore it is no great thing if his ministers also be transformed as the ministers of righteousness; whose end shall be according to their works.

2 Corinthians 11:13-15.

The Jewish origin of the Zionist millennial doctrine explains why its essence is an implicit rejection of Jesus Christ. Jesus Christ is the Chief cornerstone of the spiritual temple of God. The rebuilding of the physical temple with physical stone as expounded in the premillennial eschatology is a rejection of the rock of salvation, Jesus Christ.

> But Israel, which followed after the law of righteousness, hath not attained to the law of righteousness. Wherefore? Because **they sought it not by faith, but as it were by the works of the law. For they stumbled at that stumblingstone**; As it is written, Behold, I lay in Sion a stumblingstone and rock of offence: and whosoever believeth on him shall not be ashamed. (Romans 9:31-33)

Jesus Christ is the stone that has been rejected by the builders of this false religion; to them he is a rock of offense upon whom they will stumble to their ultimate demise. "For if they which are of the law be heirs, faith is made void, and the promise made of none effect." (Romans 4:14) Jesus is the rock of salvation. Psalms 62:6; 89:26; 95:1. Christians are spiritual stones that are incorporated into Jesus Christ to make a holy temple of the Lord.

> As newborn babes, desire the sincere milk of the word, that ye may grow thereby: If so be ye have tasted that the Lord is gracious. **To whom coming, as unto a living stone, disallowed indeed of men, but chosen of God, and precious, Ye also, as lively stones, are built up a spiritual house,** an holy priesthood, to offer up spiritual sacrifices, acceptable to God by Jesus Christ. Wherefore

> also it is contained in the scripture, Behold, I lay in Sion a chief corner stone, elect, precious: and he that believeth on him shall not be confounded. **Unto you therefore which believe he is precious: but unto them which be disobedient, the stone which the builders disallowed, the same is made the head of the corner, And a stone of stumbling, and a rock of offence, even to them which stumble at the word, being disobedient: whereunto also they were appointed.** But ye are a chosen generation, a royal priesthood, an holy nation, a peculiar people; that ye should shew forth the praises of him who hath called you out of darkness into his marvellous light: (1 Peter 2:2-9)

What is the temple of God? Each saved Christian individually and all saved Christians corporately make up the temple of God.

> Know ye not that **ye are the temple of God**, and that the Spirit of God dwelleth in you? If any man defile the temple of God, him shall God destroy; for **the temple of God is holy, which temple ye are**. (1 Corinthians 3:16-17)

> What? know ye not that **your body is the temple of the Holy Ghost** which is in you, which ye have of God, and ye are not your own? For ye are bought with a price: therefore glorify God in your body, and in your spirit, which are God's. (1 Corinthians 6:19-20)

> In whom all the **building fitly framed together groweth unto an holy temple in the Lord**: (Ephesians 2:21)

Hebrews 8:1-10:39 makes explicitly clear that Christ fulfilled the requirements of the law by sacrificing himself once for sins for all time. If the blood of animals were sufficient to satisfy God, there would be no need for him to come to the earth and sacrifice himself. "But now hath he obtained a more excellent ministry, by how much also he is the mediator of a better covenant, which was established upon better promises. For if that first covenant had been faultless, then should no place have been sought for the second." (Hebrews 8:6-7)

> So Christ was **once offered** to bear the sins of many; and unto them that look for him shall he appear the second time without sin unto salvation. (Hebrews 9:28)

> By the which will we are sanctified through the offering of the body of Jesus Christ **once for all**. And every priest standeth daily ministering and offering oftentimes the same sacrifices, which can never take away sins: But this man, after he had **offered one sacrifice for sins for ever**, sat down on the right hand of God; From henceforth expecting till his enemies be made his footstool. For **by one offering he hath perfected for ever them that are sanctified**. (Hebrews 10:10-14)

God would not have us return to the weak and beggarly elements of the Old Testament law. See Galatians 4:9-11. To teach such a thing is to blasphemously state that Christ's sacrifice was imperfect and insufficient, and that therefore there is a need to reinstate the animal sacrifices. The Old Testament law was to act as a schoolmaster until the promise of Christ. God would have no reason to reinstate something that was intended to be in place only until he came to offer his own body as a perfect sacrifice. In Christ there is neither Jew nor Gentile, we are all one by faith in Christ. He is not going to divide us once again into Jew and Gentile. His church is his body which cannot be divided. 1 Corinthians 1:13. For a kingdom divided against itself cannot stand. Mark 3:24.

> But before faith came, we were kept under the law, shut up unto the faith which should afterwards be revealed. Wherefore the law was our schoolmaster to bring us unto Christ, that we might be justified by faith. **But after that faith is come, we are no longer under a schoolmaster.** For ye are all the children of God by faith in Christ Jesus. For as many of you as have been baptized into Christ have put on Christ. **There is neither Jew nor Greek, there is neither bond nor free, there is neither male nor female: for ye are all one in Christ Jesus**. And if ye be Christ's, then are ye Abraham's seed, and heirs according to the promise. (Galatians 3:23-29)

The bible makes clear that the old covenant is to vanish, being replaced by the new covenant of faith in Jesus Christ. "In that he saith, A new covenant, he hath made the first old. Now that which decayeth and waxeth old is ready to vanish away." (Hebrews 8:13) Why would God reinstate something in which he has said would vanish away and in which he has had no pleasure? "In burnt offerings and sacrifices for sin thou hast had no pleasure." (Hebrews 10:6)

Christ made his one sacrifice on the cross, whereby those who believe in him are made perfect, consequently there will be no more offering of any kind for sin, period.

> But this man, after he had offered one sacrifice for sins for ever, sat down on the right hand of God; From henceforth expecting till his enemies be made his footstool. For **by one**

offering he hath perfected for ever them that are sanctified. Whereof the Holy Ghost also is a witness to us: for after that he had said before, This is the covenant that I will make with them after those days, saith the Lord, I will put my laws into their hearts, and in their minds will I write them; And their sins and iniquities will I remember no more. **Now where remission of these is, there is no more offering for sin.** (Hebrews 10:12-18)

Christ has set us free from the law of sin and death in our flesh. Because of the weakness of the flesh, it is not possible for us to obey God's holy law. God must change our hearts through spiritual rebirth, so that we are able to walk not after the flesh but after the spirit. Our obedience to God's law does not earn salvation, though, it is a sign of salvation. We fulfill the righteousness of his law through the obedience of Jesus and his final sacrifice. Jesus' righteousness is imputed to those who are chosen for salvation to believe in him. "And therefore it was imputed to him for righteousness. Now it was not written for his sake alone, that it was imputed to him; But **for us also, to whom it shall be imputed, if we believe on him that raised up Jesus our Lord from the dead**; Who was delivered for our offences, and was raised again for our justification. Therefore being justified by faith, we have peace with God through our Lord Jesus Christ." (Romans 4:22-5:1)

Those who try to use obedience to the law of God as a means to salvation are carnally minded, trying to earn salvation though the works of the flesh. The carnal minds that teach a return to the carnal sacrifices of the law are enmity against God.

There is therefore now no condemnation to them which are in Christ Jesus, who walk not after the flesh, but after the Spirit. For the law of the Spirit of life in **Christ Jesus hath made** me free from the law of sin and death. For what the law could not do, in that it was weak through the flesh, God sending his own Son in the likeness of sinful flesh, and for sin, condemned sin in the flesh: That **the righteousness of the law might be fulfilled in us, who walk not after the flesh, but after the Spirit.** For they that are after the flesh do mind the things of the flesh; but they that are after the Spirit the things of the Spirit. For to be carnally minded is death; but to be spiritually minded is life and peace. Because **the carnal mind is enmity against God: for it is not subject to the law of God, neither indeed can be.** So then they that are in the flesh cannot please God. (Romans 8:1-8)

Jesus blotted out the ordinances that were against us and nailed them to the cross. The law was only a shadow of Christ; he is the fulfilment of the law. Having fulfilled the law, Christ will not reinstate it.

And you, being dead in your sins and the uncircumcision of your flesh, hath he quickened together with him, having forgiven you all trespasses; **Blotting out the handwriting of ordinances that was against us, which was contrary to us, and took it out of the way, nailing it to his cross**; And having spoiled principalities and powers, he made a shew of them openly, triumphing over them in it. **Let no man therefore judge you in meat, or in drink, or in respect of an holyday, or of the new moon, or of the sabbath days: Which are a shadow of things to come; but the body is of Christ.** (Colossians 2:13-17)

The law of God was added after the promise given to Abraham. The law did not void the promise of God given to Abraham. The blessings of Abraham flow to all who believe in Jesus Christ. All who believe in Jesus are heirs of the promise given to Abraham. Galatians 3:23-29. That is, through faith in Christ one becomes the spiritual seed of Abraham. Obedience to God is the result of salvation, not the cause of it. Just as with Abraham, who believed God and it was accounted to him as righteousness, so too all others who believe God it is also accounted unto them as righteousness.

> **Even as Abraham believed God, and it was accounted to him for righteousness.** Know ye therefore that **they which are of faith, the same are the children of Abraham**. And the scripture, foreseeing that God would justify the heathen through faith, preached before the gospel unto Abraham, saying, In thee shall all nations be blessed. **So then they which be of faith are blessed with faithful Abraham**. For as many as are of the works of the law are under the curse: for it is written, Cursed is every one that continueth not in all things which are written in the book of the law to do them. **But that no man is justified by the law in the sight of God, it is evident: for, The just shall live by faith**. And the law is not of faith: but, The man that doeth them shall live in them. **Christ hath redeemed us from the curse of the law, being made a curse for us: for it is written, Cursed is every one that hangeth on a tree: That the blessing of Abraham might come on the Gentiles through Jesus Christ; that we might receive the promise of the Spirit through faith**. Brethren, I speak after the manner of men; Though it be but a man's covenant, yet if it be

confirmed, no man disannulleth, or addeth thereto. Now to Abraham and his seed were the promises made. He saith not, And to seeds, as of many; but as of one, And to thy seed, which is Christ. And this I say, that the covenant, that was confirmed before of God in Christ, **the law, which was four hundred and thirty years after, cannot disannul, that it should make the promise of none effect. For if the inheritance be of the law, it is no more of promise**: but God gave it to Abraham by promise. **Wherefore then serveth the law? It was added because of transgressions, till the seed should come to whom the promise was made**; and it was ordained by angels in the hand of a mediator. Now a mediator is not a mediator of one, but God is one. Is the law then against the promises of God? God forbid: for if there had been a law given which could have given life, verily righteousness should have been by the law. **But the scripture hath concluded all under sin, that the promise by faith of Jesus Christ might be given to them that believe**. (Galatians 3:6-22)

All the law and the prophets are summarized in two commandments.

Master, which is the great commandment in the law? Jesus said unto him, Thou shalt love the Lord thy God with all thy heart, and with all thy soul, and with all thy mind. This is the first and great commandment. And the second is like unto it, Thou shalt love thy neighbour as thyself. **On these two commandments hang all the law and the prophets**. (Matthew

22:36-40)

Jesus set believers free, by fulfilling the requirements of the law for us. Matthew 5:17; John 8:32; Ephesians 2:15; Colossians 2:14. Because believers are set free, does not mean we are free to sin. He gave his elect a new heart, so that we are free to obey the law of God, which would otherwise have been an impossibility. We are commanded to love one another and love God; upon those two commandments hang all the requirements of the law. Matthew 22:36-40. "For, brethren, ye have been called unto liberty; only use not liberty for an occasion to the flesh, but by love serve one another. For all the law is fulfilled in one word, even in this; Thou shalt love thy neighbour as thyself." (Galatians 5:13-14)

The royal law of God is that we should love our neighbors as we love ourselves. James 2:6. In fact, Jesus gave us a new commandment that goes further and tells us to what degree we are to love one another. Our obedience to this new commandment does not earn salvation, but our obedience is a sign that we are his disciples. "A new commandment I give unto you, That ye love one another; as I have loved you, that ye also love one another. By this shall all men know that ye are my disciples, if ye have love one to another." (John 13:34-35)

Righteousness is imputed to those who believe, it is not earned. The deeds of the law will never earn salvation. Salvation is a gift of God through faith in Jesus Christ. Ephesians 2:8-10.

Therefore by the deeds of the law there shall no flesh be justified in his sight: for by the law is the knowledge of sin. **But now the righteousness of God without the law is manifested**, being witnessed by the law and the prophets; **Even the righteousness of God which is by faith of Jesus Christ unto all**

> and upon all them that believe: for there is no difference: For all have sinned, and come short of the glory of God; **Being justified freely by his grace through the redemption that is in Christ Jesus**: Whom God hath set forth to be a propitiation through faith in his blood, to declare his righteousness for the remission of sins that are past, through the forbearance of God; To declare, I say, at this time his righteousness: that he might be just, and the justifier of him which believeth in Jesus. Where is boasting then? It is excluded. By what law? of works? Nay: but by the law of faith. **Therefore we conclude that a man is justified by faith without the deeds of the law. Is he the God of the Jews only? is he not also of the Gentiles? Yes, of the Gentiles also: Seeing it is one God, which shall justify the circumcision by faith, and uncircumcision through faith**. Do we then make void the law through faith? God forbid: yea, we establish the law. (Romans 3:20-31)

The true Jews are those that accept their Messiah, Jesus. The kingdom of God is a spiritual kingdom; it is not a kingdom based upon race or tribe. Those who are chosen by God to believe in Jesus Christ are the spiritual Israel of God.

> Not as though the word of God hath taken none effect. **For they are not all Israel, which are of Israel**: Neither, because they are the seed of Abraham, are they all children: but, In Isaac shall thy seed be called. That is, **They which are the children of the flesh, these are not the children of God: but the children of the promise are counted for the seed**. (Romans 9:6-8)

> For he is not a Jew, which is one outwardly; neither is that circumcision, which is outward in the flesh: But **he is a Jew, which is one inwardly; and circumcision is that of the heart, in the spirit, and not in the letter; whose praise is not of men, but of God**. (Romans 2:28-29)

Good works done to earn salvation or being born into a certain tribe or nation will not gain entrance into God's kingdom. God's kingdom is made up of those whom he has chosen by his grace.

> So then it is not of him that willeth, nor of him that runneth, but of God that sheweth mercy. (Romans 9:16)

> Therefore hath he mercy on whom he will have mercy, and whom he will he hardeneth. (Romans 9:18)

God has not cast away Israel. His Israel is made up of those whom he foreknew before the foundation of the world who would believe in Jesus unto salvation. Therefore, all Israel shall be saved.

> God hath not cast away his people which he foreknew. (Romans 11:2) And so **all Israel shall be saved**. (Romans 11:26)

Part and parcel of the belief in the renewed millennium sacrifices is the belief that there will be a rebuilding of the Jewish temple. Many believe that the supposed future temple will be rebuilt at the location of what is now known as the Wailing Wall. They believe that the Wailing Wall is a remnant of the western wall from the old temple. In fact, the wailing wall is not the western wall from the ancient Jewish temple, but in fact is the western wall of the Roman Fort Antonia.[163] Fort Antonia was a permanent Roman fort at the time of Jesus. Fort Antonia was approximately 600 feet north of the temple and the southern wall of the fort was connected to the northern wall of the temple by double colonnades.

Jesus made it clear that the temple would be destroyed so thoroughly that "[t]here shall not be left here one stone upon another, that shall not be thrown down." Matthew 24:1,2; Mark 13:1,2; Luke 19:43,44; 21:5,6. The Jews are all too happy to deceive the world into believing that Jesus was wrong. In fact, the prophecy of Jesus was fulfilled perfectly. The temple was completely destroyed down to the last stone, the remains that are left standing today are the remains of Fort Antonia, not the temple.

The Dome of the Rock is not as it is supposed the place where Mohamad ascended into heaven. The Dome of the Rock is a heathen Islamic shrine built over the Roman Praetorium, which was where Pilate sentenced Jesus.[164] The Praetorium was inside Fort Antonia, not the Jewish temple.

Just as Christ repeated throughout his new testament, so I will repeat: God has abolished the distinction between Jew and Gentile. Romans 3:28-30; 10:11-13. His church has become one spiritual temple and household of God, with Christ being the chief cornerstone. There is no more need for a physical temple, which was merely a shadow of the greater spiritual temple, his church.

> For he is our peace, who hath made both one, and hath broken down the middle wall of partition between us; **Having abolished in his flesh the enmity, even the law of commandments contained in ordinances**; for to make in himself of twain one new man, so making peace; And that he might reconcile

both unto God in one body by the cross, having slain the enmity thereby: And came and preached peace to you which were afar off, and to them that were nigh. **For through him we both have access by one Spirit unto the Father**. Now therefore ye are no more strangers and foreigners, but fellowcitizens with the saints, and of the household of God; And are built upon the foundation of the apostles and prophets, Jesus Christ himself being the chief corner stone; **In whom all the building fitly framed together groweth unto an holy temple in the Lord: In whom ye also are builded together for an habitation of God through the Spirit**. (Ephesians 2:14-22)

The theology of dispensational Zionism is rooted in the Judaic/Babylonian religion of the Jews. The churches that have been inculcated with that unbiblical doctrine are more akin to Jewish synagogues than Christian churches. Could these "Christian" Zionist churches be the "synagogue of Satan" described by God in the book of Revelation?

Jesus stated in Revelation: "I know thy works, and tribulation, and poverty, (but thou art rich) and I know the blasphemy of them which say they are Jews, and are not, but are the synagogue of Satan." (Revelation 2:9)

God explained in his New Testament that one who is saved by the grace of God through faith in Jesus Christ is a spiritual Jew.

For he is not a Jew, which is one outwardly; neither is that circumcision, which is outward in the flesh: But he is a Jew, which is one inwardly; and circumcision is that of the heart,

in the spirit, and not in the letter; whose praise
is not of men, but of God. (Romans 2:28-29)

That means that a Christian is a spiritual Jew. The reference to " them which say they are Jews, and are not" in Revelation 2:9 seems to be a reference to false spiritual Jews (false Christians), who claim to be Christians but are not. The false spiritual Jews (false Christians) are those who are in nominal "Christian" churches that have been inculcated with Judaic doctrines. The false "Christian" churches preaching Judaic Zionism seem to be the "synagogue of Satan" referenced in Revelation 2:9.

7 Tim LaHaye Left Jesus Behind

Ultimately, the new Zionist dispensational theology was introduced in the seminary schools controlled by crypto-Jews. The witting and unwitting seminary graduates then introduced their new "Christian" theology into the Protestant churches throughout the world. This new theology is the basis for the *Left Behind* series of 16 religious novels, which have sold more than 65 million copies.[165] The *Left Behind* series of books, authored by Tim LaHaye, are also very popular movies that are heavily promoted in churches throughout the world.

Tim LaHaye is more than the author of a popular book series. In 1981, Tim LaHaye founded the Council for National Policy (CNP), ostensibly as a forum for conservative Christians. The New York Times described CNP as a "little-known group of a few hundred of the most powerful conservatives in the country."[166] Something that should be of concern for all Christians is that the meetings of CNP are secret. CNP has confidential meetings three times each year and the meetings are behind closed doors at undisclosed locations. The New York Times obtained a list of rules for attendees at the meetings: "The media should not know when or where we meet or who takes part in our programs, before of after a meeting."[167]

David Kirkpatrick of the New York Times further explains:

> The membership list is "strictly confidential." Guests may attend "only with the unanimous approval of the executive committee." In e-mail messages to one another, members are instructed not to refer to the organization by name, to protect against leaks.[168]

What is CNP hiding? CNP does not act like a Christian organization doing the Lord's work; it behaves like a satanic coven doing the work of the devil. Jesus explains this behavior:

> And this is the condemnation, that light is come into the world, and men loved darkness rather than light, because their deeds were evil. **For every one that doeth evil hateth the light, neither cometh to the light, lest his deeds should be reproved.** But he that doeth truth cometh to the light, that his deeds may be made manifest, that they are wrought in God. John 3:19-21.

Who do we find attending a CNP meeting? We find in attendance a prominent member of another secret satanic society (Skull and Bones), George W. Bush. "Mr. Bush addressed the [CNP] group in fall 1999 to solicit support for his campaign, stirring a dispute when news of his speech leaked and Democrats demanded he release a tape recording. He did not."[169]

President George W. Bush, in his autobiography, *A Charge to Keep* stated: **"During my senior year I joined Skull and Bones, a secret society, so secret I can't say anything more."** What is so secret that he cannot speak any further about it? The secret is that in return for power, wealth, and fame, he must blindly obey his satanic masters in their antichrist conspiracy to enslave and rule the world. The initiation ceremony for Skull and Bones involves, but is not limited to, the inductees lying naked in a coffin and telling their deepest sexual secrets. Anton LaVey, the founder of the Church of Satan, in his *Satanic Rituals: Companion to the Satanic Bible,* states that such a coffin ritual is a satanic ritual common in many pagan orders. During the ritual a powerful spiritual force charges through the participants transforming their lives dramatically. This powerful spiritual force is a devil. The participants in these ceremonies end up possessed by a devil.

Evidence indicates that the Order of Skull & Bones founded at Yale in 1832 is a chapter of the Illuminati, which was originally founded in 1776 at the University of Ingolstadt in Germany.[170] From this we know that Skull & Bones is not American at all, but is a branch of a foreign secret society.[171]

As with the Jesuits and the Illuminati, Skull & Bones has many ostensible Gentiles who are members. From this fact most people have mischaracterized the Skull & Bones as a purely Gentile organization. That is not true. Just as with the Illuminati and the Jesuits, the Skull & Bones is controlled by and serves the interests of Zionist Jews. George W. Bush is a prime example of an ostensible Gentile member of Skull & Bones who is acting in the interests of Israel to the detriment of the United States. He is completely controlled by Zionist Jews.

The Jewish control of Skull & Bones comes from its roots as a chapter in the crypto-Jewish Illuminati. Some of the practices and terms of the Skull & Bones reveal the Jewish nature of the Order. For example, those outside Skull & Bones are referred to by Skull & Bones members as vandals and **"Gentiles."**[172] Furthermore, in an attempt to conceal the meanings of their writings from any Gentile outsider who may obtain a copy, members of the Skull & Bones often obscure key words by deleting the vowels. For example, patriarchs would be written as p-tr–rchs, bones would be written as b-n-s.[173] The Hebrew alphabet does not have vowels, they use accent marks, and so Jews are accustomed to writing without using vowels. It is not surprising that they would follow that same practice when trying to conceal the meaning in their writings from the uninitiated Gentile world.

The Skull & Bones use the Hegelian dialectic to change society into a totalitarian state. Under the Hegel's dialectic there must be a conflict, either real or perceived, between a thesis and an antithesis which is resolved by a synthesis of the two. The secret societies create these conflicts in order to move society regressively away form Christ and Christian principles and toward Satan and satanic principles. David Bay explains the origin and power behind the Cabalistic Skull and Bones:

> The Brotherhood of Death Society in the United States is the Skull and Bones Society in Yale University in New Haven, Connecticut. Its belief structure is identical to that of the Thule Society. Therefore, we can conclude that Bones Men affirm this belief about Jesus Christ, thus condemning them to committing the Unpardonable Sin. The list of some of the Families comprising Skull and Bones is frightening, for it immediately shows the extent to which America has been influenced by this Satanic organization. Remember, the men of these families have likely committed the Unpardonable Sin. (Quoting from Antony Sutton, "America's Secret Establishment", p. 22).
>
> Rockefeller Family (Standard Oil), Weyerhaeuser Family (Lumber), Sloane Family (Retailing), Pillsbury Family (Flour Milling), J.P. Morgan Family (Banking), Taft

Family (Politics), Bush Family, including former President George Bush. Wait a minute, you say, George Bush likely committed the Unpardonable Sin because of his membership in Skull and Bones? Yes. Now, you can see how easy it was for Bush to lead the charge into the Satanic New World Order. Now you can see that Bush was far different in his innermost heart than he was on his media-created surface.[174]

Before the Republican convention, the New York Times reported that the members of CNP "quietly convened in New York, holding their latest meeting almost in plain sight, at the Plaza Hotel, for what a participant called 'a pep rally' to re-elect President Bush."[175]

CNP's Zionist war mongering is evident in the fact that "not long after the Iraq invasion, Vice President Dick Cheney and Defense Secretary Donald H. Rumsfeld attended a [CNP] council meeting."[176] The CNP practice of keeping their meetings secret ensures that there is no public disclosure of their involvement in, and approval of, war decisions.

President Kennedy had this to say about secret societies:

> The very word 'secrecy' is repugnant in a free and open society; and we are as a people inherently and historically opposed to secret societies, to secret oaths and to secret proceedings.[177]

In a speech given at the Waldorf-Astoria Hotel New York City, April 27, 1961, President Kennedy explained the nature and scope of the grand conspiracy to enslave our nation and the world.

> For we are opposed around the world by a monolithic and ruthless conspiracy that relies primarily on covert means for expanding its sphere of influence--on infiltration instead of invasion, on subversion instead of elections, on intimidation instead of free choice, on guerrillas by night instead of armies by day. It is a system which has conscripted vast human and material resources into the building of a tightly knit, highly efficient machine that combines military, diplomatic, intelligence, economic, scientific and political operations. Its preparations are concealed, not published. Its mistakes are buried, not headlined. Its dissenters are silenced, not praised. No expenditure is questioned, no rumor is printed, no secret is revealed. It conducts the Cold War, in short, with a war-time discipline no democracy would ever hope or wish to match.[178]

President Kennedy was not a wild conspiracy theorist. As President of the United States, he was privy to intelligence reports that revealed plans for world conquest being executed through secret societies. He knew that the secret societies had subverted the United States Government itself, and he aimed to do something about it. One of his first steps in his fight against the conspiracy was to undermine the CIA, which he viewed as the fulcrum of the treachery within the U.S. Government. After the Bay of Pigs fiasco, President Kennedy vowed to "splinter the CIA into a thousand pieces and scatter it into the winds."[179] The treasonous conspirators knew that Kennedy presented a formidable force against them; they responded to the Kennedy threat by assassinating him.

CNP has an interlocking relationship with other secret societies. It is not surprising to find that Tim LaHaye, the founder of CNP is a central figure involving evangelical churches with the intelligence community, through intelligence operative and cult leader Sung Myung Moon. Eric Jewell reveals the following details of LaHaye's activities:

> He was a principal in the American Freedom coalition, which was a Moon sponsored group, and claimed by Moon as an arm of his network. He was also associated with the Coalition on Revival, and the Heritage foundation, both of which were also Moon sponsored. After this association was made public, he resigned from the AFC, (though his name was not removed when he resigned), and tried to distance himself from Moon in the public eye. He was also a principal in the Coalition of Religious Freedom, where he spoke out for Moon during Moon's incarceration for tax fraud, asking hundreds of evangelicals to go to prison to support Moon if allowed by authorities. He was also on the original board of directors of Falwell's Moral Majority, which was also tied through its members to the intelligence community, and Ren [sic] Moon's Unification Church. LaHaye also founded the American Coalition of Traditional Values, which was touted as a Christian organization, but was extra-ripe with Moon organization board members, and the intelligence community.[180]

He who pays the piper calls the tune. It has been reported that LaHaye received $500,000 on behalf of CNP from Mr. Bo Hi Pak, who is alleged to be a former Korean intelligence officer and Sung Myung Moon's Lieutenant. LaHaye denies the charge, although there are witnesses to LaHaye thanking Pak for the money and even an alleged tape memorializing the event.[181] LaHaye is the founder and chairman of Coalition For Religious Freedom (CRF). Eric Jewell reveals that "CRF President Don Sills admits that CRF has received no less than $500,000 from Moon sources."[182]

When one looks at LaHaye's CNP membership and its extreme secrecy, it is apparent that it is a religious front for a secret intelligence operation. We find that Lt. General Daniel Graham is on the CNP Board of Governors. General Graham was the Director of the Defense Intelligence Agency, and former Deputy Director of the CIA, as well as former Military advisor to President Reagan.[183] In addition, we find Max Hugel as a CNP Member. Hugel is a former special assistant CIA Deputy Director for Administration, and Deputy Director for Operations.[184]

The CNP was supposed to be a Christian conservative alternative to the liberal socialist agenda of the Council on Foreign Relations (CFR). Barbara Aho, however, reveals: "Profiles of other prominent CNP officers and members reveal a shocking number of CFR connections."[185]

> Early CNP membership directories were obtained by enterprising researchers, however, and these revealed that the early leadership of the CNP was, in fact, also represented in the Council on Foreign Relations -- the very organization of globalists to which the CNP was to be the conservative alternative! On the first CNP Governing Board there were no less than three, and possibly more, members of the CFR: George F. Gilder - CNP Board of Governors (1982); Dr. Edward Teller - CNP Board of Governors (1982); and Guy Vander Jagt - CNP Board of Governors (1982).[186]

CNP Board of Governor George Gilder is the Program

Director for the Rockefeller-funded Manhattan Institute, friend of David Rockefeller, and a member of the CFR.[187] CNP member Arnaul D'Borchgrave, who is the Editor in Chief of the Washington Times (owned by Sung Myung Moon), is also a member of the CFR.[188] Former Senator Jesse Helms (deceased) was one of the CNP Board of Governors; he was also a CFR member.[189]

CNP and CFR are conspiratorial affiliates. "Can two walk together, except they be agreed?" Amos 3:3. The nature of the CFR tells us a lot about the nature of the CNP. The CFR is a front group for a satanic and decidedly Zionist secret society (Illuminati). The CFR is one of several round table societies. The CFR is used to indoctrinate its members, who then infiltrate and control the U.S. government. Admiral Chester Ward was a member of the CFR for 16 years. He resigned from the CFR when he realized that its goal was to disarm and surrender the United States to an all powerful world government.[190]

Washington Post ombudsman Richard Harwood stated that the CFR is the nearest thing we have to a ruling establishment in the United States. He wrote the following in the October 30, 1993 issue of the Washington Post:

> The president is a member. So is his secretary of state, the deputy secretary of state, all five of the undersecretaries, several of the assistant secretaries and the department's legal adviser. The president's national security adviser and his deputy are members. The director of Central Intelligence (like all previous directors) and the chairman of the Foreign Intelligence Advisory Board are members. The secretary of defense, three undersecretaries and at least four assistant secretaries are members. The secretaries of the departments

of housing and urban development, interior, health and human services and the chief White House public relations man ... along with the speaker of the House [are members] ...

This is not a retinue of people who "look like America," as the President once put it, but they very definitely look like the people who, for more than half a century, have managed our international affairs and our military-industrial complex.[191]

Georgetown University history professor Carroll Quigley was granted unprecedented access to the secret records of the CFR and wrote in his 1966 book *Tragedy and Hope*, that the Republican and Democratic parties in the U.S. are completely controlled behind the scenes by the CFR. Quigley agreed with the plans of the CFR stating that "the two parties should be almost identical, so that the American people can 'throw the rascals out' at any election without leading to any profound or extensive shifts in policy."[192] That is exactly what we see with each change from a Democratic to a Republican administration and vice versa there is no real change in domestic or foreign policy. There is an unchecked treasonous march toward world government led by the Zionist pied pipers.

David Rockefeller is the former Chairman of the CFR. He is now listed on the CFR website as the Honorary Chairman of the CFR.[193] David Rockefeller is the only surviving grandchild of Standard Oil founder John D. Rockefeller. David Rockefeller stated the following in his published memoirs:

> For more than a century ideological extremists at either end of the political spectrum have seized upon well-publicized incidents such as my encounter with Castro to attack the Rockefeller family for the inordinate influence

they claim we wield over American political and economic institutions. Some even believe we are part of a secret cabal working against the best interests of the United States, characterizing my family and me as 'internationalists' and of conspiring with others around the world to build a more integrated global political and economic structure – one world, if you will. If that's the charge, I stand guilty, and I am proud of it.[194]

Tim LaHaye is an accomplice in the satanic deception that is Zionism. An amazing 1976 interview was conducted of Harold Wallace Rosenthal by Walter White Jr., the editor of the Conservative monthly Western Front. Rosenthal was a Jewish insider. He was the personal assistant to New York Senator Jacob Javits. Rosenthal felt that Jewish power was unassailable. He wanted to make some extra cash, which he needed for gambling, by revealing insight into the Zionist conspiracy for world domination. Henry Makow accurately summarizes what Rosenthal stated by concluding that "Jews have built an earthly empire partly by rejecting Christ's vision of a spiritual kingdom based on brotherly love. Jewish bankers plan to govern the world from Jerusalem according to their own interests."[195]

Rosenthal blasphemes Christ and affirms the earthly Zionist objectives of the Jews during the interview by saying "We are building and, in fact, have built an earthly empire without your kind and your disappointing Messiah."[196] One of the most revealing statements was Rosenthal's response to a question about the Jews being the chosen people. Rosenthal states that the Jews are the chosen people, chosen by their god, who is Lucifer. "Most Jews do not like to admit it, but our god is Lucifer -- so I wasn't lying -- and we are his chosen people. Lucifer is very much alive."[197]

The bible states that "the love of money is the root of all evil." 1 Timothy 6:10. It is no surprise that we find that the source of the power of Zionist Jews is in money. Rosenthal states:

> Our power has been created through the manipulation of the national monetary system. We authored the quotation. 'Money is power.' As revealed in our master plan, it was essential for us to establish a private national bank. The Federal Reserve system fitted our plan nicely since it is owned by us, but the name implies that it is a government institution. From the very outset, our purpose was to confiscate all the gold and silver, replacing them with worthless non-redeemable paper notes. This we have done![198]

The Jewish power over money and usury gives them control over the mass-media and education, from which they control the Gentile masses. Rosenthal explains:

> At first, by controlling the banking system we were able to control corporation capital. Through this, we acquired total monopoly of the movie industry, the radio networks and the newly developing television media. The printing industry, newspapers, periodicals and technical journals had already fallen into our hands. The richest plum was later to come when we took over the publication of all school materials. Through these vehicles we could mold public opinion to suit our own purposes. The people are only stupid pigs that grunt and squeal the chants we give them, whether they be truth or lies.[199]

Rosenthal explains how their control over the "Christian" Zionists is used to stifle any revelations about the nefarious plans of the Jews for a communist world government. That is where LaHaye, Haggee, and other Zionist shills play their vital roles.

> Through our influence of religion we were able to involve the ignorant white Christians in war against themselves which always impoverished both sides while we reaped a financial and political harvest. Anytime truth comes forth which exposes us, we simply rally our forces -- the ignorant Christians. They attack the crusaders even if they are members of their own families.[200]

8 The Fifth Column

It seems that LaHaye in his interlocking association with CNP, CFR, and others is involved not in a Christian ministry but rather a finely crafted intelligence operation. When that intelligence operation is viewed as a tree and its fruit is examined, it is apparent that it is for the treasonous purpose of bringing about a world government. Carol Valentine describes the aid and comfort given to Israel by "Christian" Zionists as treason against the United States. She explains that the loyalty of "Christian" Zionists to Israel has blinded them to the fact that they are abetting an enemy nation:

> The brother of a friend of mine works in the South. He was discussing US foreign policy with a fellow worker, a retired career Navy man who describes himself as a fundamentalist Christian. The Navy man is a devotee of TeeVee preacher Pat Robertson.
>
> My friend's brother was arguing that the US policy towards Israel amounts to treason to the US. During the discussion, the subject of the USS Liberty came up. Believe it or not, this

Navy man had never heard of Israel's attack on the USS Liberty in 1967. My friend's brother referred him to http://www.USSLiberty.org

The next day, the Navy man came into the office and said: "I don't care what Israel did to the USS Liberty. I put my God ahead of my country."

"Fundamentalist Christians" (sometimes called "Fundies") are, characteristically, Zionist, not Christian. In practice, they reject the teaching of Jesus in the New Testament: that each of us is equally precious in the eyes of the Lord.

* * *

Zionist Fundies will do anything for Israel and "the Jews," whom they worship as God or God's little brother. They are only too happy to be the Jews' slaves, and insist we all join in their bondage. Certainly their beliefs are anti-Christian.

More to the point: Zionist "Christians" are traitors to America. Along with Jews, they wave the American flag, urging us to spill the blood of any who stand in the way of Israeli ambition. Along with Jews, Zionist Christians scream loudest for Arab blood, even though all rational analysis shouts that Israel and Israeli agents in America were responsible for 9-11. Along with Jews, Zionist Christians would happily have America spill its own blood to help Israel realize its ambitions.

[According to the authoritative writings of the

Jewish Talmud] only "the Jews" really matter, only "the Jews" qualify as human. Thus these fundamentalists, knowingly or unknowingly, follow the teachings of the Talmud in their anti-American beliefs. . . .

In fact Jews (Talmudists) regard goyim as a lower life form, as sub-human. According to the Talmud, non-Jews can be slaughtered like cattle.

The intent to kill a non-Jew is so laudable that even if a Jew is accidently killed in an attempt to kill a non-Jew, the murderous Jew suffers no liability. (Babylonian Talmud, Soncino Edition, London, 1935. Sanhedrin 78b-79a.)

But if a Jew intends to kill another Jew and does so, he is liable. (Sanhedrin 78b-79a.)

If a Jew murders a Gentile, the Jew suffers no death penalty. (Sanhedrin 57a.)

If a Gentile strikes a Jew in the jaw, the Gentile, having stricken the "Divine Presence" (that is, a Jew) suffers the death penalty. (Sanhedrin 58b).[201]

Zionist "Christians" operate as Israeli super patriots, never questioning their own loyalties to Israel or weighing them against other principles or values. As the example of the Navy man shows, this loyalty transcends all loyalty to America (or any other native country), and even overt oaths of loyalty. Most astoundingly, few people would see the Navy man's Zionism as the fundamental treason it is, and it is unlikely that his officers would have a problem with it, much less prosecute him for treason.[202]

Carol Valentine has come to the only conclusion possible from an objective view of Zionism. Jewish Zionists and their "Christian" Zionist collaborators are a fifth column within the United States. A fifth column is "a group of people who act traitorously and subversively out of a secret sympathy with an enemy of their country."[203] It was a phrase originally coined to describe Franco sympathizers in Madrid during the Spanish Civil War. It was originally an allusion to a statement in 1936 that the insurgents had four columns marching on Madrid and a fifth column of sympathizers in the city ready to rise and betray it.[204] Christopher Jon Bjerknes summarizes the dangers of "Christian" Zionism to the United States:

> Israel has created a large fifth column of "Christian" Zionists in America, who worship Jews not Christ, and who will help Jewry to build a Jewish Temple and anoint the Jewish "Messiah" which "anti-Christ" will mock Jesus by his very existence. These fuming and foaming at the mouth genocidal maniacs are eager to attack our fellow human beings with nuclear weapons. What will happen to us when the nuclear bombs start falling, they care not. They believe in the Jewish manufactured lunacy of the "Rapture" and hope to kill us in the billions so that they will be whisked away to Heaven.[205]

Steve Van Nattan is an example of a "Christian" Zionist who puts his allegiance to Israel before his allegiance to his own country. Van Nattan is a U.S. citizen who has served in the U.S. military, yet he states that he is "delighted" at the thought that that "God will destroy America very soon," so that

God will finally exalt Israel. Van Nattan's "Christian" Zionist hope and belief is that God will leave behind his church in favor of Israel. Van Nattan states:

> Just before the Kingdom reign of Messiah Christ, which is just around the corner, God will exalt Israel and the Jews who are left after He destroys arrogant Jews and rebels in Israel (Zephaniah 3). God will exalt Israel. Thus, we are now just at the door of the next great era in human history. America is leading the rebellion against God, and America is concerned with one thing alone-- the good life and her toys. So, God WILL destroy America very soon. I am delighted, for we need to leave the profane and sloppy Agape world Church behind, and we need to get on into the glorious Kingdom of Jesus Christ. Even so, come Lord Jesus. MARANATHA.[206]

The allegiance of Zionists is to Israel first. One example of the priorities of Zionists is the statement made by Zionist and former U.S. President Bill Clinton: "If Iraq came across the Jordan River, I would grab a rifle and get in the trench and fight and die."[207] When, however, it came time for Clinton to keep his military commitment to the United States, he wrote Arkansas ROTC Commander Col. Eugene Holmes, and explained that he couldn't serve because he "loathed the military." He did all he could to avoid fighting for "his" country but he would be willing to fight and die in the trenches for Israel. His presidency was marked by one act of treason against the United States after another. Israel, on the other hand, benefitted handsomely from the Clinton presidency.

Zionists are working inside the United States to undermine American freedoms in their march toward a communist world government. For example, on December 31,

2011, President Barrack Obama signed into law the National Defense Authorization Act of 2012 (NDAA 2012), which authorizes the suspension of *habeas corpus* protection of U.S. civilian citizens inside the United States if the Department of Homeland Security deems that the person is suspected of being involved in terrorism.[208] The bill was authored and presented by Michigan Senator Carl Levin. Senator Levin is a dual citizen of Israel and part of the Zionist fifth column in the United States.[209]

    Richard Evans explains that this bill is just one bill in a long list of bills that undermine the liberty of Americans for the benefit of the Zionist world government. Evans points out that the bill's author, Senator Levin, is chairman of the Armed Services Committee. He is empowered with legislative oversight of the nation's military, including the Department of Defense, military research and development, nuclear energy (as pertaining to national security), benefits for members of the military, the Selective Service System and other matters related to defense policy.[210] Senator Levin is also *ex officio* on the Committee on Homeland Security and Governmental Affairs, and Select Committee on Intelligence. Evans properly asks how Senator Levin can be objective about the application of U.S. military policy in the Middle East when he is a citizen of Israel?[211] Evans concludes:

> There's nothing wrong with a doctor, a banker, or teacher having dual citizenship. They aren't in positions of public trust. It's entirely inappropriate for [a] public servant.[212]

    Evans points out that the NDAA 2012 is just the latest in liberty grabbing legislation brought to you by Israeli dual citizens working feverishly toward a Talmudic world government.

    On the cue of 911, the already prepared

PATRIOT Act was introduced by Republican Senators Orrin Hatch (R-UT) and Jon Kyl (R-AZ) with Democratic Senators Dianne Feinstein (D-CA) and Chuck Schumer (D-NY). Feinstein and Schumer were both Israeli dual citizens.[213]

Senators Levin, Feinstein, and Schumer are just a few of the long list of *Sayanim* who have been used in the service of Israel. *Sayanim* (plural for *Sayan*) are Jews living outside of Israel who are fanatically loyal to the Jewish state and have agreed to assist Israel. Their loyalty to Israel supplants any loyalty they have to the country in which they reside. Often, *Sayanim* are recruited by relatives living in Israel and are under the control of professional spy masters called "*katsas*." They do whatever is asked of them to assist Israel and the Mossad.

Texe Marrs explains the danger posed to the United States by treasonous Sayanims:

> At this very moment, throughout America, in every city and town of even moderate size, dedicated undercover agents are hard at work. These spies are everywhere, stealing classified material, filching "secret" documents, plotting terrorist attacks, and devising new means of how America can best be conquered and its citizens subjugated.
>
> * * *
>
> They are the Sayanim. Jews born and raised in America, who, regardless of the blessings and financial rewards bestowed on them as Americans, are turncoats and traitors.
>
> These Benedict Arnold-types willingly collude

with a foreign power and plot to damage America by serving that foreign power, the nation of Israel, as undercover spies, saboteurs, and intel agents. To most Jews, their origin of birth is of no consequence. They are Israel-firsters and are traitors.

Wherever a Jew resides, he or she is an Israeli. When the Israeli Mossad or Shin Bet, Israel's intelligence and secret police organizations, ask for his assistance, he jumps into action.

Since America has a Jewish population of 7.5 million, our nation is bulging with Israeli spies willing to steal, lie, cheat, or even kill if necessary for their chosen nation Israel. They possess no loyalty to their native born country, the U.S.A., but have, since birth, been propagandized and indoctrinated by fanatical Zionist parents, relatives, teachers, and rabbis. They are Zionist zealots through and through, and many are dual citizens of both Israel and the U.S.A.

* * *

For example, take Abraham Feinberg. According to FBI files, Feinberg, a wealthy American Jew from New York City who owned manufacturing and construction companies, led a secret cabal of seventy other Sayanim agents.

Together, Feinberg and his underlings committed numerous acts of criminality. They stole nuclear material and uranium, sending it to Israel. It was Feinberg's spying crimes in the late 1940s and early 1950s that enabled both Soviet Russia and Israel to develop atomic bombs.

American Jews Julius and Ethel Rosenberg were Sayanim agents. These two heinously stole atomic bomb plans and turned them over to the Communists. With their help, Stalin and the USSR built its first nuclear bomb. Tried in federal criminal court for espionage, the treacherous Rosenbergs were found guilty and were put to death in the electric chair.

* * *

The Jewish/Israel Sayanim are today the single most dangerous threat to our national security. It is no wonder that in country after country, these Jewish parasites, at first welcomed in as "fellow citizens" and "neighbors," are eventually found out and expelled.[214]

Former Deputy Director of the CIA, Admiral Bobby Inman said of the Israeli Sayanim: "Israeli spies have done more harm and have damaged the United States more than the intelligence agents of all other countries on earth combined. . . . They are the gravest threat to our national security."[215]

The Patriot Act is typical of the Zionist flim-flams orchestrated by Israeli Sayanim (Senators Levin, Feinstein, and Schumer) and their fellow travelers. The bill was brought to the floor of the House of Representatives on October 23, 2001 for a vote. That was the same day it was introduced. There were only two copies made available for all members of Congress to read. Prior to being considered in the House of Representatives, the bill was not made publicly available through common channels such as the Government Printing

Office (GPO) or the THOMAS legislative database.²¹⁶ Obviously, the authors did not want the provisions scrutinized. Rep. Bobby Scott said:

> I think it is appropriate to comment on the process by which the bill is coming to us. This is not the bill that was reported and deliberated on in the Committee on the Judiciary. It came to us late on the floor. No one has really had an opportunity to look at the bill to see what is in it since we have been out of our offices.²¹⁷

The Patriot Act was a massive 300 page bill that almost none of the members of the House of Representatives read. Despite their almost total ignorance of the provisions, the bill passed on October 24, 2001, by a vote of 357-66. The bill then passed the Senate the next day on October 25, 2001. President Bush signed the bill into law on October 26, 2001.

The Patriot Act is a subversive law that empowers the federal government to intrude on the liberty of all Americans. The Patriot Act was brought to you by the same people who produced the 9/11 attacks. In fact, the Patriot Act was one of the principle objectives of the 9/11 attacks.

The Patriot Act was drafted long in advance of the 9/11 attacks. That fact was confirmed by Senator Ron Paul:

> "The PATRIOT Act was written many, many years before 9/11," Paul said. The attacks simply provided "an opportunity for some people to do what they wanted to do," he said.²¹⁸

Not only was the Patriot Act written and ready to go before the 9/11 attacks, the invasions of Afghanistan and Iraq were also planned in advance of the 9/11 attacks.²¹⁹ On

September 18, 2001, the BBC reported:

> Niaz Naik, a former Pakistani Foreign Secretary, was told by senior American officials in mid-July that military action against Afghanistan would go ahead by the middle of October.[220]

The U.S. invaded Afghanistan in October 2001, right on schedule. What was the justification for the invasion of Afghanistan? The 9/11 attacks were used as the justification for the invasion; the 9/11 attacks were also right on schedule.

In addition, Former Bush Administration Treasury Secretary Paul O'Neill stated that in early 2001 the Bush Administration was already considering the use of force to oust Saddam Hussain, as well as planning for the aftermath of a post Hussain Iraq. O'Neill backed up his charges with memos of high level cabinet meetings.[221] The attacks on 9/11 and the subsequent authorization given by Congress to the President to wage war on terrorism anywhere in the world, provided President Bush the needed power and authority to invade Iraq. Declassified documents published at the National Security Archive support the allegations by O'Neill and prove that the Bush administration planned to invade Iraq as early as January, 2001.[222] That was nine months before the 9/11 attacks.

The Patriot Act is just one in a long line of liberty grabbing laws that could only be enacted after a terrorist attack. The traitors in government use war as a cover to undermine the constitution and enslave the people.

In 1966, a report was issued by the Hudson Institute, which is located at the base of Iron Mountain. The report is commonly referred to as *The Report From Iron Mountain*. The report was commissioned by the Department of Defense under Defense Secretary Robert McNamara. The purpose of the report was to determine if there was a substitute for war.

G. Edward Griffin in his book, *The Creature From Jeckyl Island, A Second Look at the Federal Reserve*, revealed that "*The Report From Iron Mountain* concludes that there can be no substitute for war, unless it possesses three properties. It must (1) be economically wasteful, (2) represent a credible threat of great magnitude, and (3) provide a logical excuse for compulsory service to the government."[223] The report did not address issues of right or wrong, constitutionality, religious precepts, or patriotism. The sole purpose of the report was to determine how to perpetuate the existing government. Griffin summarized the Machiavellian report:

> The self-proclaimed purpose of the study was to explore various ways to "stabilize society." Praiseworthy as that may sound, a reading of the Report soon reveals that the word society is used synonymously with the word government. Furthermore, the word stabilize is used as meaning to preserve and to perpetuate. It is clear from the start that the nature of the study was to analyze the different ways a government can perpetuate itself in power, ways to control its citizens and prevent them from rebelling.

* * *

The major conclusion of the report was that, in the past, war has been the only reliable means to achieve that goal. It contends that only during times of war or the threat of war are the masses compliant enough to carry the yoke of government without complaint. Fear of conquest and pillage by an enemy can make almost any burden seem acceptable by comparison. War can be used to arouse human passion and patriotic feelings of loyalty to the nation's leaders. No amount of sacrifice in the name of victory will be rejected. Resistance is viewed as treason. But, in times of peace, people become resentful of high taxes, shortages, and bureaucratic intervention. When they become disrespectful of their leaders, they become dangerous. No government has long survived without enemies and armed conflict. War, therefore, has been an indispensable condition for "stabilizing society." These are the report's exact words:

"The war system not only has been essential to the existence of nations as independent political entities, but has been equally indispensable to their stable political structure. Without it, no government has ever been able to obtain acquiescence in its 'legitimacy,' or right to rule its society. The possibility of war provides the sense of external necessity without which no government can long remain in power. The historical record reveals one instance after another where the failure of a regime to maintain the credibility of a war threat led to its dissolution, by the forces of private interest, of reactions to social injustice, or of other disintegrative elements. The organization of society for the possibility of war is its principal political stabilizer . . . It has enabled societies to maintain necessary class distinctions, and it has insured the subordination of the citizens to the state by virtue of the residual war powers inherent in the concept of nationhood."[224]

The Hudson Institute researchers considered such options to war as poverty, environmental threats, and even alien invasions from outer space. They thought that poverty would not create sufficient fear, because most of the world's population was already in poverty. The researchers felt that a threat from outer space could be contrived. The report expressed the view that such a danger could be used in "uniting mankind against the danger of destruction by 'creatures' from other planets or from outer space."[225] The report, however, concluded that such a threat was not sufficiently credible to be an adequate substitute for war.

The report made the point that the substitute threat must be credible. "Credibility, in fact, lies at the heart of the problem of developing a political substitute for war"[226] The threat, however, does not have to be real; the researchers opined that the threats could be, and in fact would probably have to be, contrived deceptions. "It is more probable, in our judgement, that such a threat will have to be invented."[227] The only threat that the researchers thought came closest to war in controlling the population was danger to the environment. Griffin explains the strategy:

> The masses would more willingly accept a falling standard of living, tax increases, and bureaucratic intervention in their lives as simply "the price we must pay to save Mother Earth." If a vision of death and destruction from pollution could be implanted in the public subconscious mind, then the global battle against it could, indeed, replace war as the mechanism for control.[228]

The Zionists have put into effect the findings in *The Report From Iron Mountain*. The myth of global warming is the centerpiece of the environmental strategy. Donn deGrand Pre states that the "'radical' environmental summits held in The

Hague [2000], in Rio [1992], and in Kyoto [1997], [were] all designed with but one thought in mind, to reduce America's tremendous productive capacities to the level of a third-world country."[229] Donn deGrand Pre concluded: "The Enemy is active today under the guise of environmentalism. Exceptionally strong forces are massed to push us over and back into the Dark Ages of totalitarian Bolshevism under the false and frightening banner of the United Nations."[230]

It seems, however, that the overlords in waiting have not been satisfied with the pace of environmentalism alone in persuading people to willingly give up their freedoms. So, they added the threat of war to their environmental strategy. They planned and executed the September 11, 2001, attacks.

We do not need the *Report From Iron Mountain* to know what war does to the combatant societies. History has shown that wars have inevitably resulted in the curtailment of freedoms that were taken for granted in times of peace. This is a truth that our founding fathers well understood, as witnessed by the writings of James Madison:

> Of all the enemies to public liberty war is, perhaps, the most to be dreaded, because it comprises and develops the germ of every other. War is the parent of armies; from these proceed debts and taxes; and armies, and debts, and taxes are the known instruments for bringing the many under the domination of the few. In war, too, the discretionary power of the Executive is extended; its influence in dealing out offices, honors, and emoluments is multiplied; and all the means of seducing the minds, are added to those of subduing the force of the people.[231]

James Madison, who was a great statesman, father of

the U.S. Constitution, and fourth President of the United States, concluded from his long study of history that "no nation could preserve its freedom in the midst of continual warfare."[232] Sadly, that is exactly the situation in which the United States finds itself today, with the perpetual war on terror. Each new tragedy of the war on terror will be used as a justification for further restrictions on our liberties.

Once the citizens are propagandized and worked into a patriotic fervor, they will gladly bear any burden to fight the perceived foe. The following quote has been attributed to Julius Caesar. Its validity, however, does not rest on the patina of Caesar; the truth of the statement is self evident.

> Beware of the leader who bangs the drums of war in order to whip the citizenry into a patriotic fervor, for patriotism is indeed a double edged sword. It emboldens the blood, just as it narrows the mind. When the drums of war have reached a fervor pitch, and the blood boils with hate and the mind is closed, the leader will have no need in seizing the rights of the citizenry. Rather, the citizenry, infused with fear and blinded by patriotism, will offer up all of their rights unto the leader, and do it gladly so. How do I know? I know, for this is what I have done. And I am Caesar.

9 Treasonous *Provocateurs*

One may think that "Christian" Zionists could not be a treasonous fifth column, because they are helping Israel, who is an ally of the United States. Looking behind the curtain of official censorship, however, reveals that Israel is not truly an ally to the United States, and that helping Israel is detrimental to the interests of the United States.

While the United States and other countries consider Israel an ally, in most instances Israel only pretends to be an ally of countries that help it. For example, Rafi Eitan, who is a Mossad spymaster, an advisor to Fidel Castro, and an Israeli cabinet minister, told one of Israel's largest daily newspapers, *Yediot Aharonot*, in June 1997: "I failed in the Pollard affair, just as I failed in other intelligence operations beyond enemy lines."[233]

Pollard is a Jewish spy who was caught spying on the U.S. for Israel. Joseph DiGenova, the U.S. attorney who prosecuted the case, said he was surprised that Eitan would admit that Pollard spying was sanctioned by Israel, since the official government position taken by Israel is that Pollard was a rogue spy operation. DiGenova added: "But this is basically all stuff that the evidence in the case shows."[234]

The most notable aspect of Eitan's statement is his characterization of the United States as Israel's enemy. The most DiGenova could bring himself to say on that matter was the fact that Eitan "does not refer to the U.S. as an ally is regrettable."[235] The political power of Israel is so great, there are limits to what a public servant will say about Israel, no matter how authoritative is the evidence. No matter what Israel says in its official pronouncements, the actions of Israel in the Pollard case are the actions of an enemy. "When Jonathan Pollard stole our nuclear secrets (which your taxes paid to develop) and sent them to Israel, Israel did not hesitate to trade those secrets to the USSR in exchange for increased emigration quotas."[236]

Spymaster Rafi Eitan's statement that Israel is the enemy of the United States is proven by the conduct of Israel toward the United States. Israel has acted as a *provocateur* to incite the United States to react in a manner beneficial to Israel's interests. Moshe Sharett, the first foreign minister of Israel and prime minister of Israel from 1954-1956, stated in his diary that Israel must use the sword as its main if not its only instrument to keep morale high and to keep a state of "moral tension." Sharett stated: "[T]oward this end -- it may no it MUST -- invent dangers, and to do this it must invent the method of provocation and revenge. . . . and above all let us hope for a new war with the Arab countries so that we may finally get rid of our troubles and acquire our space."[237]

Israel's provocations to war are primarily done through the Mossad. The Israeli Mossad is not just an intelligence agency, it is an operational agency. The Mossad runs "special operations." Aharon Sherf, the head of the Mossad training academy in Israel, explained that the full title of the Mossad is *Ha Mossad, le Modiyn ve le Tafkidim Mayuhadim*,[238] which means The Institute for Intelligence and Special Operations. The subterfuge of provocation and revenge is the core "special operation" of the Israeli Mossad. Sherf explained "our

[Mossad] motto is: 'By way of deception, thou shalt do war.'"[239] The primary tactic of the Mossad is to cause war through the deception of false-flag attacks that act as a provocation for a retaliatory response. Henry Makow states that the U.S. war on terror is a continuation of Israel's plan of "provocation and revenge."[240]

One might wonder, what the U.S. war on terror has to do with Israel and its method of "provocation and revenge?" The first question any investigator asks when trying to solve a crime, especially in the shadowy world of terrorism, is: *cui bono* (who benefits)? The New York Times reported that when former Israeli Prime Minister Benjamin Netanyahu, was asked on September 12th what the 9/11 attacks meant for the relations between the United States and Israel, Netanyahu replied with a matter-of-fact and cold assessment: "It's very good."[241] Immediately realizing that he was speaking to a reporter, Netanyahu edited himself by stating: "Well, not very good, but it will generate immediate sympathy."[242] In 2008, Netanhyahu, then leader of the Likud party, told an assembly at Bar Ilan University that the 9/11 attacks were a good thing for Israel. Israel's Ma'ariv newspaper quoted Netanyahu: "We are benefitting from one thing, and that is the attack on the Twin Towers and Pentagon, and the American struggle in Iraq."[243]

Clearly, the former Prime Minister of Israel recognizes that the 9/11 attacks benefitted Israel. If you start looking for culprits behind the 9/11 attacks from the perspective of who benefits, the first suspect on the list would be Israel. Was Israel the perpetrator of the 9/11 attacks? Israel and its partner Zionists are the clear winners from the 9/11 attacks, and the attacks fit the Israeli *modus operandi*.

In December 2001, investigative reporter Christopher Bollyn spoke with Eckehardt Werthebach, the former head of the *Verfassungsschutz*, the domestic branch of German intelligence, about the terror attacks of 9-11.[244] Werthebach stated that the deathly precision and the magnitude of planning behind the 9/11 attacks would have required years of planning. He explained that such a sophisticated operation would have required the fixed frame of a state intelligence organization.

Werthebach said that is not something that is found in the loose group like the one allegedly led by Mohammed Atta while he studied in Hamburg. The nebulous *Al Qaida* and the Taliban of Afghanistan lacked the fixed frame of a state intelligence organization. He stated that many people would have been involved in the planning of such an operation and the absence of leaks was a further indication that the attacks were state organized actions. That raises the question: which state?

When the evidence is examined, it points to Israel and the Mossad as the perpetrators of the 9/11 attacks. The scheme was to frame Arabs as patsies in order to get the U.S. to wipe out the Arab resistance and other ancillary impediments to their Zionist goals.

Former Italian President Francesco Cossiga, has told Italy's oldest and most widely read newspaper, *Corriere della Sera*, that the 9-11 terrorist attacks were run by the Mossad, which is Israel's foreign intelligence service.[245] President Cossiga stated in that newspaper that the Mossad's perpetration of the 9/11 attacks was common knowledge among global intelligence agencies. President Cossiga stated that the attacks were designed to blame the Arab countries and induce the western powers to invade Iraq and Afghanistan.[246]

In an interview only weeks after 9-11, Hamid Gul, former head of Pakistani intelligence (ISI) from 1987-1989, told UPI reporter Arnaud de Borchgrave that the Mossad and its accomplices were the perpetrators of 9/11. Gul pointed out that the U.S. spent $40 billion per year on intelligence prior to 9-11-2001 and yet claims that it was taken by surprise. Within 10 minutes of the attacks, however, the government and the media had decided that Osama Bin Laden was the perpetrator. Gul, stated that pinning the 9/11 attacks on Osama Bin Laden was a planned piece of disinformation. Gul further stated: "It created an instant mindset and put public opinion into a trance, which prevented even intelligent people from thinking for themselves."[247]

Andreas von Buelow, the former head of the parliamentary commission that oversaw the German intelligence agencies, told Christopher Bollyn that he believed that the Mossad was behind the terror attacks of 9-11.[248] Von Buelow explained that a sophisticated false-flag operation like 9/11 has an organizational structure with three basic levels: 1) architectural, 2) operational, and 3) working. He said that Atta and the 19 Arabs blamed as the hijackers of 9/11 were part of the working level. Von Buelow explained that the alleged hijackers were simply part of the deception. That is, after all, how false-flag terror works. The 9/11 attacks were designed to turn public opinion against the Arabs, and to boost military and security spending.

Von Buelow further explained: "You don't get the higher echelons," which is the architectural level that masterminds such false-flag terror attacks. At that level, the organization doing the planning, in this case the Mossad, is primarily interested in affecting public opinion, and it goes without saying that the mass media must be tightly controlled in order for such large-scale deception to succeed. He opined that "ninety-five percent of the work of the intelligence agencies around the world is deception and disinformation."[249]
He stated that the deception is widely propagated in the mainstream media, which creates an accepted version of events. One can see it in the reporting. Von Buelow explained that is why journalists don't even raise the simplest questions. He said that those who do deviate from the official story are labeled as crazy.

Dr. Alan Sabrosky stated unequivocally:

What we need to stand up and say is that not only did they [Israel] attack the USS Liberty, they did 9/11. They did it.

I have had long conversations over the past two weeks with contacts at the Army War College, at the Headquarters Marine Corps, and I have made it absolutely clear in both cases that it is 100% certain that 9/11 was a Mossad operation. Period.[250]

Who is Dr. Sabrosky? Alan Sabrosky (Ph.D., University of Michigan) was for five years the Director of Studies for the Strategic Studies Institute at the U.S. Army War College. In his capacity as director, he received the Superior Civilian Service Award. While in government service, he held concurrent adjunct professorships at Georgetown University and Johns Hopkins University School of Advanced International Studies (SAIS). Dr. Sabrosky's teaching and research appointments have included the United States Military Academy, the Center for Strategic and International Studies (CSIS), Middlebury College, and Catholic University. He was also holder of the General of the Army Douglas MacArthur Chair of Research. He is listed in WHO'S WHO IN THE EAST (23rd ed.) and is a Marine Corps Vietnam veteran and a 1986 graduate of the U.S. Army War College.[251]

Dr. Sabrosky's credibility is further enhanced by the fact that he is part Jewish. He has a grandparent who was a Jew and some in his extended family are Jewish. He acknowledged that if the American people find out that Israel did 9/11 he will suffer right along with the other Jews. Dr. Sabrosky, however, states that he has a duty to the United States and if it means that he suffers for protecting America he is willing to do that. Dr. Sabrosky stated: "If this explodes I am going to go down with the rest of them, and I know this. I flat out know this."[252]

Being Jewish, Dr. Sabrosky has every motive to conceal this information. He feels compelled by patriotism as an American first to expose the truth of the matter. Dr. Sabrosky's allegiance is to the U.S., but as he explains "a large majority of American Jews give their allegiance to a foreign country, and they have American citizenship, but their allegiance is to Israel."[253]

There is evidence that supports the opinions of the above government officials and scholars. That evidence is documented in this author's book: *9/11 - Enemies Foreign and Domestic*. The book explains in detail the secret evidence censored from the official record that proves traitors aided Israel in attacking the United States on 9/11.

The U.S. Military is fully aware of the Mossad's capabilities and ruthlessness. Just one day before the 9/11 attacks, on September 10, 2001, the Army School of Advanced Military Studies issued a report written by elite U.S. army officers. The report described the Mossad as follows: "Wildcard. Ruthless and cunning. Has capability to target US forces and make it look like a Palestinian/Arab act."[254]

The 9/11 attacks proved the truth of the U.S. military report. The military officers who prepared the report were not just guessing about the activities of the Mossad. The report was based upon hard evidence of the Mossad's long history of attacks on the United States. The Beirut Marine Barracks bombing, the Lavon Affair, the attempted sinking of the U.S.S. Liberty, and the assassination of President Kenendy are all examples of Israeli perfidy against the United States.

Jack Bernstein stated that the 23 October 1983 suicide bombing attack on the U.S. Marine barracks in Lebanon where 241 Marine personnel were killed was planned by the Israeli military intelligence (the Mossad). Bernstein stated that the purpose for the attack on the marine base was to turn the American people against the Arabs in order to draw the United States into the war to help Israel.[255]

The 1983 Marine barracks bombing was not the first time that Israel has used *agent provocateurs*. In 1954 the U.S. was beginning to favor Egypt over Israel regarding some regional issues. The Israeli government decided to use eleven Israeli agents in Egypt to blow up some American buildings and blame it on Egyptian nationalists. The hope of the Israelis was to rupture the relationship between Egypt and the United States. The plot, however, was discovered and exposed. It was referred to as the Lavon Affair, after the Defense Minister of Israel, Pinhas Lavon, who was allegedly the mastermind behind the plot. Lavon denied he was involved in the plot and blamed the Israeli military intelligence, the Mossad. It was never completely resolved which of them was responsible. What is clear was that it was an official operation of the Israeli government.

The Israelis learned their lesson from the Lavon affair. They now use unwitting Muslim Arabs to do their dirty work. The Arabs are intelligence "cut outs" that can be disavowed by their Israeli controllers. The Arab "cut outs" would be kept ignorant that they are actually acting as agent *provocateurs* for Israel. If anything went wrong with the operation, the Arab patsies would not have any meaningful information on the true masterminds of the operation.

Another clear example of the truth of Israeli spymaster Rafi Eitan's statement that Israel is the enemy of the United States is the infamous attack on the USS Liberty. On June 8, 1967, during the Israeli Six Day War, Israel used unmarked military jets to attack and attempt to sink that USS Liberty. That attack also demonstrates the power of the Jews in the U.S. government.

During the Israeli Six Day War, the USS Liberty, an American intelligence gathering ship, was sailing in international waters. Apparently the USS Liberty had discovered something that the Israeli Government did not want revealed. Israeli aircraft and torpedo boats attacked the Liberty. The attack lasted for 75 minutes, during which U.S. Defense Secretary Robert McNamara and Lyndon Johnson ordered the Admiral on a nearby aircraft carrier to recall his jets and NOT to come to the USS Liberty's aid.

Israeli aircraft flew approximately 13 close up reconnaissance sorties on a day with clear skies over the six hours between 6:00 a.m. and 12:00 p.m. Then at approximately 2:00 p.m. unmarked aircraft came in from all directions at once in a massive air attack that included machine gun fire, rocket attacks, and even the dropping of napalm bombs on the ship.

The Israeli aircraft had no identifying markings, which was in violation of the Geneva Convention. Because the aircraft were unmarked, the sailors on the USS Liberty did not know at the time of the attack who were the attacking forces. The objective of the first waive of attacks was to knock out the communications capability of the ship. The attackers succeeded, but the sailors on the USS Liberty were able to rig a communications antenna and transmit an S.O.S., which was received by the Sixth Fleet. However, MacNamara and Johnson treasonously recalled the American jets sent to defend the Liberty. The U.S. had intercepted the radio transmissions of the Israeli aircraft and so Johnson and MacNamara knew that the unmarked aircraft were from Israel.

The initial air attack was followed by a torpedo attack by three torpedo boats, which fired six torpedoes at the Liberty, with one hit. The torpedo hit produced a huge gaping hole on the side of the ship, but miraculously it did not sink. The life rafts were launched, but they were immediately shot up by machine gun fire from the jets. It was clear to those on board the Liberty that the intent was to sink the ship and leave no survivors. An Israeli helicopter gun ship made an appearance and waited nearby expecting the Liberty to sink. The inferred mission of the gun ship was to machine-gun any life boats and anyone who was floating in the water to ensure that there would be no survivors.

When the Liberty did not sink as expected, the helicopter flew off. If the Israelis had succeeded in their mission and there had been no survivors, the Israelis and the Zionists in the U.S. Government could lay the blame for the attack on Egypt and thus the U.S. would have been drawn into the war on the side of Israel. The attack on the USS Liberty is just another case in the long history of Israel acting as *agent provocateur*.

Thirty four Americans were killed and 172 were wounded in the attack. Israel claimed it was a case of mistaken identity. However, U.S. intelligence revealed that it was a deliberate attack ordered by Israeli General Moshe Dyan. Former Secretary of State Dean Rusk and former Joint Chief of Staff Chairman Admiral Thomas Moorer have both stated that the Israeli attack was deliberate.[256] That incident gives some idea of the power and control that the Jews have in the U.S. government. They can control the very apex of the executive branch of government to order the military to stand by while navy sailors are being massacred by the Israeli military.

Lieutenant Commander David E. Lewis, the officer in charge of Liberty's Research Department, had a meeting with Rear Admiral Lawrence R. Geis shortly after the Liberty attack. Admiral Geis was the officer in charge of the embarked aircraft from both the USS America and USS Saratoga. Commander Lewis recounted that Geis told him that attempts were made to come to the aid of the USS Liberty.

Admiral Geis said that he had launched aircraft from

his carriers, after which he called Washington. Secretary McNamara spoke to Geis and ordered the recall of the aircraft, which he did. Geis thought that McNamara was concerned about the jets being armed with nuclear weapons. Geis stripped the planes of nuclear weapons and relaunched the jets, reconfigured with conventional weapons, to defend the USS Liberty. Geis again called Washington to let them know what was going on. Again, Secretary McNamara ordered the aircraft recalled. Geis did not understand why he was being ordered to call-off the defense of the USS Liberty and requested confirmation of the order from President Johnson. President Johnson got on the line and instructed Geis to return the aircraft to his ship. President Johnson stated that he would not have his allies embarrassed, he didn't care who was killed or what was done to the ship.[257] The attack exposes a Zionist fifth column in the United States that controls the executive branch of government.

Most do not know that Johnson was a crypto-Jew. Investigative writer, Salvador Astucia, in his book, *Opium Lords*, explains Lyndon Johnson's Jewish heritage: "The line of Jewish mothers can be traced back three generations in Lyndon Johnson's family tree. There is little doubt that he was Jewish."[258] National disloyalty is the hallmark of a Zionist Jew. The disloyalty shown by President Lyndon Johnson towards his country during the attack on the U.S.S. Liberty is illustrative of that fact. Johnson's policies and conduct toward Israel revealed him as an ardent Zionist. As Commander in Chief of the Army and the Navy, he treasonously prevented the defense of the USS Liberty while it was under attack by Israeli forces and then ordered that the official report of the incident conceal the deliberate nature of the attack.

One thing that seems never to be discussed is the fact that the Israeli attack on the USS Liberty makes no sense unless the Israelis were certain that the USS Liberty would not be defended by the U.S. Sixth Fleet. The Israelis knew that they were no match against the U.S. fighter jets and would have been summarily wiped from the skies. The Israeli gun boats also would have been decimated. There must have been coordination between the highest levels of the U.S. and Israeli governments prior to and during the attack. The Israelis must have been assured by high U.S. Government officials that the USS Liberty would remain undefended throughout the attack. There is only one word to describe such conduct: TREASON!

Israel was also behind the assassination of President Kennedy. Jack Ruby (a/k/a Jack Rubinstein), who shot the patsy Lee Harvey Oswald, told his defense lawyer, William Kunstler: "I did this that they wouldn't implicate Jews."[259] Before Kunstler left Ruby after his last jail visit, Ruby handed him a note in which he reiterated that his motive was to "Protect American Jews from a pogrom that could occur because of anger over the assassination."[260] Ruby and his handlers knew that if Oswald were to be prosecuted for the assassination of President Kennedy, the evidence would not support his conviction but would rather have pointed directly to Israel.

It seems that Ruby was a *Sayan* who was pressed into service to eliminate a loose end (Oswald). A fair view of the facts reveals that the assassination of President Kennedy was a *coup d'etat*. Michael Collins Piper in his book, *Final Judgment*, presents a compelling case that Zionists in general, and the Israeli Mossad in particular, played a primary role in the assassination of President John F. Kennedy, and the subsequent coverup. Piper's book is chock-full of sources and evidence, with more than 1,000 endnotes, and 10 appendices. Other books have revealed the separate involvement of Lyndon Johnson, the Dallas Police Department, the CIA, the FBI, anti-Castro Cubans, French intelligence agencies, the U.S. Secret Service, and organized crime in the assassination of President Kennedy. Mr. Piper methodically explains how all of these persons and organizations were tied together in a conspiracy that at its core was set in motion by the Israeli Mossad.

The motives for the Kennedy assassination are manifold, but one of the key reasons was Kennedy's intent to put an end to the Israeli plans for developing their own nuclear weapons. The Jerusalem Post reported on July 25, 2004 that the jailed nuclear whistle blower, Mordechai Vanunu, revealed that the Israeli government was behind the assassination of President Kennedy.

> Comments by freed nuclear spy Mordechai Vanunu that Israel was behind the assassination of US President John F. Kennedy failed to bring smiles to government officials Sunday. Vanunu said that according to "near-certain indications," Kennedy was assassinated due to "pressure he exerted on then head of government, David Ben-Gurion, to shed light on Dimona's nuclear reactor."[261]

10 Protocols of the Learned Elders of Zion

By crippling the spread of the gospel, the "Christian" Zionists are fulfilling the strategy of Zionist Jews as set forth in the Protocols of the Learned Elders of Zion. Paragraph two of Protocol 17 states:

> We have long past taken care to discredit the priesthood of the "goyim," and thereby to ruin their mission on earth which in these days might still be a great hindrance to us. Day by day its influence on the peoples of the world is falling lower. Freedom of conscience has been declared everywhere, so that now only years divide us from the moment of the complete wrecking of that Christian religion.[262]

The "Christian" Zionists are being used according to the plans set forth in *The Protocols of the Learned Elders of Zion.* That document is an outline of a plan by Jews to rule the world. The Protocols are the minutes of the meetings of the Learned Elders of Zion.[263] The Protocols contain the formula used by the Zionists to launch their offensive to rule the world.

The Protocols came to light when on or about 1884 the daughter of a Russian general, Justine Glinka, living in France, paid 2,500 francs to a Jew, Joseph Schorst, who was a member of the Mizraim Lodge (Oriental Rite of Freemasonry) in Paris, for the Protocols of the Learned Elders of Zion.

Glinka forwarded the French original of the Protocols, accompanied by a Russian translation, to General Orgevskii, who was the Russian Secretary to the Minister of the Interior, in St. Petersburg.[264] General Orgevskii in turn handed the Protocols to his superior, the Minister of the Interior, General Cherevin, for delivery to the Tsar. Cherevin, however, was under the control of wealthy Jews, and he consequently refused to transmit the Protocols. Cherevin merely filed the Protocols in the Russian archives. Upon his death in 1896, Cherevin willed a copy of his memoirs containing the Protocols to Nicholas II.[265]

Years later Glinka returned to Russia and gave a copy of the Protocols to the marechal de noblesse (marshal of the nobility) of her district (Orel), Alexis Sukhotin. Sukhotin showed the document to Professor Sergius A. Nilus. In 1901, in Tsarskoe-Tselc (Russia), Professor Nilus published the Protocols in a book titled *The Great Within the Small*. On or about August 10, 1906 a copy of the Protocols was deposited in the British Museum. In addition, the minutes of the 1897 proceedings of the Zionist Congress meeting in Basel had been obtained through Jewish members of the Russian police and these were found to confirm the plans set forth in the Protocols.[266]

Some Jews have claimed that the Protocols are forgeries. We should recognize the precise way they have denied the Protocols. They have called them forgeries. A forgery is merely an unauthorized copy of an original. Others, with absolutely no evidence to support their claim, have supposed that although the Protocols are genuine, at some point they were altered to refer to the Jews. Historical events have confirmed that Talmudic Jews are following the blueprint set forth in the Protocols.

The great researcher Nesta Webster, in her *World Revolution* states:

> The truth is, then, that the Protocols have never been refuted, and the futility of the so-called refutations published, as also the fact of their temporary suppression, have done more to convince the public of their authenticity than all the anti-Semite writings on the subject put together.[267]

The treatment of Professor Nilus by the Jewish Bolsheviks speaks clearly to the authenticity of the Protocols. Professor Nilus was arrested by the Cheka (Russian Secret Police) in Kiev. He was imprisoned and tortured. The Jewish president of the court told Professor Nilus that the brutal treatment he received was as retribution for "having done them incalculable harm in publishing the Protocols." Professor Nilus was released for a few months, but was soon rearrested by the Cheka, this time in Moscow. He was confined in prison until February 1926. He died in exile in the district of Vladimir on January 13, 1929.

Jewish researcher Rose Cohen explains that if one reads the Protocols it would be clear to the reader that it is not a false anti-Semitic document but rather an authentic plan of powerful Zionists:

> [I]t takes a Jew to understand the Zionist mind as reflected in the reviled 'Elders'. Without reading this officially scorned and hated book, no one can EVER understand the Mossad and/or Israel. This is why we in Israel have

been always forbidden to read the Protocols and the government maintained a 50+ year campaign among Israelis to discredit the Protocols as a fraud. I had an Israeli professor as a guest in my house recently here in Sydney. He, too, was absolutely certain The Protocols are a fraud, but he readily admitted that he has NEVER read them! When I commented that whether the Protocols are legitimate or not, we Jews have actually behaved and accomplished almost 100% of what is written in them. He could not believe it. Ignorance is bless [sic], I guess he can sleep at night. However, in the interest of fairness to the professor, I should add that in the last 45 years of my research in this subject, I have yet to meet a single Israeli who actually read the Protocols.[268]

Please dear reader do not miss the very important fact revealed by Cohen; as in communist Russia, so also in Israel, the Protocols are forbidden. The Jewish hierarchy does not want the rank and file Jews to read their plans. It is the Jewish hierarchy that is evil, the ordinary Jews, like the gentiles, are cannon fodder in a spiritual and temporal war to rule the world. The masses of Jews are kept in ignorance of the true aims of the evil Jewish hierarchy. The Jewish hierarchy has a history of fanning the flames of antisemitism as a tool to keep the rank and file Jews in line and obedient to their commands. They portray the Protocols as another example of antisemitic hate literature, yet they do not allow the rank and file Jew to read the document for themselves.

The best evidence of the genuineness of the Protocols is that in March 1917 the Bolshevik Revolution took place in Russia and one of the first things done upon the Jewish Bolsheviks taking power was to destroy all copies of Professor

Sergius A. Nilus' book, *The Great Within the Small*, which contained *The Protocols of the Learned Elders of Zion*.

All copies of the Protocols that were known to exist in Russia were destroyed during the Kerensky regime. The law followed by Kerensky's communist successors to power was that the possession of a copy of the Protocols by anyone in the Soviet Union was a crime punishable by being shot on sight.

The lengths that the communists went to eradicate the Protocols speaks to their authenticity. Why bother destroying something if it is, as alleged by the Jews, a false document. If the document is false, one would think that the Jews would want to preserve the Protocols and use them as an exhibit to prove the falsehood of the claims made against them.

It is only if the Protocols are genuine that the Jews would want them eradicated. The Jewish Bolsheviks knew that the Protocols fall into a category of documents that are self-authenticating, by virtue of the fact that the stratagems set forth in the Protocols have been put into effect by Zionist Jews exactly in the manner set forth in the Protocols. The very actions of the Jews prove the authenticity of the Protocols. The Jewish Bolsheviks understood that fact, and so they could not allow them to be circulated.

In an interview published in the New York World on February 17, 1921, the great American industrialist Henry Ford tersely and convincingly put the case for the genuineness of the Protocols: "The only statement I care to make about the Protocols is that they fit in with what is going on. They are sixteen years old and they have fitted the world situation up to this time. They fit it now."[269] Henry Ford's statement is as true today as it was when he spoke in 1921.

The self-authenticating nature of the Protocols of Zion can be compared to a treasure map that accurately leads you to the treasure. If you follow the map and find the treasure that proves that the map is authentic. It would be ridiculous to say that the treasure map is a forgery, when the map has proven its authenticity by leading you to the treasure. The world events and the political power obtained by Zionist Jews testify to the authenticity of the Protocols.

Almost all politicians understand the political power of the Jews, few however, have the courage to reveal what they know. The former Prime Minister of Malaysia is an exception to the rule. On October 16, 2003, Prime Minister of Malaysia Tun Dr. Mahathir Mohamad gave a speech to the Tenth Islamic Summit Conference in Putrajaya, Malaysia. Mahathir was the Prime Minister of Malaysia for 22 years from 1981 to 2003. Mahathir revealed what he learned about the Zionist Jews during his many years in high political office. Prime Minister Mahathir Mohamad explained:

> [T]oday the Jews rule this world by proxy. They get others to fight and die for them. . . . They invented and successfully promoted Socialism, Communism, human rights and democracy so that persecuting them would appear to be wrong, so they may enjoy equal rights with others. With these they have now gained control of the most powerful countries and they, this tiny community, have become a world power.[270]

The Anti-Defamation League (ADL) posted Mahathir's speech on its website and, not surprisingly, alleged that it was antisemitic.[271] Anytime someone tells the truth about the political power of Jews, they are falsely labeled an "antisemite."

The details of the plan set forth in the Protocols have been implemented before the eyes of the world in Russia,

Eastern Europe, China, North Korea, Afghanistan, Iraq, Libya, and Vietnam. The plan is in the process of being implemented in Western Europe, South America, South Africa, Iran, the United States, and many countries throughout the world.[272] The religious works by the Jews also testify to the authenticity of the Protocols. For example, the evil and blasphemous nature of the Talmud parallels much of what is found in the Protocols.

The Protocols are quite frank in admitting that the Zionist strategy of rule is through deception. The second language of Zionist Jews is lying. Paragraph 11 of Protocol 1 states:

> The political has nothing in common with the moral. The ruler who is governed by the moral is not a skilled politician, and is therefore unstable on his throne. He who wishes to rule must have recourse both to cunning and to make-believe. Great national qualities, like frankness and honesty, are vices in politics, for they bring down rulers from their thrones more effectively and more certainly than the most powerful enemy. Such qualities must be the attributes of the kingdoms of the goyim, but we must in no wise be guided by them.[273]

11 Billy Graham: Zionist Shill

As previously revealed, paragraph two of Protocol 17 states that the Zionist strategy is "to discredit the priesthood of the 'goyim,' and thereby to ruin their mission on earth."[274] The Zionists consider all ministers, whether they are protestant or Catholic, part of the "priesthood of the 'goyim.'"

The aim of the Zionists, as stated in Protocol 17, is the "complete wrecking of that Christian religion."[275] The wrecking of the nominal Christian religion is being done by injecting Judaic doctrine into the churches. That is the very thing that Jesus was warning about when he said "[t]ake heed and beware of the leaven of the Pharisees and of the Sadducees." (Matthew 16:6) Once the Christian doctrine is undermined, the church ceases to be Christian. Zionists stated in Protocol 17 that they have nearly accomplished their goal of wrecking the "Christian religion." The result is that nominal Christian churches have been changed into auxiliary Jewish Synagogues.

One of the most famous Zionist agents of change in the nominal Christian community is Billy Graham. Billy Graham is one of the many Zionist preachers who sees no point in preaching the gospel of Jesus Christ to the Jews.

The Charlotte Observer reported on a press release of the Billy Graham Evangelistic Association, where Billy Graham lashes out at Southern Baptists who desire to evangelize Jews for Christ. Graham makes it clear that he firmly opposes "proselytizing" the Jews; Billy Graham's unbiblical teaching is that, if you are a Jew, you are already part of the Body of Christ, even if you reject Jesus.[276]

Eric Jewell reports that Graham "is a supporter of the National Council of Churches and the World Council of Churches, where a belief in Jesus Christ is a nonessential."[277]

Dr. Cathy Burns reveals that Billy Graham has been a Zionist stooge promoting the Zionist political program for decades.[278] Where does Billy Graham get his variety of Zionism? Graham told Larry King: "In New York, they have had me to the Rabbinical Council to . . . talk with them and Rabbi Tannenbaum, who was a great friend . . . he gave me more advice and more counsel, and I depended on him constantly, theologically and spiritually and in every way."[279]

Rabbi Marc Tannenbaum, was a leading sponsor of the Lucis Trust (formerly the Lucifer Publishing Company).[280] Lucis Trust was founded for the purpose of establishing of a "One World Religion."[281] Lucis Trust is a dangerous New Age cult that has at its core the worship of Lucifer. The Lucis Trust runs The Temple of Understanding, which is the only religious chapel at the United Nations headquarters in New York City. The Lucis Trust was originally founded as the Lucifer Trust, in London, in 1923, but the name was changed to Lucis Trust, to make the nature of the organization less conspicuous.[282]

Billy Graham is serving his masters. He gained notoriety as a direct result of media-hype. Media mogul William Randolph Hearst sent a telegram to his newspaper editors instructing them to "Puff Graham" during Graham's 1949 Los Angeles tent crusade. Within five days, Graham gained national coverage.[283]

With the massive media attention, Graham soon became a national figure. Within a year he was meeting with President Truman, of course with the major media on hand to take pictures of Graham kneeling on the White House lawn. President Truman called Graham "a counterfeit."[284] It takes one, to know one. In 1954, Henry Luce, the publisher of TIME magazine put Graham on the cover of TIME. Henry Luce was a member of the satanic Skull and Bones society.

It is notable that William Randolph Hearst got his start as a national media mogul by selling Anaconda Copper to the Rothschilds in 1895 for $7.5 million.[285] With that money Hearst acquired his first New York paper, the New York Journal.[286] The Hearst News Corporation today is controlled by Zionists. In 2008, the Hearst Corporation went so far as to prohibit its reporters from even accessing the anti-Zionist website, Rense.com. Rense reports: "This raw, unabashed, fascist censorship is indicative of a corporation under Zionist dominance and not serving the will or the interests of the people."[287] It is astounding that a company that is supposed to present unbiased news coverage takes affirmative steps to ensure that its reporters are ignorant of an opposing viewpoint. It is especially disturbing when one considers that the Zionist issue is the foremost concern today.

Texe Marrs reports that Zbigniew Brzezinski has revealed that the New World Order tyranny cannot come to power based solely upon politics and economics alone. The Zionist overlords must use religion to control the masses.

> In his revealing book, *Out of Control*, distributed privately among the elite of the Bilderbergers, Council on Foreign Relations,

Trilateral Commission and other groups, Zbigniew Brzezinski, Rockefeller operative and former National Security Advisor to President Jimmy Carter, declared that the New World Order cannot be built on a foundation of politics and economics alone. To truly establish ironclad global control over all peoples and nations, Brzezinski explained that the elite must also use the religious element.[288]

What form of government does Brzezinski have in mind for the New World Order? Brzezinski and his handlers plan on enslaving the world under a communist police state. Brzezinski wrote a book in 1970 titled Between Two Ages: *America's Role in the Technetronic Era.* In that book Brzezinski extols the supposed virtues of communism. He states that "Marxism represents a further vital and creative stage in the maturing of man's universal vision."[289] Brzezinski describes Marxism is "a victory of reason over belief."[290] He further states that Marxist communism has "supplied the best available insight into contemporary reality."[291]

Billy Graham and his ilk fulfill the need of the ruling elite to control the masses. Graham and virtually all televangelists are funded and supported by powerful Zionist interests. Marrs explains:

> It is well known that wealthy Illuminati chieftains Henry Luce (Order of Skull & Bones patriarch and head of the Time Life empire) and William Randolph Hearst (Hearst newspapers) puffed up and made evangelist Billy Graham a "star." Knights of Malta magnate, J. Peter Grace (W.R. Grace and Co. Chemicals) and his cronies, such as Ted Turner (CNN), were the prime movers behind Pat Robertson's Christian Broadcasting

Network apparatus. Other Illuminati helped set up the Crouches and their Trinity Broadcasting Network.

The Rockefellers and the heirs to the Firestone and other fortunes funded Alcoholics Anonymous. An Orthodox Jewish billionaire from Canada and the corrupt but fabulously wealthy Riady family from Indonesia secretly funded both televangelist Morris Cerullo's TV broadcast and Jim and Tammy Faye Bakker's PTL Network. The Rockefellers also ponied up millions for the work of the apostate Jesus Seminar scholars and the heretical World Council of Churches organization.

The Vatican's secret societies also were instrumental in furthering the charismatic movement. Rick Joyner, one of the popular charismatic "Kansas City Prophets," was even initiated into the Vatican's mysteriously evil order, the Knights of Malta. Meanwhile, CIA operative Reverend Sun Myung Moon has spread millions of bucks among his favorite evangelical Christian stooges, ranging from Tim and Bev La Haye (Left Behind) to the Crystal Cathedral's positive-thinking guru Dr. Robert Schuller and Christian pop singer Pat Boone.

Schuller also was rewarded with big bucks by his Illuminati pal, the late Communist-puppet oilman, Armand Hammer (Occidental Oil Corp). Meanwhile, James Dobson's Focus on the Family moved into a luxurious new Colorado facility a few years ago, paid for by a curiously secret Roman Catholic foundation.[292]

Billy Graham knows the spiritual depravity and nefarious ambitions of the Zionists with whom he has conspired. In 1972 he was recorded talking to President Richard Nixon during what Graham thought was a private conversation where Graham referred to the Jewish stranglehold on the media: "This stranglehold has got to be broken or this country's going down the drain."[293] The St. Petersburg Times reports of the conversation:

> Nixon then broaches a subject about which "we can't talk about it publicly," namely Jewish influence in Hollywood and the media. He cites Paul Keyes, a political conservative who is executive producer of the NBC hit, Rowan and Martin's Laugh-In, as telling him that "11 of the 12 writers are Jewish."
>
> "That right?" Graham says, prompting Nixon to claim that Life magazine, Newsweek, the New York Times, the Los Angeles Times and others are "totally dominated by the Jews." He calls network TV anchors, Howard K. Smith, David Brinkley and Walter Cronkite "front men who may not be of that persuasion," but said their writers are "95 percent Jewish."

* * *

> [Graham] later concurs with a Nixon assertion that a "powerful bloc" of Jews confronts Nixon in the media. "And they're the ones putting out the pornographic stuff," Graham adds.

* * *

> [Graham states that] I don't mean all the Jews, but a lot of the Jews are great friends of mine. They swarm around me and are friendly to me. Because they know I am friendly to Israel and so forth. They don't know how I really feel about what they're doing to this country. And I have no power and no way to handle them."[294]

Hugh Dougherty explains that the tapes prove that Graham had lied eight years earlier when he denied making the statements after Nixon Chief of Staff, H.R. Haldeman, revealed the comments in his 1994 memoirs. Graham thought that he would never get caught lying, because Haldeman had died before his memoirs were published and was not around to substantiate the allegation. Graham did not know that the conversation was being taped.

> The tapes confirmed a claim by one of Nixon's advisers that Mr Graham had made the comments - which was completely denied in 1994 by the preacher, who said, "I have never talked publicly or privately about the Jewish people, including conversations with President Nixon, except in the most positive terms." The evangelist, who has been a friend and spiritual counselor to a series of presidents, yesterday retracted his denial and tried to prevent lasting damage to his legacy. In a statement, he repudiated the comments and apologized for their effect.[295]

Why would Billy Graham say such things in private, when in public he was an ardent supporter of Israel and the Jews in word and deed? Texe Marrs explains that "the men and women who publicly smile and cheer on their Zionist masters actually chafe and sneer in private. They despise the fact that the Jews lord it over them."²⁹⁶ Marrs puts in context the private concerns expressed by Nixon and Graham over Jewish power:

> Both of these men were often publicly humiliated by their Jewish bosses. A cowed Billy Graham was forced to repeatedly state to the media that Jews, being "God's Chosen," do not need to accept Jesus Christ as Lord and Saviour. Graham once assured a smug and superior Israeli Prime Minister Golda Meir that he would never conduct a "Billy Graham Crusade" in Tel Aviv, Haifa, or Jerusalem. "We can't proselytize someone who already has God's blessings," Graham told Meir.
>
> Nixon, too, knew that the Jews held the power to do him in, and he was constantly watchful to make sure he didn't slight a rich Jew or displease an Israeli leader. As President, Nixon showered the nation of Israel with foreign aid money and military arms.²⁹⁷

Graham's obedience to his Jewish overlords was grudging, but he nonetheless remained obedient. Not only did Graham refuse to proselytize Jews, he even sent Jews who came to him seeking the salvation of Jesus Christ back to their Jewish synagogues. In a September 21, 1957 interview with the *San Francisco News*, Graham said, "Anyone who makes a decision at our meetings is seen later and referred to a local clergyman, Protestant, Catholic, or Jewish."²⁹⁸

12 Freemasonry: Judaism For Gentiles

The Zionism of Billy Graham is in large part explained by the fact that Graham is a Freemason.[299] Indeed, he is likely a 33rd degree Mason. Former 33rd degree Mason, Jim Shaw, has revealed that Billy Graham attended Shaw's 33rd degree induction ceremony. Only other 33rd degree Masons are permitted to attend such ceremonies. Graham's membership in the Masonic Lodge explains his unchristian view that there is no point in preaching the gospel to the Jews.

To this day Graham has refused to personally answer the many inquiries whether he is a Freemason. He has left it to his subordinates to deny his membership in Freemasonry for him. His membership in Freemasonry is one reason why Billy Graham has never spoken out against Freemasonry, when God's word states that he should do just that. "And have no fellowship with the unfruitful works of darkness, but rather reprove them." (Ephesians 5:11).

Graham's refusal to reveal himself as a Freemason is in accord with the conventions of Freemasonry. On or before

1912, The Zion News, a Masonic paper, stated:

> The public has no right to know that any man is a Mason. That he has a right to conceal the fact for business and other reasons, or for no reason at all; that it is one of the secrets of Freemasonry that no one has a right to reveal but himself.[300]

One might ask what is wrong with being a Freemason? Isn't Freemasonry just a fraternal organization? Martin L. Wagner conducted an objective and thorough study of Freemasonry and wrote a book about his findings titled *Freemasonry: An Interpretation*. Wagner's authoritative study of Freemasonry concludes that Freemasonry is not simply a fraternal organization, it is in fact a religion.

> We might multiply the citations from eminent ministers of the gospel, of almost every denomination, expressing their convictions that Masonry is a religion. In fact the most learned men of the church, irrespective of denominational affiliation, who have given this question any attention, with one voice, testify that Masonry is a religion. These men representing not only the church, but also occupying professor's chairs in seats of learning, men whose business it is to deal with religion and questions of religion, are from that fact, competent judges; and from the Masonic publications, its lexicons, rituals, encyclopedias and apologetic literature, enough of Masonry can be learned in order to judge of its nature and character. Surely the testimony of these men has weight.[301]

What kind of religion is Masonry? Wagner interviewed

many former Masons who quit Masonry because they discovered that the Masonic religion was antithetical to Christianity.

> With the testimony of these learned Christian men agrees that of those who were at one time honored members of the Masonic fraternity, but for sufficient reasons left it, and in not a few cases, exposed it. We have conversed with a large number of this class of seceding Masons, all of whom assigned as the reason for their repudiation and renunciation of Masonry, that it is a religion; that it conflicts and interferes with their views and duties as Christians; that it teaches moral and religious precepts which their Christian conscience could not approve and practice jeopardizing their souls; that its aim and tendency is to undermine their faith in the Lord Jesus Christ as their personal Saviour; that it alienates their affections and support from the church, and destroys their faith in the Bible as the word of God. Their common sense as well as their moral sense taught them that as a religion, Masonry is incompatible with Christianity; that it is another religion, and being unable to serve two masters, they were driven to renounce Freemasonry with its hidden things, in order to have peace of mind and a good. conscience toward God. From the testimony of these devout Christians, who firmly expected to obtain more light when they united with the fraternity, we are persuaded that Freemasonry is a religion. These men learned these things, came to these convictions while active members of the craft and sought earnestly its secret arts by which they might learn truth,

practice relief, and above all to subdue their passions. Finding it a religion which sought their support and loyalty over against that of their Lord Jesus Christ, they renounced its hidden works, and repudiated its claims.[302]

Wagner discovered that although Freemasonry is contrary to Christianity, it uses Christian theological terms in many of its rituals in order to hoodwink the uninitiated.

> Freemasonry is a system of cunningly devised fables whereby it deceives all except the discerning few whose wit and wisdom enable them to perceive the deeper meaning, and who alone of all those admitted into the order become the true Masons.
>
> The peculiar theological and religious ideas which Freemasonry holds and aims to inculcate while positively non-Christian, are expressed in terms of Christian theology, not to express the Christian ideas or to show their harmony with Christian thought, but to give them a Christian coloring the more effectually to deceive, mislead and hoodwink the neophyte, the conscientious member, and the non-Mason into whose hands Masonic literature may come, and also to intensify the task of the Mason to learn the real sentiments.[303]

Wagner concluded that the Christian labeling of Masonic symbolism cannot change the true character of Freemasonry, because "the essence of Freemasonry is such that it is morally and absolutely impossible to hold and to adhere to it, and to hold and to adhere to Christianity. The two are antithetical and mutually exclusive, and no juggling with or distorting of religious terms can circumvent this fact."[304] What are the beliefs of Freemasonry that are so antithetical to Christianity? Wagner explains:

> The Masonic view of the revelation of God, in the lower degrees, is deistic, but in the higher degrees it becomes pantheistic. The writings of Garrison, Buck, Pike, and other eminent Masons show this unmistakably. It is this peculiar pantheistic conception of deity which has passed from India through the secret doctrines of the Kabbalah into modern speculative Freemasonry, as Buck intimates, that constitutes the secret doctrine of the institution.[305]

Deism is the belief that the sole basis of knowledge about the creator is intellectual reason and observation of the natural world. Deists reject the revelation and authority of the Holy Bible. Deistic theology ranges from un-Christian to anti-Christian.

What is pantheism? Pantheism is a word derived from the root words pan (all) and theos (god). Pantheism literally means "all is god." Pantheism is the belief that all of creation is god. Pantheism is directly contrary to the biblical teaching that God is the eternal, omnipotent, and omniscient creator and is separate and distinct from his creation.

The Masonic pantheism flowed to Freemasonry through the secret doctrines of the Kabbalah.[306] The god of Freemasonry is a speculative pantheistic force of nature that Masons call the "Great Architect of the Universe." That Great Architect of the Universe is the generative principle in nature that has been worshiped by heathen societies from antiquity.

Freemasons state that their Great Architect of the

Universe is the same god, under a different name, as all other gods worshiped by all monotheistic religions. That concept is the basis for Freemasons deceptively claiming that the Masonic Great Architect of the Universe is the God of the Holy Bible.

It is impossible, however, to equate heathen gods with the true God of the bible. There is only one Lord God. "The LORD he is God; there is none else beside him. . . . the LORD he is God in heaven above, and upon the earth beneath: there is none else." Deuteronomy 4:35,39. The Holy God of the bible asks: "To whom will ye liken me, and make me equal, and compare me, that we may be like?" Isaiah 46:5. God makes it clear: "I am God, and there is none else; I am God, and there is none like me." Isaiah 46:9. God does not mince words; he clearly commands: "Thou shalt have no other gods before me." Exodus 20:3. Indeed, the very God who commands that there be no other gods before him, states in no uncertain terms that salvation can be had by no other but through him, the Lord Jesus Christ. "Jesus saith unto him, I am the way, the truth, and the life: no man cometh unto the Father, but by me." John 14:6.

Wagner points out that Freemasons violate God's command and employ all manner of cunning sophistry to deceive the public into believing that the Masonic Great Architect of the Universe is the same as the Lord God of the bible:

> Freemasons attempt to identify its Great Architect with Jehovah, the Father of our Lord Jesus Christ, but these attempts are simply cunning devices for misleading and deceiving both the Mason and the profane. They are examples of clever sophistry, of skillful syncretism, of cunningly devised fables and delusive fictions, which have a semblance of truth and fact, but which in reality are only veils and disguises for its refined idolatry.

They are skillful professions of adherence to the first commandment while in fact they are palpable violations of it. The Masonic god is a secret deity, whose nature, name and worship is veiled under the name and guise of Jehovah. This cunning sophistry and fiction must be seen in order to apprehend the true nature of the religion of Freemasonry. From the Christian viewpoint, the two, Jehovah and the Great Architect of the Universe, are entirely separate and different, mutually exclusive, and no syncretism can harmonize them.[307]

In order to keep up the charade that the Masonic Great Architect of the Universe is the God of the bible, Freemasons conceal from the public the name of their god. Freemasons call their Great Architect of the Universe by the name *Jabulun*[308] (a/k/a *Jah-Bul-On*[309] or *Jah-Bel-On*[310]). That name is a cryptographic word that is based upon the abbreviated names for Jehovah (*Jah*), Baal (*Bel* or *Bul*), and Osiris (*On*).[311] The Freemasons blasphemously identify Jehovah, who is the God of the bible, as the Hebrew sun god.[312] The Freemasons join that name to Baal, who was the Assyrian sun god, to whom the Jews sacrificed their children. *See* Jeremiah 32:26-36. The sixteenth century demonologist John Weir identified Baal as a devil.[313] Osiris was the Egyptian sun god. There cannot be a joining of God with Baal, Osiris, or any other heathen god. "What concord hath Christ with Belial?" 2 Corinthians 6:15. The Prophet Elijah stated "if the Lord be God, follow him: but if Baal, then follow him." 1 Kings 18:21. There is only one God and salvation is solely by the grace of God through faith in Jesus Christ. "Neither is there salvation in any other: for there is none other name under heaven given among men, whereby we must be saved" Acts 4:12.

Stephen Knight interviewed over 50 Royal Arch Freemasons in order to get a balanced view of Freemasonry for his book, *The Brotherhood*. Only one-fifth of Master Masons are "exalted" to the Royal Arch degree. Only Royal Arch Masons are told the name of the Masonic god (*Jah-Bul-On*). All but a few Royal Arch interviewees lost their composure when he asked them about *Jah-Bul-On*. Knight stated: "If I insisted on returning to *Jah-Bul-On*, almost invariably the interview would be unceremoniously terminated."[314] The reaction of the Masons was due to the fact that they had no way to discuss *Jah-Bul-On* without revealing the esoteric meaning behind that cryptograph, which would expose the true nature of Freemasonry as a decidedly satanic religion.

The bible states that Jesus is the Lord God Almighty and "is the blessed and only Potentate, the King of kings, and Lord of lords." (1 Timothy 6:15) God is a potentate who rules from heaven over his creation. God states that "Heaven is my throne, and earth is my footstool: what house will ye build me? saith the Lord: or what is the place of my rest? Hath not my hand made all these things?" (Acts 7:49-50) Clearly, God is separate from and not part of the things that he has created. Paul, in apparent reference to pantheists, explained in his letter to the Romans that ungodly men had "changed the truth of God into a lie, and worshipped and served the creature more than the Creator, who is blessed for ever." Romans 1:25.

Who is "the creature" that is referenced by Paul, whom men worshiped and served? That creature is likely a reference to Satan, because "the creature" is juxtaposed against "the Creator." Satan was created by God, and we know he seeks to be worshiped and served. We read in Isaiah how Lucifer (who became Satan after being cast out of heaven) seeks to "be like the most High." Isaiah 14:14. We see in the book of Revelation how all whose names are not written in the book of life of the Lamb will worship the dragon, who is Satan (Lucifer); they will also worship the beast, to whom the dragon has given his power. *See* Revelation 13:4-8.

Albert Pike, the theological pontiff of Masonry wrote that "[i]t is certain that its true pronunciation is not represented by the word Jehovah; and therefore that *that* is not the true name of Diety, nor the Ineffable Word."[315] God's word, however, states clearly that JEHOVAH is God's name. "That men may know that thou, whose name alone is JEHOVAH, art the most high over all the earth." (Psalms 83:18)

If the Masons do not recognize JEHOVAH as God, who is their god? The god of the Masons is Lucifer, which was Satan's name before he rebelled against God and was cast out of heaven. Albert Pike said that "[t]he doctrine of Satanism is heresy; and the true and pure philosophic religion is the belief in Lucifer, the equal of Adonay; but Lucifer, God of Light and God of Good is struggling for humanity against Adonay, the God of Darkness and Evil."[316] Adonay is the Old Testament Hebrew word for God. Pike not only acknowledges that Lucifer is the god of Freemasonry, but he also blasphemes God by calling God "the God of Darkness and Evil."

Pike wrote the official theological manual of Masonry titled *Morals and Dogma of the Ancient and Accepted Scottish Rite*. In *Morals and Dogma*, Pike calls the creator of Adam the "Prince of Darkness."[317] The Holy Bible (Genesis 2:7) is clear that God created Adam. Pike blasphemes God by calling him the "Prince of Darkness."

The Holy Bible (Genesis 2:17) states that God forbade Adam from eating of the fruit of the knowledge of good and evil. Pike blasphemes God again by referring to God as "the Demons" who forbade Adam from eating from the fruit of knowledge of good and evil.[318] The Holy Bible states that God created Eve. Pike continues his blasphemy by calling God "the Demons" who created Eve.[319]

Pike portrays the serpent (Satan) as "an Angel of Light" that induced Adam to transgress against "the Demons" and thus giving Adam "the means of victory."³²⁰ Pike calls the sin of Adam and Eve "the means of victory" over God. Whereas, God views Adams disobedience against him as the means of the fall of man, which required God to come down to earth and redeem man. (Romans 5:12-21) Christ has won the victory over Satan for all those who believe in Jesus. (1 Corinthians 15:54-58, 1 John 5:4, Revelations 15:2) While it is true that Satan can transform himself into an angel of light (see 2 Corinthians 11:14), Pike's point in calling Satan an "Angel of Light" was to distinguish him from God, whom he called the "Prince of Darkness."³²¹

To attribute the power of God to Satan is considered blaspheming the Holy Spirit, which Jesus stated was the unpardonable sin. *See* Matthew 12:24-32. Jesus stated that "all manner of sin and blasphemy shall be forgiven unto men: but the blasphemy against the Holy Ghost shall not be forgiven unto men." Matthew 12:31. Jesus made that statement in response to the allegation leveled against him by the Pharisees that he cast out devils by the power of the prince of the devils, "Beelzebub." Matthew 12:24.

Upon what authority did Albert Pike rely for writing his authoritative *Morals and Dogma of the Ancient and Accepted Scottish Rite*? Wagner states that "Albert Pike drew largely from the writings of Eliphas Levi, the Abbe Constant, a great Kabbalist, and whom Buck considers as knowing more of the occult science than any one since the days of the old initiates, for illuminating and illustrating Freemasonry."³²²

One of the key points revealed in the Protocols of the Learned Elders of Zion is the secret use of ostensibly Gentile nations and institutions in order to further Jewish Zionist aims, while hiding the Jewish influence over those institutions. In the Protocols, the Learned Elders of Zion state that they have used Masonry as a cover to hide their involvement in the plan for a "new world order." Paragraph two of Protocol 4 states:

Who and what is in a position to overthrow an invisible force? And this is precisely what our force is. Gentile masonry blindly serves as a screen for us and our objectives, but the plan of action of our force, even its very abiding place, remains for the whole people in unknown mystery. [323]

The Gentile facade of Freemasonry offers the Zionist Jews the perfect cover. We can see the same hidden control by Jews over the "Christian" Zionist movement. Freemasonry is based upon Judaism.[324] It is a Gentile front for Jewish mysticism, whose history, grades, and official appointments, are rooted in Jewish theosophy.[325]

The Zionists promote and control masonic lodges. They use those lodges as indispensable secret intelligence agencies and organs of influence. Paragraphs four and five of Protocol 15 states:

> [W]e shall create and multiply free masonic lodges in all the countries of the world, absorb into them all who may become or who are prominent in public activity, for these lodges we shall find our principal intelligence office and means of influence. All these lodges we shall bring under one central administration, known to us alone and to all others absolutely unknown, which will be composed of our learned elders.

* * *

It is natural that we and no other should lead masonic activities, for we know whither we are leading, we know the final goal of every form of activity whereas the goyim have knowledge of nothing.[326]

Zionist Jews use the lodges of Freemasonry as recruiting grounds for their Gentile front-men. The Gentile nature of freemasonry is only a cover; freemasonry is wholly based upon the Jewish Cabala. Using the Gentile front of freemasonry is explained in paragraphs four and seven of Protocol 11.

> The goyim are a flock of sheep, and we are their wolves. And you know what happens when the wolves get hold of the flock? ... For what purpose then have we invented this whole policy and insinuated it into the minds of the goy without giving them any chance to examine its underlying meaning? For what, indeed, if not in order to obtain in a roundabout way what is for our scattered tribe unattainable by the direct road? It is this which has served as the basis for our organization of secret masonry which is not known to, and aims which are not even so much as suspected by, these "goy" cattle, attracted by us into the "show" army of masonic lodges in order to throw dust in the eyes of their fellows.[327]

The statements in the Protocols that Freemasonry is rooted in Judaism is confirmed by Wagner, in his study of Freemasonry. Wagner quotes Masonic authorities that reveal that "Masonry in its purity, derived as it is from the old Hebrew Kabbala as a part of the great universal wisdom religion of remotest antiquity."[328] Wagner concludes:

> A candid investigation convinces us that Freemasonry is indebted in a very large measure to the Kabbalah for its philosophical ideas, its methods of interpreting the

scriptures, its doctrines of emanations, its art speech, its cosmogonical views, and its veils and glyphs. In a certain sense it is a continuation of the Kabbalah under a different name and guise.[329]

Further confirmation of the Judaic foundations of Freemasonry comes from the authoritative Rabbi Isaac Wise. Wise confirms that the Gentile nature of Freemasonry is only a cover: "Freemasonry is a Jewish establishment, whose history, grades, official appointments, passwords, and explanations are Jewish from beginning to end."[330]

The October 28, 1927 Jewish Tribune of New York stated: "Masonry is based on Judaism. Eliminate the teachings of Judaism from the Masonic Ritual and what is left?"[331] Michael Hoffman concluded: "It is from these [Cabalistic and Talmudic] recondite doctrines of Judaism that the Freemasons and other occult workers of iniquity derive their beliefs."[332] Henry Makow describes Freemasonry as "Judaism for Gentiles."[333] Makow states that it is "a way for the Cabalistic Jewish elite to enlist Gentiles in their conspiracy."[334]

Albert Pike, who is the preeminent authority on masonic liturgy and creeds, explains the Jewish underpinnings of Masonry in the doctrinal bible of Freemasonry, *Morals and Dogma*: "Masonry is a search for Light. That leads us directly back, as you see, to the Kabalah [*sic*]."[335]

What is the theology of the Kabbalah that forms the basis for Freemasonry? Cabalic Judaism and all ancient mystery religions are based upon phallicism.[336] Phallicism is the pantheistic worship of procreation in nature, with a focus on genitalia. Phallicism is a fetish theology, wherein the generative principle is represented through images of phalli and yonis.

Phallicism incorporates a mythology based upon heathen gods who engage in sexual deviance, including incest, rape, and mutilation. For example, in one myth "Demeter, the earth mother, the feminine or nourishing power, in an act of stealth and violence, is violated by her son, the god Zeus."[337] Kora was the offspring of Zeus' rape of Demeter. The depravity continues with Zeus violating his daughter, Kora.[338] The offspring of that incestuous union is Dionysus. Each new offspring is a regeneration; Kora is the reappearance of Demeter and Dionysus is the reappearance of Zeus. Phallicism is the pantheistic deification and worship of the procreative act. Wagner explains:

> Phallicism, fundamentally, is the deification, adoration and worship of the procreative or self propagating power of the life of nature, that secret mysterious energy, endowment or power which animates all vegetable and animal creatures, and which perpetually dying, renews itself in new, similar yet different forms. Phallicists view this mysterious energy as the divine nature, and usually in the conception of the divine triad, the creator, the preserver and the destroyer of life, and worship and adore it as the deity. Phallicists recognize no author of life separate and apart from this energy in nature, but adore it as a great self-originating, self-preserving, self-destroying, self-reproducing, unifying and united divine power, pervading the universe.[339]

The Kabbalah identifies the heathen god of the Jews as *Ein Sof*. *Ein Sof* consists of 10 *sefirot* (plural of *sefirah*); each *Sefirah* is a god in its own right. *Ein Sof*'s lower portion is made up of three *sefirot*: 1) *Netzach* (Endurance/Victory), 2) *Hod* (Majesty/Glory), and 3) *Yesod* (Foundation).[340] Athol Bloomer reveals that *Netzach* and *Hod* are the right and left legs of *Ein Sof*, and *Yesod* is *Ein Sof*'s phallus.

Yesod is both the phallus of *Ein Sof* and a god in its own right. Bloomer explains that the light and power of the *sefirot* are channeled through the phallic god *Yesod* to the last *Sefirah*, which is the *Shekinah* (a/k/a *Malkuth*).[341]

This phallic god is part of the blatantly erotic interpretation of the Jewish god found in the Kabbalah.[342] RabbiW. Dennis in *The Encyclopedia of Jewish Myth, Magic, and Mysticism* explains: "The *Zohar* includes multiple interpretations built around the concept of God's genitals."[343]

Dan Cohn-Sherbok and Lavinia Cohn-Sherbok explain the development of the esoteric sexual meanings concealed within the orthodox Jewish liturgy:

> Likewise, Phallic symbolism was employed in speculations about the ninth *Sefirah*, *Yesod*, from which all the higher *Sefirot* flowed into the *Shekinah* as the life force of the cosmos. In later centuries erotic terminology was used in the Hasidic works to describe movement in prayer which was depicted as copulation with the *Shekhinah*.[344]

The Kabbalah infuses orthodox Judaism with a powerful undercurrent of phallic worship and practice, including sex magic.[345] The sex magic is an offshoot of the secret doctrine in Judaism, which is a common doctrine found in secret societies, that the mystic can find redemption through an "heroic" willingness to do evil.[346] The secret rabbinic doctrine is that evil can be redeemed by embracing it; there is a spiritual good in doing evil.[347] That explains why Jesus said to the Jews: "Ye are of your father the devil, and the lusts of your father ye will do."John 8:44.

Phallicism and sensualism are the esoteric core of Judaism. The Jewish Encyclopedia states that the Kabbalah (Zohar) brought into the Jewish liturgy allegorical and symbolic "use of erotic terminology to illustrate the relations between man and God" that includes "sensuous pleasures, and especially intoxication." Wagner explains that "the Kabbalah was the phallicized Judaism."[348] Wagner states that "Gnosticism was an attempt to phallicize Christianity."[349] Wagner determined that the ceremonies of Freemasonry, being based in large part upon the Kabbalah, involve esoteric phallicism.

> In the light of the Kabbalah, then, the Masonic altar is the symbol of the genital, the local dwelling place of the deity; the spot where all the wisdom of the ages are synthetized, and from which it ever goes forth into new entities; the object upon which all the speculations of the institution are centered, and the place where all Masonic life originates. Around this altar and that which it symbolizes, all Masonic religion, ethics and philosophy, revolve. It is the "foundation" of Freemasonry as well as the "foundation" of the Kabbalah.[350]

There is a reason that Wagner put "foundation" in quotation marks. That word has an esoteric meaning. Wagner explains that the "root and principle the cause and maker of all things was in the Kabbalah the Foundation, the genital in the archetypal man."[351] Wagner expounds further on the esoteric meaning of "foundation" in Freemasonry:

> Foundation is the genital of the archetypal man. This organ is the basis and source of all things, "all marrow, all sap, and all power are congregated in this spot. Hence all powers which exist originated through genital organs." (C. D. Ginsberg). "Foundation" in the

> Kabbalah is the reproductive principle, the root of all existence. "Foundation" is the medium of the union of sexes, and the means by and through which these emanations are continued throughout time and in the animate world.[352]

The meaning of the Masonic altar (the "foundation") is that it represents the genitals of their pantheistic god. That genital symbolism flows from the Kabbalah. Wagner explains that the Kabbalah is the principal source of Masonic phallicism:

> These cults were esoteric, and phallic, and the Kabbalah naturally partook of the same character, for the pagan conception of the mystery of sex, passed in a refined form through the Talmud into this Jewish speculation. So also the Gnostic idea of pairs, was adopted by the Talmud and was later developed into a system by the Kabbalah. The doctrines of the Kabbalah were communicated to the few only.[353]

The altar is among the symbols used in Masonry, the exoteric meaning of which conceals the true esoteric phallic nature of its religion.[354] There is a reason that Freemasonry uses symbols to convey meanings. That is so that the true but hidden meaning that is only shared with those initiated into its secrets can be concealed from the uninitiated, who are deceived into believing the publicly proclaimed meaning of the symbols. Having two meanings for each symbol (one exoteric and the other esoteric) is necessitated by the sense of shame felt if the true (but hidden) nature of the worship was publicly known.[355] The esoteric and true interpretation of the Masonic symbols, glyphs, and ideographs reveal the true phallic character of Freemasonry.

Thus it is seen that the mysteries of Freemasonry parallel so perfectly with the mysteries of antiquity and the phallic cults, that the conclusion is irresistible and the demonstration complete, that Freemasonry is not an imitation but a restoration of the mysteries of antiquity, in rite, symbol, and in its essential religious ideas and doctrines.[356]

Phallicism was the central theme of the ancient mystery religions upon which the Kabbalah and Freemasonry are based. Wagner explains:

The phallus was an essential part in the rites and symbolism of the mysteries. Its office was to convey to the initiated a profound and sacred meaning. It was a common object of worship and of ornament. Originally it had no other meaning than that union of male and female upon which depended the procreation of life.[357]

The gods were male and female, and the worship of the sexual was prominent in these cults. The religious ideas were based upon the sexual facts, and grew out of a profound veneration for the generative principle. Ritual prostitution which was possibly a decadence, was a recognized and wide spread institution, and grew out of a purely religious point of view. At the shrine of Baal and Astarte in Phoenicia and similar sanctuaries elsewhere, sexual intercourse was a part of the rite.[358]

Phallus worship is in fact the oldest form of idolatry. Wagner explains:

Monumental, historical, and philological evidence shows that phallus worship is among the oldest, if not the oldest form of idolatry. Reverence for the phallus or for phallic emblems shows itself in the earliest historic remains of Babylonia, Assyria, India, China, Japan, Persia, Phrygia, Scandinavia, France, Spain, Great Britain, North and South America, Africa, and in the islands of the sea. Phallicism is the bond that unites all forms of idolatry into one great system. It is the essential principle that pervades them. It is the basis of tree worship, animal worship, serpent worship, sun worship, and man worship. It was the basis of the mysteries of Phrygia, Egypt, Greece and Rome. It is the basis of all the mythology of the past ages, for as Weiss says "Freemasonry (Phallicism?) may be traced in all the mythology to the remotest part of the globe."[359]

Wagner states: "A number of other Masonic authorities agree with Pike and concede that the symbolism of the institution in its original and proper meaning refers above all to the solar and phallic worship of the ancient mysteries."[360] Masonry is heathen phallicism cloaked in the imagery of the Jewish temple. Wagner calls it "a Jewish mask for the Egyptian phallicism."[361] Wagner states that "the mysteries of Freemasonry are the ancient mysteries translated into scripture imagery and story, and so colored, veiled and transposed as to prevent detection of the trick."[362] The trick is that Masonic symbols used in its ceremonies have esoteric meanings that conceal the phallic nature of Masonry from the uninitiated. Wagner details the parallels between the mythology in heathen mystery religions and Freemasonry:

In the Egyptian when Osiris is found, the

phallus is lost. In the Masonic when Hiram is found, the 'word' is lost. Isis furnishes a substitute for the phallus, the master furnishes a substitute word. "Isis raises the prostrate form of him who was slain, she takes from him his essence, she conceives and brings forth a son." In the Masonic rite the master raises the prostrate form of him who was slain, whispers in his ear the mystic word, and a son, a Mason, is born into the lodge. In the Egyptian rite Osiris lived again in his son Horus, in the Masonic the slain. Hiram lives again in the newly made Master Mason, who is frequently termed the widow's son.[363]

Wagner further concludes that "upon Masons' own confessions and declarations, the proof is conclusive that Freemasonry is a sex-cult, in which the generative powers are adored and worshiped under the disguised phallic rites and symbols. Phallicism is the essence of the religion of the mysteries, and phallicism is the essence of the religion of Freemasonry. This we believe we can demonstrate beyond a reasonable doubt."[364] That fact is a closely guarded secret within Freemasonry. Its rites and ceremonies act as secure puzzle against revelation of the occult secrets of Freemasonry. Wagner states:

Having now gone to the sources from which Freemasonry claims to be derived, and studied them in their several aspects and relations one to another, we find the one thing that is common and runs through them all, is phallicism. We are led therefore to the conclusion, that Freemasonry is a cult, a religion in which all religions are esoterically synthetized under the garb, imagery and terms of operative masonry, but whose real essence is phallicism; that phallicism is the essence of Freemasonry, the real secret which is symbolized by its entire ceremonial, and that this being the fact, the perpetuity of the institution depends upon keeping this secret doctrine concealed from the knowledge of all except a tested few. Phallicism as the key, interprets consistently every rite, symbol and ceremony and monitorial lecture in the institution. It unlocks this synthesis of all knowledge and of all religions.[365]

In 1843, the Jews decided that the coast was clear to publically proclaim an overtly Jewish branch of Freemasonry. People generally mark 1843 as the date that *B'nai B'rith* was formed as a Jewish offshoot of Scottish Rite Freemasonry.[366] It is generally accepted that the Anti-Defamation League was formed in 1914 as a sub-lodge and the enforcement arm of *B'nai B'rith*.[367] It is more likely that the formation of *B'nai B'rith* as an overtly Jewish form of Freemasonry was done to help solidify in the public mind the fact that all other Masonic lodges are completely Gentile and not in any way under Jewish control.

What are the foundational beliefs of Judaism upon which Freemasonry is built? It would surprise most to learn that Judaism is in essence witchcraft. The *Sefer Yezirah* (a/k/a Book of Formation or Book of Creation), which is one of the earliest and most important books of the Kabbalah, teaches fortune telling, numerology, and astrology by means of contacting devils.[368] The Talmud *Sanhedren* 65b, acknowledges that the *Sefer Yezirah* "has affinities with Babylonian, Egyptian, and Hellenic mysticism."[369] It is no wonder that Jesus upbraided the Jews: "Ye are of your father the devil, and the lusts of your father ye will do." John 8:44.

Most Masons would object to characterizing

Freemasonry as a Judaic/Luciferian religion. That is because, in Freemasonry, as with Judaism, only the upper echelons know about its Judaic/Luciferian essence. Wagner cites to Charles Hecketron, who states that "in the first three degrees nothing but the exoteric doctrines are revealed."[370] Heckethorn explains that "the members of the first three degrees of Freemasonry are not initiated in the grand so-called secrets of Freemasonry. Only in the royal arch degree are they informed of it."[371] Wagner further explains the general ignorance of the lower degrees of Freemasonry. He cites the authority of Dr. J.D. Buck and explains:

> [N]ot one Mason in ten thousand understands the real key to Masonry . . . [Buck] asserts that it is in the ancient symbols of Freemasonry that its real secrets lie concealed and that these are as densely veiled to the Mason as to any other, unless he has studied the science of symbolism in general, and Masonic symbolism in particular . . . the secrets lie in the ancient symbols, that the candidate is debarred from possessing the secrets solely by his inattention to the hints everywhere given in the ritual of the lodge . . . their deeper meaning is still unknown to the craft, it is equally unknown to all others, except is the result of genuine initiation.[372]

Billy Graham is a 33rd degree Mason and is accordingly an initiate into its Luciferian occultism. Graham is under a Masonic duty, sealed through a blood oath, to inculcate his Masonic theology into his preaching. This point was explained by Dr. J.D. Buck, an authority in Freemasonry, in his book titled *The Genius of Freemasonry and the Twentieth Century Crusade*. Dr. Buck "charges cowardice or treason on all Masons who refuse to use their controlling influence in the churches, and their two million votes in the nation."[373]

Graham is one of the Masonic minions whose true mission is the destruction of Christianity. On September 20, 1902, French Senator Delpech the President of the Grand Orient Lodge of Freemasonry gave a speech before fellow Freemasons where he stated that the Christian religion is dying and Freemasons should take credit for its demise. Senator Delpech stated:

> The triumph of the Galilean [Jesus Christ] has lasted twenty centuries. But now he dies in his turn. The mysterious voice . . . today announces the death of the impostor God who promised an era of justice and peace to those who believe in him. The illusion has lasted a long time. The mendacious God is now disappearing in his turn; he passes away to join in the dust of ages the divinities of India, Egypt, Greece, and Rome, who saw so many creatures prostrate before their altars. Brother Masons, we rejoice to state that we are not without our share in this overthrow of the false prophet.[374]

As previously revealed, in the year before he died, Senator Joseph McCarthy revealed that Freemasonry was the vehicle through which the Judaic religion was inculcated into the nominal Christian churches in the United States.[375] The subversion of Christian doctrine is the means by which the Jews will gain the cooperation of nominal Christians in their own slavery under the Zionist New World Order.

Recall that Senator McCarthy stated that "Darby and the Plymouth Brethren brought a Jewish Christianity to America."[376] He explained that Joseph Franklin Rutherford (1869-1942) and Charles Taze Russell (1852-1916) were Freemasons and their Masonic religion was the source of the Judaism that is the foundation of the "divine kingdom" theology of the Jehovah Witness cult.

Senator McCarthy revealed that Joseph Smith (1805-1844), who was the founder of the Mormon Church, was a Freemason. The Theology of the Mormon Church is completely based upon the Judaism of Freemasonry. The Mormon Church stems from Joseph Smith's publication of the Book of Mormon in March 1830.

Smith's publication of the Book of Mormon was curiously timed after the anti-Freemason movement that followed the murder of Captain William Morgan (1774-1826). Captain Morgan was a former Freemason who was murdered in 1826, after revealing some of the Masonic ceremonies and customs. His murder was a national sensation. There was even an anti-Masonic political party established in 1828.

The anti-Masonic movement caused memberships in Masonic Lodges to plummet and it looked like the end of Freemasonry in the United States. The revelations by Morgan and his subsequent murder caused 45,000 of the 50,000 Freemasons in the United States to leave the order.[377] It seems that Mormonism was a way to save a remnant of Freemasonry under the guise of a "Christian" church. Indeed, Senator McCarthy states that the Mormon millenialism is a Judaic construct that came from the occult Freemasonry of Joseph Smith.[378] Freemasonry survived and the Mormon Church has since thrived in the United States. With over 14 million members today, the National Council of Churches lists the Mormon Church as the fourth largest "Christian" denomination in the United States.

Freemasonry ultimately recovered from the Captain Morgan controversy; by 1912 there were approximately 1.5 million Masons in the United States.[379] Today, there are an estimated 3 million Freemasons in the United States, with a worldwide membership of approximately 6 million.

Senator McCarthy avers that all of the large denominations in the United States are actually inculcated with occult Judaic doctrines that flowed from Freemasonry. McCarthy points to the Scofield Bible, with its Jewish interpretation of the prophecies as the primary means for subverting the churches. Senator McCarthy stated that due to their Judaic doctrines "all the American churches have silently become synagogues."[380] He stated: "We now have Baptist Jews, Methodist Jews, Church of God Jews, apostate Catholic Jews, and many Protestant Jews throughout America. We are aliens in our own country because of false religion."[381]

McCarthy's observation suggests that mainline churches have become, in a sense, Synagogues of Satan. This seems to be evidence of what Jesus said in the book of Revelation? "Behold, I will make them of the synagogue of Satan, which say they are Jews, and are not, but do lie; behold, I will make them to come and worship before thy feet, and to know that I have loved thee." (Revelation 3:9)

God explained in his New Testament that one who is saved by the grace of God through faith in Jesus Christ is a spiritual Jew. One is not a Jew physically; one is a Jew spiritually. It is not the circumcision of the flesh that makes one a Jew. "But he is a Jew, which is one inwardly; and circumcision is that of the heart, in the spirit." (Romans 2:28-29)

A spiritual Jew is a Christian. In Revelation 3:9, the reference to those who "say they are Jews, and are not, but do lie" seems to be a reference to those who falsely claim to be spiritual Jews; that is they are falsely claiming to be Christians. The false spiritual Jews (false Christians) are those who are in nominal "Christian" churches that have been inculcated with Judaic Zionist doctrines. The false "Christian" churches are actually auxiliaries to Jewish Synagogues, teaching Jewish fables based on the traditions of men that flowed from

Babylonian mysticism. The "Christian" Zionist churches are in a very real sense synagogues of Satan, as described in Revelation 3:9.

13 Proofs of a Conspiracy

John Robison, Professor of Natural Pholosophy, who was General Secretary of the Royal Society of Edinborough was one of the leading intellectuals of his day. He was a witness to the influence of the Illuminati and the Jesuits within Freemasonry. In 1798 he published a book titled, *Proofs of a Conspiracy*. In his book, Professor Robison stated the following regarding the amalgamation of Freemasonry and a nefarious secret society known as the Illuminati: "an association has been formed for the express purpose of rooting out all religious establishments and overturning all the existing governments of Europe. I have seen this association exerting itself zealously and systematically, till it has become almost irresistible: and I have seen that the most active leaders in the French Revolution were members of this association, and conducted their first movements according to its principles."[382]

George Washington, himself, was convinced of the nefarious force and influence of the Illuminati and its threat to the United States. Washington, who was also a Freemason, wrote a letter on October 24, 1798, to George Snyder, who had sent him a copy of Robison's book. Washington wrote: "It was not my intention to doubt that, the Doctrines of the Illuminati, and principles of Jacobinism had not spread in the United States. On the contrary, no one is more truly satisfied of this fact than I am."[383]

Professor Robison revealed in his book that he witnessed the Jesuits begin their interference in Freemasonry after the Jesuits were suppressed by the pope in 1773. He stated that the Jesuits were using Freemasonry as a way of maintaining their power.[384] Professor Robison stated that the influence of the Jesuits over Freemasonry was considerable. The Jesuit control over Freemasonry was so complete that the Jesuits even changed many of the promotional ceremonies and degrees in Freemasonry.[385]

Robison perceived the separate influences of the Illuminati and the Jesuits within Freemasonry, but he did not understand that those two organizations were two horns on the head of the same beastly cabal. John Torell, founder and president of European-American Evangelistic Crusades, explains that the Illuminati was a reconstitution of the Jesuit order, which had been suppressed in 1773 by Pope Clement XIV. Torrell further reveals that the Jesuit order was a reincarnation of a secret society known as the Alumbrados. The Alumbrados can be traced to 1492; it was organized by Spanish Jews, known as Marranos.[386]

Torell states that Marranos were Jews who concealed the fact that they were Jews in order to avoid the persecution of Jews in Spain and Portugal, which began in 1391. Marranos became known as crypto-Jews, because they concealed their Judaism. Torell reveals that publicly these Jews appeared to be Roman Catholics, but secretly they practiced Judaism, including following the Talmud and the Cabala.[387] Torell states that "as is the custom with all Jewish people, it did not matter in what nation they lived, their loyalty was to themselves and Judaism."[388]

San Ignacio De Loyola was born in 1491 to a wealthy Marrano Jewish family in the Basque province of Guipuzcoa.[389] Loyola became a member of the Alumbrados in Spain. As was typical of crypto-Jews, Loyola was very active as a Roman Catholic. In 1539, Loyola founded the Jesuit Order. In 1540, Pope Paul III approved the Jesuits as a Roman Catholic order of priests.[390]

The Jesuits engaged in all manner of political subversion. In response to the Jesuit subversive activities they were banned throughout the Portuguese Empire in 1759.[391] On April 6, 1762 the French Parliament issued the following "statement of arrest" (indictment):

> [The Jesuits' doctrine is] perverse, a destroyer of all religious and honest principles, insulting to Christian morals, pernicious to civil society, hostile to the rights of the nation, the royal power, and even the security of the sovereigns and obedience of their subjects; suitable to stir up the greatest disturbances in the States, conceive and maintain the worst kind of corruption in men's hearts.[392]

In 1764 the Jesuits were outlawed in France, and in 1767 they were banned from Spain.[393] Such great political pressure was brought by the European nations that were the objects of Jesuit subversion that Pope Clement XIII decided on the 3rd of February 1769 to dissolve the Jesuits. The night before he was to execute the dissolution, however, he suddenly fell ill and died. Prior to his death he cried out "I am dying . . . It is a very dangerous thing to attack the Jesuits."[394]

His successor, Pope Clement XIV, was also put under tremendous political pressure to dissolve the Jesuits, but he resisted doing so for three years until the political tension finally forced his hand. Pope Clement XIV issued the papal brief of dissolution, *Dominus ac Redemptor,* on August 16, 1773.[395] Pope Clement XIV knew the significance of such an act to the papacy, he exclaimed: "I have cut off my right hand."[396] In addition, Pope Clement XIV knew that by signing the brief dissolving the Jesuits he was signing his own death warrant. Soon after signing the brief, the letters I.S.S.S.V. appeared on the palace walls in the Vatican.[397] Pope Clement XIV knew what it meant and explained that it stood for *In Settembre, Sara Sede Vacante.* Which translated means "in September, the See will be vacant (the pope will be dead)."[398] Pope Clement XIV was poisoned and died on September 22, 1774.[399]

The Jesuits immediately sought revenge against the Vatican and all the monarchs of Europe. Their first step was to reconstitute themselves in 1776 under the banner of the Illuminati. Torell explains that the Illuminati was an alliance between the crypto-Jewish Jesuits and the very powerful Ashkenazi Jewish Banking House of Rothschild.[400] Meyer Amschel, the head of the House of Rothschild, was a rabbinically trained German Jew, who later took the name Rothschild.[401]

We find Lorenzo Ricci and Jakob Frank instrumental in the establishment of the Illuminati. Frank was a Polish born Jew. His family name was originally Leibowicz. He lived in the German city of Offenbach and was the leader of the secret Jewish Cabala at that time.[402] Ricci was the Jesuit General deposed by Pope Clement XIV.[403]

Ricci and Frank tapped Adam Weishaupt as the leader of their reconstituted Jesuit secret society.[404] Weishaupt was born on February 6, 1748, in Ingolstadt. His parents were crypto- Jews. Weishaupt was educated in the Jesuit order where he was exposed to the Jesuit organization and its political agenda. Weishaupt learned from early childhood to have a secret allegiance to the Jewish Talmud and the Cabala, while outwardly he was a dedicated Roman Catholic.[405]

Weishaupt was a professor of canon law at the Jesuit Ingolstadt University, which was the center of the Jesuit counter-reformation.[406] Some historians have alleged that Weishaupt became a Jesuit after the Jesuits were suppressed in 1773.[407] That is strong evidence that he was to be the Jesuit's hand-picked front man for the reconstituted Jesuit society under the banner of the Illuminati.

Robison had a contrary view of Weishaupt. Robison claims that although Weishaupt had been educated among the Jesuits, "the abolition of their order made him change his views, and from being their pupil, he became their most bitter enemy."[408] That is contrary to the account of other historians. What is the truth between these two accounts? Robison gives more detail which sheds some light on resolving the issue. He states that Weishaupt was establishing an order (the Illuminati) to govern the world and that he had tried to recruit several former Jesuits to join him. Robison claims that since only two Jesuits joined him that he and the other Jesuits became enemies.[409]

Arguably, Robison had imperfect knowledge of the situation and made too much of a falling out between individuals of the same camp. There is conflict in all organizations. For example, Generals Bedford Forest and Braxton Bragg had a falling out during the civil war. Bragg was the commanding general over the able and intrepid Forest, when Forest threatened the life of Bragg. Despite their personal animosity, they put their differences aside to fight for their common cause, against their common enemy.

If there can be conflict between two honorable generals engaged in open warfare against a common foe, it would not be surprising that there would also be conflict in a Satanic conspiracy engaged in secret warfare against all mankind.

Indeed, it is the very nature of Satan's kingdom for there to be conflict. That is how Satan works. His kingdom is the opposite of the Kingdom of God, which is one of love and obedience. The kingdom of Satan is one of hate and rebellion. An example would be the relationship between Hitler and Stalin. Stalin assisted Hitler in coming to power. At the beginning of World War II Russia and Germany were allies. Stalin assisted Hitler so that he could ultimately destroy him. That was a fact that Hitler learned too late; once hear realized he was being set up by Stalin for invasion from Russia, he launched his desperate Operation Barbarossa attack on Russia.

Those facts are documented in a very revealing book titled, *Icebreaker: Who Started the Second World War?*, by Viktor Suvorov. Hitler and Stalin were both integral parts of Satan's conspiracy toward a Zionist new world order. Communism (world socialism) and Nazism (national socialism) are two arms of the same Zionist body. Yet those two arms alternately cooperated and then warred against each other. It is no surprise that Weishaupt and the Jesuits had a falling out, but it would be inaccurate to characterize the Jesuits and Illuminati as implacable enemies.

The Jesuits, through the Illuminati, rampaged against the Vatican, capturing many of its church properties the world over. The Vatican had learned its lesson, and on August 7, 1814, the Jesuits were restored as a Catholic order by Pope Pius VII.[410] The Jesuits were now stronger and more powerful than ever.

John Adams wrote to Thomas Jefferson in 1816 "I am not happy about the rebirth of the Jesuits. ... Swarms of them will present themselves under more disguises ever taken by even a chief of the Bohemians, as printers, writers, publishers, school teachers, etc. If ever an association of people deserved eternal damnation, on this earth and in hell, it is the Society of Loyola. Yet, with our system of religious liberty, we can but offer them a refuge."[411] Thomas Jefferson answered Adams: "Like you, I object to the Jesuits' reestablishment which makes light give way to darkness."[412]

The crypto-Jewish Jesuit infiltration of Freemasonry has rendered Freemasonry a Gentile front for Jewish Illuminism. This is in accord with the plans of the Learned Elders of Zion. In Protocol 15, the Learned Elders of Zions state that "we shall create and multiply free masonic lodges in all the countries of the world."[413] The Masonic lodges would then be controlled by the Learned Elders through their Illuminati. Protocol 15 further reveals that while the Masonic lodges would be under the complete control of the Learned Elders of Zion, the Jewish control would be unknown to the Gentile members of the lodge. "All these lodges we shall bring under one central administration, known to us alone and to all others absolutely unknown, which will be composed of our learned elders."[414]

To ensure that crimes committed by Masons are not prosecuted Masonic lodges actively recruit members from the legal and law enforcement communities. Paragraph 4 of Protocol 15 reveals that the Zionists use Masonic lodges to gain control of a nation's law enforcement agencies:

> Among the members of these lodges will be almost all the agents of international and national police since their service is for us irreplaceable in the respect that the police is in a position not only to use its own particular measures with the insubordinate, but also to screen our activities and provide pretexts for discontents.[415]

Stephen Knight in his book *Jack the Ripper: The Final Solution*, documents that infiltration of police forces is a high priority within Freemasonry. He quoted from a Masonic document: "The services of the police are of extreme importance to us as they are able to throw a screen over our enterprises . . . as well as punish those who refuse to submit."[416] He presented evidence that the infamous Ripper killings were Masonic ritual murders directed by a conspiracy involving the highest officials in the British government itself.

Because of this, communities should not permit anyone who is a Mason to hold the offices of sheriff, judge, prosecutor, or police investigator. When one hears of seemingly unexplainable behavior of the police, a judge, a prosecutor, or any politician that allows a criminal go free, one should not overlook the hidden hand of Masonry.

For example, Albert Pike, the "Sovereign Grand Commander of the Ancient and Accepted Scottish Rite of Freemasonry of the Southern Jurisdiction, U.S.A.," was convicted of treason. But in April 22, 1866, Pike was granted a full pardon by President Andrew Johnson. The next day Pike visited the president in the White House. Pike visited Johnson again in 1867, after the impeachment proceedings had begun against Johnson. General Gordon Granger was present at the 1867 meeting and was summoned before the U.S. Congress to testify about the meeting. General Granger testified that Johnson and Pike discussed Masonry and that he understood from the conversation that Pike was Johnson's superior in Masonry. Shortly thereafter, on June 20, 1867, a delegation of Masons granted Johnson the fourth through the 32nd degrees of the Scottish Rite of Masonry in his bedroom at the White House.[417]

Millard Fillmore, the thirteenth president of the United States and a former Mason, said that "[t]he Masonic fraternity tramples upon our rights, defeats the administration of justice, and bids defiance to every government which it cannot control."[418] A joint committee of the Massachusetts legislature investigated Freemasonry in 1834 and concluded that Masonry was "a distinct independent government within our government, and beyond the control of the laws of the land by means of its secrecy."[419]

Adam Wieshaupt died in 1830 at the age of 82. Giuseppe Mazzini, who was an Italian revolutionary, then became the leader of the Illuminati. He held this position from 1834 until his death in 1872. On August 15, 1871, while Giuseppe Mazzini was the head of the Illuminati in Europe, he wrote a letter to Albert Pike, who was then the Sovereign Grand Commander of the Ancient and Accepted Scottish Rite of Freemasonry of the Southern Jurisdiction U.S.A. Pike succeeded to that Masonic position from Isaac Long, a Jew, who in 1801, brought a statue of Baphomet (Satan) to Charleston, South Carolina, where he helped established the Ancient and Accepted Scottish Rite.[420] In Mazzini's letter to Pike, Mazzini gives the details for a plan for world conquest, through three world wars. The first war would destroy Czarist Russia and place that vast territory under the control of the Illuminati. The second war would be caused by the differences between the Political Zionists and the German Nationalists. This would lead to the expansion of Russian Communist power and the creation of a state of Israel in Palestine. The third war would be caused by the conflict between the predicted State of Israel and the Arab Muslims.[421]

Paragraph 4 of Protocol 15 reveals that the Zionists use Masonic lodges to foment and control political plots and revolutions:

> In these lodges we shall tie together the knot which binds together all revolutionary and liberal elements. Their composition will be made up of all strata of society. The most secret political plots will be known to us and fall under our guiding hands on the very day of their conception.[422]

Are Freemasons involved government subversion today to the degree expressed over 200 years ago by Washington and Robison? The answer is, yes. Stephen Knight, an expert on Freemasonry and author of *The Brotherhood*, concluded that the communist revolution in Russia was provoked by Freemasons. The Tsar of Russia knew full well that the Masonic lodges were fomenting revolution against his government, and he made efforts to suppress them. The few lodges that remained in Russia were hotbeds of communist revolutionary activity. The communist revolution of 1917, initially saw a provisional government where Alexander Kerensky was the first Minister of Justice and second Prime Minister. Kerensky was, of course, a Freemason.

Knight explains that Kerensky appointed fellow Freemasons to all of the important government posts in the provisional government. However, Kerensky was soon removed from power by the more hard-core Bolsheviks. Once the Bolsheviks came to power, they immediately proscribed Freemasonry.[423] The communists had used the Gentile Freemasonry to gain power, and once they had obtained their objective, there was no need for Freemasonry, and so it was outlawed. Many of the Gentile Masons were executed and the others had to flee Russia for their lives. Kerensky survived and lived until 1970.

The KGB feverishly suppressed Freemasonry within Russia. However, once the communists solidified their hold on the reigns of government in Russia, they infiltrated Masonic lodges in other countries. For example, Stephen Knight reveals that the *Propaganda Due* (a/k/a P2) Masonic lodge in Italy was completely controlled from the top by the KGB in the 1980s.[424] Licio Gelli began in 1969 to gain control of what became known as the P2 lodge. Gelli was a KGB asset. The lodge was discovered to be a subversive society undermining the ordered government in Italy.

In analyzing the rise and fall of the P2 lodge, it became apparent to the intelligence agencies that the P2 lodge was set up and then exposed by the KGB in order to destabilize the Italian government and bring the communists to power in Italy.[425] The members of the P2 lodge were described by an interior ministry official as "the most potent hidden power center" in the country.[426] One prosecutor investigating the P2 lodge concluded: "Lodge Propaganda Due is a secret sect that has combined business and politics with the intention of destroying the country's constitutional order."[427]

Knight described the P2 lodge as "a very real state within the state," and concluded that Gelli was using that power base to overthrow the Italian republic.[428] The P2 lodge membership included Admiral Giovanni Torrisi, who was the Commander of the Armed Forces, along with 30 army generals, 8 navy admirals, 43 members of parliament, 19 judges, the directors of the three main intelligence agencies, 54 top civil servants, including cabinet ministers, among them, Justice Minister Adolfi Sarti, several political party leaders, three former prime ministers, 58 university professors, leading bankers, and newspaper proprietors.[429]

One of the notable and suspicious aspects of the P2 lodge was that high officials in all of the political parties in Italy were represented among the 953 members of the P2 lodge, except for the communist party. There was not a single member of the communist party found as a member of the P2 lodge. That fact was particularly notable in light of the fact that the P2 lodge was controlled by a businessman (Gelli) who had frequent and close business relationships with high officials in communist countries. One would expect that there would be communist members in his lodge, unless of course the lodge was set up to be exposed for the benefit of the communist party. That would seem to be the case, and it is the settled judgement of the intelligence community. The P2 conspiracy destabilized the Italian government and came close to bringing the communist party to power in Italy.

Another example of the KGB using Masonic lodges for intelligence purposes is the case of Sir Roger Hollis, who was the Director-General of MI5 from 1956-65. MI5 (Military Intelligence, Section 5) is the British intelligence agency in charge of domestic national security. It turns out that Hollis was a KGB spy.

People wondered how Hollis was ever accepted into MI5 as he had poor health, had traveled to China in 1926 and to communist Russia in 1935, had unremarkable skills, and an inadequate academic background, having dropped out of college after two years. His travel to communist Russia alone should have been an insuperable barrier to his entry into MI5. Stephen Knight opined that Hollis was the very opposite of what was required to be an MI5 agent. Hollis gained his entry into MI5 through his connections that he made as a Freemason. The Director-General of MI5 at the time Hollis applied to the agency was fellow Freemason Major General Sir Vernon Kell.

Even more remarkable than MI5 accepting Hollis was his meteoric rise within MI5 that was not based upon his performance. His colleagues, not knowing of his secret Masonic connection, were mystified by his advancement in MI5. Sir Dick Goldsmith White, was the MI5 chief before Hollis was appointed to that position. White recommended Hollis to be his successor. White was a Freemason. However, when Stephen Knight asked White if he knew Hollis was a Freemason, he not only denied knowing that Hollis was a Freemason, he argued that Hollis could not have been a Freemason, because he was not the type. That was just the opposite of what other people had told Knight; people who knew Hollis said he was exactly the type to join a Mason lodge. White also tried to deceive Knight by denying that he, himself, was a Freemason.[430]

14 The Love of Money is the Root of All Evil

God makes it clear that "the love of money is the root of all evil."(1 Timothy 6:10) Jews love money above all else. In paragraph seven of Protocol 1, the Learned Elders reveal the source of their power, gold. "In our day the power which has replaced that of the rulers who were liberal is the power of Gold."[431]   Jewish power is not spiritual, it springs from their control of immense wealth.

The political power and influence of the Jews stems directly from their control of banking. The historical events in the United States demonstrate that fact. Representative Louis T. McFadden in a May 2, 1934 radio address stated:

> It would be a monstrous mistake for any intelligent citizen of whatever nation to close his eyes to the evident fact that for nigh sixty years, the Jews have surely and rapidly though almost invisibly climbed to the heights of government wherefrom the masses are ruled. Politically, financially and economically they have seized the reigns of governments of all

nations and their invasion in the realms of social, educational and religious fields [is] not less important.[432]

Congressman McFadden, who was Chairman of the U.S. House of Representatives Banking and Currency Committee, knew the power that the Jews wielded and the calamities that they caused. Just as the Protocols of the Learned Elders of Zion provided, the Talmudic Jews controlled the money supply through a central bank (The Federal Reserve Bank). Congressman McFadden sated: "It [the depression] was not accidental. It was a carefully contrived occurrence. . . . The international bankers sought to bring about a condition of despair here so that they might emerge as the rulers of us all. . . . The end result, if the Insiders have their way, will be the dream of Montagu Norman of the Bank of England 'that the Hegemony of World Finance should reign supreme over everyone, everywhere, as one whole super-national control mechanism.'"

Representative McFadden addressed the U.S. House of Representatives on June 10, 1932. "Some people think the Federal Reserve Banks are U.S. government institutions. They are not government institutions. They are private credit monopolies which prey upon the people of the U.S. for the benefit of themselves and their foreign and domestic swindlers, and rich and predatory money lenders."[433]

The international Jewish money power used corrupt politicians to push through the Federal Reserve Act, which gave them a monopoly to print the money of the nation.[434] The Federal Reserve Act legalizes theft for a select few commercial banks that make up the Federal Reserve. McFadden's exposed the methods that the Jews used to obtain their immense power over the government of the United States.

Representative McFadden revealed, in a 1932 speech

before the House of Representatives, that the communist revolution in Russia was financed by the Federal Reserve.[435] In addition, billions of dollars and millions of ounces of the gold deposits of the United States were stolen by the Federal Reserve Banks and sent to Germany.[436] As he spoke in 1932, huge amounts of gold were being sent to Germany on a weekly basis. Why was this money being sent to Germany? It was sent to fund the Nazis. It was only a little more than eight months later, on January 30, 1933, that Adolph Hitler was sworn in as Chancellor of Germany. Within a year, Hitler had consolidated enough power, with the help of the Federal Reserve, that he declared himself "Fuhrer" (leader) of Germany. The gold he received from the Federal Reserve was used to build planes, ships, tanks, and guns that were used to kill brave Americans during World War II. The Federal Reserve Board and Banks funded both the communists in Russia and the Nazis in Germany, all at the expense of the hard labor of the American middle class.

Due to the treasonous actions of the Federal Reserve, in addition to its own financial burdens of the war, the United States funded the communist Russians (through the "Lend-Lease Program") and the German Nazis. The Jewish Bankers, having used the U.S. Treasury to fund both sides of the war, made out like bandits by collecting interest on the massive debt incurred by the United States Government. That debt was then put on the backs of the American middle class to pay through the, communist inspired, graduated income tax.

Representative McFadden was Chairman of the House Banking and Currency Committee and was in a position to do something about the banking monopoly. On May 23, 1933, he brought formal criminal charges against the Board of Governors of the Federal Reserve Bank, the Comptroller of the Currency, and the Secretary of the United States Treasury. The petition for Articles of Impeachment was, thereafter, referred to the Judiciary Committee.

The Zionist Jews could not allow such a powerful person to oppose their plans. They tried several times to assassinate Representative McFadden. They were ultimately successful; in 1935 they poisoned him. After Representative McFadden's death, the petition for Articles of Impeachment introduced by him was pigeonholed in the Judiciary Committee and has never seen the light of day since.

God admonished the Jews against the destructive practice of usury (i.e., interest). See, e.g., Exodus 22:25, Leviticus 25:36-37, Deuteronomy 23:19, Nehemiah, Psalms 15:5, Proverbs 28:8. Why would the Jews ignore the commands of God against usury? They ignored God's commands because the orthodox Jews do not follow the Old Testament. They have replaced God's laws with their traditions. They follow their oral traditions, which in part have been memorialized in the Talmud. Israel Shahak explains that although the Talmud forbids a Jew, on pain of severe punishment, to take interest on a loan made to another Jew, the rabbis have figured a contrivance to get around that restriction.[437] A business dispensation called *heter 'isqa* was devised for an interest-bearing loan between Jews.[438] In any event, the Talmud grants a license to charge interest to Gentiles; according to a majority of Talmudic authorities, it is a religious duty to take as much interest as possible on a loan made to a Gentile.[439]

The influence of the Talmud over the Jewish banking practices is witnessed by the fact that when Alan Greenspan, who is an atheist Jew, took his oath of office as Chairman of President Nixon's Council of Economic Advisers, he did so on a volume of the Talmud.[440] He later went on to be appointed Chairman of the Federal Reserve by Ronald Reagan. Greenspan was instrumental in creating the housing crisis and resulting economic collapse of 2006-2008 that saw the transfer of wealth from the middle class to the upper class in part through massive bailouts paid for by the hidden tax of inflation.

Spreading the gospel among the Jews is the answer to the Jewish issue. However, what can the people do to protect the body politic while the Jews are being evangelized? The government cannot discriminate against Jews by enacting special laws that apply only to Jews, because such a response plays into the hands of the Jewish hierarchy. Any law must apply across the board to Jew and Gentile alike. What laws can protect a country from the Jewish crimes without naming the Jews as targets of those laws?

God gives us the answer to addressing the Jewish issue. God states: "The love of money is the root of all evil." 1 Timothy 6:10. The way to address the Jewish issue is to strike at the root of their power, their love of money. They have the world in their service through usury. "The rich ruleth over the poor, and the borrower is servant to the lender." Proverbs 22:7. The only effective laws that a country can enact to end Jewish power are those that apply Christian principles to the regulation of finance and banking.

First, the nation should enact laws that prohibit usury (charging interest on a loan).

Second, fractional reserve banking should be outlawed.

Third, the Federal Reserve Act should be repealed.

Fourth, the only national legal tender money (which is money that by law must be taken in payment of debt or obligation) should be silver coin and gold coin.

Fifth, no party to a contract should be required to accept as payment of a debt any private bank or government notes (e.g., Federal Reserve Notes or U.S. Notes), unless the contract specifies otherwise.

Sixth, the nation should prohibit the government from taxing the labor of its citizens.

Doing those things will cut off the Jewish power at its root. All of their influence over the media, education, religion, and government flows from their immense economic power, which is derived from dishonest money, created out of thin air, and loaned at interest. Establishing honest money and prohibiting usury would end Jewish power. Such an environment of honesty would put Gentiles on equal economic footing with the Jews. The Jews would not need to be an insular group, because they could very easily assimilate into society. The Jewish hierarchy would lose its power base, as it loses its grip over the rank-and-file Jews. They would still be a criminal element in society, but on a much smaller scale.

The above steps would put into practice Christian principles. With the present spiritual condition of the United States, however, the chances of the above things happening without a war are remote. We must do what we can to bring about a spiritual awakening in the country, so that the populace understands the need to follow those Christian principles. The only way to do that is to spread the gospel of Jesus Christ; teaching all men the proper attitude toward money:

> Sell that ye have, and give alms; provide yourselves bags which wax not old, a treasure in the heavens that faileth not, where no thief approacheth, neither moth corrupteth. For where your treasure is, there will your heart be also. (Luke 12:33-34)

15 Zionism is Communism

Zionists have created all manner of antichrist philosophies designed to propagandize and enslave the masses. One of the principal satanic movements propagated by Zionists is communism. Paragraph three of Protocol 2 states: "think carefully of the successes we arranged for Darwinism (Evolution), Marxism (Communism), Nietzsche-ism (Socialism). To us Jews, at any rate, it should be plain to see what a disintegrating importance these directives have had upon the minds of the goyim."[441]

Rabbi S. Wise stated in the May 5, 1935, American Bulletin: "Some call it Marxism I call it Judaism."[442] On April 4, 1918, The Jewish Chronicle stated that "the ideals of Bolshevism are consonant with the finest ideals of Judaism."[443]

The fact that communism is actually a religious philosophy born of the Talmud and put into practice has been concealed from the ignorant Gentiles. In a 1971 White House recording released by the National Archives in 1999, President Richard Nixon revealed: "The only two non-Jews in the communist conspiracy were Chambers and Hiss. . . . Every other one was a Jew and it raised hell with us."[444] The Talmudic Jews have been successful in preventing any revelations about their involvement in establishing a new communist world order by labeling anyone who exposes their efforts an antisemite.

Many think that Zionism is the struggle by the Jews for a homeland. Zionism is much more than the Jews establishing a homeland. That is merely a cover for a much grander plan to rule the world. Zionism is the child of the Talmud, and Talmudism is communism. The communist revolution in Russia was planned and executed by Jews according to the doctrines of their Talmud.

Make no mistake about it, the communists stated at the outset that their aim is world domination. The 1919 World Congress of the Communist International stated that it intended to wage a "fight by all available means, including armed force, for the overthrow of the international bourgeoisie and for the creation of an international Soviet republic."[445] That statement was in essence a declaration of war against all countries in the world. Once one understands that communism is a cloak for Zionism, it becomes clear that the Zionists have declared war on the world and plan on ruling the world with an iron fist after their victory.

Communism is essentially Talmudic Judaism. The exoteric communism portrays itself as an atheistic political movement. The persecution of the Christian churches wherever communists have been brought to power seems to prove that point. However, the real nature of communism as a Judaic religious movement is manifest by the fact that Jewish synagogues do not suffer the same fate as Christian churches in communist countries. Communism reveals Judaism as a satanic conspiracy against God and man.

Jewish scholar Henry Makow, Ph.D., was asked why when the Bolsheviks took over Russia and tried to eliminate religion, Christian churches were destroyed, and the Christian clergy were killed or imprisoned, yet the Jewish synagogues and rabbis remained untouched. If communism was a political movement that was antagonistic to all religion, why was Judaism given a pass? Makow researched that issue:

> Last week I stumbled across the answer in a book by American historian Edwin Schoonmaker:
>
> "Fifteen years after the Bolshevist Revolution was launched to carry out the Marxist program, the editor of the 'American Hebrew' could write: 'According to such information that the writer could secure while in Russia a few weeks ago, not one Jewish synagogue has been torn down, as have hundreds-perhaps thousands of the Greek Catholic Churches. . . . In Moscow and other large cities one can see Christian churches in the process of destruction . . . [whenever] the Government needs the location for a large building.' (American Hebrew, Nov. 18, 1932, p. 12) Apostate Jews, leading a revolution that was to destroy religion as the 'opiate of the people' had somehow spared the synagogues of Russia." ("Democracy and World Dominion," 1939, p.211)
>
> If the Communists hated God and religion so much, why didn't they destroy synagogues too? Do Christianity and Judaism worship the same God? Or can a religion that claims an exclusive ownership of God be a religion? Could it be that Judaism is a really a secret society like Freemasonry where the members don't know the hidden agenda, which is in fact expressed by Communism? Although many religious Jews were indeed anti-Communist,

Schoonmaker's information suggests there may be an affinity between Talmudic Judaism and pagan Satanic Communism.[446]

V.I. Lenin's maternal grandfather, Israel Blank, was Jewish. Researcher Wayne McGuire of Harvard University wrote: "Lenin was a Jew by the standards of Israel's Law of Return: he possessed a Jewish grandparent."[447] Lenin, in apparent reference to himself, said: "The clever Russian is almost always a Jew or has Jewish blood in him."[448] Leon Bronstein (Trotsky), supreme commander of the Soviet Red Army, was also Jewish.[449]

The Bolshevik revolution was Jewish from top to bottom. Of 556 leading conspirators in the Bolshevik state in 1918-19 there were 17 Russians, two Ukrainians, eleven Armenians, 35 Latvians, 15 Germans, one Hungarian, ten Georgians, three Poles, three Finns, one Czech, one Karaim, and 457 Jews.[450] As pointed out by Robert Wilton in his book The Last Days of the Romanovs, the communist revolution was not an insurrection by Russians, but rather a secret invasion by Jews. As of 1983, the Premier of the Soviet Union was a Jew (Andropov) and 23 out of 25 members of the Politburo (the Soviet ruling clique) were Jews. In addition, every top member of the Soviet military and police was a Jew.[451] Robert Wilton explains:

> The Germans knew what they were doing when they sent Lenin's pack of Jews into Russia. They chose them as agents of destruction. Why? Because the Jews were not Russians and to them the destruction of Russia was all in the way of business, revolutionary or financial. The whole record of Bolshevism in Russia is indelibly impressed with the stamp of alien invasion. The murder of the Tsar, deliberately planned by the Jew Sverdlov (who

came to Russia as a paid agent of Germany) and carried out by the Jews Goloschekin, Syromolotov, Safarov, Voikov and Yukovsky, is the act not of the Russian people, but of this hostile invader.[452]

Colonel Jack Mohr states: "One of the greatest difficulties of the Talmudic Pharisees has been that of bringing communism into power while trying to conceal its Talmudic origin."[453] However, the direct and circumstantial evidence that the communist revolution in Russia was a conspiracy perpetrated by Talmudic Jews is overwhelming. Circumstantial evidence that points to Jewish control of the communist revolution is that once the communists in Russia seized power, the first law they passed made antisemitism a crime punishable by death.[454] While Christian church buildings were turned into animal stables, slaughter houses, and dance halls, the Jewish synagogues were untouched. [455] Christian pastors were removed from their pastoral duties and made to work on roads and in slave labor camps, yet the Jewish rabbis were permitted to continue their clerical duties.[456] "Some 200,000 (Christian) clergy, many crucified, scalped and otherwise tortured, were killed during the approximately 60 years of communist rule in the former Soviet Union, a Russian commission reported Monday (Nov. 27, 1995) . . . 40,000 churches (were) destroyed in the period from 1922 to 1980."[457]

Historian Michael Hoffman II exposed the hidden meaning behind some of the bloodthirsty communist propaganda:

> Lenin declared, "We are exterminating the bourgeoisie as a class." His partner in crime, Apfelbaum (Zinoviev) stated: "The interests of the revolution require the physical annihilation of the bourgeoisie class." Who were these bourgeoisie? Certainly not Jews. Trotsky

gave a clue to their identity in a 1937 interview in the New York Jewish newspaper, *Daily Forward:* "The longer the rotten bourgeoisie society lives, the more and more barbaric will anti-Semitism become everywhere."

Bourgeoisie was a Bolshevik code-word for Gentile. The first law passed after the Communists seized power in Russia made anti-semitism a crime punishable by death. (*Izvestia,* July 27, 1918).

* * *

The Jewish Bolsheviks regarded politics as a branch of Gentile pest control. Hatred of Christians, especially the peasant "bourgeoisie" was their prime motivation. The systematic destruction of the Christian peasantry of Russia as so many vermin, beginning with Lenin's attack on them in the summer of 1918 and his forced starvation in 1921, has been almost completely ignored in Western history.[458]

Henry Makow explains that the brutality of the Bolshevik Revolution in Russia was inspired and led by Talmudic Jews. Makow estimates that the Cheka (later renamed OGPU, then NKVD and finally KGB) was responsible for at least 20 million deaths.[459] The primary foci of the slaughter were Gentiles in general and Christians in particular. According to Slava Katamidze: "The Church became the target of Bolshevik hostility from the very beginning."[460]

Makow quotes Jewish writer Sever Plocker, who stated that the brutal Cheka was led and staffed mainly by Jews.[461] The Cheka was empowered by Lenin and Trotsky, who were

Illuminati Jews and financed by Illuminati Jewish bankers. "Many Jews sold their soul to the devil of the Communist revolution and have blood on their hands for eternity," Plocker writes. "We mustn't forget that some of the greatest murderers of modern times were Jews."[462]

Plocker gives the example of Genrikh Yagoda, who was a bloodthirsty Jew who oversaw the slaughter of millions of Russians:

> An Israeli student finishes high school without ever hearing the name "Genrikh Yagoda," the greatest Jewish murderer of the 20th Century, the GPU's deputy commander and the founder and commander of the NKVD. Yagoda diligently implemented Stalin's collectivization orders and is responsible for the deaths of at least 10 million people. His Jewish deputies established and managed the Gulag system.[463]

Moses Mordecai Marx Levi, alias Karl Marx, was a Jew, a Satanist, and a member of the "League of the Just," which was a branch of the Illuminati.[464] In 1847, Marx was commissioned by the Illuminati to write the *Communist Manifesto*, which is an outline of their plans for world domination.[465]

Paragraph seven of Protocol 3 states that the Gentile communists and socialists are dupes that are helping the Zionist Jews bring about the destruction of the Gentiles.

> We appear on the scene as alleged saviours of the worker from this oppression when we propose to him to enter the ranks of our fighting forces - Socialists, Anarchists, Communists - to whom we always give support in accordance with an alleged

brotherly rule (of the solidarity of all humanity) of our social masonry. The aristocracy, which enjoyed by law the labor of the workers, was interested in seeing that the workers were well fed, healthy, and strong. We are interested in just the opposite - in the diminution, the killing out of the goyim.[466]

The Talmudic Jews have been successful in preventing any revelations about their involvement in establishing a new communist world order by labeling anyone who exposes their efforts an antisemite. What most do not understand is that many who claim to be objects of antisemitism are not Semites at all. Semites are those who are descended from Shem, the oldest son of Noah. Most Jews living in Israel and throughout the world today are eastern European converts to a religion that they call Judaism, but in fact is Babylonian Talmudism. The Europeans who later converted to this Babylonian form of Judaism are known as Ashkenazi or Khazar Jews.

Dr. Benjamin H. Freedman, a former Jew, states that the Khazars were a pagan nation whose religious worship was a mixture of phallic worship and other forms of idolatry. In the 7th century their King Bulkan chose Talmudism, which most now call Judaism, as the state religion.[467] Today Khazar Jews are called "Yiddish."

These Ashkenazi Jews are people without any allegiance to any nation. Their primary objective is to own the entire world. To get an idea of the nefarious objective of these Talmudists, let us read an 1879 letter from Baruch Levy to Karl Marx:

> The Jewish people as a whole will be its own messiah. It will attain world dominion by the dissolution of other races, by the abolition of frontiers, the annihilation of monarchy, and by

the establishment of a world republic in which the Jews will everywhere exercise the privilege of citizenship. In this new world order the children of Israel will furnish all the leaders without encountering opposition. The governments of the different peoples forming the world republic will fall without difficulty into the hands of the Jews. It will then be possible for the Jewish rulers to abolish private property, and everywhere to make use of the resources of the state. Thus will the promise of the Talmud be fulfilled, in which it is said that when the messianic time is come, the Jews will have all the property of the whole world in their hands.[468]

Many think that communism could not be the work of Talmudic Jews because Russia is allied with the Arab countries. Things, however, are not what they appear. Jack Bernstein, an American Ashkenazi Jew who moved to Israel shortly after its founding in 1948, returned in disgust to the United States after witnessing the duplicity of Israel. He revealed that the aboriginal Jews of Palestine, who are called Sephardic Jews, are discriminated against in modern Israel. They are second class citizens at the bottom strata of society in Israel, along with Christians and Muslims. In his book, *The Life of an American Jew in Racist Marxist Israel*, explains the Machiavellian strategy of Israel.[469]

Bernstein found out that communist Russia's support for the Arab countries is a Jewish subterfuge.[470] He stated that part of the Machiavellian plan is for communist Russia to appear to support the Arabs by furnishing them with military aid. However, the communists will never provide enough aid to allow the Arabs to destroy Israel. Since 1949, there has been a free-flow of intelligence sharing between Israel and communist Russia.[471] Bernstein obtained this information directly from the horse's mouth: the Secretary-Treasurer of the Communist Party in Northern Tel Aviv.[472]

Bernstein pointed out that Israel presents itself as a democracy, but in fact Israel is a communist country to its core. He stated that Zionism and communism are one and the same. The purest form of communism is found in Jewish kibbutzim in Israel.

Michael Collins Piper reveals in his book, *Final Judgment*, that Israel's communist ties are not limited to the former Soviet Union. There has been a long, albeit secret, history of mutual cooperation between communist China and Israel in the development of nuclear and other military weapons. In fact, Israel has been cited as one of the primary conduits for the flow of U.S. and other western technologies to communist China.

16 The Dark Secret of Judaism

When the Zionist Jews gain control of their world government, they will not allow for any religion other than their religion. Paragraph one of Protocol 14 explains that point.

> When we come into our kingdom, it will be undesirable for us that there should exist any other religion than ours of the One God with whom our destiny is bound up by our position as the Chosen People and through whom our same destiny is united with the destinies of the world. We must therefore sweep away all other forms of belief.

What is that religion? Paragraph four of Protocol 14 states that the religion is a secret.

> Our philosophers will discuss all the shortcomings of the various beliefs of the "goyim," but no one will ever bring under discussion our faith from its true point of view since this will be fully learned by none save ours who will never dare to betray its

secrets.[473]

Why would they keep their religion a secret? It is because their religion is the mystical worship of Satan. That fact must be kept secret until they have full control of all of the organs of government. According to John Torell, in the Jewish Cabala (a/k/a Kabbalah), the Jewish god consists of one male being and one female being. The male part of the Jewish god (called "En-Sof" by the Cabalists) withdrew himself into himself and created a vacuum in his own structure, which created a bottomless pit (this abyss is called the "kelipot" by the Cabalists). The Cabala teaches that the female part of the Jewish god has fallen into this pit, and has taken the form of the "holy serpent."

The Cabala further teaches that the "holy serpent" is surrounded by evil spirits and she is tempted at all times. The "holy serpent" is trying to set herself free from the bottomless pit. Once she does this she can enter the earth as "the messiah." Cabalists teach that "the messiah" will only appear on earth in one of two ways. One way is for the Cabalistic Jews to destroy all evil on the earth and make it totally good. The other alternative is for the Cabalistic Jews to destroy all good on earth and make it totally evil.[474]

The Cabalistic Jews have decided that is harder to make things good and so they have chosen the alternative of destroying all goodness and making the world evil. This Cabalistic religion is grounded in the commission of sins in order to bring about the ascension of their messiah, the "holy serpent," out of the bottomless pit to make "her" appearance on earth. These Jews believe that only by breaking the laws of God can they serve their god.

Do not think that Jews are ignorant of the fact that Satan is the god of their religion. Harold Wallace Rosenthal, Administrative Assistant to United States Senator from New

York, Jacob K. Javits, in a 1976 interview with Walter White Jr. stated: "Most Jews do not like to admit it, but our god is Lucifer."[475] That explains the revelation by Albert Pike, the theological pontiff of Freemasonry, in his doctrinal bible of Masonry, that the god of Freemasonry is Lucifer. The evidence is that Freemasonry flows from Cabalistic Judaism. It makes sense that the god of Freemasonry would be the same as the god of the religion upon which it is based. Jesus was not using hyperbole when he told the Jews: "Ye are of your father the devil, and the lusts of your father ye will do." John 8:44.

The modern day Pharisees go to great lengths not only to sin themselves, but also to lead as many others into sin as they serve their evil god, Satan. Jesus revealed their nature when he said to the Pharisees: "Woe unto you, scribes and Pharisees, hypocrites! for ye compass sea and land to make one proselyte, and when he is made, ye make him twofold more the child of hell than yourselves." (Matthew 23:15)

The fact that Judaism is a religion of sin and rebellion that embraces evil is confirmed by Jewish "rabbi" David Cooper, who spent eight years studying the Cabala in Jerusalem's Old City.

> The lesson is that even the heart of Satan has a divine spark; even the heart of evil yearns to be redeemed. This is important, because we learn that our job is not to set up the battleground to eradicate evil, but search out its spark of holiness. Our task is not to destroy but to build.[476]

* * *

> The mystical teaching of the Baal Shem Tov, however, presents us with a new paradigm. It says that evil has a divine nature within it. As

the Zohar describes, 'there is no sphere of the Other Side (evil) that entirely lacks some streak of light from the side of holiness.' [Zohar II:69a-b] Rather than destroy it, our task is to uplift it.[477]

The purposeful promotion of evil by Jews is the reason that we find vice, death, and destruction, at every turn of the Zionist screw. Near the top of the Zionist power pyramid we find the Rothschild banking family. Henry Makow reveals that the Rothschilds were Sabbatean-Frankists, which is a sect of Judaism. Sabbateans are followers of Rabbi Sabbatai Zevi (1626-1676), who claimed to be the Jewish Messiah. Frankists are followers of Jacob Frank (1726-1791). Frank was a popular Jewish Cabalist, who claimed to be the reincarnation of Sabbatai Zevi. Sabatean-Frankists are "characterized by their 'liberated' sexual practices, incest, pedophilia, etc. They believed the Messiah would return only when the world descended into sin and chaos. They would advance this process."[478] Sabbatean-Frankists adhered to the code of "what had been prohibited would be allowed: adultery, incest, pedophilia. (This is the occult origin of our 'sexual liberation.'). Inspired by the Cabala, they practiced 'holiness through sin.' Good would come through the annihilation of Western civilization and the triumph of Evil."[479]

Surely Satan has an end in mind for constructing such a sinister religious doctrine. He does, and it is nothing short of the subjugation of all men under the dictatorial rule of his antichrist! He uses the escalating sin and crime in society as a justification to bring about more government regulation and control of the masses. As explained by Edmond Burke: "Men are qualified for civil liberty in exact proportion to their disposition to put moral chains on their own appetites. Society cannot exist unless a controlling power upon will and appetite be placed somewhere, and the less of it there is within, the more there is without. It is ordained in the eternal constitution of things that men of intemperate minds cannot be free. Their passions forge their fetters."

This evil doctrine can also be seen in the Talmud, where incest, fornication, adultery, etc. are promoted as virtues and something to be desired. It is difficult for the Gentile world to fully comprehend what is happening in this Jewish netherworld of conspiracy unless they understand the nature of Cabalistic Judaism. It is a religion that is based on the promotion, propagation, and commission of sin as a means to world domination.[480]

The Cabala, like the Talmud, graphically blasphemes Jesus. For example, in Zohar III, 282a, the Cabala refers to Jesus as a dog who resides among filth and vermin.[481]

There is a hidden link between Judaism and "Christian" Zionism, which the Jews would just as soon keep concealed. Some "Christian" Zionists have spoiled the game by revealing that they have taken their doctrine from the Cabala and Talmud.[482] For example, the Cabala and Talmud played an essential role in the thought and practice of noted dispensational theologian Freiderich Christoph Oetinger.[483] Oetinger taught that Jesus Christ would reign bodily on earth after his second coming. He also taught that the church was wrong in teaching that the unconverted were subjected to eternal punishment after death.[484]

The satanic rebellion of the Jews against God is something the leaders in the "Christian" Zionists movement cannot help but see. They hold themselves out as expert theologians. Assuming they are the experts that they claim to be, they must know the satanic nature of Judaic Zionism.

The misguided flocks in "Christian" Zionist churches are largely ignorant about the Babylonian core of Judaism, which is in every sense an antichrist religion. Hence, Zionist church members are oblivious to their role in aiding and abetting a conspiracy against God and man. Others are not so innocent and could properly be described as wilfully ignorant. They stumble across the truth, but they get back up, dust themselves off, and continue on their merry way, disregarding the plain evidence that "Christian" Zionism is neither Christian nor Zionist in the biblical sense.

Individual Jews can be saved only by the grace of God through faith in Jesus Christ. Such a saved Jew, will reject Judaism, just as a saved Satanist will reject Satanism. Judaism is irreformable. The Jews who follow Judaism to their death, will die in their sins. Such Jews are described by Stephen as stiff-necked people, who are in perpetual rebellion against God.

> Ye stiffnecked and uncircumcised in heart and ears, ye do always resist the Holy Ghost: as your fathers did, so do ye. Acts 7:51.

"Christian" Zionists are doing the work of the devil by forgoing preaching the gospel of Jesus Christ to the Jews, encouraging Jews to continue their heathen practice of Judaism, and aiding the Zionist aims of the Jews.

Henry Makow, in his book *Illuminati, The Cult that Hijacked the World*, explains the occult nature of Judaism:

> The "secret society" appears to be the organizational model for Judaism as well as Freemasonry, Zionism and Communism (which are Masonic orders.). Essentially, the leadership deceives and manipulates the membership with idealistic-sounding goals. Only those corruptible (and blackmail-able) are let in on the true agenda and allowed to rise.

This model now applies to the whole world. "Successful" people have often accepted the Devil's Bargain-"Serve me and I will give you the world."

This view of Judaism is confirmed by the author of the "Protocols of Zion" who says:

"No one will ever bring under discussion our faith from its true point of view since this will be fully learned by none save ours, who will never dare to betray its secrets." (Protocol 14)

* * *

Edith Starr Miller, an expert on religion and the occult, called Judaism "a secret society posing as a religion," and "a sect with Judaism as a rite."

The real purpose of Judaism and all secret societies, Miller says, is to con people into advancing the agenda of the super rich. "Regardless of their exoteric objects, the esoteric aims of most societies are all directed toward the same end, namely: the concentration of political, economic and intellectual power into the hands of a small group of individuals, each of whom controls a branch of the International life, material and spiritual, of the world today." ("Occult Theocracy," 1933, p.661)

Flavien Brenier compares the goals of Judaism with Freemasonry: securing political power and gradually modifying "the conceptions of the people in the direction of their secret doctrine." ("Occult Theocracy," 80)

The secret aim of Judaism is the same as Freemasonry.[485]

Part and parcel of Zionism is the Judaic religious philosophy based upon the occult worship of a type of god known as an egregore. An egregore is an autonomous god of the collective group mind. The egregore influences the thoughts of a group of people. In the case of Judaism, it is the Jewish people. Henry Makow opines that this Judaic egregore is Lucifer:

> Perhaps the Jewish elite has a different God. A reader, "George," knew the heiress of a rich Jewish banking family "not the Rothschilds, although her family dwelled in a palace neighbouring the Rothschilds."
>
> "Leah was one of my classmates in the Geneva University (Switzerland) where I was studying psychology . . . She was an attractive blue-eyed blonde lady. . . . As she was wearing a Star of David, I asked if she was a believer. She answered "yes and no" and added that she believed in a god of the Jews who was serving the Jews rather than served by them. I immediately asked whether she was speaking of an egregore . . . Her only response was "yes" and she broke that conversation. Never again did we mention the subject."[486]

* * *

George speculates that elite Jews created the Jewish God as their "egregore," i.e., an instrument of their collective will, i.e., their desire to vanquish the heathens and rule supreme:

"Could it be possible that the ancient Levite priests found a way to create a supernatural entity from the collective mind of the tribe of Judah? An entity born from a collective mind the Levites were shaping into self-isolationism and segregationist a.k.a., extreme ethno-centrism?... An entity designed to help the "chosen people" destroy the 'alien' nations and provide it with material rewards? An entity resulting from the black magic of the Levite priests who, as the first indoctrinated atheists, were denying the universal God of Moses because they didn't want to submit to a 'Lord and Master' but rather become themselves 'Lords and Masters' through their slavish 'egregorious' god?"

This "egregore" is Lucifer. Elite Jews have made him the master meme of the New World Order. The elite Jews are the "Communist Capitalist International," the intermarried German Jewish banking families who, according to Christian Rakovsky include the Rothschilds, Warburgs, Schiffs and many others.

They have also intermarried with the corrupt gentile elites of Europe and America, many of whom think they are Jews.[487]

Makow's opinion that the Jewish egregorious god is Lucifer is substantiated by occult authorities. Philip Gardiner quotes Sir Osmond IV, *Saturnian Principles,* who explains that an egregore is a spirit that is used to maintain a link to the

Prince of Darkness. The Prince of Darkness, of course, is Satan (i.e., Lucifer).

> The egregore is a group spirit that serves to remind the initiate of his or her goals. It informs and guides the individual and it protects the living chain of brotherhood. The living chain of brotherhood is entered into when a Setian performs a rite of their own creation intended to protect and enhance the Temple of Set. The egregore protects the brotherhood by letting them know their enemies are there. A symbolic representation of the egregore is used to maintain a link to the Prince of Darkness.[488]

All egregorious gods are evil and under the command of Satan. John Kominski quotes Diane Vera, who in *Intro to Satanism* states that Satan is the most powerful magical egregore.

> Satan is not an actual discarnate, sentient being, but is more than just a symbol. Satan is, at the very least, today's most powerful magic(k)al egregore.[489] (parenthesis in original)

Vera is wrong that Satan is not a sentient being. She is, however, correct that there is a direct link between Satan and egregores. Egregores are a manifestation of the evil of Satan and are under the control of Satan.

The Jewish egregore is viewed within Jewry as a serpent that is gaining control of nation after nation as it slithers across the globe in its journey toward world domination. Texe Marrs reveals: "In the religion of Judaism, the Sacred Serpent is said to rise from the abyss. Through his power and guidance, a divine World Jewry will triumph over the Gentiles, and the Jews' Messiah will reign supreme."[490] Makow's opinion that the egregore of Judaism is Lucifer is perceptive, since Lucifer controls all egregores. That fact is implicitly supported by the writings of eminent Jewish Rabbis. Marrs explains:

> Take, for example, the celebrated rabbi known throughout the Jewish religious world as the "Gaon of Vilna." It was he who taught of the Kabbalah's doctrine that inside Judaism's vaunted Tree of Life there resides a great and Sacred Serpent whose masculine name is Leviathan and whose feminine name is Malkut. It is this Sacred Serpent, the Kabbalah teaches, that in the coming Messianic age shall rise from the abyss to conquer the Gentiles and exalt God's Chosen, the Jews. This Leviathan, the holy and piercing serpent, is the expected Messiah prophesied to appear, the one who will supernaturally possess the bodies of the world's Jews and lead them to global domination and glory.
>
> This strange doctrine, accepted by the vast majority of today's Orthodox Rabbis, also makes the bold claim that the Jews are a Holy Race of wise and virtuous serpent beings. Collectively, World Jewry is claimed to be the very incarnation on earth of the Holy Serpent.
>
> Could this be what the true Messiah and Lord of the Universe, Jesus Christ, meant when he confronted the wicked pharisaic Jews—equivalent to today's Orthodox Jewry—by flatly declaring:
>
> "Ye serpents, ye generation of vipers, how can

ye escape the damnation of hell?" (Matthew 23:33)

* * *

The Jews themselves, in their devilish religion of Judaism, admit their god is the Serpent. Their leaders well know that this is the Devil, or Satan. In some type of creepy and eerie doctrinal confession, the rabbis are even discovered to be boasting of their Sacred Serpent and they say that all Jews live inside its belly! Is this not unbelievable and revelatory?[491]

Who do we see described in the bible as the serpent? It is none other than Satan himself. "And the great dragon was cast out, that old serpent, called the Devil, and Satan, which deceiveth the whole world: he was cast out into the earth, and his angels were cast out with him." Revelation 12:9.

Dr. Chika Flint examined the Jewish esoteric teaching about Leviathan and concluded that the Jewish god is not the holy God of the bible, but is rather a heathen god made up of both good and evil.[492] Flint states:

> Jehovah is said to be a cruel and oppressive deity whose strict rules and laws must be obeyed if he is to be appeased. In contrast, Jehovah's "other half" the Serpent, whom they call Lucifer, is a god of freedom of enlightenment and liberty. Whereas Jehovah is merciless and foreboding, the Serpent god is claimed to be freespirited; he encourages pleasure and his motto is, "Do as thou wilt."[493]

The earthly god of Judaism, who is androgynous, is known as Leviathan or Malkut.[494] Leviathan is an evil god, adopted by the rabbis as the god of the Jews during their captivity in ancient Babylon.[495] Flint explains:

> Leo Schaya, in The Universal Meaning of the Kabbalah, says that the wisdom of the Kabbalah returned to Israel after the captives were set free by Cyrus, Persian conqueror of Babylon, and some rabbis and many of the people returned to Jerusalem to rebuild the destroyed Temple. This is why the Talmud, the Halakah (Law) books of the Jews, are called The Babylonian Talmud. This is also why centuries later, Jesus, in Jerusalem, bluntly told the Jews that their religion, Phariseeism, or what we call today "Orthodox Judaism" was based on "man-made traditions" and not the God-given teachings of the Old Testament prophets. Jesus further said theirs were the commandments of hell and that new converts to Judaism thus became "twice the devils" that their teachers were! What a stunning, yet entirely truthful, indictment of the Jews' religion.[496]

The Jews exoterically depict Leviathan as an evil beast from the sea who will be hunted and killed by the Jews. His flesh will provide food for the Jews of Jerusalem and his hide will be a tent for the pious.[497] This is clearly an exoteric portrayal, with much deeper occult meaning. If the Leviathan is the egregorious god of the Jews, it makes no sense that the Leviathan would be hunted down and eaten by the Jews, unless the hunting of the Leviathan is a metaphor for the antisemitic persecution of the Jewish people that is fostered and furthered by the Zionist Jews themselves (e.g., the Nazi persecution). Is the eating of the flesh of Leviathan a satanic twist on what

Jesus said? Recall that Jesus stated: "Whoso eateth my flesh, and drinketh my blood, hath eternal life; and I will raise him up at the last day. For my flesh is meat indeed, and my blood is drink indeed. He that eateth my flesh, and drinketh my blood, dwelleth in me, and I in him." John 6:54-56.

Flint explains the esoteric teaching within the Kabbalah that accepts the evil of Leviathan, who is a god of war that will subjugate the earth under Jewish rule.

> God gives the Righteous (Jews) serpentine protection through the magical ability to summon serpents from the lower regions to come and do their bidding. Ultimately, say the rabbis, through supernatural magic, Leviathan himself will take up their cause, encircle the earth, destroy their enemies, and finally, serve both as Light of the World and as covering (defender) for the Holy City of Jerusalem.[498]

The worship of Leviathan (the Jewish serpent deity) is the esoteric worship of Satan. Flint explains:

> More pertinent to the discussion at hand is the revelation that the Judaic religion, in its kabbalistic aspects, literally advocates and practices veneration, admiration, and worship of the Serpent as Deity. Jesus' bold and truthful declaration to the Jews was that by their wicked acts and as a result of their religion being man-made and based on "the traditions of the elders," they had proven to be a "generation (that is, a nation of people and offspring) of vipers." The Lord's exact words were: Ye serpents, ye generation of vipers, how can ye escape the damnation of hell? (Matt. 23:33; 2Cor. 2:11).[499]

Rabbi Joel David Bakst, in *Journey To the Center of the Torah: The Secret In the Serpent's Belly* quotes from Rabbi Shlomo Eliyashav's (1841-1925) interpretation of the Kabbalah, *Sifra DiZtenuta*, Chapter 1, which is the Zohar's Book of Concealment. The highly respected Rabbi Eliyashav's interpretation is found in his work titled *Leshem Shevo VeAchlama*. The language of Rabbi Eliyashav's interpretation is almost indecipherable to those uninitiated in occult Kabbalism. According to Rabbi Eliyashav, the "holy serpent" is the root and essence of the Jewish god's revelatory light. That means that the holy serpent (Leviathan) is the god of the Jews.

> The Holy [macro] Serpent is the fountainhead, root and essence for all of God's sacred, revelatory Light from which emanates all dimensions of reality. This is the ray of Light of the *Ain Sof* that extends into the *Ztimztum*. This ray of light is what becomes the "supernal pathways of the image of the elongating [macro] Serpent who stretches out on both sides with its tail [united] in its head, its head "returning upon its shoulders."
>
> The kabbalists explain: This [serpent] is the *sod* of the Cosmic Balance, the *Supernal Da'at* (the middle brain of the Godhead). This is Leviathan.[500] (brackets and parenthesis in original)

The occult Judaism, which is hidden from the uninitiated, is that the Jews view themselves as the very manifestation of their egregore god, whom they call Leviathan. This collective god, Leviathan, also known as the "holy serpent," will subjugate the world under the rule of the Jews.

The egregore of the Jews is confirmed in paragraph one

of Protocol 3, which refers to the "Symbolic Snake" and depicts it as an egregorious symbol of the Jewish people:

> Today I may tell you that our goal is now only a few steps off. There remains a small space to cross and the whole long path we have trodden is ready now to close its cycle of the Symbolic Snake, by which we symbolize our people. When this ring closes, all the States of Europe will be locked in its coil as in a powerful vice.

Professor Nilus in the epilogue to the 1905 edition of his book, *The Great Within the Small*, explains the symbolism of the snake with the head of the snake being those initiated in the Zionist plan to conquer the world and the body of the snake being the mostly unwitting body of Jewry. The snake symbolized the slyness of the Jews to penetrate into the hearts of nations in order to undermine and subdue them under Jewish power. Nilus' describes the egregorious "Symbolic Snake" as follows:

> [T]he Symbolic Snake, whose head was to represent those who have been initiated into the plans of the Jewish administration, and the body of the Snake to represent the Jewish people—the administration was always kept secret, even from the Jewish nation itself. As this Snake penetrated into the hearts of the nations which it encountered, it undermined and devoured all the non-Jewish power of these States.[501]

John Torell has revealed that in the Jewish Cabala, the "holy serpent" is mystically trying to set itself free from the bottomless pit in order to enter the earth as "the messiah."[502] The "holy serpent" of the Jews is an egregorious god, which means the Jews believe they are their own messiah. In 1879

Baruch Levy wrote to Karl Marx and stated that the Jews will, in the end, have all of the world's property in their hands. Levy stated that the promise of the Talmud would then be fulfilled, which is that "the Jewish people as a whole will be its own messiah."[503]

The Messianic promise of the Talmud to which Levy referred can be found in the Babylonian Talmud at Folio 111a of Tractate Kethuboth, where it states in pertinent part: "We have a tradition that Babel will not witness the sufferings that will precede the coming of the Messiah." A footnote to that passage explains: "These are the throes of mother Zion which is in labor to bring forth the Messiah - without metaphor, the Jewish people." The Jewish hierarchy plan to establish a Messianic reign over a new world order tyranny from their earthly Zion in Israel.

What does the bible say about Leviathan? In Job 41:34 we read that "He beholdeth all high things: he is a king over all the children of pride." God has stated that "[p]ride goeth before destruction, and an haughty spirit before a fall." Proverbs 16:18. Whereas, Jesus Christ calls on his followers not to be prideful, but rather to be humble. "Whosoever therefore shall humble himself as this little child, the same is greatest in the kingdom of heaven." Matthew 18:4.

So, we know that the Leviathan, who is king over the children of pride, must be the very opposite of God. Leviathan must be "the great dragon was cast out, that old serpent, called the Devil, and Satan" mentioned in Revelation 12:9.

Please note that it was the serpent in the garden of Eden who beguiled Eve. The serpent was the most subtle of the beasts. He told Eve that she and Adam could become as gods if they ate the fruit from the tree. Genesis 3:4-5. That is exactly what the Jews are claiming for themselves. They have believed the lie of the serpent that they are gods. Each Jew believes that he is a god who is part of the collective Jewish egregorious god. The Jewish view of themselves as gods is found in the Jewish religious doctrine. For example, the Talmud at Tractate Sanhedrin, Folio 58b refers to Jews as a "Divine Presence."[504] Rabbi Shimon ben Yohai declared his godhood by stating: "I am beyond the jurisdiction of any angel or judge in heaven."[505]

Satan is the adversary of God. He tries to be like God and his earthly kingdom is a devilish imitation of God's heavenly kingdom. God's kingdom is a spiritual kingdom that is not of this earth. John 18:36. God has a heavenly Jerusalem (containing a heavenly Zion). Revelation 21:10. Satan's kingdom is a kingdom of the flesh that is headquartered in the earthly Jerusalem (containing an earthly Zion). The gospel of Jesus Christ explains that Jesus is in believers and believers are in Jesus. John 14:20; 17:20-23. There is one spiritual body of Christ, with Jesus the head. Colossians 1:18. As with the earthly imitation Zion, Satan also has a fleshly imitation body of satanic believers. That body is not a spiritual body. It is the fleshly body of the Jews. It is the egregore of the "holy serpent" of the Jewish people. As the church is the body of Christ, so also in a perverse way is the egregore of the Jews the body of Lucifer.

The Jewish egregore, or group god, is a communist beast that is kept together through antisemitism. Antisemitism is the means by which the head of the snake keeps the body of Jews following in lockstep its leadership. Without antisemitism, the body of Jews would disperse and be assimilated into the Gentile nations. That simply cannot be allowed by the Jewish hierarchy. The Jews must be kept as an insular body separated from the Gentiles. The power of the Jewish hierarchy is centered in its control of the egregorious body of Jews. Henry Makow explains:

[Nicholas] Lysson discusses how the Jewish

leadership actively provoke anti-Semitism because it is indispensable for Jewish cohesion and survival. Jews acknowledge this. Are they saying that, without its "egregore" i.e. its predatory agenda, Jews would have no corporate raison d'etre? Of course this secret is kept from the rank-and-file, as in Freemasonry which Rakovsky said is designed to bring about "the triumph of Communism."[506]

The language of witchcraft always carries two meanings. There is the exoteric meaning for the uninitiated public, and there is the esoteric meaning that is only understood by the inner circle of initiates. For example, Jewish communists claim that they are atheists. That is the exoteric meaning of communist doctrine. However, the occult meaning of communism is hidden. The esoteric meaning of communism is that the collective body of Jews make up the egregore, who is the collective god of communism. So when communists talk about atheism, they only mean that there is no God outside of themselves. The egregore, however, only includes the Jewish communists; the Gentile communists are simply the skin of the serpent that will ultimately be shed after they have served their purpose.

As of the year 2000 there were 268 kibbutzim in Israel.[507] A Kibbutz is a collective Jewish society. According to the Jewish Virtual Library, Kibbutz is "the fulfillment of the idea 'from each according to his ability, to each according to his needs.'"[508] That is a direct quote from Karl Marx.[509] The Kibbutz collective is the purest form of communism. The Kibbutz is one manifestation of the Jewish egregore. When the Jewish egregore is allowed unrestrained aggression against Gentiles, the exoteric term used to describe it is "communism." It is not a surprise that as one gets closer to the head of the egregorious serpent in Israel, we find the purest form of communism.

What does this Jewish egregore leave in its path? History has shown that it is nothing but merciless death and destruction. The egregorious religious doctrine of the godhood of the Jews is how the Jewish communists could be so bloodthirsty. They do not believe that there are any moral constraints on their conduct. They are imbued with an ethnic superiority complex, where they are gods over the Gentiles. They view Gentiles, particularly Christians, as their enemies to be enslaved and exterminated. Makow explains:

> The greatest mass slaughter in history was not the Jewish holocaust but the Ukrainian holodomor, i.e., the "hunger." By Stalin's own estimate, ten million Ukrainians died, mostly at the hands of Bolshevik Jews.
>
> The holodomor took place because the Bolsheviks confiscated all the grain. Lysson writes:
>
> "A quarter of the rural population, men, women and children, lay dead or dying in a great stretch of territory with some forty million inhabitants, like one vast Belsen. The rest, in various stages of debilitation, had no strength to bury their families or neighbours. [As at Belsen] well-fed squads of police or party officials supervised the victims."
>
> The extermination of the Ukrainian Kulaks was directed from the Kremlin where the Bolshevik leadership lived in family apartments and maintained a fraternal atmosphere suffused by collectivist idealism, i.e., their egregore. This is how historian Simon Sebag Montefiore, the scion of an elite

British Jewish family, describes the scene during the holomodor. Of course he doesn't mention that most of the main players were Jews.

"The Party was almost a family business. Whole clans were members of the leadership. ... This pitiless fraternity lived in a sleepless frenzy of excitement and activity, driven by adrenalin and conviction. Regarding themselves like God on the first day, they were creating a new world in a red-hot frenzy." ("Stalin: The Court of the Red Tsar," p. 40, 45)

The Soviets didn't raze synagogues because Communism expressed the Jewish "egregore." Christians and Jews apparently do not worship the same God. The Christian God represented by Jesus is universal love and brotherhood. The Jewish God has been supplanted by a Cabalistic egregore that "serves" elite Jews only. It represents their ruthless sociopathic urge for world dominion. The same egregore- the desire to supplant God- animates the New World Order.[510]

The idealism of brotherhood and comradery that is commonly propagandized in communist circles is just so much window dressing that conceals a satanic deception. The real agenda of communism is the destruction of religion, family, and nation; the accumulation of all wealth and the enslavement of mankind.[511]

The idealistic Gentile followers of communism are dupes, who are viewed by the Jewish leaders as "useful idiots," who will be summarily executed when the Jews come to power. That has been the pattern in all communist revolutions in the past, and it will continue to be the practice in the future. The Zionist Leviathan is a cunning and diabolical egregorious viper bent on nothing short of world rule based upon Jewish supremacy.

The core doctrine of Judaism is the rejection of Jesus Christ. Harmony Daws explains that the Jewish religion is diametrically opposed to Christianity.

> As we have said many times, the modern Jewish religion is extremely aware of the inherent hostility between itself and Christianity. The two faiths could hardly be more opposed in their basic tenets. Judaism absolutely rejects the deity of Christ, which is (or should be) the central foundation on which all other Christian beliefs are built. Modern Judaism exalts the Jewish people as the correct representations of God in this world while Christians call for a spiritual revolution that extends to all people of all races. Jewish leaders and sacred texts know that these two faiths are diametrically opposed; unfortunately, Christians seem completely ignorant.[512]

Jesus criticized the Pharisees for their religious traditions. Those traditions were oral traditions at that time. Later they were memorialized in the Talmud and the Kabbalah (a/k/a Cabala). The Kabbalah and the Talmud today span numerous volumes. Jesus called the pharisees hypocrites, who masqueraded as religious men, but who were in reality irreligious frauds.

> Then came to Jesus scribes and Pharisees, which were of Jerusalem, saying, Why do thy disciples transgress the tradition of the elders?

for they wash not their hands when they eat bread. But he answered and said unto them, **Why do ye also transgress the commandment of God by your tradition?** For God commanded, saying, Honour thy father and mother: and, He that curseth father or mother, let him die the death. But ye say, Whosoever shall say to *his* father or *his* mother, *It is* a gift, by whatsoever thou mightest be profited by me; And honour not his father or his mother, *he shall be free.* **Thus have ye made the commandment of God of none effect by your tradition.** *Ye* **hypocrites**, well did Esaias prophesy of you, saying, This people draweth nigh unto me with their mouth, and honoureth me with *their* lips; but their heart is far from me. But **in vain they do worship me, teaching** *for* **doctrines the commandments of men.** (Matthew 15:1-9)

The Pharisees had an outward appearance of piety, in order to gain political and religious control of the Jews. In secret, however, they practiced an occult doctrine that was only known to its initiates. Lady Queenborough (Edith Miller) explains in her book *Occult Theosophy*:

> The Chaldean science acquired by many of the Jewish priests, during the captivity of Babylon, gave birth to the sect of the Pharisees whose name only appears in the Holy Scriptures and in the writings of the Jewish historians after the captivity (606 B. C). The works of the celebrated scientist Munk leave no doubt on the point that the sect appeared during the period of the captivity. "From then dates the Cabala or Tradition of the Pharisees. For a

long time their precepts were only transmitted orally but later they formed the Talmud and received their final form in the book called the *Sepher ha Zohar*."[513]

The scrupulous observance by the Pharisees of Jewish religious tradition was only a cover for their secret doctrine. They had rejected Jehovah and had adopted the pantheism of Babylon. They pretended that their many rituals were necessary for the worship of Jehovah, but those were only man-made rules to conceal their secret Babylonian religion. Jesus rebuked them for it; calling them hypocrites for their vain worship of God through man-inspired rituals and honoring God with fine words, when their hearts in fact were focused on the heathen gods of Babylon. See Mark 7:5-7. The Pharisees had accepted the satanic lie that they had become "as gods." See Genesis 3:5. Their new Babylonian (a/k/a Chaldean) religion was to be exclusive to the Jews, who were to rule the world. Edith Miller explains:

> The Pharisees, then, judging it wiser to capture the confidence of their compatriots by taking the lead in the religious movement, affected a scrupulous observance of the slightest prescriptions of the law and instituted the practice of complicated rituals, simultaneously however cultivating the new doctrine [i.e., secret doctrine] in their secret sanctuaries. These were regular secret societies, composed during the captivity of a few hundred adepts. At the time of Flavius Josephus which was that of their greatest prosperity, they numbered only some 6,000 members. This group of intellectual pantheists was soon to acquire a directing influence over the Jewish nation. Nothing, moreover, likely to offend national sentiment ever appeared in their doctrines.

However saturated with pantheistic Chaldeism they might have been, the Pharisees preserved their ethnic pride intact. This religion of Man divinised, which they had absorbed at Babylon, they conceived solely as applying to the profit of the Jew, the superior and predestined being. The promises of universal dominion which the orthodox Jew found in the Law, the Pharisees did not interpret in the sense of the reign of the God of Moses over the nations, but in that of a material domination to be imposed on the universe by the Jews. The awaited Messiah was no longer the Redeemer of original Sin, a spiritual victor who would lead the world, it was a temporal king, bloody with battle, who would make Israel master of the world and 'drag all peoples under the wheels of his chariot.' The Pharisees did not ask this enslavement of the nations of a mystical Jehovah, which they continued worshipping in public, only as a concession to popular opinion, for they expected its eventual consummation to be achieved by the secular patience of Israel and the use of human means.[514]

Jesus cursed the Pharisees to their face: "Woe unto you, scribes and Pharisees, hypocrites! for ye are as graves which appear not, and the men that walk over them are not aware of them." (Luke 11:44) The Babylonian traditions of the Pharisees, which were traditions passed down orally from generation to generation, were eventually (in part) memorialized in the Kabbalah and Talmud. The double aim of the Pharisees was to wrestle political control over the Jews from the Sadducees and "to modify gradually the conceptions of the people in the direction of their secret doctrine."[515] They accomplished both goals. Today Orthodox Jewry is an insular authoritarian society that is completely given over to the practice of the Babylonian religion of the ancient Pharisees.

The twisted Babylonian god of modern Jewry as expressed in the Talmud and Kabbalah is a god of vengeance and hatred of Gentiles and particularly Christians. Edith Miller summarizes the nature of the Jewish god as being "just and merciful only to his own people, but foe to all other nations, denying them human rights and commanding their enslavement that Israel might appropriate their riches and rule over them."[516]

The Talmud sets forth clear distinctions between Gentiles and Jews. Jews are viewed as gods, whereas Gentiles are viewed as animals. For example, in Talmud Tractate Sanhedrin, Folio 58b it states that smiting a Jew on the jaw is like assaulting a "Divine Presence."[517] If the assailant happens to be a gentile, he is "worthy of death."[518] A Gentile child is considered to be subhuman.[519]

Judaism is a religion of hate. The hatred of Christians and all Gentiles of all races runs through the warp and woof of Judaism. The Jews recite *Amidah*, which is a set of eighteen (by some accounts nineteen) weekly Jewish prayers. The twelfth prayer is called *Birkat ha-minim*. The *Birkat ha-minim* is actually a hateful curse against heretics and enemies of the Jews, particularly Christians. The curse was first introduced in the *Amidah* in the first century at Jabneh by Samuel ha Katan, at the request of Rabban Gamaliel II in order to drive followers of Jesus Christ from the synagogues.

The book of Acts records the successful efforts of the early Christians in converting Jews to Christianity. The early Christian disciples would meet with the Jews in the synagogues and explain the gospel. Many Jews became followers of Christ. Acts 17:1-13. The bible records that the chief ruler of the synagogue at Corinth believed in Jesus and was saved. Acts 18:8. The Jewish leadership saw Christianity as a threat to

Judaism and could not allow the spread of Christianity to continue. They instituted the *Birkat ha-minim* as a means of making clear to the Jews that Judaism was incompatible with Christianity. They wanted to keep the newly converted Christians out of the synagogue and stop Christianity from spreading.

Min is a pejorative that is commonly used to refer to a Christian, with *minim* being the plural form of *min*. According to the Encyclopedia Judaica, the *Birkat ha-minim* has to be recited during public worship by the *hazzan* so as to avoid any suspicion of heresy.[520] The *hazzan* is a Jewish cantor who leads the congregation in prayer. If the *hazzan* makes an error and omits the *Birkat ha-minim*, he is required to return to the *Birkat ha-minim* and recite the curse. That regulation requiring return to the omitted curse does not apply to any of the other benedictions recited as part of the *Amidah*.[521]

The *Birkat ha-minim* is a clear impediment to the spread of the philosemitism (love of Jews) of "Christian" Zionism.[522] The Jews know this, and so they make every effort to keep Christians ignorant about the true nature and beliefs of Judaism. The Zionist Jews benefit greatly from the support of the "Christian" Zionists and they do not want the Christians to know what they really think of them. The "Christian" Zionists are "useful idiots" to the Zionist Jews, and they would like to keep them in ignorant bliss.

Not only do Jews include curses against Christians in their weekly prayers, they have corrupted the yearly Passover celebration into a hate-fest against Christians. Ariel Toaff, explains in his book *Pasque di Sangue* (*Blood Passover*), that In orthodox Judaism Passover has become a ritual of detestation against Jesus.[523]

Ariel Taoff is a professor of Jewish renaissance and medieval history at Bar Ilan University[524] in Israel, just outside of Tel Aviv. Professor Toaff is a Jewish insider, who comes from a rabbinic bloodline that is highly respected among Jews. He is the son of one of the most revered rabbis in the world, Elio Toaff. He is the former chief rabbi of Rome and was considered the dean of Italian Jewry. Some have called Elio Toaff the "Pope of the Jews." So influential was Rabbi Taoff in Rome, he was one of only two people that Pope John Paul II mentioned by name in his will.[525]

Toaff explains how over time the Judaism and the Passover memorial in particular had been corrupted into a hate-fest against Christ and Christians.

> In this Jewish-Germanic world, in continual movement, profound currents of popular magic had, over time, distorted the basic framework of Jewish religious law, changing its forms and meanings. It is in these "mutations" in the Jewish tradition – which are, so to speak, authoritative – that the theological justifications of the commemoration in mockery of the Passion of Christ is to be sought, which, in addition to its celebration in the liturgical rite, was also intended to revive, in action, vengeance against a hated enemy continually reincarnated throughout the long history of Israel (the Pharaoh, Amalek, Edom, Haman, Jesus).[526]

Toaff explains that the Passover meal was transformed into a ceremonial curse upon Christians. He explains how during the middle ages, the orthodox Jews sprinkled the Passover table with wine to signify the blood hatred of Christians by the vengeful Jews. The Jews made wine an integral part of the ceremony of Passover, which is intended as a disdainful twist on the last supper of Christ. Wine was not part of the Passover celebration as laid down by God. The

Passover was intended to be a memorial that was to celebrate God having freed the Jews from Egyptian slavery. Passover also looked forward to the coming of Christ, who is the sacrificial Lamb of God, who takes away the sins of the world. *See* John 1:29.

The fourteenth day of the first month is the Passover (Leviticus 23:4-5, Exodus 12:17-18). Passover is immediately followed by the seven days of unleavened bread (Leviticus 23:6-7, Exodus 12:15-16). There is no mention of using wine as part of the Passover ceremony. Jesus instituted wine at the last supper. Matthew 26:27-29. The Jews have now instituted wine as an integral part of their Passover ceremony; it is intended as a contemptuous mockery of the last supper. The Passover ceremony included cursing Christians with the ten curses that were brought upon Egypt during the Jewish captivity there. Toaff explains:

> At this point, in the traditional reading of the *Haggadah*, according to the custom of the Ashkenazi Jews, the curses against the Egyptians were transformed into an invective against all the nations and enemies hated by Israel, with explicit reference to the Christians.[527]

Toaff was quick to point out that this cursed ceremony was not practiced by the Sephardic or Italian Jews, but as far as he knew, it was only practiced among the German Orthodox Ashkenazi Jews. Toaff explained that the Ashkenazi tradition was that the head of the family would state at the table: "Thus we implore God that these ten curses may fall on the gentiles, enemies of the faith of the Jews."[528] Toaff stated that was a clear reference to the Christians. The orthodox Jews call on God to cast his anger upon the Gentiles and let the fury of his anger persecute and destroy them.[529]

Toaff came to the ineluctable conclusion, based upon careful examination of authoritative evidence, that in the middle ages blood from Christian boys, who were ritually murdered, was used in some orthodox Jewish communities as part of the yearly Passover ceremony. The evidence is that the Jewish ritual murders continued long after the middle ages. In the 1941 book, *Jewish Ritual-Murder, A Historical Investigation,* Hellmut Schramm, Ph.D., documented over 130 cases of Jewish ritual murder of gentile children between the years 1144 A.D. and 1913 A.D. The cases documented that Jewish doctrine requires the victim to first undergo the most unimaginably sadistic tortures before his blood is drained, in order for the blood to be efficacious. The Jewish ritual concludes with the victim's blood being drained while the victim's heart is still beating. Dr. Schramm quoted the sworn testimony directly from trial transcripts of the gruesome details of the torture and bleeding of the victims. Dr. Schramm also documented the bribery of the high government officials by rich, powerful Jews in order to undermine investigations and prosecutions of Jewish ritual murderers. The blood, once drained from the victim, is carried away and then later distributed within the Jewish community to be used by Jewish families in the Jewish Passover ceremony. Toaff explained that only a small nut-sized amount of dried blood was shaken from a glass vial into the wine. The head of the family would announce: "This is the blood of a Christian child." He then would recite the ten plagues of Egypt as curses against Christians and gentiles. Toaff states:

> The head of the family takes a bit of the blood of the Christian child and drops it in his glass full of wine [...] then, putting his finger in the wine, with that wine where the blood of the Christian child has been shaken, he sprinkles the table and food on the table with it, pronouncing the Hebraic formula in commemoration of the ten curses, which God

sent to the refractory Egyptian people who refused to liberate the Jewish people. At the end of the reading, the same head of the family, referring to the Christians, utters the following words (in Hebrew): 'thus we beseech God that he may similarly direct these ten curses against the gentiles, who are enemies of the Jewish faith.'

Toaff obtained evidence of the Jewish practice of a blood Passover from testimony of Jewish witnesses at the trial of the murder of a Christian child in the 1400's. Expert testimony of Mosè of Würzburg at trial explained that "the Jews naturally require the blood of a Christian child, but if they were poor and could not afford any blood, they were relieved of the expense."

The witnesses at the trial testified that a small amount of blood of the Christian child was also mixed with the dough of the unleavened bread that was eaten during the Passover meal. There was testimony from a witness named Israele, who was identified as Samuele of Nuremberg's son, who stated that the mixing of the blood into the unleavened bread was a memorial of the blood with which the Lord commanded Moses to paint the door-posts of the doors. However, Toaff found another deeper meaning.

Vitale of Weissenburg, Samuele's agent, preferred to confer a second meaning upon the rite, that is, that of an upsidedown memorial to the Passion of Christ, considered as an emblem and paradigm of the fall of Israel's enemies and of divine vengeance, forewarning of final redemption. "We use the blood", he declared, "as a sad memorial of Jesus ... in outrage and contempt of Jesus, God of the Christians, and every year we do the memorial of that passion

> ... in fact, the Jews perform the memorial of the Passion of Christ every year, by mixing the blood of the Christian boy into their unleavened bread."

The curses pronounced against Christians by the Jews during their Passover ceremony are symptomatic of the orthodox Jewish antipathy of Gentiles in general and hatred of Christians in particular. The most revered rabbis (*gedolim*) view Gentiles as garbage. According to orthodox Judaism, Gentiles are not only an inferior species, but a species that is "completely evil." For example, Rabbi Saadya Grama of Beth Medrash Govoha in his book *Romemut Yisrael Ufarashat Hagalut* (Jewish Superiority and the Question of Exile) states: "The Jew by his source and in his very essence is entirely good. The *goy* [Gentile], by his source and in his very essence, is completely evil. This is not simply a matter of religious distinction, but rather of two completely different species."[530]

Rabbi Grama is simply stating the philosophy contained in the Talmud. He explains that according to his understanding of Jewish religious doctrine "The difference between Jews and gentiles is not historical or cultural, but rather genetic and unalterable."[531]

Rabbi Grama's opinion cannot be dismissed as a fringe view within orthodox Jewry. His assertion is backed up by other esteemed Rabbis. For example, Rabbi Shneur Zalman, the esteemed founder of *Chabad-Lubavitch*, taught that the difference between Jew and Gentile is not merely religious or racial, but that the souls of Jews and Gentiles are completely different in kind. "Gentile souls are of completely different and inferior order. They are totally evil, with no redeeming qualities whatsoever... Indeed they themselves are refuse.... All Jews are innately good, all gentiles are innately evil."[532]

According to the Talmud, Christians are allied with

hell,⁵³³ and Jesus is not only cursed,⁵³⁴ he is described as being tormented in boiling hot semen.⁵³⁵ The Talmud, however, gives immunity to rabbis from ever going to hell.⁵³⁶ Chagigah 27a (a/k/a Hagigah 27a) states: "As to disciples of the wise, the flame of Gehenna [hell] has no power over them."⁵³⁷ The Talmud explains in Tractate Baba Bathra that "disciples of the wise men" means scholars or distinguished students.⁵³⁸ That means that not only are rabbis immune from hell, but also all scholars or distinguished students of the Talmud. Rabbi Shimon ben Yohai declared: "I am beyond the jurisdiction of any angel or judge in heaven."⁵³⁹

Rabbi ben Yohai, who believed he was beyond the jurisdiction of God, did not think Gentiles were even worthy to live. His views regarding Gentiles were that "even the best of gentiles should all be killed."⁵⁴⁰ Rabbi ben Yohai is not a rabbi on the fringes of Judaism; he is in fact one of the most revered of rabbis in Judaism; his grave is a shrine in Israel. He authored the Zohar, which is the principal work of the Kabbalah.

While the Jewish clergy consider Gentiles subhuman, they will turn on Jews who do not adhere to their dictates. Jewish rabbis have nothing but contempt for Jews who do not follow the Jewish traditions.⁵⁴¹ This overbearing attitude by Jewish rabbis is nothing new. One can sense the contempt that the Pharisees had for the common Jews in John 7:49, where common Jews were impressed by what Jesus had to say, and the Pharisees responded by cursing the Jews for not knowing the "law." The law to which the Pharisees referred was their oral tradition.

William Wotton explains the undue burdens placed on the Jews through the laws of the Pharisees:

> They were absurdly minute in the literal observance of their vows, and as shamefully

subtle in their artful evasion of them. The Pharisees could be easy enough to themselves when convenient, and always as hard and unrelenting as possible to all others. They quibbled and dissolved their oaths with experienced casuistry.[542]

William Wotton (1666-1727) was a rare genius; he undertook foreign language translation at age five, attended Cambridge University at age 10, being graduated at age 13.[543]

The common Jews are as much victims of the Jewish hierarchy as are the Gentiles and Christians. The common Jews are being spiritually brainwashed to do the bidding of their rabbis. Jesus explained the process: "Woe unto you, scribes and Pharisees, hypocrites! for ye compass sea and land to make one proselyte, and when he is made, ye make him twofold more the child of hell than yourselves." (Matthew 23:15) Jesus cursed the Pharisees and scribes; he could have, but did not, curse all Jews. It is the reprobate spiritual leaders who were the targets of Jesus' epithets. He came to set Jew and Gentile alike free from spiritual bondage. "Then said Jesus to those Jews which believed on him, If ye continue in my word, then are ye my disciples indeed; And **ye shall know the truth, and the truth shall make you free.**" (John 8:31-32)

According to Orthodox Judaism Gentiles have no property or other rights that can be asserted against a Jew. Baba Bathra 54b: Property of Gentiles is like the desert; whoever gets there first gets it.

Sanhedrin 57a: If a Gentile robs a Jew, he must pay him back; but if a Jew robs a Gentile, the Jew may keep the loot. Likewise, if a Gentile kills a Jew, the Gentile is to be killed; but if a Jew kills a Gentile, there is no death penalty.

Sanhedrin 52b: Adultery forbidden with the neighbor's

wife, but is not forbidden with the wife of a heathen (Gentile). The implication is that a heathen is not a neighbor.

Talmudic Judaism has the most intense hatred for Jesus.[544] While some Jews will deny that the Talmud teaches such things, Benjamin Freedman, a former Talmudic Jew, stated that: "there have never been recorded more vicious an vile libelous blasphemies of Jesus, of Christians and the Christian faith than you will find between the covers of the 63 books of the Talmud which forms the basis of Jewish religious law, as well as being the textbook used in the training of rabbis."[545] For example:

Sanhedrin 106a & b: Mary was a whore; Jesus was an evil man.

Shabbath 104b: Jesus was a magician and a fool. Mary was an adulteress.

Sanhedrin 43a: Jesus was guilty of sorcery and apostasy; he deserved execution. The disciples of Jesus deserve to be killed.

Gittin 57b: Jesus was sent to hell, where he is punished by boiling excrement for mocking the Rabbis.

Michael Hoffman explains that "[l]ike the Talmud, the Kabbalah supersedes, nullifies and ultimately replaces the Bible."[546] Lawrence Fine, Professor of Jewish Studies and prominent scholar of medieval Judaism and Jewish mysticism, reveals that the Kabbalah contains the "true" meaning of the Old Testament. The "simple" meaning of the biblical language recedes into the background as the symbolic meaning contained in the Kabbalah supercedes the bible and takes control. There is a code to the true meaning in the bible that can only be unlocked through the Kabbalah.

[T]he reader must become accustomed to regarding biblical language in a kabbalistically symbolic way. The Kabbalists taught that the Torah is not only the speech or word of God, but is also the many names of God or expression of God's being. It is a vast body of symbols, which refers to the various aspects of divine life, the sefirot, and their complex interaction. **The simple meaning of biblical language recedes into the background as symbolic discourse assumes control**. The true meaning of Scripture becomes manifest only when it is read with the proper (sefirotic) code. **Thus the Torah must not be read on the simple or obvious level of meaning; it must be read with the knowledge of a kabbalist who possesses the hermeneutical keys with which to unlock its *inner* truths.**[547]

The Kabbalah at Zohar III, 152a states: "Thus the tales related to the Torah are simply her outer garments, and woe to the person who regards that outer garb as the Torah itself! For such a person will be deprived of a portion in the world to come."[548] That passage in the Kabbalah puts a curse on anyone who tries to read the bible for what it actually says, instead of with the mystical gloss put on it by the Kabbalah.

The Kabbalah is Judaic mystical practices that were adopted by the Jews from Babylon. H.P. Blavatsky described the Kabbalah as:

The hidden wisdom of the Hebrew Rabbis of the middle ages derived from the older secret doctrines concerning divine things and cosmogony, which were combined into a theology after the time of the captivity of the Jews in Babylon. All the works that fall under the esoteric category are termed Kabalistic.[549]

Magic and occult mysticism runs throughout the Kabbalah. Judith Weill, a professor of Jewish mysticism stated that magic is deeply rooted in Jewish tradition, but the Jews are reticent to acknowledge it and don't even refer to it as magic.[550]

Gershom Scholem (1897-1982), Professor of Kabbalah at Hebrew University in Jerusalem, admitted that the Kabbalah contains a great deal of black magic and sorcery, which he explained involves invoking the powers of devils to disrupt the natural order of things.[551] Professor Scholem also stated that there are devils who are in submission to the Talmud; in the Kabbalah these devils are called *shedim Yehuda'im*.[552]

The *Jewish Chronicle* revealed that occult practices such as making amulets, charms, and talismans are taught in Jerusalem at the rabbinic seminary Yeshivat Hamekubalim.[553] That is why Jesus said to the Jews: **"Ye are of your father the devil, and the lusts of your father ye will do."** John 8:44. The bible states clearly that the magic arts are an abomination to the Lord.

> There shall not be found among you any one that maketh his son or his daughter to pass through the fire, or that useth divination, or an observer of times, or an enchanter, or a witch, Or a charmer, or a consulter with familiar spirits, or a wizard, or a necromancer. For all that do these things are an abomination unto the LORD: and because of these abominations the LORD thy God doth drive them out from before thee. (Deuteronomy 18:10-12)

17 Catholic Judaism

Dr. Chika Flint explains that the Kabbalah contains an esoteric revelation that the Messiah of the Jews is to be possessed by the "holy serpent." This seems to be a reference to the antichrist being possessed by Satan.

> Thus, the Kabbalah, at its rotten core, contains the ultimate kernel of knowledge to be discovered in the Mystery teachings—the great secret that the Holy Serpent is God. He is destined, the rabbis disclose to the initiates, to incarnate the body and mind of their Christ-Messiah to come. This will be the same one the New Age mystics call the Lord Maitreya, whom the Babylonians knew as Tammuz, and the Greeks as Hermes. Christians who are not wrapped up in the deceit of idolatrous Zionism recognize this being for whom he really is. The antichrist, or beast, given the number 666 (Rev. 13) who is to wreak havoc and usher in an age of horrors. His power, the Scriptures say, comes from the Dragon and Serpent, Satan.[554]

It seems that the Zionists have plans for the entry of the antichrist. Protocol 3, in pertinent part, states:

> [W]hen the hour strikes for our sovereign lord of all the world to be crowned it is these same hands which will sweep away everything that might be a hindrance thereto. . . . Ever since that time we have been leading the peoples from one disenchantment to another, so that in the end they should turn also from us in favor of that king-despot of the blood of Zion, whom we are preparing for the world.[555]

In Paragraph 3 of Protocol 23, this antichrist is called: "The supreme lord who will replace all now existing rulers."[556] The beast is further described in paragraph nine of Protocol 3: "When the hour strikes for our sovereign Lord of all the world to be crowned it is these same hands which will sweep away everything that might be a hindrance thereto."[557] Is there any clue from the Protocols as to who the antichrist would be? In fact, there is. Paragraph four of Protocol 17 states:

> The King of the Jews will be the real Pope of the Universe, the patriarch of the international church.[558]

It is revealing that the Protocols describe their leader of the world as "King of the Jews" and "Pope of the Universe." Is there a corollary to those titles in the world today? In fact there is, and it is none other than the Pope of Rome.

It seems that the Vatican plays a central role in the Zionist plans for world rule from Jerusalem. Barry Chamish reveals that in March 1995 a secret cable from the Israeli embassy in Rome to the Israeli Foreign Ministry was leaked to an Israeli radio station (Arutz Sheva).[559] The cable documents negotiations between the Israelis and the Vatican, wherein the Vatican will gain control of Jerusalem. This cable was printed on the front page of the Israeli newspaper, *Haaretz* two days later.[560]

The Jerusalem Post reported that under Israeli Labor Party Leader Shimon Peres' plan, the old walled city would become a "world capital," with the U.N. Secretary-General serving as mayor. Chamish states that *"The Jerusalem Post* added that under the Peres plan, the sovereignty of the holy places would revert to their owners. And since the Vatican has the lion's share of real estate claims, guess who gets to own the most holy land in Jerusalem?"[561]

That plan caused a political scandal when the cable was revealed. Rabbis who had invited Peres for Passover services cancelled their invitations in protest of the perceived treachery. Peres reacted by claiming that the cable was real but that someone had whited-out the word, "not" in the cable. He claimed that the cable really said that Israel would "not" hand Jerusalem over to the Catholic Pontiff.[562] Chamish characterized Peres' statement as a "cockamamie excuse." Chamish based his assessment on the fact that in "widely distributed minutes of a meeting with Clinton in 1997, Peres reiterated his diplomacy, ending with the words, 'as I had previously promised the Holy See.'"[563]

The Zionists know that they cannot rule the world from Jerusalem without it appearing to the world as gentile rule. That is where the Vatican comes in. It is a gentile front for a Judaic religion, which is completely under the control of Zionist interests. That fact, however, is not generally known. When the Vatican has served its purpose, the Zionists will destroy it. Destruction is the fate of all the gentile fronts, once they are no longer needed; they are considered "useful idiots" by the Zionist Jews.

It is no surprise to see the Protocols use "Pope" to describe their coming antichrist world ruler. What is at root of the traditions of the Roman Catholic Church? It is the Jewish Cabala (a/k/a Kabbalah). Cabala is a Hebrew word, which literally translated means "tradition." Nesta Webster in her classic book *Secret Societies and Subversive Movements* explained how the Jewish theology of the Cabala was introduced into the Roman Catholic Church by Pope Sixtus IV (1471-1484).

> It was likewise from a Florentine Jew, Alemanus or Datylus that Pico della Mirandola, the fifteenth-century mystic, received instructions in the Cabala and imagined that he had discovered in it the doctrines of Christianity. This delighted Pope Sixtus IV, who thereupon ordered Cabalistic writings to be translated into Latin for the use of divinity students.[564]

Pope Sixtus' use of the Cabala was not the institution of something new but rather a progression of Judaic principles in the Catholic Church. This author's book, *Solving the Mystery of Babylon the Great*, proves beyond any doubt that the Roman Catholic Church is a "Christian" front for a Judaic/Babylonian religion. The Bible states that the Devil is at war with Christians, who are the spiritual seed of Jesus. Revelation 12:17. The Catholic priesthood, who impose the fleshly Judaic rules of the Roman church, are soldiers in a war against Christ and Christians. Galatians 4:29.

Jesus Christ is the rock upon which the church is built. Ephesians 2:20, 1 Corinthians 3:11. The Pope of Rome, however, claims that Peter is the rock upon the church is built and that the Pope of Rome is his successor. By claiming that Peter is the rock, the pope has denied that Jesus is the rock, which is essentially a denial that Jesus is the Christ. The pope has fulfilled the prophecy in 1 John 2:22-23, which states that the antichrist will deny that Jesus is the Christ.

Who then does the pope claim is the Christ? The answer is found when we compare what the Holy Bible says about Christ with what the pope has said. What does it mean when we say that Jesus is Christ? It means that he is the one anointed "God with us." In Matthew 1:23, Jesus is identified as "Emmanuel, which being interpreted is, God with us." The pope, however, claims that he is God with us. **"[W]e hold upon this earth the place of God Almighty."** *Pope Leo XIII* (emphasis added).[565]

Jesus Christ is "an advocate with the Father" for us. 1 John 2:1. In fact he is the "one mediator between God and men." 1 Timothy 2:5. The pope, however, claims the title of Supreme Pontiff. Pontiff means literally bridge builder; it connotes that the pontiff is one who is a bridge or intermediary between God and man. The pope has stated: "To be subject to the Roman Pontiff is to every human creature altogether necessary for salvation." *The Bull Sanctum*, November 18, 1302.

In addition, the Catholic Church teaches that Mary and the saints are advocates before the throne of God for us. "[The saints'] . . . intercession is their most exalted service to God's plan. **We can and should ask them to intercede for us and for the whole world.** *CATECHISM OF THE CATHOLIC CHURCH*, § 2683, 1994." Jesus Christ is the "author and finisher of our faith." Hebrew 12:2. "For by grace are ye saved through faith; and that not of yourselves: it is the gift of God: Not of works, lest any man should boast." (Ephesians 2:8-9) The pope, however, states that faith comes from man and it must be joined with works, i.e., started and finished by man, not Jesus. The Catholic Church even teaches that works done after death by others are effective for the salvation of the deceased. "[T]he souls . . . are cleansed after death by purgatorial

265

punishments; and so that they may be relieved from punishments of this kind, namely, the sacrifices of Masses, prayers, and almsgiving, and other works of piety, which are customarily performed by the faithful for other faithful according to the institutions of the Church." COUNCIL OF FLORENCE, 1439.[566]

Jesus Christ is the "blessed and only Potentate." 1 Timothy 6:15. Pope Innocent II claimed ownership of the entire universe as the "TEMPORAL SOVEREIGN OF THE UNIVERSE."[567] Pope Boniface VIII pronounced: "**I have the authority of the King of kings. I am all in all and above all, so that God, Himself and I, The Vicar of God, have but one consistory, and I am able to do almost all that God can do. What therefore, *can* you make of me but God.**" *The Bull Sanctum*, November 18, 1302 (emphasis added).[568] Even today the Pope wears a triple crown because he claims to rule as king over Heaven, Hell, and Earth. Jesus Christ is the "great high priest" of God almighty. Hebrews 4:14. The pope claims to be the great high priest. As already mentioned above, the pope claims the title of Supreme Pontiff. He is the successor of the emperors of Rome who were seriatim the Supreme Pontiff (*Pontifex Maximus*),[569] which was the high priest of the pagan religions of Rome.[570] Jesus is higher than the kings of the earth. Psalms 89:27. The pope claims, however, authority over the kings of the earth. "[T]he Roman pontiff possess **primacy over the whole world.**" *The Vatican Council*, Session IV, chapter III, July 18, 1870 (emphasis added).

Jesus is "Lord of all." Acts 10:36. The pope, though, claims that all must submit to him: "The Roman Pontiff judges all man, but is judged by no one. We declare, assert, define and pronounce: to be subject to the Roman Pontiff is to every human creature altogether necessary for salvation. . . . That which was spoken of Christ . . . 'Thou hast subdued all things under His feet,' may well seem verified in me." *The Bull Sanctum*, November 18, 1302 (emphasis added).[571] The pope has claimed every attribute of Christ for himself. He has essentially denied that Jesus is the Christ and laid claim himself to being Christ. The Holy Bible identifies such a one as antichrist. 1 John 2:20-23.

The Bible says that the antichrist will deny the Son and, implicitly, deny the Father. 1 John 2:20-23. The pope makes his identity as the antichrist clear by expressly denying the Father.

The pope claims the title "Holy Father." *See Catechism of the Catholic Church*, at § 10. Holy Father is a title that appears only once in all the Holy Scriptures and is reserved for God the Father. John 17:11.

Just as there is no commonality between Judaism and Christianity, so also, there is no commonality between Catholicism and Christianity. As is Judaism, so also, Catholicism is an overtly antichrist religion.

The Elders of Zion chose their words carefully, when identifying their future world-leader as the "pope." There is a direct historical connection between Judaism and Roman Catholicism. Most people do not understand that Judaism is polytheistic. That Babylonian polytheism of Judaism is the foundational theology of the Roman Catholic church.

Judaism concealed its polytheism beneath the guise of worshiping Jehovah. It was, therefore, easier for the Judaizers to establish their own version of the ersatz "Christian" church. The heathen poison was disguised beneath the Jewish customs, and therefore it was found more palatable to those without the unction of the Holy Spirit. Those who had the unction of the Holy Spirit gagged on the poisonous Babylonian/Judaic customs and spewed it from the true church of Christ. Those same Babylonian/Judaic customs found a home in the Catholic Church.

Ezekiel was taken by the Lord and shown how the Jews had turned from him and worshiped idols and heathen gods. *See* Ezekiel 8:1-17. The Jews thought that the heathen worship was hidden from God. "Then said he unto me, Son of man, hast thou seen what the ancients of the house of Israel do in the dark, every man in the chambers of his imagery? for they say, The LORD seeth us not; the LORD hath forsaken the earth." Ezekiel 8:12.

It was not the common Jews who were engaging in the secret worship of heathen gods, it was the "seventy of the ancients of the house of Israel." Ezekiel 8:11. Who were the seventy ancients? They were the members of the Jewish Sanhedrin. There were seventy members of the Sanhedrin, who select the high priest, who is considered the 71st member.

The common Jews were kept in the dark about the secret heathen worship. They were exposed to the oral traditions of the Jews, which they ignorantly followed, not realizing that they nullified God's laws. Jesus revealed this in Mark. "And he said unto them, Full well ye reject the commandment of God, that ye may keep your own tradition." (Mark 7:9) The oral Jewish traditions had esoteric meanings that were hidden from the uninitiated common Jews. That is the way it is today both among Jews and Catholics.

The heathenism of the Jews was ever so subtle. Jesus warned about that subtlety. He likened the false Judaic mixing of heathen worship with God's laws to leaven. A little leaven works its way through the whole loaf. The Jews created a mixture that on the surface appeared godly, but was in fact a wholly leavened loaf of heathenism. "Then Jesus said unto them, Take heed and beware of the leaven of the Pharisees and of the Sadducees. . . . Then understood they how that he bade them not beware of the leaven of bread, but of the doctrine of the Pharisees and of the Sadducees." (Matthew 16:12) Paul also warned about the Judaizers that were trying to inject their

Judaic doctrine into the church. He warned: "A little leaven leaveneth the whole lump." (Galatians 5:9)

The subtlety of the Judaizers even deceived Peter. In Galatians 2:11-13, we read how Paul had to upbraid Peter for being deceived to follow after the subtle dissimulation of the Jews. Peter caused Barnabas to fall into the same Judaizing error. That same Barnabas, however, was quick to recognize the clear heathenism when the Lycaonians sought to worship Paul and him as gods in Acts 14:11-15. Both Barnabas and Paul rent their clothes and ran among the people telling them to stop their heathen worship. The exoteric heathen worship of the Lycaonians was obvious to Barnabas, but the esoteric heathenism of the Jews was so subtle that Barnabas was taken in by it. *See* Galatians 2:13.

The Judaizing strategy resulted ultimately in the establishment of the Catholic Church. There is historical evidence for the common Babylonian lineage between Judaism and Roman Catholicism. After the fall of Jerusalem, Cabalistic Jews migrated to Alexandria where they synthesized their Chaldean witchcraft with Neo-Platonic philosophy and cloaked that religion in Christian terminology. They then tried to introduce this new heathen gnostic philosophy into the fledgling Christian Church. The penetration of the true spiritual church of Christ was futile. What this Jewish gnosticism did accomplish was the creation of a new ersatz "Christian" church, which grew into what we know today as the Roman Catholic Church. Those facts have been concealed from the historical accounts of the Catholic Church.

Maurice Pinay in his book *The Plot Against the Church* explains the spiritual fight waged by Irenaeus of Lyons (circa 130-202) against the gnostic heresy that was being injected into the church.[572] Maurice Pinay is alleged to be a pseudonym for a group of Catholic priests. According to Pinay, one of the lead purveyors of the gnostic heresy was Valentinus.[573] Valentinus was a crypto-Jew, who tried to keep his Jewish roots secret when he migrated from Alexandria to Rome. He migrated with the intention of portraying himself as a Christian in order to undermine the Christian church at Rome with his gnostic doctrines. Valentinus gained great influence in Rome and was even a candidate for bishop of Rome in 143 A.D.[574] Irenaeus discovered the Jewish roots of Valentinus and found out what Valentinus was up to. Irenaeus exposed Valentinus' anti-Christian heresy.

Paul warned about the Jewish heresy. He described their actions. "And that because of false brethren unawares brought in, who came in privily to spy out our liberty which we have in Christ Jesus, that they might bring us into bondage." (Galatians 2:4) Notice that the false brethren came in secretly pretending to be Christians as a way to bring them into bondage. Bondage to what? The passage makes it clear that they were spying out the liberty in Christ and so the bondage would be to inject into the church a false gospel that strikes at the heart of that liberty. That false gospel is salvation by works, which is the heart of the Jewish gnosticism.

Paul made that clear in his epistle to the Romans, which was a church that was being particularly targeted for corruption. Paul explained how the Jews were trying to rebel against God's plan of grace as a means of salvation and instead institute a salvation by obedience to the law. "For they being ignorant of God's righteousness, and going about to establish their own righteousness, have not submitted themselves unto the righteousness of God." (Romans 10:3) Paul warned about those who were bent on perverting Christ's gospel of grace.

> For I know this, that after my departing shall grievous wolves enter in among you, not sparing the flock. Also of your own selves shall men arise, speaking perverse things, to draw away disciples after them. Therefore

> watch, and remember, that by the space of three years I ceased not to warn every one night and day with tears. And now, brethren, I commend you to God, and to the word of his grace, which is able to build you up, and to give you an inheritance among all them which are sanctified. (Acts 20:29-32).

Notice that Paul commended the church to "God, and the word of his grace." It is the word of grace that the Judaizers would try to corrupt. The corrupt gospel is salvation by works, which was eventually given life in the Roman church.

Paul repeats the point more directly in his letter to the Galatians. The Jewish gnostics argued that obedience to the law was necessary for salvation. Paul, on the other hand, states emphatically that works of the law will not justify a person.

> Knowing that a man is not justified by the works of the law, but by the faith of Jesus Christ, even we have believed in Jesus Christ, that we might be justified by the faith of Christ, and not by the works of the law: for by the works of the law shall no flesh be justified. (Galatians 2:16).

Justification is by God's grace through faith alone. "For by grace are ye saved through faith; and that not of yourselves: it is the gift of God: Not of works, lest any man should boast." (Ephesians 2:8-9) For more detailed information on salvation by the Grace of God alone read: *The Anti-Gospel, The Perversion of Christ's Grace Gospel*.[575] The false doctrine of salvation by works was founded upon gnostic philosophy that found its way out of Alexandria.[576]

Irenaeus, who died in 202 A.D., identified the Jews as the inventors of the Gnostic philosophy that threatened to spin the early church into apostasy.

> Arising among these men, Saturninus (who was of that Antioch which is near Daphne) and Basilides laid hold of some favourable opportunities, and promulgated different systems of doctrine—the one in Syria, the other at Alexandria.... These men, moreover, practise magic; and use images, incantations, invocations, and every other kind of curious art.... **They declare that they are no longer Jews, and that they are not yet Christians**; and that it is not at all fitting to speak openly of their mysteries, but right to keep them secret by preserving silence.[577]

A theological view that Jesus was not the Son of God, born of a virgin, was nurtured in the early church by the Jewish sect called Ebionites. The Ebionites followed the corrupted Theodotion and Pontus text in support of their argument that Jesus was the son of Joseph.[578] Ebionites were Jews that accepted Jesus as the Messiah, but did not believe him to be God. Irenaeus stated that the Ebionites had an opinion of the Lord similar to that of Carpocrates, and that the Ebionites "practice circumcision, persevere in the observance of those customs which are enjoined by the law, and are so Judaic in their style of life, that they even adore Jerusalem as if it were the house of God."[579]

The doctrines that we see described by Irenaeus in the first and second centuries of the Ebionites and the followers of Carpocrates were almost identical to the idolatry of the modern Catholic Church.[580] At the very inception, the Judaizers were creeping into the church with all of their Babylonian witchcraft. The Ebionites were "so Judaic in their style of life, that they even adore Jerusalem as if it were the house of God."[581] They were in no way Christians. Irenaeus identifies Marcellina, who brought the Gnostic heresy to Rome and led multitudes to follow those idolatrous practices. They possessed graven images and even crowned these images.[582] Those are the very things that are practiced within the Roman Catholic Church today.

Irenaeus wrote extensively against the Judaizers who crept into the church, trying to inject one heresy or another. He explains in one of his writings how two Jewish proselytes, Theodotion of Ephesus and Aquila of Pontus, tried to undermine the prophecy regarding the virgin birth of Jesus by changing the passage in Isaiah 7:14.[583] That passage in Isaiah states: "Therefore the Lord himself shall give you a sign; Behold, a **virgin** shall conceive, and bear a son, and shall call his name Immanuel." *Id.* Theodotion and Pontus corrupted the passage to read "Behold, a **young woman** shall conceive, and bring forth a son." This Jewish corruption had never before been manifested in scripture until after the fulfillment of the prophecy in Isaiah by the birth of Jesus Christ was memorialized in the New Testament.

Irenaeus quite properly points out that the change in Isaiah from "virgin" to "young woman" makes no sense. The prophecy in Isaiah is supposed to be a sign from God of the birth of Christ. Matthew explains that Immanuel means God with us. "Behold, a virgin shall be with child, and shall bring forth a son, and they shall call his name **Emmanuel, which being interpreted is, God with us.**" (Matthew 1:23) If the passage states that the sign is to be that a "young woman" is to conceive, it loses all meaning since that is not a "sign," since young women conceive regularly. The sign must be something unusual in order for it to be a sign; the virgin birth of Jesus was that sign as prophesied by Isaiah.

The virgin birth of Christ is fundamental to Christianity. If Jesus was merely a man, born of natural processes, then his death on the cross could not atone for the sins of others. He could not be the perfect unblemished sacrifice. Hence, Jesus could not be the savior.

Jews today argue that the correct rendering of the Hebrew word in the passage should be "young woman" instead of "virgin."[584] They are wrong, the Hebrew word is *"alma"* and it means "virgin." The argument of the Jews makes no sense. Since Jews reject Jesus as the Messiah, they are still looking forward to the birth of the Messiah. How can they tell who that Messiah is, since it is not a sign to be born of a "young woman?" The passage specifically states that "the Lord himself shall give you a sign." The virgin birth is the sign that the child born of the virgin is the Messiah. It is very simple. If there is no virgin birth, there is no sign; if there is no sign, there is no Messiah.

The Jews have painted themselves into a corner; if they maintain their position that the prophecy in Isaiah means that a young woman will give birth, then they have lost the sign for the coming of the Messiah. Why would they do that? It is because their position is really an attack on Christianity. They cannot have Christ being born of a virgin. Rather than argue whether Jesus was born of a virgin, they change the passage of the prophecy of the virgin birth, thus making the virgin birth irrelevant. If there is a prophecy of a virgin birth and the New Testament records a virgin birth, that means Jesus is the Messiah. They cannot change the account in the New Testament, so they do the next best thing, they remove the prophecy of a virgin birth from the Old Testament.

Crypto-Jews and their Catholic fellow travelers are still pushing this corruption of the bible today. There are corrupt bible versions that maintain this gnostic fiction and corrupt Isaiah 7:14 to remove the virgin birth: Revised Standard Version (RSV), New Revised Standard Version (NRSV), New World Translation (NWT), Jerusalem Bible (JB), New Jerusalem Bible (NJB).

AV (KJV)	NJB
Therefore the Lord himself shall give you a sign; Behold, **a virgin shall conceive**, and bear a son, and shall call his name Immanuel. Isaiah 7:14 AV (KJV)	The Lord will give you a sign in any case: It is this: **the young woman is with child** and will give birth to a son whom she will call Immanuel. Isaiah 7:14 (NJB)

In the case of the Holy Bible, it is the New and Old Testaments of God Almighty. They are the most important legal documents ever written. God Almighty is the testator. He wrote both testaments. In addition, he created the languages into which his original testaments would be written. He also created the languages into which those testaments would be translated. Genesis 11:7-9. He has supernaturally controlled the process from beginning to end. **"All scripture is given by inspiration of God**, and is profitable for doctrine, for reproof, for correction, for instruction in righteousness." (2 Timothy 3:16) In addition, he has promised to supernaturally preserve his testaments. **"[T]he word of the Lord endureth for ever**. And this is the word which by the gospel is preached unto you." (1 Peter 1:25) The heirs of Christ are Christians. "The Spirit itself beareth witness with our spirit, that we are the children of God: And if children, then heirs; heirs of God, and joint-heirs with Christ; if so be that we suffer with *him*, that we may be also glorified together." (Romans 8:16-17)

Crypto-Jews and Catholics cannot eradicate the word of God, because God has promised to preserve it forever. They, therefore, have created a whole population of corrupt bible versions, so that it will be difficult for Christians to figure out what is the true word of God. **The pure word of God in the English language is the Authorized (King James) Version (AV or KJV).**

The new bible versions are based upon corrupt

transcripts and the translators use a method of translation known as dynamic equivalence, rather than the formal equivalence used in the Authorized Version (AV), which is also known as the King James Version (KJV). Formal equivalence is a word for word translation, whereas dynamic equivalence is a thought for thought translation. A translator using dynamic equivalence is less a translator and more an interpreter. Thus, the new versions of bibles should more accurately be called interpretations, rather than translations. The dynamic equivalent interpreters of the new bible versions have often made unfounded assumptions as to the meaning of particular passage. Rather than translate what God wrote, they have, with some frequency, twisted passages by injecting their own personal bias. Some of these interpreters have displayed malicious intent and caused great mischief.

The subjective biases of the interpreters in the new bible versions have caused changes in the new version English bibles that are not supported by any of Greek or Hebrew texts. For example, dynamic equivalencies caused 6,653 English word changes in the New International Version (NIV), approximately 4,000 word changes in the New American Standard Bible (NASB), and approximately 2,000 word changes in the <u>New King James Version (NKJV), none of which are supported by the words in any of the Greek or Hebrew texts.</u>[585] Those word changes reflect the subjective bias of the interpreters. The combined effect of having a corrupted text and then having that text interpreted using dynamic equivalence has been that the NIV has 64,098 fewer words than the AV.[586] That is a 10% loss in the bible. That means that an NIV bible would have 170 fewer pages than a typical 1,700 page AV bible.[587] The new versions of the bible are materially different; they are the product of the imaginations of interpreters who have applied their personal prejudices to slant already corrupted texts to comport with their own ideas. They are truly counterfeit bibles. For more detailed information on the corruption of God's word in the new counterfeit bibles read *Antichrist Conspiracy, Inside the Devil's Lair.*[588]

We can see the Judeo/Babylonian influence in the organization of the Roman Catholic Church. The Vatican College of Cardinals is the Roman Catholic version of the Jewish Sanhedrin. The College of Cardinals, like the Sanhedrin, has traditionally had 71 members. However, that number has been expanded in modern times. The members of the College of Cardinals are called Cardinals for a reason. Cardinal means "**Chief**, principal, preeminent, or fundamental."[589] The Catholic Cardinals fill the office of the Jewish "**Chief**" Priests who, along with the scribes and elders, were members of the Sanhedrin. The Sanhedrin selected the High Priest[590] who was the head of the Sanhedrin, just as the Cardinals select a Pope who is the head of the College of Cardinals. The seventy-first member of the Sahehdrin is the High Priest.[591] The Catholic corollary to the High Priest is the Pope, who as head has traditionally been the seventy-first member of the College of Cardinals.[592]

In addition to his other priestly responsibilities, the high priest's principal duty was to perform the service on the Day of Atonement. On the Day of Atonement he entered the holy of holies in the Jewish Temple to make expiation for the people by sprinkling blood of the animal sacrifice on the mercy seat.[593] Hebrews 9:7.

Recall that it was the Jewish High Priest who had Jesus arrested and condemned to death.

> But he held his peace, and answered nothing. Again the high priest asked him, and said unto him, Art thou the Christ, the Son of the Blessed? And Jesus said, I am: and ye shall see the Son of man sitting on the right hand of power, and coming in the clouds of heaven. **Then the high priest rent his clothes, and**

> saith, **What need we any further witnesses? Ye have heard the blasphemy: what think ye? And they all condemned him to be guilty of death.** And some began to spit on him, and to cover his face, and to buffet him, and to say unto him, Prophesy: and the servants did strike him with the palms of their hands. (Mark 14:61-65)

With the destruction of the temple on or about 70 A.D. there was no more need for an earthly high priest; no temple, no high priest. There has not been a Temple high priest since the destruction of the Temple. The Temple was destroyed by God using the Roman army because there was no need for the symbolic animal blood atonement, since Christ who was the real lamb of God as the actual atonement sacrificed once for all time. Hebrews 9:8-9. There is no more need for continual animal sacrifices and thus no need for an earthly High Priest.

> But Christ being come an high priest of good things to come, by a greater and more perfect tabernacle, not made with hands, that is to say, not of this building; Neither by the blood of goats and calves, but by his own blood he entered in once into the holy place, having obtained eternal redemption for us. (Hebrews 9:11-12)

Jesus is now our High Priest in the holy of holies in heaven. Hebrews 4:14.

> **For Christ is not entered into the holy places made with hands, which are the figures of the true; but into heaven itself, now to appear in the presence of God for us:** Nor yet that he should offer himself often, as the high priest entereth into the holy place

every year with blood of others; For then must he often have suffered since the foundation of the world: but now once in the end of the world hath **he appeared to put away sin by the sacrifice of himself**. And as it is appointed unto men once to die, but after this the judgment: So **Christ was once offered to bear the sins of many**; and unto them that look for him shall he appear the second time without sin unto salvation. (Hebrews 9:24-28)

There is a Temple mentioned in scripture. It is a Temple wherein the antichrist is seated.

Let no man deceive you by any means: for that day shall not come, except there come a falling away first, and that man of sin be revealed, the son of perdition; **Who opposeth and exalteth himself above all that is called God, or that is worshipped; so that he as God sitteth in the temple of God, shewing himself that he is God.** (2 Thessalonians 2:3-4)

The temple of God is not a physical temple but rather each saved Christian individually and all saved Christians corporately. "Know ye not that **ye are the temple of God**, and that the Spirit of God dwelleth in you?" 1 Corinthians 3:16. *See also* 1 Corinthians 6:19-20; Ephesians 2:21.

Who is it that sits in God's temple claiming the authority of God? None other than the Pope of Rome. The Pope claims that he is the head of the Catholic church. Catholic church means universal church.[594] God, not the Pope, is the head of the universal church.

The leader of the Roman Catholic organization, the pope, has claimed that he not only is he the leader of the Roman

Catholics but also claims that he is the head of the true church of God including Protestant Christians whom he refers to as "separated brethren." He boldly claims that entrance into Heaven is dependant on submission to his authority.

> **We declare, state and define that it is absolutely necessary for the salvation of all human beings that they submit to the Roman Pontiff.** *Bull Unum Sanctum,* Pope Boniface VIII, 1302.

Such a doctrine reveals the Pope as the antichrist. Pope Boniface VIII implied by the statement in *Bull Unum Sanctum* that he holds the position and authority of God Almighty. Further on you will read where the Pope expressly claims the authority of God. Jesus, however, made it clear that he, being God, was the only way to heaven.

> Jesus saith unto him, **I am the way, the truth, and the life: no man cometh unto the Father, but by me.** (John 14:6)

> This is the stone which was set at nought of you builders, which is become the head of the corner. **Neither is there salvation in any other: for there is none other name under heaven given among men, whereby we must be saved.** (Acts 4:11-12)

Not only has the pope claimed the authority to save but he also claims to sit in place of Almighty God with equal authority and infallibility of the Lord Jesus Christ.[595] Not just in spiritual matters but in all matters. The pope claims power over the governments of the earth. During the coronation ceremony the Pope is crowned with these words: "Take thou the tiara adorned with the triple crown, and know that thou art the father of princes and kings and the governor of the world"[596]

The Roman Pontiff judges all man, but is judged by no one. We declare, assert, define and pronounce: to be subject to the Roman Pontiff is to every human creature altogether necessary for salvation. . . . That which was spoken of Christ . . . 'Thou hast subdued all things under His feet,' may well seem verified in me. **I have the authority of the King of kings. I am all in all and above all, so that God, Himself and I, The Vicar of God, have but one consistory, and I am able to do almost all that God can do. What therefore,** *can* **you make of me but God**. *The Bull Sanctum*, November 18, 1302 (emphasis added).[597]

[W]e hold upon this earth the place of God Almighty. *Pope Leo XIII* (emphasis added).[598]

This one and unique Church, therefore, has not two heads, like a monster, but one body and one head, viz., Christ and his **vicar**, Peter's successor. *Bull Unum Sanctum,* Pope Boniface VIII, 1302 (emphasis added).

[T]he apostolic see and the Roman pontiff possess **primacy over the whole world**; and that the Roman pontiff is the successor of Blessed Peter, Prince of the Apostles, and is true **Vicar** of Christ, and Head of the whole Church, and **Father** and Teacher of all Christians; and that full power was given to him in Blessed Peter by Jesus Christ our Lord, to **rule**, feed and govern the universal Church. . . . **This is the teaching of Catholic truth, from which no one can deviate without loss of faith and of salvation.** And since, by the divine right of Apostolic primacy, one Roman pontiff is placed over the universal Church, We further teach and declare that he is the **supreme judge** of the faithful . . . none may reopen the judgment of the Apostolic See, than whose authority there is no greater. *The Vatican Council*, Session IV, chapter III, July 18, 1870 (emphasis added).

[R]oyal power derives from the Pontifical authority.[599] *Pope Innocent III.*

[T]emporal power should be subject to the spiritual.[600] *Pope Boniface VII.*

The pope claims primacy over the whole world, but when the disciples asked Jesus who is the greatest in the Kingdom of heaven, Jesus did not say "Peter." He said whoever humbles himself as a little child shall be the greatest. *See* Matthew 18:1-4. Christ is the head of the church, not Peter or his alleged successor, the pope. *See* Ephesians 5:23.

The pope considers himself the vicar of Christ. What does it mean to be a vicar? The word vicar means one who acts in place of another. We derive the English word vice from vicar. For example the Vice President acts in place of the President during those times when the President himself cannot act. The Bible talks about one who would come and deceive the world into believing that he is in place of Christ. He is identified as the **antichrist.** The pope himself is acknowledging that he is the antichrist by claiming to be the vicar of Christ. Vicar of Christ means antichrist. Noah Webster defined the prefix "anti" as a preposition meaning not only against but also in place of the noun it follows.[601] The Oxford English Dictionary[602] defines "anti" as meaning "opposite, against, in exchange, instead, representing, rivaling, simulating." Antichrist means one who is against Christ and at the same time purports to take the place of Christ. **Therefore, vicar of Christ = antichrist.**

Is there one who Jesus promised would act in his name? Yes, the Holy Ghost, not the pope of Rome!

> These things have I spoken unto you, being *yet* present with you. **But the Comforter, which is the Holy Ghost, whom the Father will send in my name, he shall teach you all things, and bring all things to your remembrance, whatsoever I have said unto you**. (John 14:25-26)

> Nevertheless I tell you the truth; It is expedient for you that I go away: for **if I go not away, the Comforter will not come unto you; but if I depart, I will send him unto you**. (John 16:7)

Jesus warned his disciples time and again about many who would come in his name.

> And Jesus answered and said unto them, Take heed that no man deceive you. For **many shall come in my name, saying, I am Christ**; and shall deceive many. (Matthew 24:4-5)

Pope John Paul II made an incredible claim: that the Pope is the fulfilment of Christ's promise that he will be with us until the end of the world. John Paul II says that Jesus is personally present in his church, implying that Jesus is present through the Pope. As we see from the above passages in John 14:25-26 and 16:7, the fulfillment of that prophecy in Matthew is through the presence of the Holy Spirit, who dwells in all believers. The Pope is essentially claiming to be both Jesus and the Holy Spirit.

> Once again, concerning names: The Pope is called the 'Vicar of Christ.' This title should be considered within the entire context of the Gospel. Before ascending into heaven, Jesus said to the apostles: 'I am with you always, until the end of the age' (Matthew 28:20). Though invisible, He is personally present in His Church." *Pope John Paul II.*[603]

The Pope even takes the title of God the Father. For example, the *Catechism of the Catholic Church*, at § 10 refers to Pope John II as the "Holy Father, Pope John II." The pope goes by other majestic titles such as "Your Holiness." Pope John Paul II, himself, admitted that such titles are inimical to the Gospel. He even cited the Bible passage that condemns such practices. He simply explained that the Catholic traditions of men implicitly authorize this violation of God's commands.

> Have no fear when people call me the 'Vicar of Christ,' when they say to me 'Holy Father,' or 'Your Holiness,' or use titles similar to these, which seem even inimical to the Gospel. Christ declared: 'Call no one on earth your father; you have one Father in heaven. Do not be called 'Master;' you have but one master, the Messiah' (Mt 23:9-10). These expressions, nevertheless, have evolved out of a long tradition, becoming part of common usage. One must not be afraid of these words either. *Pope John Paul II.*[604]

The term "Holy Father" was used in the Holy Scripture only one time, it was used by Jesus the night before his crucifixion to refer to God the Father. Implicit in taking God's name is taking his position and authority. As Jesus said in John 14:28, God the Father is greater than Jesus. By taking the title

"Holy Father," the Pope is implicitly presenting himself as greater than Jesus Christ.

> And now I am no more in the world, but these are in the world, and I come to thee. **Holy Father**, keep through thine own name those whom thou hast given me, that they may be one, as we are. (John 17:11)

> Ye have heard how I said unto you, I go away, and come again unto you. If ye loved me, ye would rejoice, because I said, I go unto the Father: for **my Father is greater than I.** (John 14:28)

The very title "Pope" is a Latin word which means papa. It is the term used by small children to refer to their father. It is the Latin equivalent of "dada" or "daddy." In Aramaic Hebrew "papa" would be translated "abba." Abba is used 3 times in the Holy Bible. Each time abba refers to God the Father.

> And he said, **Abba, Father**, all things *are* possible unto thee; take away this cup from me: nevertheless not what I will, but what thou wilt. (Mark 14:36)

> For ye have not received the spirit of bondage again to fear; but ye have received the Spirit of adoption, whereby we cry, **Abba, Father**. (Romans 8:15)

> And because ye are sons, God hath sent forth the Spirit of his Son into your hearts, crying, **Abba, Father**. (Galatians 4:6)

Note the trusting humility connoted in the above

passages. The Pope of Rome wants his subjects to humble themselves before him as trusting children. He is the papa of their faith. He has taken the name that is rightfully God's in his attempt to turn men from God to him. The Pope not only desires submission to his authority, but it is not uncommon for the Pope to humiliate his subjects by requiring them to kiss his feet.[605]

> Whosoever therefore shall humble himself as this little child, the same is greatest in the kingdom of heaven. (Matthew 18:4)

> Verily I say unto you, Whosoever shall not receive the kingdom of God as a little child, he shall not enter therein. (Mark 10:15)

Babylonian polytheism has been injected by crypto-Jews into the Roman Catholic religion. An example of this Babylonian/Judaic polytheism in the Roman Catholic Church is the worship of Mary. Catholics pray to Mary because she is a goddess in the Catholic Church. Catholics will acknowledge that they pray to Mary, but deny that she is a goddess. That is because this truth has largely been veiled from them.

The Mary of the Catholic Church is not the Mary of the bible. She is in fact the Jews' queen of heaven. Athol Bloomer reveals that Mary is equivalent to the Sabbath Queen in Judaism.[606] The Kabbalah also has a warrior queen called Matronita who commands the hosts of heaven on behalf of Israel against its enemies.[607] Bloomer states that "Matronita is an image of both Mother Church and the Mother of God."[608]

Bloomer equates Matronita with Shekinah and Mary. Daniel Matt in his book *Zohar, The Book of Enlightenment* reveals that the Sabbath Queen and Shekinah are one and the same.[609] The Catholic goddess Mary is the "queen of heaven" in the Kabbalah, to whom the Jews have been making cake and drink offerings since the time of Jeremiah. "And when we burned incense to the **queen of heaven**, and poured out drink offerings unto her, did we **make her cakes to worship her**, and **pour out drink offerings unto her**, without our men?" (Jeremiah 44:19)

The Mary of the bible is not a goddess, she was a woman elected by God to be the mother of Jesus. She died like everyone else and any attempt to communicate with her through prayer is the sin of necromancy. Deuteronomy 18:10-12. "**For there is one God, and one mediator between God and men, the man Christ Jesus**; (1 Timothy 2:5).

The practice of communicating with Mary is part and parcel of the general practice of praying to a pantheon of Catholic gods and goddesses, which the Catholic Church calls "saints," who purport to join along with Mary as the queen of heaven to answer the prayers of the faithful.

> The holy council . . . orders all bishops and others who have the official charge of teaching. . . to instruct . . . the faithful that the **saints**, reigning together with Christ, **pray to God for men** and women; **that it is good and useful to invoke them humbly and to have recourse to their prayers, to their help and assistance, in order to obtain favours from God** through his Son our lord Jesus Christ, who alone is our Redeemer and Saviour. Those who deny that the saints enjoying eternal happiness in heaven **are to be invoked**, or who claim that saints do not pray for human beings or that **calling upon them to pray for each of us** is idolatry or is opposed to the word of God and is prejudicial to the honour of Jesus Christ, the one Mediator between God and humankind; or who say that it is foolish to

> make supplication orally or mentally to those who are reigning in heaven; all those entertain impious thoughts. *THE GENERAL COUNCIL OF TRENT, TWENTY FIFTH SESSION, DECREE ON THE INVOCATION, THE VENERATION AND THE RELICS OF SAINTS AND ON SACRED IMAGES*, 1560.

> [The saints'] . . . intercession is their most exalted service to God's plan. **We can and should ask them to intercede for us and for the whole world.** *CATECHISM OF THE CATHOLIC CHURCH*, § 2683, 1994.

The prayers to the dead so -called "Catholic saints" is simply an attempt to communicate with the dead. God has expressly commanded that we not attempt to communicate with the dead. To communicate with the dead is a sin called **necromancy**. There is only one mediator between man and God to whom we should pray, and that is Jesus Christ.

> There shall not be found among you any one that maketh his son or his daughter to pass through the fire, or that useth divination, or an observer of times, or an enchanter, or a witch, Or a charmer, or a consulter with familiar spirits, or a wizard, or a **necromancer**. **For all that do these things are an abomination unto the LORD**: and because of these abominations the LORD thy God doth drive them out from before thee. (Deuteronomy 18:10-12)

> **For there is one God, and one mediator between God and men, the man Christ Jesus;** (1 Timothy 2:5)

Why would one pray to the saints? God won't listen to their counsel, because he doesn't need counsel. Ephesians 1:11. God puts no trust in his saints.

> Behold, **he putteth no trust in his saints**; yea, the heavens are not clean in his sight. (Job 15:15)

How did this clearly sinful practice of communicating with the dead through so-called prayer originate? It is a direct outgrowth of the necromancy practiced by the Jews. Necromancy is so ingrained in Judaism that among ancient Jews some Rabbis considered knowledge in necromancy to be a necessary qualification for a seat in the Sahhendrin, which was the grand counsel and court of justice among the ancient Jews.[610]

The Roman Catholic Church has a different gospel, with a different Jesus than that which is found in the Bible. *See* 2 Corinthians 11:4. Their different gospel was born of the Kabbalah and has different doctrines and a different Mary from the Mary in the Bible. In the Bible, Mary is the handmaid of the Lord. *See* Luke 1:38. The Roman Catholic Church Mary, however, is an imperious queen of heaven, who rules over all things.

The Catholic Mary (as distinguished from the biblical Mary) is a heathen goddess, who in 1950 was "infallibly" declared by Pope Pius XII to have been assumed body and soul into heaven and crowned **"Queen over all things."**

> Finally the Immaculate Virgin, preserved free from all stain of original sin, when the course of her earthly life was finished, was taken up body and soul into heavenly glory, and exalted by the Lord as **Queen over all things**, so that she might be the more fully conformed to her

Son, the Lord of lords and conqueror of sin and death. Pope Pius XII -- *Munificentissimus Deus*, 1950.

The problem with that "infallible" pronouncement of the pope is that it is impossible for Mary to be "queen over all things." The Bible states unequivocally that Jesus Christ "is the blessed and **only Potentate**, the Lord of lords and King of kings." 1 Timothy 6:15. A potentate is a sovereign monarch.[611] Jesus Christ is the "only Potentate." Only means only! There is not room in heaven for another Potentate. Mary, therefore, cannot be "queen over all things." Jesus is the **"only Potentate"** over all things!

Satan is using his Catholic Church and its doctrine of Mariolatry to attempt a futile spiritual *coup d'etat* to supplant Jesus and enthrone its Mary as the "Queen of Heaven." The Catholic Church is dedicated to the worship and service of "Mary," the queen of heaven. Jesus is ancillary and almost incidental to the worship of the Catholic queen of heaven. For example, the coin commemorating the pontificate of John Paul II has on the front has a declaration that he is the Pontifex Maximus. "On the reverse side is his papal heraldic shield. The large letter M on the shield stands for Mary, the mother of God. The words at the bottom 'TOTUS TUUS' are transposed and excerpted from a latin prayer composed by Saint Louis-Marie Grignion de Montfort: *tuus totus ego sum, et omnia mea tua sunt, O Virgo super omnia benedicta*, which in English reads 'I belong to you entirely, and all that I possess is yours, Virgin blessed above all.'"[612] The pope dedicates his fealty not to Jesus but to "Mary," the Catholic "Queen of Heaven."

In 1978, on the feast day of the Immaculate Conception, Pope John Paul II dedicated and entrusted the Roman Catholic Church and all its property not to their Catholic version of Jesus, but rather to their Catholic version of Mary:

> The Pope, at the beginning of his episcopal service in St. Peter's Chair in Rome, wishes to entrust the Church particularly to her in whom there was accomplished the stupendous and complete victory of good over evil, of love over hatred, of grace over sin; to her of whom Paul VI said that she is ' the beginning of the better world;' to the Blessed Virgin. He entrusts to her himself, as the servant of servants, and all those whom he serves, all those who serve with him. **He entrusts to her the Roman Church, as token and principle of all the churches in the world, in their universal unity. He entrusts it to her and offers it to her as her property.** Insegnamenti Giovanni Paolo II (1978), Vatican City: Libreria Editrice Vaticana, 313.[613]

The Catholic Church has a series of ritualistic mysteries that are recited after each of 15 Catholic "stations of the cross." These "mysteries" are said while counting beads that are called the rosary. The primary focus of the Catholic Rosary is not Jesus, it is Mary. Mary's roles in Christ's birth, death, and resurrection are highlighted, exaggerated, and in some instances fabricated in 12 of the 15 "mysteries." In fact, the formal title of the Rosary is: **"The Roses of Prayer for the Queen of Heaven."**[614] The prayers to Mary outnumber the supposed prayers to God by roughly 10 to 1. After each mystery is recited, Catholics say one "Our Father" prayer followed by ten "Hail Mary" prayers. The "Hail May" is a rote prayer to the Catholic goddess, whom they call Mary. They blaspheme God by praying to their Mary goddess and prove themselves heathen by repeating the blasphemous prayers over and over again. "But when ye pray, use not vain repetitions, as the heathen do: for they think that they shall be heard for their much speaking." (Matthew 6:7)

It is notable that the rosary said in honor of the queen of heaven has stations of the cross called "mysteries." There is a woman mentioned in the Bible whose very name is "mystery."

> And the woman was arrayed in purple and scarlet colour, and decked with gold and precious stones and pearls, having a golden cup in her hand full of abominations and filthiness of her fornication: And upon her forehead *was* a name written, **MYSTERY, BABYLON THE GREAT, THE MOTHER OF HARLOTS AND ABOMINATIONS OF THE EARTH.** (Revelation 17:4-5)

Later, when the Bible speaks of the destruction of the "mystery" harlot, the harlot says in her heart that she sits as a **"queen."**

> Reward her even as she rewarded you, and double unto her double according to her works: in the cup which she hath filled fill to her double. How much she hath glorified herself, and lived deliciously, so much torment and sorrow give her: **for she saith in her heart, I sit a queen**, and am no widow, and shall see no sorrow. Therefore shall her plagues come in one day, death, and mourning, and famine; and she shall be utterly burned with fire: for strong *is* the Lord God who judgeth her. (Revelation 18:6-8)

God reveals the mystery of the woman. God identifies the woman as a great city. "And the woman which thou sawest is that great city, which reigneth over the kings of the earth." (Revelation 17:18) God also reveals the mystery of the woman.

I will tell thee the mystery of the woman, and of the beast that carrieth her, which hath the seven heads and ten horns. The beast that thou sawest was, and is not; and shall ascend out of the bottomless pit, and go into perdition: and they that dwell on the earth shall wonder, whose names were not written in the book of life from the foundation of the world, when they behold the beast that was, and is not, and yet is. And here *is* the mind which hath wisdom. **The seven heads are seven mountains, on which the woman sitteth**. (Revelation 17:7-9)

So we know that the mystery harlot is a great city that sits on seven mountains. There is only one city that matches that description and that is Rome. Rome is famous for the seven mountains upon which it sits (the Capitoline, the Quirinal, the Viminal, the Esquiline, the Caelian, the Avenue, and the Palatine).[615] The glorification of the queen of heaven is in a sense a glorification by proxy of the Roman Catholic Church. That is why the Catholic hierarchy refers to their organization as "Mother Church."[616] It is true that the Catholic Church is a mother, **"THE MOTHER OF HARLOTS AND ABOMINATIONS OF THE EARTH."** (Revelation 17:4-5) That mother of harlots "saith in her heart, I sit a **queen**." Revelation 18:7. There is a spiritual parallel between the wicked harlot queen in the book of Revelation and Mary the queen of heaven glorified by the Catholic Church. The harlot of Revelation and Mary the queen of heaven both draw men from Jesus Christ, who "is the blessed and only Potentate, the Lord of lords and King of kings." 1 Timothy 6:15.

One of the "mysteries" recited during the Catholic rosary is called "the Fifth Glorious Mystery - The Coronation." In that mystery it is claimed by the Catholic Church that "**Mary is the Queen of Heaven.**"

Mary had served Jesus all her life. She had loved and served God with her whole heart and soul. She had never committed the slightest sin. So in heaven she was to have her reward. Body and soul, Mary entered heaven. Her Son, Jesus, met her and took her in His grateful arms. The heavenly Father said, "This is My dear devoted daughter." The Divine Son said, "This is My dear faithful Mother." The Holy Spirit said, "This is my sweet, pure bride." And the saints and angels all cried, **"This is our Queen!"** So Jesus, the King of Kings, seated her on her throne. On her head He placed a glorious crown of stars. But Mary looked down to see her children on earth. For now she could help her sons and daughters to reach heaven. **Mary is the Queen of Heaven**. But she is our loving Mother who protects us with her power.[617]

One of the final prayers of the Rosary is a prayer to the Catholic goddess "Mary" called "**Hail Holy Queen**."

Hail, holy Queen, Mother of Mercy! Our life, our sweetness, and our hope! To thee do we cry, poor banished children of Eve; to thee so we send up our sighs, mourning and weeping in this valley of tears. Turn, then, most gracious Advocate, thine eyes of mercy toward us; and after this our exile show unto us the blessed fruit of thy womb, Jesus; O clement, O loving, O sweet Virgin Mary.[618]

The Catholics also have other prayers not said during the rosary to their goddess, the Queen of Heaven:

Queen of heaven, rejoice. Alleluia. The Son

whom you were privileged to bear, Alleluia, has risen as he said, Alleluia. Pray to God for us, Alleluia. Rejoice and be glad, Virgin Mary, Alleluia. For the Lord has truly risen, Alleluia. O God, it was by the Resurrection of your Son, our Lord Jesus Christ, that you brought joy to the world. Grant that through the intercession of the Virgin Mary, his Mother, we may attain the joy of eternal life. Through Christ, our Lord. Amen.[619]

The Catholic "Mary" (queen of heaven) is viewed by the Roman Catholic Church as "the **restorer of the world that was lost, and the dispenser of all benefits** . . . the **most powerful mediator (*mediatrix*) and advocate (*conciliatrix*) for the whole world** . . . **above all others in sanctity and in union with Christ** . . . **the primary minister in the distribution of the divine graces**,"[620] "**the beloved daughter of the Father and Temple of the Holy Spirit**,"[621] "**the mother of all the living**,"[622] "**the new Eve**,"[623] "**Mother of the Church**,"[624] "the '**Mother of Mercy**,' the **All Holy One**."[625] She supposedly "**surpasses all creatures, both in heaven and on earth**,"[626] conquered death and was ". . . raised body and soul to the glory of heaven, to **shine refulgent as Queen** at the right hand of her Son, the immortal King of ages."[627]

> [I]ndeed, she is clearly the **mother of the members of Christ since she has by her charity joined in bringing about the birth of believers in the Church** who are members of its head. Wherefore she is hailed as pre-eminent and as a wholly unique member of the Church, and as its type and outstanding model in faith and charity. The Catholic Church taught by the Holy Spirit, honours her with filial affection and **devotion as a most beloved mother.** THE SECOND VATICAN

COUNCIL, 1964 (emphasis added).[628]

What does God think of this Catholic goddess, Mary?

> Thou shalt worship the Lord thy God, and him **only** shalt thou serve. (Luke 4:8)

> Thou shalt have **no other gods** before me. . . . Thou shalt not bow down thyself to them nor serve them: for I the LORD thy God am a jealous God. (Exodus 20:3-5)

When a woman praised Mary loudly, Jesus corrected her, making it clear that the woman who gave birth to him is not blessed above those who are saved by the grace of God.

> And it came to pass, as he spake these things, a certain woman of the company lifted up her voice, and said unto him, Blessed *is* the womb that bare thee, and the paps which thou hast sucked. But he said, Yea rather, blessed *are* they that hear the word of God, and keep it. (Luke 11:27-28)

Roman Catholic Mariolatry is derived from the goddess worship performed by the Jews when they worship Matronita, the queen of heaven. The Catholic Church has simply changed the name of the Jewish queen from Matronita to Mary. The Catholic Mary has nothing in common with the biblical Mary. The Catholic queen of heaven, however, has everything in common with the queen of heaven described in the Bible. In the Bible, God condemns homage and service to the queen of heaven.

> Seest thou not what they do in the cities of Judah and in the streets of Jerusalem? The

children gather wood, and the fathers kindle the fire, and the women knead their dough, to make cakes to the **queen of heaven**, and to pour out drink offerings unto other gods, that they may provoke me to anger. Do they provoke me to anger? saith the LORD: do they not provoke themselves to the confusion of their own faces? Therefore thus saith the Lord GOD; Behold, mine anger and my fury shall be poured out upon this place, upon man, and upon beast, and upon the trees of the field, and upon the fruit of the ground; and it shall burn, and shall not be quenched. (Jeremiah 7:17-20)

Serving the queen of heaven is an abomination to God. There are consequences for that great sin against the Lord. In chapter 44 of Jeremiah we read that the Jews burned incense and served the **"queen of heaven."** This great sin kindled the fury and anger of the Lord, who responded by wasting and bringing desolation upon the cities of Judah, including Jerusalem. The Jews have not learned, they have inculcated their queen of heaven anew into their Roman Catholic Church.

The official doctrine of the Catholic church goes beyond Mary as a co-mediatrix with Christ. According to Catholic dogma, Mary is also co-redemptrix with Christ. That means that the Catholic Church blasphemously teaches that Mary suffered in our stead as a propitiation for our sins. The Catholic Church teaches that when Jesus was on the cross, Mary suffered with him and therefore her suffering was an atonement for our sins. This is known as the "5th Marian Dogma." An explanation carrying the Official Roman Catholic Imprimatur from Ernesto Cardinal Corripio Ahumada is found on the website *Vox Populi Mariae Mediatrici*:

> But the climax of Mary's role as Co-redemptrix under her divine son takes place at the foot of

the Cross, where the total suffering of the mother's heart is obediently united to the suffering of the Son's heart in fulfillment of the Father's plan of redemption (cf. Gal. 4:4). As the fruit of this redemptive suffering, Mary is given by the crucified Savior as the spiritual mother of all peoples: "Woman, behold your son!' Then he said to the disciple, 'behold, your mother!" (Jn. 19:27). As described by Pope John Paul II, Mary was "spiritually crucified with her crucified son" at Calvary, and "her role as Co-redemptrix did not cease with the glorification of her Son." John Paul II, Papal Address, Jan. 31, 1985, Guayaquil, Ecuador, (O.R., March 13, 1985). Even after the accomplishment of the acquisition of the graces of redemption at Calvary, Mary's co-redemptive role continues in the distribution of those saving graces to the hearts of humanity.[629]

Dr. Mark Miravalle, Professor of Theology and Mariology at the Franciscan University of Steubenville states:

> Are you afraid to call Mary the Co-redemptrix? You shouldn't be. John Paul II, Mother Teresa, Padre Pio, Sr. Lucia, and the endless list of other saints, mystics, popes, theologians, and Christian faithful who refer to her as Co-redemptrix do so with the assurance of Scripture, the Papal Magisterium, and the consolation of the Holy Spirit. It is safe, it is true, and it is a title that she overwhelmingly deserves in virtue of the greatest human suffering in the history of man after that of her Son.[630]

The problem with the Roman Catholic heathen belief in the co-atonement of Mary is that the bible makes it clear that the atonement was attained only by the blood of Jesus Christ. It was The one and only sacrifice of Christ on the cross that atones for the sins of the believers. In Romans 5:8-21, God drives home the point several times that we receive the free gift of salvation, through the **one** atonement of Jesus Christ, who is the only **one** who could atone for our sins, because he is the **one** and only man who is the obedient **one** and the righteous **one**.

> But God commendeth his love toward us, in that, while we were yet sinners, Christ died for us. Much more then, being now justified by his blood, we shall be saved from wrath through him. For if, when we were enemies, **we were reconciled to God by the death of his Son**, much more, being reconciled, we shall be saved by his life. And not only so, but we also joy in God through our Lord Jesus Christ, **by whom we have now received the atonement**. Wherefore, as by one man sin entered into the world, and death by sin; and so death passed upon all men, for that all have sinned: (For until the law sin was in the world: but sin is not imputed when there is no law. Nevertheless death reigned from Adam to Moses, even over them that had not sinned after the similitude of Adam's transgression, who is the figure of him that was to come. But not as the offence, so also is the free gift. For if through the offence of one many be dead, much more the grace of God, and **the gift by grace, which is by one man, Jesus Christ**, hath abounded unto many. And not as it was by one that sinned, so is the gift: for the judgment was by one to condemnation, but the free gift is of many offences unto justification.

> For if by one man's offence death reigned by one; much more they which receive abundance of grace and of **the gift of righteousness shall reign in life by <u>one</u>, Jesus Christ.**) Therefore as by the offence of one judgment came upon all men to condemnation; even so by **the righteousness of <u>one</u> the free gift came upon all men unto justification of life.** For as by one man's disobedience many were made sinners, so **by the obedience of <u>one</u> shall many be made righteous.** Moreover the law entered, that the offence might abound. But where sin abounded, grace did much more abound: That as sin hath reigned unto death, even so **might grace reign through righteousness unto eternal life by Jesus Christ our Lord.** (Romans 5:8-21)

It seems that the Jews have long planned on controlling the Roman Catholic Church. The following is a passage from paragraph three of Protocol 17:

> When the time comes finally to destroy the papal court the finger of an invisible hand will point the nations towards this court. When, however, the nations fling themselves upon it, we shall come forward in the guise of its defenders as if to save excessive bloodshed. By this diversion we shall penetrate to its very bowels and be sure we shall never come out again until we have gnawed through the entire strength of this place.[631]

Bella Dodd was a high government official in the Communist Party USA and sat on its National Council. She later left the communist party and in 1953 testified before the United States Senate about widespread communist infiltration of labor unions and other institutions, including public education, all of which were designed to undermine and demoralize the United States.

Dodd revealed in a speech that one of her jobs as a Communist agent was to encourage young radicals to enter Catholic seminaries. She stated that during her time in the communist party, she had encouraged more than 1,000 young radicals to infiltrate the seminaries and religious orders. Dodd stated:

> In the 1930's, we put eleven hundred men into the priesthood in order to destroy the Church from within. The idea was for these men to be ordained, and then climb the ladder of influence and authority as Monsignors and Bishops.[632]

Manning Johnson confirmed Dodd's account. Johnson belonged to the Communist party in the 1940s and early 50s. He later defected from the communists and testified in 1953 before the House un-American Activities Committee regarding the communist infiltration of the Catholic Church. Johnson stated that the Kremlin organized the infiltration of the Catholic Church principally through the seminaries. That way, as the communists in the Catholic Church advanced, they would be able to influence the Catholic ideology. Johnson stated that the plan succeeded beyond the expectations of the communists.[633]

Communism is essentially Talmudic Judaism. The communist infiltration is just one prong of a manifold strategy to maintain Jewish control of the Roman Catholic Church. Today the Jews have almost complete dominion over the Roman Church. Another prong of the Zionist strategy was for Jews to obtain control over Vatican finances. Researcher Eustace Mullins determined that the Rothschilds took over all the financial operations of the worldwide Catholic Church in

1823.[634] He who pays the piper calls the tune. The communist infiltration of the Catholic Church was to ensure that the Jewish financial control over the Vatican is put into practical effect in maintaining the Catholic Church as an auxiliary of Judaism.

The Zionists have in like manner undermined the theology in the Protestant churches. The Judaic influence in the Protestant churches has elements common to the Judaized Catholic Church. It is no surprise, therefore, that we see Zionist Protestant preachers of one mind with the Roman Catholic Church. For example, Billy Graham has stated that "I find that my beliefs are essentially the same as those of orthodox Roman Catholics"[635]

In 1980, Billy Graham called Pope John Paul II, the greatest spiritual leader of the modern world.[636] Graham usually has Catholics on the platform during his "gospel" crusades and has a regular practice of giving the decision cards that are handed in during the crusade to the area Catholic bishop for follow up by Catholic priests.[637] In Graham's 1994 Crusades in Minneapolis and Cleveland 6,000 respondents at each crusade were referred to the Catholic Church. In Graham's September 1996 Charlotte, North Carolina crusade 1,700 respondents were referred back to the Catholic Church.[638]

With Graham, it gets worse, in a 1978 McCall's Magazine interview Graham stated: "I used to think that pagans in far-off countries were lost -- were going to hell -- if they did not have the Gospel of Jesus Christ preached to them. I no longer believe that ... I believe there are other ways of recognizing the existence of God -- through nature, for instance -- and plenty of other opportunities, therefore, of saying yes to God." Graham's theology is directly contrary to the gospel of Jesus. "Jesus saith unto him, I am the way, the truth, and the life: no man cometh unto the Father, but by me." (John 14:6) "But if our gospel be hid, it is hid to them that are lost: In whom the god of this world hath blinded the minds of them which believe not, lest the light of the glorious gospel of Christ, who is the image of God, should shine unto them." (2 Corinthians 4:3-4)

Graham has even praised the blasphemous Catholic mass. "This past week I preached in the great Catholic cathedral a funeral sermon for a close friend of mine who was a Catholic, and they had several Bishops and Archbishops to participate. And as I sat there going through the funeral Mass, that was a very beautiful thing, and certainly straight and clear in the gospel. There was a wonderful little priest that would tell me when to stand and when to kneel and what to do."[639] God states: "Can two walk together, except they be agreed?" (Amos 3:3) Graham walks hand in hand with the false teachers of the Roman Church.

Billy Graham's affinity for the Roman Catholic Mass can be understood in light of the fact that Graham is a 33rd Degree Mason. Freemasonry and Roman Catholicism are both based upon ancient mystery religions. As has been proven in a previous chapter, Freemasonry is based upon the Kabbalah. The Kabbalah is also the doctrinal source for the liturgy of the Roman Catholic Mass.[640]

18 The Occult Catholic Liturgy

The central concept of both Jewish and Catholic mysticism is what the Jews call the "Divine Presence," which is also known as *Shekinah*.[641] The Eucharistic presence of Jesus is the Catholic corollary to the *Shekinah* presence of God in Judaism.[642] *The Catholic Encyclopedia* reveals that the Jewish liturgy is the source for the Eucharistic liturgy of the Catholic Church.[643] The word *Shekinah* appears nowhere in either the Old or New Testaments. *Shekinah* is a wholly Jewish concept that was born of their Kabbalah; it is also found in the Jewish Talmud and Targums.

The exoteric meaning of the Catholic Eucharist is that the Eucharist is God actually present as *Shekinah* in the form of bread, and is to be worshiped as God.[644] That doctrine was confirmed by Cardinal Ratzinger. Before becoming Pope Benedict XVI, Cardinal Ratzinger explained how the attendant worship of the host during the Catholic liturgy is based upon the Eucharist being *Shekinah*. Cardinal Ratzinger stated: "His presence (Shekinah) really does now dwell among us - in the humblest parish church no less than in the grandest cathedral."[645]

The publicly proclaimed doctrine of the Roman Catholic liturgy is that it is based upon the belief that the Eucharist contains the body, blood, soul, and divinity of the Lord God Almighty Jesus Christ in the form of bread. The church teaches that the appearance of bread and wine remain, but that they have actually been transubstantiated into a god, whom they call Jesus.

> **In the most blessed sacrament of the Eucharist 'the body and blood, together with the soul and divinity, of our Lord Jesus Christ and, therefore, *the whole Christ is truly, really, and substantially* contained.'** CATECHISM OF THE CATHOLIC CHURCH, § 1374, 1994 (italics in original, bold emphasis added).

The Catholic Church is saying, in no uncertain terms, that Jesus Christ himself, God Almighty, is present during the Catholic mass in the outward form of bread and wine.

> By the consecration the transubstantiation of the bread and wine into the Body and Blood of Christ is brought about. Under the consecrated species of bread and wine **Christ himself, living and glorious, is present in a true, real, and substantial manner: his Body and his Blood, with his soul and his divinity.** CATECHISM OF THE CATHOLIC CHURCH, § 1413, 1994 (emphasis added).

That Catholic Jesus is not the Jesus of the bible. The Eucharistic Host is idolatry, and it violates God's commandments. The Second Commandment is very specific as to what conduct toward graven images is prohibited. "Thou shalt not make unto thee any graven image, or any likeness of any thing that is in heaven above, or that is in the earth beneath, or that is in the water under the earth: Thou shalt not bow down thyself to them, nor serve them." Exodus 20:4. That same command was repeated in the New Testament. "Little children, keep yourselves from idols. Amen." 1 John 5:21. Christians are not even to come near to idolatry. "Wherefore, my dearly beloved, flee from idolatry." 1 Corinthians 10:14.

It seems that God was addressing the very idolatry of the Catholic Church by commanding us to abstain from blood, which the Catholic Church teaches is present in the Eucharist. "But that we write unto them, that they abstain from pollutions of idols, and from fornication, and from things strangled, and from blood." (Acts 15:20) This re-crucifixion of Christ during the Catholic mass is a re-enactment of the humiliation suffered by Christ on the cross. This re-enactment is not only unnecessary, it is a blasphemy. The bible states that we are to look to Jesus in faith, not in ceremony. Jesus despised the shame of the cross. "Looking unto Jesus the author and finisher of our faith; who for the joy that was set before him **endured the cross, despising the shame**, and is set down at the right hand of the throne of God." (Hebrews 12:2)

Jesus was crucified once for all time. The Catholic mass is a demonstration that the Catholic Church does not believe in the sufficiency of Jesus' sacrifice on the cross. They require that he be crucified over and over again, day after day, week after week, month after month, year after year. The Catholic mass is more than an affront to Christ, it is a ceremonial attack on Christ. It is an anti-Christ ceremony, whereby the Roman church puts Christ to an open shame by crucifying him anew. The bible states that it is a terrible sin to crucify Jesus again, because it once again puts him to an open shame. "If they shall fall away, to renew them again unto repentance; seeing **they crucify to themselves the Son of God afresh, and put him to an open shame."** (Hebrews 6:6)

As bad as that is, the blasphemous exoteric doctrine of

the Eucharist does not approach the depravity of the esoteric meaning of the Eucharist. The esoteric meaning of the *Shekinah* presence in the Eucharist is only understood by those initiated into the occult theology of Judaism and Catholicism. Michael Hoffman explains that the charter objective of Cabalistic Judaism is the consummation of the spiritual and sexual union of the female goddess, *Shekhinah*, with her male consort, *Tif'eret*, into one androgynous god.[646] That objective is accomplished esoterically during the Roman Catholic Mass. Athol Bloomer explains that the esoteric meaning behind the Catholic Mass, which is hidden from the Catholic faithful, but is understood by those initiated into the secret doctrine, is that the Mass is a mystical/sexual union between the god, *Tif'eret*, and the goddess, *Shekinah*, through the divine phallus, *Yesod*.[647]

This esoteric mystical/sexual union transubstantiates the Eucharistic Host into an androgynous amalgam of gods and goddesses. Alexander Hislop explains that the Eucharistic host actually carries the initials of the heathen trinity of gods and goddesses that it symbolizes. The host carries the Symbol IHS, which refers to Isis, Horus, and Seb.[648] That fact is explained in great detail in this author's book *Solving the Mystery of Babylon the Great*.

What is the exoteric meaning of IHS presented to the public by the Catholic Church? Catholic Priest Ryan Erlenbush explains that a popular explanation for IHS often given is simply wrong: "It is popular legend that the IHS stands for the Latin phrase *Iesus Hominum Salvator*, "Jesus the Savior of (all) Men". While this is a fine devotion, it is not historically accurate."[649] *The Catholic Encyclopedia* confirms Erlenbush's position: "IHS was sometimes wrongly understood as '*Jesus Hominum* (or *Hierosolymae*) *Salvator*', i.e. Jesus, the Saviour of men (or of Jerusalem=*Hierosolyma*)."[650]

That tells us what the Roman Catholic Church states that IHS does not mean, but what does the Catholic Church say it means? The public exoteric meaning for IHS as expressed in *The Catholic Encyclopedia* (carrying the official imprimatur of John Cardinal Farley, Archbishop of New York) is that the letters represent "a monogram of the name of Jesus Christ."[651] The explanation given in the encyclopedia is that Jesus' name was represented by "IC and XC or IHS and XPS for *Iesous Christos*."[652] That explanation, however, is unhelpful. It does not explain where the letters IHS come from. That section of the encyclopedia then explains how through the ages, IHS has been used by certain religious orders but does not explain its derivation. The encyclopedia simply states that IHS was used. It purports to be an explanation, but it explains nothing.

In another section of the *The Catholic Encyclopedia*, under the same imprimatur of John Cardinal Farley, it states: "In the Middle Ages the Name of Jesus was written: IHESUS; the monogram [IHS] contains the first and last letter of the Holy Name."[653] The problem with that explanation is that it is based upon a misspelling of Jesus' name. In fact, that point is made in another section of *The Catholic Encyclopedia*, where it states: "Eventually the right meaning was lost, and erroneous interpretation of IHS led to the faulty orthography 'Jhesus.'"[654] The modern Latin "J" is equivalent to the ancient Latin "I" in the Latin alphabet. "IHESUS" contains all uppercase letters and is intended by the Catholic Church as equivalent to "Jhesus." The problem is that Jesus has never been spelled anywhere in the Holy Scriptures with all uppercase letters.

The Catholic authorities cannot seem to get their exoteric explanation straight. In one section of *The Catholic Encyclopedia* it states that "Jhesus" is erroneous, yet in another section of that same encyclopedia, it cites that same misspelling "IHESUS" as the basis for IHS.

It is clear that "Jhesus" and "IHESUS" are both misspellings of Jesus. "Jhesus" ("IHESUS") is a combination of Greek and Latin letters, which makes no sense. The "h"

("H") is a redundant letter; it duplicates the Latin "e" ("E"). All of the other letters in Jhesus (IHESUS) are Latin except for the Greek letter "h" ("H").

What is the exoteric explanation for IHS? Catholic Priest Ryan Erlenbush presents the standard Catholic exoteric explanation for IHS:

> The insignia 'IHS' comes from the Latinized version of the Greek Iησους . . . taking the first three letters in capitals IHS(ous). . . This is the true meaning of IHS, it is the first three letters of the Greek spelling of the Holy Name of Jesus. The insignia is nothing more (and nothing less) than the symbol of the Holy Name.[655]

A letter-by-letter analysis of Erlenbush's standard Catholic explanation proves that it is a fraud. The first letter in Greek "I" is iota and carries the consonant "J" sound for the English, Latin, and Greek in the context of Jesus' name. In ancient Latin, there was no letter "J" and so it seems that the transliteration of the Greek "I" to Latin "I" makes sense. "I" is the same letter in both Greek and Latin.

The long "e" sound in Greek was represented by the letter η (eta), and so the Greek spelling of Jesus' name would appear in Greek as Iησοῦς. That would tend to offer an explanation for the "I" and the "h" as the first two letters of Jesus' name in the Greek alphabet. However, it makes no sense to represent Jesus' name as IHS in the Greek alphabet, since the second letter of his name is a lowercase Greek letter (eta) which appears as a lower case "h" (η) and not as an uppercase letter "H." Further, if IHS is supposed to be a Latinized monogram for the first three letters of Jesus' name, the second letter should be an "E" not an "H," because the Greek eta (η) is translated to "E" in Latin (and English), not "H."

The third Greek letter in Jesus name is sigma, which looks like a small letter "o" with a tail at the top (σ). The lowercase sigma has a different appearance when it is the last letter in a word (ς), as in Jesus' name, Ιησοῦς. The Greek uppercase letter for sigma, however, is always the same (Σ). Sigma has the "s" sound in English, Latin, and Greek. However, the "S" in IHS is not the Greek uppercase sigma (Σ), it is the Latin (and English) uppercase letter "S." The Greek uppercase sigma (Σ) is unique and does not look like a Latin uppercase letter "S."

This is where the Catholic exoteric explanation falls apart. If the letters are supposed to be Latinized Greek letters, why leave the second letter in its original Greek and not translate it into Latin? The second letter is changed from a Greek small eta (η) to a Greek capital eta (H), but it is not translated into Latin, which if done so would make it an "E." The third letter was translated from the Greek small sigma (σ) to the Latin capital "S," but that was not done with the second Greek letter eta (η). The second letter was capitalized, but it remained a Greek letter. Each letter is treated differently in order to create the contrivance of IHS.

If IHS is a Latinized monogram for the first three letters of Jesus' name, as claimed by Erlenbush, then it should be written IES and not IHS. It makes no sense to mix Greek and Latin letters in a monogram. Even if one accepts that the "I" and the "S" are Latinized Greek letters, it makes no sense not to Latinize the Greek eta (η) from a Greek "H" to a Latin "E." The monogram is a mixture of Latin and Greek letters. IHS contains a Latin "I," a Greek "H," and a Latin "S." That simply makes no sense.

Finally, it is absurd to represent Jesus' name with a monogram for his first three letters. That was never a practice of the Christian Church. Monograms traditionally represented the first letters of a person's given name (often including a middle name) and the surname; it was generally not a practice to represent a person in a monogram by the first three letters of his given name. Ron Byerly draws the obvious conclusion that "[o]ne wouldn't write 'PET' for Peter, or 'MOS' for Moses, or 'JAM' for James. So why IHS for Jesus."[656] The Roman Catholic exoteric explanation for IHS is thus revealed as a deception that conceals its true esoteric meaning.

The difficulty in coming up with a good exoteric explanation for IHS is not lost on the Catholic Church. That has made it necessary for *The Catholic Encyclopedia* to come up with several competing explanations for the initials, none of which are definitive. As explained above, one of the exoteric explanations has been contradicted in another section of the encyclopedia. How can the Catholic Church be so uncertain about what the initials on its Eucharistic Host mean? Obviously, the several competing public explanations are intended as smokescreens to conceal the true esoteric meaning. The true meaning of IHS was revealed by Hislop. IHS represent the heathen gods Isis (mother god), Horus (son god), and Seb (father god).

It is clear the reason why the great harlot of Babylon described in Revelation 17:5 has "MYSTERY" written across her forehead is because this ostensibly gentile church of Rome actually practices the Cabalistic Jewish religion of the Pharisees, which is derived from the occult sorceries of Babylon. This truth is concealed from the uninitiated masses of Catholics. It is truly a "MYSTERY" to them.

As the book of *Revelation* points out, the Vatican has become the habitation of devils and every foul spirit. Revelation 18:2. Former Catholic Archbishop Emmanuel Milingo revealed before the Fatima 2000 International Congress on World Peace in Rome on November 18-23, 1996 that Satan worship is practiced within the very walls of the Vatican.[657] Former Jesuit Malachi Martin, a well respected

311

scholar of considerable renown, who is considered an expert on the Vatican, had this to say about Archbishop Milingo's allegations:

> Archbishop Milingo is a good Bishop and his contention that there are Satanists in Rome is completely correct, Anybody who is acquainted with the state of affairs in the Vatican in the last 35 years is well aware that the prince of darkness has had and still has his surrogates in Rome.[658]

Martin wrote a novel titled *Windswept House*. He states that he had to write the book as a novel but that the novel is 85 % based on fact. One of the revelations in his book is that there are sodomites and Satanists among the cardinals of Rome. He also recounts the actual occurrence of a Satanic "Black Mass" in which members of the Vatican hierarchy participated.[659]

A troubling aspect of the revelations by Archbishop Milingo is that they went completely unreported by the newspapers and large circulation magazines. That is further evidence that the corporate press is controlled. The A.P. Vatican bureau reporter, Dan Walkin, when asked about the lack of coverage of such sensational news, had no acceptable explanation for not covering the story.[660]

The Vatican today is following the dictates of its Jewish overlords. For example, Zionism is the official position of the Roman Catholic Church. Cardinal Christoph Schoenborn repeated the allegedly infallible pronouncement of Pope John Paul II that the Jews have an everlasting right to Palestine. The Washington Post reported from Jerusalem, Israel:

> Archbishop of Vienna Cardinal Christoph Schoenborn, part of a visiting Austrian

delegation, made the remarks in an address Wednesday at the Hebrew University of Jerusalem, the Jerusalem Post reported Thursday.

Schoenborn said it was doctrinally important for Christians to recognize Jews' connection to the "Holy Land" and Christians should rejoice in Jews' return to Palestine as a fulfillment of biblical prophecy.

He also said Pope John Paul II had himself declared the biblical commandment for Jews to live in Israel an everlasting covenant that remained valid today.[661]

The recent announcement by the Roman Hierarchy went beyond its agreement with Jewish Zionism to stating that any criticism of Zionism cannot be tolerated. Shlomo Shamir, a reporter for the Jewish newspaper *Haaretz*, which is published in Israel, reported that the Roman Catholic Church has officially equated anti-Zionism with antisemitism.[662]

The Roman Church is aiding and abetting Israel in using the age-old trick of deflecting any criticism of Israel by equating such criticism as antisemitism. It is just as stated by former Israeli government official Shulamit Aloni who described the claim of antisemitism as "a trick we [Jews] always use."[663] The article by Shamir mentions that the Roman Church also condemns terrorism, thus subtly associating in the minds of the readers anti-Zionism with terrorism. Shamir reported in *Haaretz*:

> The Catholic Church condemned anti-Zionism as a cover for anti-Semitism by means of a joint statement issued by a forum of Catholic-Jewish intellectuals this week.

The announcement was made at a gathering of religious, academic and other leading Jewish and Catholic figures in Buenos Aires.

"We oppose anti-Semitism in any way and form, including anti-Zionism that has become of late a manifestation of anti-Semitism," the statement said.

* * *

The statement also includes a stern condemnation of terrorism, particularly terror in the name of faith.

* * *

Senior Jewish figures called the announcement a significant, public statement of support by the Catholic Church in the face of anti-Zionism.

"In the past, Zionism was equated with racism, and this statement turns anti-Zionism statements to a form of racism," a Jewish leader said in New York.

The statement joins a prior European Union announcement and UN declaration of war against anti-Semitism as part of a global front fighting the scourge.[664]

The influence of the Jews through the crypto-Jewish Jesuits in the Roman Catholic Church has been manifested for centuries in Catholic doctrine. The Council of Trent (circa 1545-1563) was an attack on Christianity with anathema after anathema against Christian doctrine that was orchestrated by the crypto-Jewish Jesuits. The control of the Jews over the Vatican is so complete that Cardinal Joseph Ratzinger (now Pope Benedict XVI), who is the prefect of the Congregation for the Doctrine of the Faith, issued an official doctrine of Catholic faith that accepts the Jewish view that the messiah is yet to come. There is apparently much double talk in the document, as it accepts the Jewish view of a coming messiah without overtly rejecting Jesus. Some have interpreted the document as denying the redemptive role of Jesus. The Catholic Church long ago implicitly denied the redemptive role of Jesus. The document is contained in a small book titled "The Jewish People and the Holy Scriptures in the Christian Bible." It is no surprise that this Jewish/Catholic doctrine was drafted by a Jesuit named Albert Vanhoye.[665]

The great harlot of Babylon in Revelation 17:5 has Mystery written upon her forehead. She is called Babylon because she is Babylonian. She is a mystery because she is masquerading as "the" Christian religion. Christian labels have been applied to Babylonian paganism to come up with the mystery religion we know as the Roman Catholic Church. Both the Talmudic Jews and the Vatican share that common Babylonian root. The Jesuits nurtured the Babylonian Cabalism in Roman Catholic doctrine. The similarities between the imperious whorish woman in Ezekiel 16:14-40 and the Mother of Harlots in Revelation 17:5 are unmistakable. They are one and the same. Roman Catholicism is an esoteric version of Babylonian Judaism. The Roman Church appears Gentile to the uninitiated, but it is Jewish to its core. Orthodox Judaism appears to the uninitiated to be the Old Testament theology, but it is actually Babylonian to its core.

19 Censoring the Gospel

The Jewish influence over the Roman Catholic institution and its doctrines is manifest in *The Document of the Vatican Commission for Religious Relations with Judaism* § 4, which states: **"We propose, in the future, to remove from the Gospel of St. John the term, 'the Jews' where it is used in a negative sense, and to translate it, 'the enemies of Christ.'"**[666]

At a speech at Hebrew University in Jerusalem, Roman Catholic Cardinal Joseph Bernadine stated:

> [T]here is need for . . . theological reflection, especially with what many consider to be the problematic New Testament's texts . . . Retranslation . . . and reinterpretation certainly need to be included among the goals we pursue in the effort to eradicate anti-semitism.
>
> [T]he gospel of John . . . is generally considered among the most problematic of all New Testament books in its outlook towards Jews and Judaism . . . this teaching of John

about the Jews, which resulted from the historical conflict between the church and synagogue in the latter part of the first century C.E., can no longer be taught as authentic doctrine or used as catechesis by contemporary Christianity . . . Christians today must see that such teachings . . . can no longer be regarded as definitive teachings in light of our improved understanding.[667]

The effort by the Catholic Church to change the gospel in order to remove any mention of the Jewish rebellion against God is just one part of a manifold strategy by Zionist Jews to conceal their antichrist agenda. Zionist Jews view the New Testament as antisemitic hate literature.[668] That is why the Jewish hierarchy prohibits Jews from reading the New Testament. In the Talmud at Sanhedrin 90a, 100b, it states that those who read the gospels are doomed to hell. Furthermore in Shabbath 116a, it states that the New Testament is blank paper and should be burned.

Orthodox Jews consider Shabbath 116a as a command to burn New Testaments. In Israel, they can get away with burning New Testaments, so that is what they do. For example, in 2008 *USA Today* reported that "Orthodox Jews set fire to hundreds of copies of the New Testament in the latest act of violence against Christian missionaries in the Holy Land."[669] When Or Yehuda Deputy Mayor Uzi Aharon heard that hundreds of New Testaments were distributed by Christian missionaries, he took to the roads in a loudspeaker car and drove through the city urging people to turn over the New Testaments to Jewish religious students, who were going door to door to collect them. The New Testaments were then dumped into a pile and set afire in a lot near a synagogue. Aharon said it was a commandment to burn books that urge Jews to convert to Christianity.[670]

The Zionists Jews have influenced the United States Government to implicitly agree that the New Testament in antisemitic. The official U.S. Government position on antisemitism is memorialized in a March 13, 2008, report from the U.S. State Department to the U.S. Congress. The U.S. Government thinks that it is antisemitism to tell the truth about Jewish control of global financing, media, the U.S. Government, or Hollywood. The evidence is that Jews in fact control global financing, media, the U.S. Government, and Hollywood. The report, however, does not let the evidence get in the way of the Zionist political agenda. The report carries a dedication from two Zionist lackeys, President George W. Bush and Vice President Richard B. Cheney. The report was released by the United States State Department Special Envoy to Monitor and Combat Anti-Semitism, Gregg J. Rickman. The report states:

> The tactics of many anti-Semitic groups include the propagation of conspiracy theories, Holocaust denial, and the attribution to Jews of a satanic and "cosmic" evil. Traditional conspiracy theories claiming Jewish control of global financial systems, the media, the U.S. government, or Hollywood remain widespread. May and July 2007 Anti-Defamation League polls found that 39% of Polish respondents and 26% of Hungarian respondents, respectively, agrees that the Jews are responsible for the death of Christ.[671]

The State Department report cites to the Jewish Anti-Defamation League. That suggests that the government political agenda is being dictated by the Anti-Defamation League, which is under the control of *B'nai Brith*, which is Jewish Freemasonry. Notice that the report implies by the cited Anti-Defamation League survey that to agree "that the Jews are responsible for the death of Christ" constitutes antisemitism.

That indicates that the U.S. Government agrees with the Anti-Defamation League position that the New Testament is antisemitic. In fact, in an earlier 2005 Report on Global Anti-Semitism, the U.S. State Department listed the following example of antisemitism: "In April, the pastor of St. Brigid Church in Gdansk told parishioners during services that 'Jews killed Jesus and the prophets.'"[672] The report states that the Archbishop of Gdansk removed the offending priest for saying that and for other alleged "improprieties."[673] In fact, that pastor was merely repeating the truth as stated clearly in the New Testament:

> For ye, brethren, became followers of the churches of God which in Judaea are in Christ Jesus: for ye also have suffered like things of your own countrymen, even as they have of **the Jews: Who both killed the Lord Jesus, and their own prophets**, and have persecuted us; and they please not God, and are contrary to all men. 1 Thessalonians 2:14-15.

That truth stated in the New Testament is considered antisemitic by the ADL and the U.S. Government. Abraham H. Foxman, National Director of the Anti-Defamation League of *B'nai B'rith*, believes that the historical record is that Jesus was crucified by the Romans, not the Jews. Foxman states:

> Over the last century a growing preponderance of evidence and scholarly study has demonstrated that the execution of Jesus was instigated primarily by the Roman authorities who ruled Palestine in the first century C.E., not by the Jewish people.[674]

Let's see what the inerrant word of God in the New Testament says. We read in the following passage, how the Jewish religious leaders conspired to kill Jesus.

> Then assembled together the chief priests, and the scribes, and the elders of the people, unto the palace of the high priest, who was called Caiaphas, And consulted that they might take Jesus by subtilty, and kill him. (Matthew 26:3-4)

Who did Judas go to and arrange to betray Jesus? Did he go to the Romans? Judas did not go to the Romans, he went to the chief priests of the Jewish Sanhedrin.

> And Judas Iscariot, one of the twelve, went unto the chief priests, to betray him unto them. And when they heard it, they were glad, and promised to give him money. And he sought how he might conveniently betray him. Mark 14:10-11.

The inerrant New Testament records that it was the chief priests of the supreme ruling council of the Jews (the Sanhedrin) who were behind the crucifixion of Jesus Christ. The chief priests and the elders persuaded the Jewish mob to demand that Jesus be crucified, despite Pontius Pilate's determination to set Jesus free because he was innocent.

> **But the chief priests and elders persuaded the multitude that they should ask Barabbas, and destroy Jesus.** The governor answered and said unto them, Whether of the twain will ye that I release unto you? They said, Barabbas. Pilate saith unto them, What shall I do then with Jesus which is called Christ? **They all say unto him, Let him be crucified.** And the governor said, Why, what evil hath he done? **But they cried out the more, saying, Let him be crucified.** When Pilate saw that he could prevail nothing, but

that rather a tumult was made, he took water, and washed his hands before the multitude, saying, I am innocent of the blood of this just person: see ye to it. **Then answered all the people, and said, His blood be on us, and on our children.** Then released he Barabbas unto them: and when he had scourged Jesus, he delivered him to be crucified. (Matthew 27:20-26)

There is no question regarding the record contained in the infallible word of God. The Jewish leaders conspired to crucify Jesus and they persuaded the Jewish mob to demand that the Roman governor, Pontius Pilate, crucify Jesus.

Ye men of Israel, hear these words; Jesus of Nazareth, a man approved of God among you by miracles and wonders and signs, which God did by him in the midst of you, as ye yourselves also know: Him, being delivered by the determinate counsel and foreknowledge of God, **ye have taken, and by wicked hands have crucified and slain**. (Acts 2:22-23)

God states in Acts 2:22-23 that the "men of Israel . . . have taken, and by wicked hands have crucified and slain" Jesus Christ. That fact is repeated in Acts 2:36, which states: "Therefore **let all the house of Israel know** assuredly, that God hath made that same **Jesus, whom ye have crucified**, both Lord and Christ." (Acts 2:36) The U.S. Government and the *B'nai Brith's* Anti-Defamation League think that the truth in God's word is antisemitic. Those are not the only passages that reveal that the Jews crucified Christ.

And when Peter saw it, he answered unto the people, **Ye men of Israel**, why marvel ye at this? or why look ye so earnestly on us, as though by our own power or holiness we had made this man to walk? The God of Abraham, and of Isaac, and of Jacob, the God of our fathers, hath glorified his Son Jesus; whom **ye delivered up, and denied him in the presence of Pilate, when he was determined to let him go. But ye denied the Holy One and the Just, and desired a murderer to be granted unto you; And killed the Prince of life**, whom God hath raised from the dead; whereof we are witnesses. (Acts 3:12-15)

God states in Acts 3:12-15 that the "men of Israel . . . delivered up and . . . killed the Prince of life," although Pontius Pilate "was determined to let him go." The truth that the Jews crucified Christ is repeated over and over again in the bible.

Then Peter, filled with the Holy Ghost, said unto them, **Ye rulers of the people, and elders of Israel** . . . Be it known unto you all, and to all the people of Israel, that by the name of **Jesus Christ of Nazareth, whom ye crucified**, whom God raised from the dead, even by him doth this man stand here before you whole. (Acts 4:8-10)

For of a truth against thy holy child Jesus, whom thou hast anointed, **both Herod, and Pontius Pilate, with the Gentiles, and the people of Israel, were gathered together**. (Acts 4:27)

And when they had brought them, **they set them before the council: and the high priest** asked them, Saying, Did not we straitly command you that ye should not teach in this name? and, behold, ye have filled Jerusalem with your doctrine, and intend to bring this man's blood upon us. Then Peter and the other apostles answered and said, We ought to obey God rather than men. **The God of our fathers raised up Jesus, whom ye slew and hanged on a tree**. Him hath God exalted with his right hand to be a Prince and a Saviour, for to give repentance to Israel, and forgiveness of sins. (Acts 5:27-31)

Which of the prophets have not your fathers persecuted? and they have slain them which shewed before of the coming of the Just One; of whom ye have been now the betrayers and murderers. (Acts 7:52)

And we are witnesses of all things which he did both in the land of the Jews, and in Jerusalem; **whom they slew and hanged on a tree**. (Acts 10:39)

Men and brethren, children of the stock of Abraham, and whosoever among you feareth God, to you is the word of this salvation sent. **For they that dwell at Jerusalem, and their rulers**, because they knew him not, nor yet the voices of the prophets which are read every sabbath day, **they have fulfilled them in condemning him. And though they found no cause of death in him, yet desired they Pilate that he should be slain.** And when they had fulfilled all that was written of him, they took him down from the tree, and laid him in a sepulchre. But God raised him from the dead. (Acts 13:26-30)

Abraham Foxman states that the New Testament

inaccurately records that Jesus was crucified by the Jewish hierarchy.[675] Foxman characterizes the New Testament as antisemitic hate literature.[676] God states that the U.S. Government, the Roman Catholic Church, *B'nai Brith's* Anti-Defamation League, and Abraham Foxman are liars for contradicting God's perfect word. "He that believeth on the Son of God hath the witness in himself: he that believeth not God hath made him a liar; because he believeth not the record that God gave of his Son." (1 John 5:10) The position of all Christians should be "let God be true, but every man a liar." (Romans 3:4) Just as the Jews persuaded the government of Rome to crucify Jesus Christ, they are now convincing the government of the United States to coverup their roll in that crucifixion. The Jews also work hand in glove with the Roman Catholic Church to censor their misdeeds from Christ's gospel.

20 Zionist Nazis

Jewish international bankers funded the communists in Russia. In addition, they were the hidden hand behind the rise of Adolph Hitler to power.[677] He who pays the piper calls the tune. We see in the rise to power of Hitler, the strategy set forth in Paragraph two of Protocol 9 of the *Protocols of the Learned Elders of Zion*, which states:

> Nowadays, if any states raise a protest against us it is only *pro forma* at our discretion and by our direction, for their anti-Semitism is indispensable to us for the management of our lesser brethren.[678]

Hitler was under the direction of the Zionists. Hitler's fiery rhetoric against the Jews and antisemitism of Nazi Germany was orchestrated by the Zionists in order to serve the ends of Zionism. Zionist Jews colluded with Hitler through their front organizations during World War II to drive the Jews from Europe to Palestine. Jewish scholar Dr. Henry Makow explains that, as odd as it may seem, Zionist Jews welcomed the Nazis' antisemitic policies. "Like the Nazis, they believed in a Master Race, just a different one."[679]

Makow details five pre-war meetings between 1929 and 1933 Hitler had with Max Warburg. The meetings were revealed by an insider believed to be James Warburg, son of Paul Warburg, who was the founder of the Federal Reserve. Paul Warburg represented the interests of Zionist bankers affiliated with the Rothschild banking consortium. The Zionist bankers agreed to fund Hitler. The process of bringing war to Europe and gaining control of Palestine began with the agreements that flowed from the meetings between Hitler and Paul Warburg. Makow concluded:

> The bottom line is that both Nazism and Zionism were sponsored by the same banking cartel and had complementary goals. The rise of anti-Semitism in Europe served to create the State of Israel, which President Assad of Syria described as a "dagger in the heart of the Arab nations."[680]

Cooperation between the Zionist Jews and the Nazis extended to political and economic spheres. Makow explains:

> Adolph Eichmann [who was the Nazi Transportation Administrator for the deportation of Jews to Palestine] set up agricultural training camps in Austria to prepare young Jews for Kibbutz life. He visited Palestine and conferred with Zionist leaders who confessed their true expansionist goals. There was even talk of a strategic alliance between Nazi Germany and Jewish Palestine. His report is in Himmler's Archives.[681]

Eichmann stated that he was an ardent Zionist.[682] His actions on behalf of the Zionist cause certainly support his claim. Furthermore, Hennecke Kardel alleged in his book,

Adolf Hitler: Begruender Israels (translation: *Adolf Hitler: Founder of Israel*), that Eichmann was not only a Zionist, but that he was also a full-blooded Jew.[683] Eichmann, being a Jew and persecuting Jews only makes sense if one realizes that Eichmann was a Zionist. Zionists wanted to drive the Jews from Europe in order to force them to immigrate to Palestine, to create Jewish hegemony over the Arabs there.

Christopher Jon Bjerknes stated that "Zionist Jews around the World delighted in the rise of the Nazis and celebrated the Nazis' Jewish-inspired segregationist laws. This fact was recorded in Eichmann and Hagen's own reports."[684] Bjerknes quotes from Eichmann and Hagen's report:

> Nationalist Jewish circles expressed their great joy over the radical German policy towards the Jews, as this policy would increase the Jewish population in Palestine, so that one can reckon with a Jewish majority in Palestine over the Arabs in the foreseeable future.[685]

Jewish author Emil Ludwig (a/k/a Emil Cohn) stated:

> Hitler will be forgotten in a few years, but he will have a beautiful monument in Palestine. You know the coming of the Nazis was rather a welcome thing. So many of our German Jews were hovering between two coasts; so many of them were riding the treacherous current between the Scylla of assimilation and the Charybdis of a nodding acquaintance with Jewish things. Thousands who seemed to be completely lost to Judaism were brought back to the fold by Hitler, and for that I am personally very grateful to him.[686]

Zionism was the prime aim of Nazi Germany. Hitler's

deputy, Rudolph Hess, *Reichmarshal* Hermann Goering, Gregor Strasser, Alfred Rosenberg, Hans Frank, *Reichminister* von Ribbentrop, top SS leader Reinhard Heydrich, Hitler's bankers Ritter von Strauss and von Stein, as well as a majority of Hitler's top officers and associates, were Jews. The Third Reich was modeled after the papacy and was controlled by crypto-Jews, just as is the papacy.[687]

Bryan Mark Rigg, has served as a volunteer in the Israeli Army and as an officer in the U.S. Marine Corps. He is a history professor at the American Military University. Based upon his research, Rigg estimated that there were 150,000 Jewish soldiers in the Wehrmacht, the regular Nazi army, as distinct from the Nazi SS.[688] The service of the Jewish soldiers was with the full knowledge of the Nazi hierarchy. There were two Jewish field marshals, fifteen Jewish generals, two Jewish full generals, eight Jewish lieutenant generals, five Jewish major generals, major generals commanded up to 100,000 troops in the Nazi German Army. One of the Jewish field marshals was Erhard Milch. He was deputy to Luftwaffe Chief Hermann Goering. 20 Jewish soldiers in the Nazi army were awarded Germany's highest military honor, the Knight's Cross.[689]

Helmut Schmidt, former Chancellor of Germany, said this about Rigg's findings:

> Rigg's extensive knowledge and the preliminary conclusions drawn from his research impressed me greatly. I firmly believe that his in-depth treatment of the subject of German soldiers of Jewish descent in the Wehrmacht will lead to new perspectives on this portion of 20th century German military history.[690]

It seems like an oxymoron to have Nazi Jews, but it

makes sense when one realizes that both the Nazis and the Zionists had the same objective of persecuting the Jews of Europe in order to force them to emigrate from Europe to Palestine. The Nazis worked out secret arrangements with the Zionist Jews to facilitate the immigration of Jews to Palestine. Henneke Kardel explained the arrangement between the Nazis and the Zionist Jews in his book *Adolf Hitler: Founder of Israel.*

> The cooperation which existed between Heydrich's Gestapo and the Jewish self-defense league in Palestine, the militant Haganah, would not have been closer if it was not for Eichamn who made it public . . . The commander of Haganah was Feivel Polkes, born in Poland, with whom in February 1937 the S. D. trooper leader Adolph Eichman met in Berlin in a wine restaurant Traube (Grape) near the zoo. These two Jews made a brotherly agreement. Polkes, the underground fighter, got in writing this assurance from Eichman: "A body representing Jews in Germany, will exert pressure on those leaving Germany to emigrate only to Palestine. Such a policy is in the interest of Germany and will be executed by the Gestapo."[691]

Why did the Zionist Jews force the Jews living in Europe to emigrate from Europe to Palestine? They did it because they wanted to increase the population of Jews in that area in order to establish a beachhead for eventual control of the entire middle east. The only way for the Jews to establish hegemony in Palestine would be to increase the population of Jews there.

After the defeat of the Ottoman Empire in World War I, Britain controlled Palestine through a mandate from the

League of Nations. On November 2, 1917, Arthur James Lord Balfour, Foreign Secretary of Britain sent a letter to prominent Zionist Lord Rothschild promising the establishment of a Jewish homeland in Palestine. The letter became known as the Balfour Declaration. It was the first recognition by a major world power of a Jewish homeland.

The Jews at the time were a minority in Palestine and consequently could not hope to control the area, which was their goal. They needed large numbers of Jews to immigrate into Palestine in order to begin the process of Jewish conquest of the Middle East.

The problem for the Jews was that they could not persuade Jews living comfortably and prosperously in Europe to leave Europe and go to third-world Palestine. It was decided that they would be driven out of Europe so that they would have no choice but to flee to Palestine. Enter Hitler and his Nazi "final solution," which had as its objective not the extermination of Jews as is commonly believed, but rather driving the Jews from Europe to Palestine.

Jewish author Edwin Black spent years researching documents in Israel, Germany, and Israel. He was shocked to discover cooperative agreements between Zionist Jews and Nazis. He determined that the Zionists and Nazis agreed to the transfer of 60,000 Jews and $100 million to Palestine. He documented his findings in his book titled *The Transfer Agreement*.[692] The evidence was so compelling that even Abraham Foxman, the National Director of *B'nai Brith's* Anti-Defamation League, acknowledged that a transfer agreement was entered into between the Nazis and Zionists. Foxman stated in the afterword to Black's book:

> In my mind, the Transfer Agreement's most important and indispensable element was the rescue of people. The rescue of assets comes

second. But clearly, the Zionists could rescue people only if they had assets and once rescued, assets were needed to maintain those people in Palestine, it was the Zionists' duty to deal in assets. The cruel reality was that the price of salvaging these lives and assets was widespread trafficking in German goods.[693]

Foxman will admit to the transfer agreement between the Nazis and the Zionists. He can dress it up and justify it as a Machiavellian way to save Jewish lives. What he hopes to conceal is the fact that the persecution of the Jews was also agreed upon by the Nazis and Zionists. There is no way to justify that. That is a deep dark secret upon which Zionist Jews like Foxman want to keep a lid.

The best evidence that the Zionist collaboration with Jews was not to save Jews is the fact that powerful Zionists thwarted a British Parliamentary initiative to send Jewish refugees to Mauritius.[694] The Zionists demanded that they be sent to Palestine.[695]

Henry Makow describes the Zionist bloody mindset, where their fellow Jews became cannon fodder in their effort to create an earthly Zion in Palestine:

> Zionists did not believe in the Jewish Diaspora and actively sabotaged rescue attempts. If Jews could escape to other countries, what would be the purpose of Israel? Thus the Zionist Rabbi of Sweden Dr. Ehrenpreis scuttled a Swedish attempt to rescue 10,000 Jews. Zionists torpedoed a similar move by the British Parliament. They also rejected numerous legitimate ransom attempts and discouraged resistance.[696]

The Zionists' claim to have run a humanitarian mission to save Jews from Nazi persecution is false propaganda designed to deceive the ignorant masses. The Zionists did not care to save Jews if those Jews were not going to be sent to Palestine. That is because the whole point of the Nazi (Zionist) "final solution" was to drive the Jews from Europe to Palestine. Any other plan undermined the Zionist strategy for hegemony over Palestine.

For example, on November 25, 1940, a boat, *The Patra*, carrying Jewish refugees exploded and sunk off the coast of Palestine, killing 252 people. *The Patra* was headed to Mauritius.[697] The Jewish *Haganah* initially claimed that the passengers committed suicide to protest the alleged British refusal to allow them to disembark. The *Haganah* later admitted that they (The *Haganah*) blew up the vessel rather than allow it to get to Mauritis. At a 1958 memorial service for the 252 people who died on *The Patra*, former Israeli Prime Minister Moshe Sharett tried to justify the Zionists' mass-murder of innocent Jews by explaining: "Sometimes it is necessary to sacrifice the few in order to save the many."[698]

On November 19, 1947, the United Nations partitioned Palestine into three sections: one for Palestinians, one for the Jews, and an international zone in Jerusalem. On May 14, 1948, the state of Israel officially came into being. Today, the Jews control all of Palestine, including Jerusalem, which is now the capital of Israel. The Zionist dream is that Jerusalem will be the capital of the world. Three quarters of the population of Jerusalem is now Jewish, with the remaining residents being Palestinians. The Jews plan on absorbing the West Bank, Gaza Strip, and the Golan Heights into Israel.

The Zionist Jews not only worked with the Nazis to force Jews to emigrate from Europe to Israel, they have also instigated other governments to persecute Jews in order to force their immigration to Israel. The Jewish scholar, Israel Shahak, discovered that "[t]he Israeli government induced Jewish immigration from Iraq by bribing the government of Iraq to strip most Iraqi Jews of their citizenship and to confiscate their property."[699] The close relationship between the Zionist Jews and the Nazis comes into focus when one looks at the characters who have assisted Israel. Most are surprised to learn that the person who was most instrumental in establishing and training the notorious Mossad (Israeli Military Intelligence) was none other than Reinhard Gehlen, former head of Hitler's Nazi Intelligence for the Eastern front.[700]

A Jewish insider broke ranks and exposed the Zionist plan for world dominion. Benjamin H. Freedman was a Jewish insider in the world Zionist conspiracy. He was a successful Jewish businessman of New York City who was at one time the principal owner of the Woodbury Soap Company. He broke with organized Jewry in 1945. He spent the remainder of his life and the great preponderance of his considerable fortune exposing the Jewish conspiracy against the United States and the world.

Mr. Freedman knew what he was talking about because he had been an insider at the highest levels of Jewish organizations and Jewish machinations to gain power over our nation. Mr. Freedman was personally acquainted with Bernard Baruch, Samuel Untermyer (also spelled Untermeyer), Woodrow Wilson, Franklin Roosevelt, Joseph Kennedy, John F. Kennedy, and many more movers and shakers of his time. In the following excerpt from a 1961 speech given at the Willard Hotel in Washington, D.C. on behalf of Conde McGinley's patriotic newspaper of that time, *Common Sense*, Freedman revealed how the Zionists double-crossed Germany in order to establish Israel. He further explains the Zionist threat to the United States and the Zionist plans for World War III.

> What I intend to tell you tonight is something that you have never been able to learn from

any other source, and what I tell you now concerns not only you, but your children and the survival of this country and Christianity. I'm not here just to dish up a few facts to send up your blood pressure, but I'm here to tell you things that will help you preserve what you consider the most sacred things in the world: the liberty, and the freedom, and the right to live as Christians, where you have a little dignity, and a little right to pursue the things that your conscience tells you are the right things, as Christians.

Now, first of all, I'd like to tell you that on August 25th 1960 -- that was shortly before elections -- Senator Kennedy, who is now the President of the United States, went to New York, and delivered an address to the Zionist Organization of America. In that address, to reduce it to its briefest form, he stated that he would use the armed forces of the United States to preserve the existence of the regime set up in Palestine by the Zionists who are now in occupation of that area.

In other words, Christian boys are going to be yanked out of their homes, away from their families, and sent abroad to fight in Palestine against the Christian and Moslem Arabs who merely want to return to their homes. And these Christian boys are going to be asked to shoot to kill these innocent [Palestinian] people who only want to follow out fifteen resolutions passed by the United Nations in the last twelve years calling upon the Zionists to allow these people to return to their homes.

Now, when United States troops appear in the Middle East to fight with the Zionists as their allies to prevent the return of these people who were evicted from their homes in the 1948 armed insurrection by the Zionists who were transplanted there from Eastern Europe. . . . when that happens, the United States will trigger World War III.[701]

Benjamin Freedman did not know that Senator Kennedy's August 25, 1960, speech before the Zionist Organization of America was political window dressing by Kennedy. Kennedy was playing a very dangerous political game. He was a ruthless politician, but he was also a patriotic American. Kennedy's speech was a speech that Kennedy felt he had to give in order to curry favor with the powerful Zionist financial and media interests, which he needed to get elected President.

Anthony Hmura was World War II veteran who decided to find out what was behind that unnecessary war. He discovered the interlocking worldwide Zionist conspiracy. Hmura had a newsletter that exposed the Zionist conspiracy. He had many private meetings with then-Senator John Kennedy on or around 1955. Kennedy was well acquainted with the Zionist threat.

Kennedy was an anti-Zionist, but he was also a shrewd politician. He was keeping his true anti-Zionist feelings private in order to further his political career. His plan was to do something about the Zionist threat once he reached the high office of President of the United States. Kennedy double-crossed the Zionists, once he was elected President. Among other things, Kennedy put the squeeze on Israel to stop its development of nuclear weapons. That led to his assassination.

It is questionable whether Kennedy ever intended to send U.S. troops to defend the Zionist regime in Palestine. At the time Freedman gave his 1961 speech at the Willard Hotel he did not know the dangerous game Kennedy was playing. Freedman, however, was absolutely accurate regarding the historical events controlled by Zionists. Freedman explained those events and their future implications during his 1961 Willard Hotel speech:

> The Zionists and their co-religionists have complete control of our government. For many reasons too many and too complex to go into here at this time -- I'll be glad to answer questions, however, to support that statement -- the Zionists and their co-religionists rule this United States as though they were the absolute monarchs of this country.
>
> Now, you say, 'well, that's a very broad statement to make', but let me show what happened while you were -- I don't want to wear that out -- let me show what happened while we were all asleep. I'm including myself with you. We were all asleep. What happened?
>
> **-The First World War-**
>
> What happened? World War I broke out in the summer of 1914. There are few people here my age who remember that. Now that war was waged on one side by Great Britain, France, and Russia; and on the other side by Germany, Austria-Hungary, and Turkey.
>
> Within two years Germany had won that war: not only won it nominally, but won it actually.

The German submarines, which were a surprise to the world, had swept all the convoys from the Atlantic Ocean. Great Britain stood there without ammunition for her soldiers, with one week's food supply— and after that, starvation. At that time, the French army had mutinied. They had lost 600,000 of the flower of French youth in the defense of Verdun on the Somme. The Russian army was defecting, they were picking up their toys and going home, they didn't want to play war anymore, they didn't like the Czar. And the Italian army had collapsed.

Not a shot had been fired on German soil. Not one enemy soldier had crossed the border into Germany. And yet, Germany was offering England peace terms. They offered England a negotiated peace on what the lawyers call a *status quo ante* basis. That means: "Let's call the war off, and let everything be as it was before the war started." England, in the summer of 1916 was considering that— seriously. They had no choice. It was either accepting this negotiated peace that Germany was magnanimously offering them, or going on with the war and being totally defeated.

-1916 Stalemate-

While that was going on, the Zionists in Germany, who represented the Zionists from Eastern Europe, went to the British War Cabinet and— I am going to be brief because it's a long story, but I have all the documents to prove any statement that I make— they said: "Look here. You can yet win this war. You don't have to give up. You don't have to accept the negotiated peace offered to you now by Germany. You can win this war if the United States will come in as your ally." The United States was not in the war at that time. We were fresh; we were young; we were rich; we were powerful. They told England: "We will guarantee to bring the United States into the war as your ally, to fight with you on your side, if you will promise us Palestine after you win the war." In other words, they made this deal: "We will get the United States into this war as your ally. The price you must pay is Palestine after you have won the war and defeated Germany, Austria-Hungary, and Turkey." Now England had as much right to promise Palestine to anybody, as the United States would have to promise Japan to Ireland for any reason whatsoever. It's absolutely absurd that Great Britain, that never had any connection or any interest or any right in what is known as Palestine should offer it as coin of the realm to pay the Zionists for bringing the United States into the war. However, they did make that promise, in October of 1916. And shortly after that— I don't know how many here remember it— the United States, which was almost totally pro-German, entered the war as Britain's ally.

I say that the United States was almost totally pro-German because the newspapers here were controlled by Jews, the bankers were Jews, all the media of mass communications in this country were controlled by Jews; and they, the Jews, were pro-German. They were pro-German because many of them had come from

Germany, and also they wanted to see Germany lick the Czar. The Jews didn't like the Czar, and they didn't want Russia to win this war. These German-Jew bankers, like Kuhn Loeb and the other big banking firms in the United States refused to finance France or England to the extent of one dollar. They stood aside and they said: "As long as France and England are tied up with Russia, not one cent!" But they poured money into Germany, they fought beside Germany against Russia, trying to lick the Czarist regime.

Now those same Jews, when they saw the possibility of getting Palestine, went to England and they made this deal. At that time, everything changed, like a traffic light that changes from red to green. Where the newspapers had been all pro-German, where they'd been telling the people of the difficulties that Germany was having fighting Great Britain commercially and in other respects, all of a sudden the Germans were no good. They were villains. They were Huns. They were shooting Red Cross nurses. They were cutting off babies' hands. They were no good. Shortly after that, Mr. Wilson declared war on Germany.

-USA Railroaded Into World War I After Balfour Declaration-

The Zionists in London had sent cables to the United States, to Justice Brandeis, saying "Go to work on President Wilson. We're getting from England what we want. Now you go to work on President Wilson and get the United

States into the war." That's how the United States got into the war. We had no more interest in it; we had no more right to be in it than we have to be on the moon tonight instead of in this room. There was absolutely no reason for World War I to be our war. We were railroaded into— if I can be vulgar, we were suckered into— that war merely so that the Zionists of the world could obtain Palestine. That is something that the people of the United States have never been told. They never knew why we went into World War I.

After we got into the war, the Zionists went to Great Britain and they said: "Well, we performed our part of the agreement. Let's have something in writing that shows that you are going to keep your bargain and give us Palestine after you win the war." They didn't know whether the war would last another year or another ten years. So they started to work out a receipt. The receipt took the form of a letter, which was worded in very cryptic language so that the world at large wouldn't know what it was all about. And that was called the Balfour Declaration.

The Balfour Declaration was merely Great Britain's promise to pay the Zionists what they had agreed upon as a consideration for getting the United States into the war. So this great Balfour Declaration, that you hear so much about, is just as phony as a three dollar bill. I don't think I could make it more emphatic than that.

-Versailles-

That is where all the trouble started. The United States got in the war. The United States crushed Germany. You know what happened. When the war ended, and the Germans went to Paris for the Paris Peace Conference in 1919 there were 117 Jews there, as a delegation representing the Jews, headed by Bernard Baruch. I was there: I ought to know. Now what happened? The Jews at that peace conference, when they were cutting up Germany and parceling out Europe to all these nations who claimed a right to a certain part of European territory, said, "How about Palestine for us?" And they produced, for the first time to the knowledge of the Germans, this Balfour Declaration. So the Germans, for the first time realized, "Oh, so that was the game! That's why the United States came into the war." **The Germans for the first time realized that they were defeated, they suffered the terrific reparations that were slapped onto them, because the Zionists wanted Palestine and were determined to get it at any cost.**

-Germans Discovered Jewish Activity-

That brings us to another very interesting point. When the Germans realized this, they naturally resented it. Up to that time, the Jews had never been better off in any country in the world than they had been in Germany. You had Mr. Rathenau there, who was maybe 100 times as important in industry and finance as is Bernard Baruch in this country. You had Mr. Balin, who owned the two big steamship lines, the North German Lloyd's and the Hamburg-

American Lines. You had Mr. Bleichroder, who was the banker for the Hohenzollern family. You had the Warburgs in Hamburg, who were the big merchant bankers— the biggest in the world. The Jews were doing very well in Germany. No question about that. The Germans felt: "Well, that was quite a sellout."

It was a sellout that might be compared to this hypothetical situation: Suppose the United States was at war with the Soviet Union. And we were winning. And we told the Soviet Union: "Well, let's quit. We offer you peace terms. Let's forget the whole thing." And all of a sudden Red China came into the war as an ally of the Soviet Union. And throwing them into the war brought about our defeat. A crushing defeat, with reparations the likes of which man's imagination cannot encompass. Imagine, then, after that defeat, if we found out that it was the Chinese in this country, our Chinese citizens, who all the time we had thought were loyal citizens working with us, were selling us out to the Soviet Union and that it was through them that Red China was brought into the war against us. How would we feel, then, in the United States against Chinese? I don't think that one of them would dare show his face on any street. There wouldn't be enough convenient lampposts to take care of them. Imagine how we would feel.

Well, that's how the Germans felt towards these Jews. They'd been so nice to them: from 1905 on, when the first Communist revolution in Russia failed, and the Jews

342

had to scramble out of Russia, they all went to Germany. And Germany gave them refuge. And they were treated very nicely. And here they had sold Germany down the river for no reason at all other than the fact that they wanted Palestine as a so-called "Jewish commonwealth."

Now Nahum Sokolow, and all the great leaders and great names that you read about in connection with Zionism today, in 1919, 1920, 1921, 1922, and 1923 wrote in all their papers— and the press was filled with their statements— that the feeling against the Jews in Germany is due to the fact that they realized that this great defeat was brought about by Jewish intercession in bringing the United States into the war. The Jews themselves admitted that. It wasn't that the Germans in 1919 discovered that a glass of Jewish blood tasted better than Coca-Cola or Muenschner Beer. There was no religious feeling. There was no sentiment against those people merely on account of their religious belief. It was all political. It was economic. It was anything but religious. Nobody cared in Germany whether a Jew went home and pulled down the shades and said "Shema' Yisroel" or "Our Father." Nobody cared in Germany any more than they do in the United States. Now this feeling that developed later in Germany was due to one thing: the Germans held the Jews responsible for their crushing defeat.

* * *

And at that time, mind you, there were 80 to

90 million Germans, and there were only 460,000 Jews. About one half of one per cent of the population of Germany were Jews. And yet they controlled all the press, and they controlled most of the economy because they had come in with cheap money when the mark was devalued and bought up practically everything.

The Jews tried to keep a lid on this fact. They didn't want the world to really understand that they had sold out Germany, and that the Germans resented that.

The Germans took appropriate action against the Jews. They, shall I say, discriminated against them wherever they could. They shunned them. The same way that we would shun the Chinese, or the Negroes, or the Catholics, or anyone in this country who had sold us out to an enemy and brought about our defeat.

-1933: Jews Declare Trade War on Germany-

After a while, the Jews of the world called a meeting in Amsterdam. Jews from every country in the world attended this meeting in July 1933. And they said to Germany: "You fire Hitler, and you put every Jew back into his former position, whether he was a Communist or no matter what he was. You can't treat us that way. And we, the Jews of the world, are serving an ultimatum upon you." You can imagine what the Germans told them. So what did the Jews do?

In 1933, when Germany refused to surrender to the world conference of Jews in Amsterdam, the conference broke up, and Mr. Samuel Untermyer, who was the head of the American delegation and the president of the whole conference, came to the United States and went from the steamer to the studios of the Columbia Broadcasting System and made a radio broadcast throughout the United States in which he in effect said, "The Jews of the world now declare a Holy War against Germany. We are now engaged in a sacred conflict against the Germans. And we are going to starve them into surrender. We are going to use a worldwide boycott against them. That will destroy them because they are dependent upon their export business." And it is a fact that two thirds of Germany's food supply had to be imported, and it could only be imported with the proceeds of what they exported. So if Germany could not export, two thirds of Germany's population would have to starve. There was just not enough food for more than one third of the population. Now in this declaration, which I have here, and which was printed in the New York Times on August 7, 1933, Mr. Samuel Untermyer boldly stated that "this economic boycott is our means of self-defense. President Roosevelt has advocated its use in the National Recovery Administration," which some of you may remember, where everybody was to be boycotted unless he followed the rules laid down by the New Deal, and which was declared unconstitutional by the Supreme Court of that time. Nevertheless, the Jews of the world declared a boycott against Germany, and it was so effective that you couldn't find one thing in any store anywhere in the world with the words "made in Germany" on it. In fact, an executive of the Woolworth Company told me that they had to dump millions of dollars worth of crockery and dishes into the river; that their stores were boycotted if anyone came in and found a dish marked "made in Germany," they were picketed with signs saying "Hitler," "murderer," and so forth, something like these sit-ins that are taking place in the South. At a store belonging to the R. H. Macy chain, which was controlled by a family called Strauss who also happen to be Jews, a woman found stockings there which came from Chemnitz, marked "made in Germany." Well, they were cotton stockings and they may have been there 20 years, since I've been observing women's legs for many years and it's been a long time since I've seen any cotton stockings on them. I saw Macy's boycotted, with hundreds of people walking around with signs saying "murderers," "Hitlerites," and so forth. Now up to that time, not one hair on the head of any Jew had been hurt in Germany. There was no suffering, there was no starvation, there was no murder, there was nothing.

Naturally, the Germans said, "Who are these people to declare a boycott against us and throw all our people out of work, and make our industries come to a standstill? Who are they to do that to us?" They naturally resented it. Certainly they painted swastikas on stores owned by Jews. Why should a German go in and give his money to a storekeeper who was part of a boycott that was going to starve

Germany into surrendering to the Jews of the world, who were going to dictate who their premier or chancellor was to be? Well, it was ridiculous.

-Reichskristallnacht and Rearmament-

The boycott continued for some time, but it wasn't until 1938, when a young Jew from Poland walked into the German embassy in Paris and shot a German official, that the Germans really started to get rough with the Jews in Germany. And you found them then breaking windows and having street fights and so forth.

Now I don't like to use the word "anti-Semitism" because it's meaningless, but it means something to you still, so I'll have to use it. The only reason that there was any feeling in Germany against Jews was that they were responsible for World War I and for this world-wide boycott. Ultimately they were also responsible for World War II, because after this thing got out of hand, it was absolutely necessary for the Jews and Germany to lock horns in a war to see which one was going to survive. In the meanwhile, I had lived in Germany, and I knew that the Germans had decided that Europe is going to be Christian or Communist: there is no in between. And the Germans decided they were going to keep it Christian if possible. And they started to re-arm. In November 1933 the United States recognized the Soviet Union. The Soviet Union was becoming very powerful, and Germany realized that "Our turn was going to come soon, unless we are strong." The same as we in this country are saying today, "Our turn is going to come soon, unless we are strong." Our government is spending 83 or 84 billion dollars for defense. Defense against whom? Defense against 40,000 little Jews in Moscow that took over Russia, and then, in their devious ways, took over control of many other countries of the world.

-World War III-

* * *

What do we face now? If we trigger a world war that may develop into a nuclear war, humanity is finished. **Why might such a war take place? It will take place as the curtain goes up on Act 3: Act 1 was World War I, Act 2 was World War II, Act 3 is going to be World War III. The Jews of the world, the Zionists and their co-religionists everywhere, are determined that they are going to again use the United States to help them permanently retain Palestine as their foothold for their world government.** That is just as true as I am standing here. Not alone have I read it, but many here have also read it, and it is known all over the world.

-Zionist Double Cross of the USA-

What are we going to do? The life you save may be your son's. Your boys may be on their way to that war tonight; and you don't know it any more than you knew that in 1916 in London the Zionists made a deal with the

British War Cabinet to send your sons to war in Europe. Did you know it at that time? Not a person in the United States knew it. You weren't permitted to know it. Who knew it? President Wilson knew it. Colonel House knew it. Other insiders knew it.

Did I know it? I had a pretty good idea of what was going on: I was liaison to Henry Morgenthau, Sr., in the 1912 campaign when President Wilson was elected, and there was talk around the office there. I was "confidential man" to Henry Morgenthau, Sr., who was chairman of the finance committee, and I was liaison between him and Rollo Wells, the treasurer. **So I sat in these meetings with President Wilson at the head of the table, and all the others, and I heard them drum into President Wilson's brain the graduated income tax and what has become the Federal Reserve, and I heard them indoctrinate him with the Zionist movement. Justice Brandeis and President Wilson were just as close as the two fingers on this hand. President Woodrow Wilson was just as incompetent when it came to determining what was going on as a newborn baby. That is how they got us into World War I, while we all slept. They sent our boys over there to be slaughtered. For what? So the Jews can have Palestine as their "commonwealth." They've fooled you so much that you don't know whether you're coming or going.** [702]

21 Carroll Quigley's Limited Hangout

Carroll Quigley was an insider who was given access to the documentary evidence of the operational arm of the oligarchs who rule the world. He wrote his findings in a 1966 book titled, *Tragedy and Hope: A History of the World in Our Time*.[703] Quigley was a professor at Georgetown University. During Bill Clinton's Democratic presidential nomination acceptance address delivered on July 16, 1992, He described Quigley by name as an influential mentor to him when he was a student at Georgetown University.

Quigley was a true believer in the aims of the world oligarchs about whom he wrote. Those oligarchs were Jewish, and Quigley knew it. Quigley did not realize that those shadowy powers considered him a "useful idiot." Quigley was an ignorant zealot doing the bidding of his masters. Quigley stated: "I have no aversion to it or to most of its aims and have, for much of my life, been close to it and to many of its instruments." The principle aim to which he refers is the goal of complete world domination. Quigley disagreed with the wishes of these powerful men ruling the world from behind the scenes to remain secret in their identity and goals. Quigley stated that "in general my chief difference of opinion is that it wishes to remain unknown, and I believe its role in history is significant enough to be known." Keep in mind that Quigley, being an insider, was not going to reveal who these people really were. He understood that his study and writing about the group was to be a "limited hangout," designed to reveal only some things but conceal the most important thing: who was really behind the world conspiracy. He used deception throughout his book when referring to the world conspirators. He was not going to reveal their true identities. He thus misleadingly described them as an "international Anglophile network." He falsely claimed that while they might work with communists, they were not communists.

During a 1974 interview with the Washington Post's Rudy Maxa, Quigley explained his objection to a book written by conservative anti-communist author W. Cleon Skousen. Quigley claimed that Skousen had violated his copyright and misinterpreted what Quigley wrote in *Tragedy and Hope*. Quigley stated:

> The group that I'm writing about was originally, in my mind, the group established secretly by Lord Milner in 1908, 1909, called The Round Table Group, which still publishes a quarterly magazine called the ?The Round Table' in London, which is one of the world's best sources of international relations information since 1910.[704]

Quigley had constructed his view of history by cutting off any inquiry beyond the secretive round table groups. Those round table groups (the Council on Foreign Relations and the Royal Institute of International Affairs) were merely front groups set up by Zionist Jews to carry out their global plans for a New World Order. Quigley objected to Skousen taking the next step and looking behind the curtain at those that funded and controlled the round table groups.

William F. Jasper explained in an August 13, 2001 *New American* magazine article titled *The Power Behind the Presidency* that the Council on Foreign Relations (CFR) is one of several round table societies. The CFR is used to indoctrinate its members, who then infiltrate and control the U.S. government. Admiral Chester Ward was a member of the CFR for 16 years. He resigned from the CFR when he realized that its goal was to disarm and surrender the United States to an all-powerful world government.

Fritz Springmeier reveals in *Bloodlines of the Illuminati*[705] that the round table groups, including, but not limited to, the Council on Foreign Relations (CFR) based in New York, and the Royal Institute for International Affairs (RIIA), based in London, were funded and established by Edmond de Rothschild of the Rothschild Jewish banking empire, his affiliates, and other powerful Jewish bankers. Edward Mandell House was the Rothschild agent who established and initially steered the CFR, headquartered in New York. The original funding for the CFR came through Rothschild agent J.P. Morgan, Jewish financier Bernard Baruch, Jewish banker Otto Kahn, Jewish banker Jacob Schiff, and Jewish banker Paul Warburg, who sat on the original board of directors of the CFR. Quigley knew this, but he was not about to breathe a word of it in his book, *Tragedy and Hope*.

It is notable that Jacob Schiff, who also funded the Bolshevik Revolution in Russia to the tune of $20 million (equivalent to more than $1 billion in today's money), is not mentioned at all by Quigley in his book, *Tragedy and Hope*. Quigley mentions the Jewish banking house of Warburg only once and then only to identify it as a Jewish Banking house. Although Paul Warburg was the Governor of the Federal Reserve Board from 1914 to 1918, Quigley never mentions Paul

Warburg in particular.

In addition to his involvement in the founding of the CFR, Rothschild agent Edward Mandell House was a close advisor to President Woodrow Wilson. Edward Mandell House shepherded Woodrow Wilson's signing of the Federal Reserve Act into law. And House counseled Wilson to petition Congress to declare war on Germany, entering the U.S. into what became World War I. Quigley makes no mention of Edward Mandell House whatsoever in his book.

Figure 2: Edward Mandell House was the Rothschild agent who established and initially steered the CFR, headquartered in New York. Edward Mandell House's role in world history was sufficient for him to be put on the cover of Time Magazine in 1923. But Carroll Quigley did not mention House in his book, *Tragedy and Hope: A History of the World in Our Time*, which was supposed to be a detailed history of the CFR.

Why would Quigley exclude all mention of such a pivotal character as Edward Mandell House? Because if Quigley revealed House's role in the founding of the CFR it would give up the game and reveal the Zionist core to the CFR.

A single quote from Rabbi Stephen Wise is all one needs to read to understand this point. Wise was an influential Zionist Jew who founded the American Jewish Congress in 1920 and became president of the Zionist Organization of America in 1936.[706] Rabbi Wise and another Zionist Jew, Louis Brandeis, convinced President Woodrow Wilson to support the Balfour Declaration.[707]

Rabbi Wise reveals that Edward Mandell House carried the water for the Zionist Jews in the Woodrow Wilson Administration. According to Rabbi Wise, "House not only made our cause the object of his very special concern but served as liaison officer between the Wilson administration and the Zionist movement."[708]

President Wilson became House's puppet, nay, his alter-ego. Douglas Reed explains that "[a]fter his election Mr. House took over his correspondence, arranged whom he should see or not receive, told Cabinet officers what they were to say or not to say, and so on."[709] President Wilson was putty to be molded in the hands of his Zionist controllers, chief of which was Edward Mandell House. Indeed, the control of the Zionists over Wilson was so complete that Benjamin Freedman described Wilson as being "just as incompetent when it came to determining what was going on as a newborn baby." Reed explains that "Mr. House did not guide American State policy, but deflected it towards Zionism, the support of the world-revolution, and the promotion of the world-government ambition. The fact of his exercise of secret power is proven."[710]

The revelation of House's influence over Wilson to guide American policy to favor the interests of powerful Zionist bankers is something that Quigley's Zionist handlers needed to be concealed. And it was Quigley's mission to spin the world conspiracy away from Zionism. Exclusions by Quigley of players instrumental in the funding and establishment of the round table groups from a tome that is allegedly based upon 20 years of deep research into those groups can only be described as purposeful. Quigley was trying to conceal the Jewish funding and communist philosophies behind the seditious activity of the round table groups.

In the interview with Washington Post's Rudy Maxa, Quigley warned Maxa that he had to be discrete. Quigley said "look. You've gotta be discrete … you know you have to protect my future … as well as your own."[711] Maxa agreed with Quigley's admonition. Quigley knew he was being recorded and his responses were guarded. He wanted to make sure that Maxa was careful with his questions as well.

Further evidence that Quigley's mission was to conceal and not reveal was the bizarre statement he made during that same interview with Rudy Maxa. Quigley stated that he "generally would think that any conspiracy theory of history is nonsense."[712] But his book reveals a massive world conspiracy that covers a large swath of history! Why would he make a statement that is so clearly contrary to the assertions in his book, which was supposed to be based upon 20 years of research? Apparently, he forgot that his mission in *Tragedy and Hope* was to only conceal the Jewish conspiracy, not all conspiracies. "A double minded man is unstable in all his ways." (James 1:8)

Immediately after Quigley made his statement that he thought that the conspiratorial theory of history was nonsense, the questioner, Rudy Maxa, brought up "the international banking conspiracy." Maxa stated: "If I could play the Devil's

Advocate, I think, you, [with] talking about the 'international banking conspiracy', they have not lost out, they simply don't want any attention." As Quigley begins to respond to the questioner's statement, the recording abruptly ends.[713] Quigley's statement on that topic was not allowed to be memorialized.

Why would powerful Zionist Jews allow Quigley to even write about some of their front organizations and machinations? In principle part, because the Jewish nature of the world conspiracy was being revealed and the public was becoming informed; the Jewish elite had to put a stop to that. For example, Benjamin Freedman, who was a Jewish insider, had been exposing the Zionist plan for world dominion.[714] Word was getting out, and the responsibility for the world communist conspiracy had to be spun away from the Jewish elite who controlled international banking. Enter Carroll Quigley, whose job was to establish his bona fides by revealing the nefarious plans for world domination but steer it away from the Jewish Zionists as the perpetrators and put it on an "international Anglophile network."

Carroll Quigley claimed that it was not true that Germany was politically stabbed in the back by international Jews during the events of World War I by orchestrating the entry of the U.S. into the war after an unvanquished Germany had previously offered peace on favorable terms to all parties.[715] That false claim by Quigley was clearly designed to address the claim made by Benjamin Freedman. As Freedman explained, the only reason World War I was prolonged and was not ended on the favorable terms for peace offered by Germany was a behind-the-scenes promise by the powerful international Jews to arrange for the U.S. to enter the war against Germany. The Jews did just that and received as their compensation in the form of the Balfour Declaration from England, promising to the Jews a homeland in Palestine.[716] Indeed, the verifiable historical facts are that the terms of the Balfour Declaration were dictated to the British Government by the powerful Jewish banker, Lord Lionel Walter Rothschild, who was later President of the Board of Deputies of British Jews.

> 148 Piccadilly,
> W. 1.
> July 18th, 1917.
>
> Dear Mr. Balfour,
>
> At last I am able to send you the formula you asked me for. If His Majesty's Government will send me a message on the lines of this formula, if they send you approve of it, I will hand it on to Zionist Federation and also announce it at a meeting called for that purpose. I am sorry to say our opponents have commenced their campaign by a most reprehensible manoeuvre, namely to excite a disturbance by the cry of British Jews versus Foreign Jews, they commenced this last Sunday when at the Board of Deputies they challenged the new elected officers as to whether they were all of English birth (myself among them).
>
> Yours sincerely,
> (Signed) ROTHSCHILD.
>
> II.
>
> Enclosure to (1).
>
> Draft Declaration.
>
> 1. His Majesty's Government accepts the principle that Palestine should be reconstituted as the National Home of the Jewish people.
>
> 2. His Majesty's Government will use its best endeavours to secure the achievement of this object and will discuss the necessary methods and means with the Zionist Organisation.

The Balfour Declaration was a declaration from the British Foreign Secretary Arthur James Balfour to Lord Lionel Walter Rothschild indicating the favor of the British Government toward establishing a "national home for the Jewish people" in Palestine with the British Government facilitating that objective, just as dictated by Lord Rothschild.[717] The Balfour declaration contained a clause that protected the civil and religious rights of the non-Jewish communities in Palestine, which was something for which Lord Rothschild did not provide in his dictated terms.

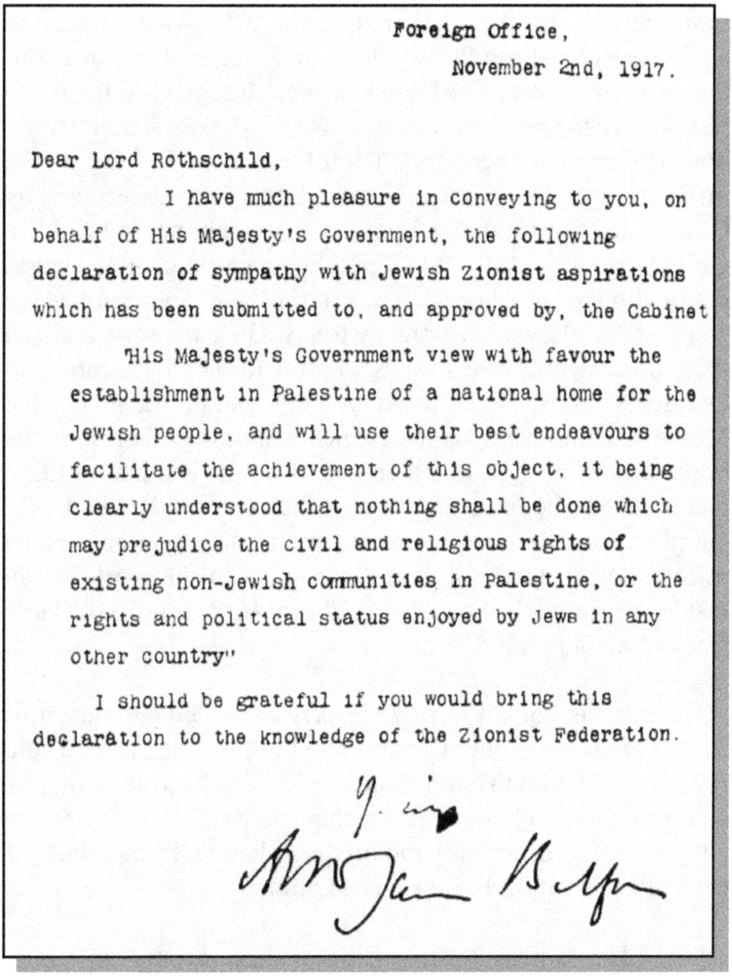

> Foreign Office,
> November 2nd, 1917.
>
> Dear Lord Rothschild,
>
> I have much pleasure in conveying to you, on behalf of His Majesty's Government, the following declaration of sympathy with Jewish Zionist aspirations which has been submitted to, and approved by, the Cabinet
>
> "His Majesty's Government view with favour the establishment in Palestine of a national home for the Jewish people, and will use their best endeavours to facilitate the achievement of this object, it being clearly understood that nothing shall be done which may prejudice the civil and religious rights of existing non-Jewish communities in Palestine, or the rights and political status enjoyed by Jews in any other country"
>
> I should be grateful if you would bring this declaration to the knowledge of the Zionist Federation.

Figure 4: The Balfour Declaration from the British Foreign Secretary Arthur James Balfour to Lord Lionel Walter Rothschild indicating the favor of the British Government toward establishing a "national home for the Jewish people" in Palestine.

Once Quigley's book was published, the Jewish

communist hierarchy was initially satisfied that the book represented only a limited hangout where they were concealed as the power pulling the strings in international intrigue. But they were mistaken. The book had enough substance for astute researchers to pierce the veil, connect the dots, and identify the powerful Jewish operators behind the scenes. It did not take much further investigation beyond the bare assertions by Quigley to identify the real powers that ought not to be. Also, Quigley was a little too specific regarding how world domination was going to be accomplished. That knowledge could not be allowed to circulate freely. Once the Jews realized their mistake they took steps to stop further publication of Quigley's book. Despite very high public demand, the MacMillan publishing house immediately stopped printing the book. The printing house then destroyed the original printing plates for the book in violation of the contract they had with Quigley. Some enterprising souls realized the importance of the information in the book being presented to the world by an insider reprinted the book. *Tragedy and Hope* is now available free online in PDF.[718]

In his book, Quigley cleverly described certain truths as though they are only myths and fables. But he, later, would reveal that the myths and fables were actually true. Now, he couldn't come right out and say they were true, so he used the contrivance of describing the myths as having "a modicum of truth" (wink-wink). For instance, Quigley states:

> The radical Right version of these events as written up by John T. Flynn, Freda Utley, and others, was even more remote from the truth than were Budenz's or Bentley's versions, although it had a tremendous impact on American opinion and American relations with other countries in the years 1947–1955. This radical Right fairy tale, which is now an accepted folk myth in many groups in

America, pictured the recent history of the United States, in regard to domestic reform and in foreign affairs, as a well-organized plot by extreme Left-wing elements, operating from the White House itself and controlling all the chief avenues of publicity in the United States, to destroy the American way of life, based on private enterprise, laissez faire, and isolationism, in behalf of alien ideologies of Russian Socialism and British cosmopolitanism (or internationalism). This plot, if we are to believe the myth, worked through such avenues of publicity as The New York Times and the Herald Tribune, the Christian Science Monitor and the Washington Post, the Atlantic Monthly and Harper's Magazine and had at its core the wild-eyed and bushy-haired theoreticians of Socialist Harvard and the London School of Economics. It was determined to bring the United States into World War II on the side of England (Roosevelt's first love) and Soviet Russia (his second love) in order to destroy every finer element of American life and, as part of this consciously planned scheme, invited Japan to attack Pearl Harbor, and destroyed Chiang Kai-shek, all the while undermining America's real strength by excessive spending and unbalanced budgets.

This myth, like all fables, does in fact have a modicum of truth. There does exist, and has existed for a generation, an international Anglophile network which operates, to some extent, in the way the radical Right believes the Communists act. In fact, this network, which we may identify as the Round Table

Groups, has no aversion to cooperating with the Communists, or any other groups, and frequently does so. I know of the operations of this network because I have studied it for twenty years and was permitted for two years, in the early 1960's, to examine its papers and secret records. I have no aversion to it or to most of its aims and have, for much of my life, been close to it and to many of its instruments. I have objected, both in the past and recently, to a few of its policies (notably to its belief that England was an Atlantic rather than a European Power and must be allied, or even federated, with the United States and must remain isolated from Europe), but in general my chief difference of opinion is that it wishes to remain unknown, and I believe its role in history is significant enough to be known.[719]

One astounding revelation in Quigley's book explains the end-game of those behind the New World Order conspiracy, and that end game suggests who they are. It could only be the Jewish international banking houses that control the central banks, as they are the only ones powerful enough to pull off the monumental goal of world hegemony described by Quigley. Quigley uses the label "powers of financial capitalism" to describe what could only be powerful international Jewish banking houses.

Quigley reveals that their goal is to "create a world system of financial control in private hands able to dominate the political system of each country and the economy of the world as a whole." These Jewish bankers want to destroy capitalism and replace it with a world socialist system that they control from the top-down. That is what the COVID-19 false pandemic and the poisonous COVID-19 vaccines are all about. This Satanic conspiracy for world dominion has been centuries in the making. Recall, that Quigley published Tragedy and Hope in 1966. Quigley explains in Tragedy and Hope:

> [T]he powers of financial capitalism had another far-reaching aim, nothing less than to create a world system of financial control in private hands able to dominate the political system of each country and the economy of the world as a whole. This system was to be controlled in a feudalist fashion by the central banks of the world acting in concert, by secret agreements arrived at in frequent private meetings and conferences. The apex of the system was to be the Bank for International Settlements in Basle, Switzerland, a private bank owned and controlled by the world's central banks which were themselves private corporations. Each central bank, in the hands of men like Montagu Norman of the Bank of England, Benjamin Strong of the New York Federal Reserve Bank, Charles Rist of the Bank of France, and Hjalmar Schacht of the Reichsbank, sought to dominate its government by its ability to control Treasury loans, to manipulate foreign exchanges, to influence the level of economic activity in the country, and to influence cooperative politicians by subsequent economic rewards in the business world.[720]

When learned scholars dissected Quigley's book and uncovered a Jewish communist conspiracy to rule the world, Quigley came out and spoke against any such notion. In a 1974 interview by Rudy Maxa,[721] Caroll Quigley stated:

> So the right said that these guys are Communist sympathizers, and are for world

domination, anti-capitalists. They want to destroy America. And a number of other things. Carroll Quigley proved everything', they said. And they constantly misquote me to this effect: that this group financed the Bolsheviks. I can see no evidence that there was any financing of the Bolsheviks by the group I'm talking about. You see, to give you one example of what it in this book. But they'll all say this. People wrote to me. They said ?Do you know about this?' They were mostly students.[722]

Quigley came under some pressure. He was called on to campaign against the revelation of the Jewish hegemony over the world conspiracy against God and man. Several books that sourced material from his book, although not overtly referring to the Jewish hierarchy, were nevertheless sufficient in detail for an astute reader to glean who was responsible for the subversion of the United States economy, government, and other institutions.

During his interview with Rudy Maxa the following exchange took place:

QUIGLEY: "And said they were having a hard time with the anti-semites using this book ['None Dare Call It Conspiracy'] as an argument against Wall Street, against bankers, against Jews, against the Communists, and everything else. And they wanted me to debate, with this fellow who'd gotten in touch with me, who was a professor at the university."[723]

MAXA: "Who believes this?"[724]

QUIGLEY: "Eh. Oh, no, he doesn't believe it. He was trying to get rid of it. The same way the fellow who called me from Brigham Young was trying to stop this hysteria which was sweeping that mountain area, apparently."[725]

Understand what is being revealed by Quigley. The debate was being set up with an opponent who was also trying to conceal information about the Jewish communist conspiracy. The entire point of the debate was to bury any notion of powerful Jews running financial institutions being involved in a communist conspiracy to subvert the United States. They knew that Quigley could be counted upon. Both sides of the debate agreed to debate the issues that were viewed as fair game for the public to know as long as they could not consider the actual players. The debate was a limited hangout to acknowledge a conspiracy but to spin the public's attention away from the actual conspirators. The debaters would only debate the scope and penetration of the conspiracy, and this was it.

They had to hope for an ignorant audience. An informed audience would see through the scam since another insider, Benjamin Freedman, had already exposed the Jewish core of the world communist conspiracy.[726] Indeed, it is likely that the revelations by Freedman prompted the Jewish hierarchy to allow Carroll Quigley to present the limited hangout of the facts in his book.

22 The Tyranny of Zionism

One can see the method of Zionist rule in Israel and other communist states. Their philosophy is that might makes right. Paragraph 12 of Protocol 1 states:

> Our right lies in force. The word "right" is an abstract thought and proved by nothing. The word means no more than: Give me what I want in order that thereby I may have a proof that I am stronger than you.[727]

The Zionist mind has no moral compass. The ends justifies the means. Whatever will accomplish the result is politically acceptable, regardless of its immorality. Paragraph 16 of Protocol 1 states:

> The result justifies the means. Let us, however, in our plans, direct our attention not so much to what is good and moral as to what is necessary and useful.[728]

These methods have been put to plans that have been nurtured in a diabolical conspiracy that has spanned centuries.

Paragraph 17 of Protocol 1 states:

> Before us is a plan in which is laid down strategically the line from which we cannot deviate without running the risk of seeing the labor of many centuries brought to naught.[729]

When the Jews thrive, then also does the nation in which they reside in like-manner fade. The idea of a restored Israel with a resulting world of harmony and justice is just a cover story to conceal the macabre plan for world dominion from the ignorant *goyim*. Yesaiah Tishbi, who is a religious authority on the Jewish Kabbalah, reveals that "the presence of Israel among the nations mends the world, but not the nations of the world . . . it does not bring the nations closer to holiness, but rather extracts the holiness from them and thereby destroys their ability to exist. . . . The purpose of the full redemption is to destroy the vitality of all the peoples."[730] This destructive influence stems from the Jewish core belief that the souls of non-Jews are evil.[731]

By supporting the state of Israel, Dispensational Zionists are furthering the cause of a world antichrist religion and oppressive political system. In Israel, the laws give Jews special status and privileges not accorded to Gentiles.[732] Identification cards issued by the Interior Ministry of Israel once listed more than 130 different categories of nationality (the most common being "Arab"). Whereas if a person was an Israeli Jew, the Identification card simply indicated that the person is Jewish. By Israeli law there cannot be a designation on the ID card for someone to be identified simply as an Israeli national.

In the year 2000 the nationality section on ID cards was phased out, because the interior ministry, which was run by an Orthodox Jewish religious party, objected to non-Orthodox Jews being identified as "Jewish" on the ID cards.[733] However, with the new ID cards any Israeli government official can instantly tell if he was looking at the card of a Jew or Arab because the date of birth on the IDs of Jews is given according to the Hebrew calendar and in addition, the ID of an Arab, unlike a Jew, includes the grandfather's name.[734]

What is the purpose of this systematic identification of Gentiles and Jews in Israel? Prejudicial discrimination. By this method, the Israeli government can determine who is Jewish and who is not. The government then selectively enforces its laws for the benefit of Jews. Jonathan Cook explains:

> [T]he special status of Jewish nationality has been a way to undermine the citizenship rights of non-Jews in Israel, especially the fifth of the population who are Arab. Some 30 laws in Israel specifically privilege Jews, including in the areas of immigration rights, naturalisation, access to land and employment.[735]

While a Gentile may be a citizen of Israel, he cannot claim his nationality as Israeli. Shimon Agranat, the President of the Supreme Court of Israel stated in a court ruling over the issue of Israeli nationality for Gentiles: "There is no Israeli nation separate from the Jewish people. ... The Jewish people is [sic] composed not only of those residing in Israel but also of diaspora Jewries."[736] Israel cannot recognize an Israeli nationality because the theory behind the state of Israel is that it is the state of the Jewish nation, which belongs to Jews all over the world. Jews are granted special legal privileges over longtime Arab citizens of Israel, once the Jews set foot in Israel, simply because they are Jews.

Professor Israel Shahak, a Jewish dissident scholar who immigrated to Israel and served in the Israeli military, explains the ingrained official institutional racism by the Jewish state of Israel:

The principle of Israel as 'a Jewish state' was supremely important to Israeli politicians from the inception of the state and was inculcated into the Jewish population by all conceivable ways. When, in the early 1980s, a tiny minority of Israeli Jews emerged which opposed this concept, a Constitutional Law (that is, a law overriding provisions of other laws, which cannot be revoked except by a special procedure) was passed in 1985 by an enormous majority of the Knesset. By this law no party whose programme openly opposes the principle of 'a Jewish state' or proposes to change it by democratic means, is allowed to participate in the elections to the Knesset.[737]

That means that no politician who seeks to hold office as a representative in the Israeli Knesset is allowed to run for office if he opposes the concept of Israel being a "Jewish state." Can anyone imagine a law in the United States that would disqualify a politician from holding office if he opposed the principle of the United States being a Catholic state, a Mormon state, or any other religious state? The very idea is antithetical to all concepts of ordered and just government.

Once a person is officially recognized as Jewish, he is given special status and rights superior to any other Gentile citizen of Israel. Professor Shahak explains:

> Let me begin with the official Israeli definition of the term 'Jewish', illustrating the crucial difference between Israel as 'a Jewish state' and the majority of other states. By this official definition, Israel 'belongs' to persons who are defined by the Israeli authorities as 'Jewish', irrespective of where they live, and to them alone. On the other hand, Israel doesn't

officially 'belong' to its non-Jewish citizens, whose status is considered even officially as inferior. This means in practice that if members of a Peruvian tribe are converted to Judaism, and thus regarded as Jewish, they are entitled at once to become Israeli citizens and benefit from the approximately 70 per cent of the West Bank land (and the 92 per cent of the area of Israel proper), officially designated only for the benefit of Jews. All non-Jews (not only all Palestinians) are prohibited from benefitting from those lands. (The prohibition applies even to Israeli Arabs who served in the Israeli army and reached a high rank.) The case involving Peruvian converts to Judaism actually occurred a few years ago. The newly-created Jews were settled in the West Bank, near Nablus, on land from which non-Jews are officially excluded. All Israeli governments are taking enormous political risks, including the risk of war, so that such settlements, composed exclusively of persons who are defined as 'Jewish' (and not 'Israeli' as most of the media mendaciously claims) would be subject to only 'Jewish' authority.[738]

Discrimination by a private party is one thing, discrimination by the government is quite another. A private party who discriminates cannot force others to also discriminate. The government, however, can enforce discrimination across its territory. George Washington famously said: "Government is not reason; it is not eloquent; it is force. Like fire, it is a dangerous servant and a fearful master." The government of Israel is using its force to discriminate in favor of Jews across its territory. That necessarily means that Israel discriminates against Gentiles and that discrimination is enforced. The Israeli government denies rights to reside, to open a business, and often to work, to anyone who is not Jewish in Israel. That is not hyperbole. Professor Shahak explains the Israeli government enforced discrimination against Gentiles:

> But there is another urgent necessity for an official definition of who is, and who is not 'Jewish'. The State of Israel officially discriminates in favour of Jews and against non-Jews in many domains of life, of which I regard three as being most important: residency rights, the right to work and the right to equality before the law. Discrimination in residency is based on the fact that about 92 per cent of Israel's land is the property of the state and is administered by the Israel Land Authority according to regulations issued by the Jewish National Fund (JNF), an affiliate of the World Zionist Organization. In its regulations the JNF denies the right to reside, to open a business, and often to work, to anyone who is not Jewish, only because he is not Jewish. At the same time, Jews are not prohibited from taking residence or opening businesses anywhere in Israel. If applied in another state against the Jews, such discriminatory practice would instantly and justifiably be labeled antisemitism and would no doubt spark massive public protests. When applied by Israel as a part of its 'Jewish ideology', they are usually studiously ignored or excused when rarely mentioned.[739]

Gentiles in Israel do not have equality before the law. Because the injustice of the discrimination against Gentiles is embarrassing to Israel, they have found a way to conceal the discrimination in official documents. One way the discrimination is concealed is that the official government documents that bestow benefits on Jews do not identify the beneficiaries as "Jews." Instead, the Israeli laws use the phrase: "anyone who can immigrate in accordance with the Law of Return" to refer to Jews. The Israeli laws use the phrase: "anyone who is **not** entitled to immigrate in accordance with the Law of Return" (emphasis added) to refer to Gentiles. Professor Shahak explains:

> Other Israeli laws substitute the more obtuse expressions 'anyone who can immigrate in accordance with the Law of Return' and 'anyone who is not entitled to immigrate in accordance with the Law of Return'. Depending on the law in question benefits are then granted to the first category and systematically denied to the second.[740]

The Israeli laws have as their objective to increase the population of Jews and decrease the population of Gentiles in Israel. There is a basic concept in government that whatever the government subsidizes will increase. Professor Shahak explains how this principle is used to increase the population of Jews in Israel and hence Jewish hegemony over that land.

> There are so many laws and regulations in Israel which discriminate in favour of the persons defined in Israel as those 'who can immigrate in accordance with the Law of Return' that the subject demands separate treatment. We can look here at one example, seemingly trivial in comparison with residence restrictions, but nevertheless important since it reveals the real intentions of the Israeli legislator. Israeli citizens who left the country for a time but who are defined as those who 'can immigrate in accordance with the Law of

Return' are eligible on their return to generous customs benefits, to receive subsidy for their children's high school education, and to receive either a grant or a loan on easy terms for the purchase of an apartment, as well as other benefits. Citizens who cannot be so defined, in other words, the non-Jewish citizens of Israel, get none of these benefits. The obvious intention of such discriminatory measures is to decrease the number of non-Jewish citizens of Israel, in order to make Israel a more 'Jewish' state.[741]

This Jewish institutional racism is part and parcel of the traditions of the Jews. Orthodox Jews are also religious chauvinists, who do not tolerate any deviation from their oral traditions. The authority of the Jewish rabbis was absolute in ancient Israel. People were so afraid of the Jews in Christ's time that they feared to even be caught speaking about Jesus. John 7:13. After the crucifixion of Jesus, Christians would meet in secret, because the Jews were actively hunting them down. *See* John 20:19 and Acts 8:1-4, 91-2. Orthodox Jews in Israel exercise the same iron rule today.

When Jews are not subjected to discrimination by the majority Gentile government, the Jewish religious leadership loses much of its coercive power. That is because a Jew who is excommunicated from the Jewish community can then find his own way as a free man in Gentile society. The shunned Jew can survive quite nicely outside the cloistered Jewish community. That is why the Jewish hierarchy tries at every turn to increase antisemitism. Increased persecution and discrimination of Jews by Gentiles creates an environment where the Jews are caught between a rock and a hard place. The fear of the Gentiles encourages the Jews to submit to the authoritarian rule of the rabbis.

Paragraph two of Protocol 9 of the *Protocols of the Learned Elders of Zion* states that antisemitism is necessary for the Zionists to keep the Jews in line. "Their anti-Semitism is indispensable to us for the management of our lesser brethren."[742] Jewish scholar Henry Makow, Ph.D., explains that "from childhood, Jews are taught that they are disliked for no rational reason and Israel is insurance against another holocaust."[743]

Antisemitism has a manifold role in the Jewish scheme. The Jewish hierarchy uses antisemitism to keep Jews from assimilating into Gentile society; they want their Jews cloistered from Gentiles. They have historically used antisemitism as a means of herding Jews to Israel. The organization *Jews Against Zionism* explains how antisemitism is used by Zionists to further their ends:

> Theodor Herzl (1860-1904), the founder of modern Zionism, recognized that anti-Semitism would further his cause, the creation of a separate state for Jews. To solve the Jewish Question, he maintained "we must, above all, make it an international political issue."
>
> Herzl wrote that Zionism offered the world a welcome **"final solution of the Jewish question."** In his "Diaries," page 19, Herzl stated "Anti-Semites will become our surest friends, anti-Semitic countries our allies."[744] (emphasis added)

Notice the language used by Herzl long before World War II and the rise of the Nazis. He described the **"final solution of the Jewish question."** That language and concept did not originate with the Germans, it originated with Jewish Zionists. The "final solution" was not the extermination of the

Jews, as is commonly believed, it was the persecution of the Jews in order to drive them out of Europe into Israel. The Nazis were simply unwitting tools in the hands of the Zionist Jews in their Machiavellian plan to gain hegemony over Palestine. All who engage in persecution of Jews, simply because they are Jews, are unwitting accessories to the Zionists.

Herzl explained in his diary how antisemitism furthers Zionist goals:

> "It is essential that the sufferings of Jews . . . become worse . . . this will assist in realization of our plans. . . . I have an excellent idea . . . I shall induce anti-semites to liquidate Jewish wealth. . . . The anti-semites will assist us thereby in that they will strengthen the persecution and oppression of Jews. The anti-semites shall be our best friends."[745] (Herzl's Diary, Part I, pp. 16)

So-called antisemitism is also a tool of the Jewish hierarchy used to keep the common Jews in line. Do not fall for that trick. If the Gentile world persecutes Jews, then the Jews will feel that they must seek the protection of the Jewish hierarchy. This gives the Jewish leaders power over the common Jews, because they cannot thrive outside the insular Jewish community. The common Jews must follow the evil dictates of the Jewish leaders who scheme against the Gentiles.

Jesus holds the answer to the Jewish issue. As Christians, we are to love our enemies. We are to be innocent in our conduct, but we should recognize and reprove the evils of Judaism. Do not allow the sin of hatred to overcome you. "Be ye angry, and sin not: let not the sun go down upon your wrath." (Ephesians 4:26) The only weapon to be used by Christians in this spiritual warfare is the gospel truth of Jesus

Christ.

> Finally, my brethren, be strong in the Lord, and in the power of his might. Put on the whole armour of God, that ye may be able to stand against the wiles of the devil. For we wrestle not against flesh and blood, but against principalities, against powers, against the rulers of the darkness of this world, against spiritual wickedness in high places. Wherefore take unto you the whole armour of God, that ye may be able to withstand in the evil day, and having done all, to stand. Stand therefore, having your loins girt about with truth, and having on the breastplate of righteousness; And your feet shod with the preparation of the gospel of peace; Above all, taking the shield of faith, wherewith ye shall be able to quench all the fiery darts of the wicked. And take the helmet of salvation, and the sword of the Spirit, which is the word of God: Praying always with all prayer and supplication in the Spirit, and watching thereunto with all perseverance and supplication for all saints. (Ephesians 6:10-18)

Antisemitism is not that answer to the Jewish hatred of Christians and Gentiles. The solution is not to strike back at the Jews, it is to love your enemy and share with him the gospel of Jesus Christ. "But I say unto you, Love your enemies, bless them that curse you, do good to them that hate you, and pray for them which despitefully use you, and persecute you." (Matthew 5:44) If you suffer persecution as a Christian at the hands of the Jews and their fellow travelers, rejoice and be glad that you are worthy to suffer for Christ's sake.

> Blessed are ye, when men shall hate you, and

> when they shall separate you from their company, and shall reproach you, and cast out your name as evil, for the Son of man's sake. Rejoice ye in that day, and leap for joy: for, behold, your reward is great in heaven: for in the like manner did their fathers unto the prophets. (Luke 6:22-23)

Jesus thought it important that we be wise about the source of our trials, but he also stated that Christians are to be harmless. "Behold, I send you forth as sheep in the midst of wolves: be ye therefore wise as serpents, and harmless as doves." (Matthew 10:16) Jesus explained that those who hate him also hate God the Father. The Jews hate Jesus and therefore they also hate the Father. The Jews reject Jesus, and therefore their god is not the Father. That leaves only Satan as their god. Do not be surprised by the unrelenting hatred of Jews toward Christians; Jesus clearly warned us that Christians would be hated by the Jews.

> If the world hate you, ye know that it hated me before it hated you. If ye were of the world, the world would love his own: but because ye are not of the world, but I have chosen you out of the world, therefore the world hateth you. Remember the word that I said unto you, The servant is not greater than his lord. **If they have persecuted me, they will also persecute you**; if they have kept my saying, they will keep yours also. But all these things will they do unto you for my name's sake, because they know not him that sent me. If I had not come and spoken unto them, they had not had sin: but now they have no cloke for their sin. **He that hateth me hateth my Father also.** If I had not done among them the works which none other man did, they had not had sin: but

now have they both seen and hated both me and my Father. But this cometh to pass, that the word might be fulfilled that is written in their law, They hated me without a cause. (John 15:18-25)

Jesus explained how to respond to the hatred of the Jews:

> But I say unto you which hear, Love your enemies, do good to them which hate you, Bless them that curse you, and pray for them which despitefully use you. And unto him that smiteth thee on the one cheek offer also the other; and him that taketh away thy cloke forbid not to take thy coat also. (Luke 6:27-29)

Do not misinterpret what Jesus was saying in Luke 6:27-29. You must read Jesus' words in the context of the whole gospel. Jesus was not saying that you should not defend yourself against physical attack by Jews or anyone else. Turning the other cheek means that you not take offense against an insult, which Jesus illustrated by the example of a slap on the cheek. Jesus point is that you "resist not evil." *See* Matthew 5:39. Jesus does not mean in Luke 6:27-29 that you should allow someone to physically harm you. In fact, Jesus advised his disciples to be armed so that they could defend themselves against those who would seek to physically harm them. Jesus said unto them, "he that hath a purse, let him take it, and likewise his scrip: and he that hath no sword, let him sell his garment, and buy one." (Luke 22:36)

Why do the Jews hate Christians so much? It is because the children of the flesh will always hate the children of the spirit. **"But as then he that was born after the flesh persecuted him that was born after the Spirit, even so it is now."** (Galatians 4:29)

Jews are victims of spiritual charlatans who have frightened them into following their heathen religion. Orthodox Jews are made by their religious leaders to hate Christ and Christians. Romans 11:28. Christians, however, are to love them and pray for them. "But I say unto you which hear, Love your enemies, do good to them which hate you, Bless them that curse you, and pray for them which despitefully use you." (Luke 6:27-28) God has chosen a remnant of Jews for salvation. Christians should preach the gospel to the lost world, including the Jews.

Jews are powerful and ruthless, but they lack wisdom. That is their weakness. They have convinced the world through their control of the media that they are exceedingly intelligent. Nothing could be further from the truth. God tells us that "[t]he fear of the LORD is the beginning of wisdom: and the knowledge of the holy is understanding." (Proverbs 9:10) The Jews reject the Lord and have no fear of him. They are in darkest ignorance. The Jewish leadership does not want the common Jew to see the light, which is why they prohibit Jews from reading the New Testament.

Our charge from the Lord is to preach God's word and reprove and rebuke those that have strayed from the sound doctrine of the Gospel of Jesus Christ. Jesus should be our model. He did not hesitate to rebuke the Jews for their religious errors. Jesus did not compromise and Christians are not to compromise with the world. We are not to be lukewarm about the gospel of Jesus Christ. Revelation 3:16. The gospel of Jesus Christ is the only effective weapon to the Jewish issue.

> For the word of God is quick, and powerful, and sharper than any twoedged sword, piercing even to the dividing asunder of soul and spirit, and of the joints and marrow, and is a discerner of the thoughts and intents of the heart. (Hebrews 4:12)

Jews and "Christian" Zionists respond to revelations of Jewish malfeasance with a cry that the bearer of the evidence is an antisemite. False claims of antisemitism are used as a shield to protect the Jewish hierarchy when evidence of their crimes are uncovered. Former Israeli government official Shulamit Aloni succinctly described the epithet antisemite as "a trick we [Jews] always use."[746] She explained that Jews hide behind it like a smokescreen, which is used to conceal evidence of Jewish malefaction.

Shulamit Aloni knows what she is talking about. She was a member of the Israeli Knesset from 1965 to 1969 and again from 1974 to 1996. She served on the Knesset Constitution Committee, Law and Justice Committee; State Audit Committee; Education and Culture Committee; and the Finance Committee. She served briefly as Minister without Portfolio from June to October 1974. From 1992 to 1996, Aloni served as Minister of Communications and the Arts, Science and Technology.[747]

By the trick of labeling a person as an antisemite, the accused person's credibility is undermined, and the focus shifts from the evidence against wrongdoing by Israel or the Jews to the motives of the accused antisemite. The Jewish controlled media then destroys the reputation of the accused antisemite, and he becomes an object lesson for anyone who might consider criticizing Israel or Jews.

Antisemitism is a versatile tool that is fashioned in the Machiavellian foundry of Judaism. It is used in different ways by the Jewish hierarchy. It is used to bludgeon its enemies with false allegations, and it is also used to control the common Jews. A close examination of Neo-Nazi hate groups reveals that there are Jews throughout their leadership. The Neo-Nazis act as *agent provocateurs* in the hands of the controlling Jews in order to fan the flames of antisemitism.

For example, Frank Collin was the leader of the National Socialist Party of America (NSPA), an anti-Semitic Neo-Nazi group. Collin created a national furor in 1977 by organizing a march in predominately Jewish Skokie, Illinois, which resulted in a First Amendment case that went all the way to the U.S. Supreme Court. It turns out that Collin was actually Jewish; his real name was Frank Cohen.[748] Before leading the NSPA, he had previously been a member of another Neo-Nazi anti-Semitic group called the National Socialist White Peoples Party (NWPP) (formerly the American Nazi Party (ANP)). Leonard Holstein was commander of the ANP's Los Angeles unit. It was discovered that Holstein was a Jew and a sodomite.[749]

There has been a resurgence of the power of the Jewish hierarchy in Israel because of the hostile Arab nations that surround Israel. That hostility is secretly encouraged by the Israeli government. For example, the Israeli government secretly funded and encouraged the growth and activities of the rabidly anti-Jewish terrorist organization, Hamas. Hamas fulfills a two-fold goal: undermining the influence of the secular Palestinian liberation organization, Fatah (Movement for the National Liberation of Palestine), and creating a hostile Islamic religious opposition to the Jewish state that was affiliated with the surrounding hostile Islamic countries. Hassane Zerouky explains:

> According to the Israeli weekly Koteret Rashit (October 1987), "The Islamic associations as well as the university had been supported and encouraged by the Israeli military authority" in charge of the (civilian) administration of the West Bank and Gaza. "They [the Islamic associations and the university] were authorized to receive money payments from abroad. Meanwhile, the members of Fatah (Movement for the National Liberation of

Palestine) and the Palestinian Left were subjected to the most brutal form of repression."

The Islamists set up orphanages and health clinics, as well as a network of schools, workshops which created employment for women as well as system of financial aid to the poor. And in 1978, they created an "Islamic University" in Gaza. "The military authority was convinced that these activities would weaken both the PLO and the leftist organizations in Gaza." At the end of 1992, there were six hundred mosques in Gaza. Thanks to Israel's intelligence agency Mossad (Israel's Institute for Intelligence and Special Tasks) , the Islamists were allowed to reinforce their presence in the occupied territories.

* * *

The Hamas then launched a carefully timed campaign of attacks against civilians, one day before the meeting between Palestinian and Israeli negotiators, regarding the formal recognition of Israel by the National Palestinian Council. These events were largely instrumental in the formation of a Right wing Israeli government following the May 1996 elections.

* * *

The Hamas had built its strength through its various acts of sabotage of the peace process, in a way which was compatible with the interests of the Israeli government. In turn, the latter sought in a number of ways, to prevent the application of the Oslo accords. In other words, Hamas was fulfilling the functions for which it was originally created: to prevent the creation of a Palestinian State. And in this regard, Hamas and Ariel Sharon, see eye to eye; they are exactly on the same wave length.[750]

Hamas acts as *agent provocateurs* under the control of the Mossad. The subterfuge of provocation by Hamas justifying a retaliatory response by Israel is exactly the strategy of Israel as explained by Moshe Sharett, the first foreign minister of Israel and prime minister of Israel from 1954-1956. Sharett stated that Israel must keep a state of "moral tension."[751] Sharett said that in order to keep that moral tension it is necessary for Israel to "invent dangers."[752] The invented dangers act as provocations for Israel to retaliate. Hamas is just such an invented danger. That is in keeping with the Mossad motto: "By way of deception, thou shalt do war."[753]

The control by the Jewish hierarchy is centered around Judaic religious traditions. Michael Hoffman explains:

> Judaism's obligation to punish Judaic heretics and its prohibition against allowing them to live in peace is unknown to the world at large, which almost exclusively associates this heresy-hunting mentality with the Spanish Inquisition and Islam's attitude toward "infidels" and "apostates." The Talmudic heresy-hunt, advocated by Orthodox rabbis historically, is not just a theory without application or real life (*yehoreig ve' al yaavor*). Where *apikorsim* can be denied life, limb or freedom, or suffer penury by being

denied the means of earning a decent livelihood.[754]

Extreme Jewish chauvinism so permeates the character of Zionists that their very language is sprinkled with racial suspicion and hatred against Palestinians. The inflammatory language of the Zionists deceptively justifies what would otherwise be inexcusable brutality. Charles Carlson calls this jingoish language "Zionese."

> "Zionese" is the unofficial spoken language of the State of Israel. Most Israelis learn and use the Zionese language, but one need not be Jewish to speak it; today it is also the language that's spoken in many Judeo-Christian and Messianic churches in America, often without church leaders realizing it.
>
> The first cab driver I rode with in Israel pointedly called the Philistines "animals" in the course of polite conversation . . . that's Zionese. He was cautioning me to keep away from Palestinians while in Israel. "They will kill you in there," he told me, when he learned I was going into Gaza. More Zionese.
>
> Zionese is not a language of letter, syllable, and punctuation. It is the delivery of a few so-called "truths" that must be learned and repeated forcefully without reservation. The trick is in the delivery. Zionese is the art of telling a story that most will reject, and repeating it as if most believe it.
>
> The teller must not worry about being thought a liar by most, so long as there are listeners who will believe because they think others

believe. Common Zionese statements are "our warfare is self-defense," "they hit us first (usually with "rockets"), "they are animals," and "Israelis are holocaust survivors." Zionese paints all Arabs as inferior. It is a language of racist superiority, and it is no stretch to call it verbal brutality.[755]

Charles Carlson wondered why Israel chose the name "Operation Cast Lead" for its 30-day Christmas war on Gaza in 2008. He could not find out why that term was used for the operation. Israel claimed that the phrase was named after a little holiday song about a toy maker who cast toys out of lead at Hanukkah. However, Carlson found out that the toy story was simply a Zionese deception. Carlson found out the real meaning of "Operation Cast Lead."

> It turns out that an old friend, Cesar Aharon, unraveled this puzzle eight years before Operation Cast Lead, when he told me about the use of molten lead as a prescribed method of killing Gentiles referred to as "burning." . . . [I]n the Talmud is described in details in the Sanhedrin . . . four ways to kill a mortal enemy, each gruesome. "Burning" it says, consists of tying the victim in a pit full of human excrement, pulling open his jaws with forceps, and pouring molten lead down his throat to his bowels.
>
> Is that not what Israel did to the people of Gaza at Christmas 2008? When Israel's military actions ended on January 18, some 1,400 Palestinians had been killed. Among the dead were hundreds of unarmed civilians, including about 300 children. Burning was the most common cause of death.[756]

23 License to Kill

The Zionist Jews view Gentiles in Israel as vermin to be exterminated. That is not hyperbole. The behavior of the Israeli Defense Force (IDF) proves the truth of the assertion. Chris McGreal, the Washington correspondent for the Guardian, who had previously been posted in Jerusalem, reported that over a three-year period "more than 400 children had been killed by the Israeli army. Nearly half were in Rafah and neighbouring Khan Yunis. One in four were under the age of 12."[757]

What is the possible justification for killing 400 children? What were the circumstances of these killings? During his research, McGreal found out that the IDF would typically claim that the shootings of children happened during gun battles between the IDF and Palestinians. McGreal researched the deaths of six children who were killed over a 10-week period.[758] He discovered that they were all in circumstances far from combat and that the IDF claims of combat were false coverups for cold-blooded murder.

McGreal reported that "[t]he dead included a 12-year-old girl, Haneen Abu Sitta, killed in Rafah as she walked home from school near a security fence around one of the fortified Jewish settlements in Gaza at the time. The army made up an explanation by falsely claiming Haneen was killed during a gun battle between Israeli forces and Palestinians."[759] McGreal interviewed the Israeli military commander in southern Gaza, Colonel Pinhas "Pinky" Zuaretz. McGreal reported that Zuaretz conceded "that there was no battle and that the girl was shot by a soldier who had no business opening fire. It was the same with the killings of some of the other children."[760]

Another example of the cold-blooded murder of a child by the IDF is the death of an 11-year-old boy, Khalil al-Mughrabi. McGreal determined that "[t]he 11-year-old boy was playing football when he was shot dead in Rafah by an Israeli soldier. The respected Israeli human rights organisations, B'Tselem, wrote to the army demanding an investigation. Several months later, the judge advocate general's office wrote back saying that Khalil was killed by soldiers who had acted with 'restraint and control' to disperse a riot in the area."[761]

McGreal, however, discovered a copy of the judge advocate general's own confidential investigation that was mistakenly attached to the false public report. The confidential report was never meant to be publicly revealed. The judge advocate general's own report impeaches the official public pronouncement of innocence. The judge advocate general's confidential investigation found "that the riot had been much earlier in the day and the soldiers who shot the child should not have opened fire. In the report, the chief military prosecutor, Colonel Einat Ron, then spelled out alternative false scenarios that should be offered to B'Tselem. The official account was a lie and the army knew it."[762]

The soldiers know that they will be protected from any punishment for cold-blooded murder and they consequently act as though they have a license to kill Palestinians with impunity. For example, McGreal reports that "an Israeli army officer who emptied the magazine of his automatic rifle into a 13-year-old Palestinian girl, Iman al-Hams, and then said he would have done the same even if she had been three years old was cleared by a military court. Iman was shot and wounded after crossing the invisible red line around an Israeli military base in Rafah, but she was never any closer than 100 yards. The officer then left the base in order to 'confirm the kill' by pumping the wounded girl full of bullets. An Israeli military investigation concluded he had acted properly."[763]

By the way, the "invisible red line" that McGreal references is a red line that appears only on IDF maps. There is no warning to the Palestinian population where such lines begin or end. Palestinians are often killed for the simple reason that they have strayed past an arbitrary and invisible red line known only to the soldier who sees it on his map.

Troublesome foreigners are also marked for death. On March 16, 2003, 23-year-old U.S. citizen Rachel Corrie was purposely run over and crushed by an Israeli military bull dozer as she protested the destruction of a Palestinian home. However, the Israeli courts have ruled that Corrie's death was an accident, despite clear and convincing eyewitness accounts that it was cold-blooded murder. Harriet Sherwood, of *The Guardian*, reported from Haifa, Israel that "the US government believed the military investigation was flawed, she added. Last week, the US ambassador to Israel, Dan Shapiro, told the Corrie family that Washington remained dissatisfied with the inquiry."[764] McGreal reports:

> She [Rachel Corrie] wasn't the only foreign victim at about that time. In the following months, Israeli soldiers shot dead James Miller, a British television documentary journalist, and Tom Hurndall, a British photographer and pro-Palestinian activist. In November 2002, an Israeli sniper had killed a

British United Nations worker, Iain Hook, in Jenin in the West Bank.

British inquests returned verdicts of unlawful killings in all three deaths, but Israel rejected calls for the soldiers who killed Miller and Hook to be held to account. The Israeli military initially whitewashed Hurndall's killing but after an outcry led by his parents, and British government pressure, the sniper who shot him was sentenced to eight years in prison for manslaughter.[765]

The outcome in the Hurndall homicide was unusual. Almost all killings of Gentiles in Israel are whitewashed in the Israeli investigations and then justified in the Israeli courts. These are just a few examples of what can only be properly described as genocide.

24 Teaching Religious Myths as Science

The Zionists have injected into the educational system principles that undermine Christian morals and order. Once the Zionists are in position of rule over the world they will teach nothing but submission to their authority. Paragraph three of Protocol 16 states:

> We must introduce into their education all those principles which have so brilliantly broken up their order. But when we are in power we shall remove every kind of disturbing subject from the course of education and shall make out of the youth obedient children of authority, loving him who rules as the support and hope of peace and quiet.[766]

It is indispensable to the Zionists' plans for world domination to undermine all religion. That is why they need to control the education of our children. That is where they instill the first ideas of atheism through the theories of evolution and heliocentricity. Paragraph three of Protocol 4 states:

> It is indispensable for us to undermine all faith, to tear out of the mind of the "goyim" the very principle of god-head and the spirit, and to put in its place arithmetical calculations and material needs.[767]

Heliocentrism, which theorizes that the earth orbits the sun as it also spins, is the seminal scientific theory from which all scientific deception flows. Heliocentrism is not based upon science; it is based upon religious superstition. So-called scientists have concluded that the earth orbits the sun. Nicolaus Copernicus died in 1543 on the day his book, *On the Revolutions of the Celestial Spheres*, was published. Most people do not know that Copernicus did not originate the theory that the earth revolves around the sun. Aristarchus of Samos (310 – 230 B. C.) is the first person known to have postulated that the earth rotates on an axis daily and orbits the sun annually. Aristarchus' model had been rejected until Copernicus' book was published. There was initially strong resistance to Copernicus' heliocentric system. However, over time the heliocentric view, with the earth and the other planets rotating around sun, has won popular acceptance.

The heliocentric theory removed the earth as the center of creation and challenged the entire ancient authority of the Bible regarding the universe and its origins. Under the heliocentric model the earth is supposed to be rotating on an axis at approximately 1,000 mph at the equator while at the same time it supposed to be traveling approximately 66,000 mph (which would be 30 times the speed of a rifle bullet) as it revolves around the sun once each year. Heliocentricity is the progenitor of the theory of evolution.

Tycho Brahe (1546 – 1601), who was born three years after Copernicus died, was the most brilliant astronomer in all of history. His observations and models established that the earth is stationary and the sun revolves around the earth, with the other planets revolving around the sun. Scientists have through objective experiments confirmed Brahe's findings. Today many of the astrophysical equations used to launch and navigate satellites assume a stationary earth.

Satan has been successful in suppressing the fact that in 1898, physicists A. A. Michelson (1852 – 1931) and chemist E. W. Morley (1838 – 1923) proved that the earth does not move. The series of Michelson/Morley experiments, using an interferometer, which measured light rays, established that the earth is stationary.[768] Throughout history scientists have conducted experiments that each time gave results that were not only consistent with a stationary earth but indicative of a stationary earth, from the light polarization experiments of E. Muscart in 1872 to the mutual inductance experiments of Theodore de Coudres in 1889 to the 1903 *Touton-Noble* experiments.[769] Dr. Neville Thomas Jones, Ph.D. explains that "George Airy proved that the world was stationary and the stars are moving."[770] Because his experiment proved that the earth does not move, which was the opposite of the expected outcome, Airy's experiment is commonly known as "Airy's failure."

Evidence that the earth is stationary is all around us. For example, assuming the heliocentric model with the earth traveling at more than 1000 mph at the equator, if one were to take a plane flight from Buffalo, New York to Miami, Florida, by the time the airplane arrived in Miami more than two hours after taking off from New York, due to the Coriolis effect Miami would have rotated more than 2000 miles to the East. That would put the plane over the Pacific Ocean, just off the west coast of Mexico's Baja Peninsula. Yet, in reality, the flight arrives in Miami on time and without the pilot having to adjust for the rotation of the earth.

The reason that the pilot does not have to adjust for the rotation of the earth is that the earth is not rotating, it is stationary just as God has said in his Holy Bible. Some who accept that the earth rotates have argued that the atmosphere moves with the earth and therefore it keeps the plane synchronized with the earth. The problem with that argument is that nobody has ever identified or measured this mysterious force that keeps the plane synchronized with the rotation of the earth. The reason that the force has never been discovered is that it does not exist. This mystical (or rather fictional) lateral force does not exist because there is no need for it; the earth is not moving.

Not only is the earth stationary, it is at the center of God's creation. In 1976 Y.P. Varshi did an extensive study of the distribution of Quasars and published his conclusion in the *Astrophysics and Space Science Journal*. Varshi was forced by the evidence to conclude that "the cosmological interpretation for the red shift in the spectra of quasars leads to yet another paradoxical result: namely, that the earth is the center of the Universe."[771] Varshi calculated the odds for of the distribution of Quasars around the earth happening by chance at 3×10^{86} to one.

God's word makes clear that the earth is God's creation and it is fixed and cannot be moved. "Fear before him, all the earth: the world also shall be stable, that it be not moved." (1 Chronicles 16:30) "The LORD reigneth, he is clothed with majesty; the LORD is clothed with strength, wherewith he hath girded himself: the world also is stablished, that it cannot be moved." (Psalms 93:1) Satan and his minions have convinced the world that the earth is not God's special creation, but just another planet.

The reason that Satan wants to convince people that the earth is just another planet is that once people can be convinced to believe that there is nothing special about the earth, it is easy to also convince them that there is nothing special about man. Whereas the bible states that "God created man in his own image, in the image of God created he him; male and female created he them." Genesis 1:27. Once people are convinced that the earth is just another of many planets, it is much easier to convince people of the fiction that man evolved from apes. With the theory of evolution, there is no room for the intelligent design of God. The ultimate aim is to deceive people into believing that there is no God. It is, therefore, not surprising that atheism is the state religion of Talmudic communism.

The theory of evolution is not only contrary to God's word, but it is not based on true science; its origins are from pagan religious beliefs. According to the established laws of science, evolution is an impossibility. The second law of thermodynamics, also known as the law of entropy, is that all matter, living or inanimate, goes from a state of order to disorder. The theory of evolution reverses that sequence and states that over time organisms go from a state of disorder to order; from the simple to the complex.

To illustrate the conflict between evolution and the laws of science, suppose one were to write each letter of one's name on a separate card. If those cards were then thrown out a second story they would scatter and fall to the ground in a chaotic display. The scattering of the cards over time as they fall to the ground illustrates the law of entropy.

The evolutionist would say that the reason that the cards did not fall to the ground in order, spelling out the persons name, is that they were not given enough time to become orderly. The evolutionist would advise one to get into an airplane and throw the cards out of the plane when it reached an altitude of 10,000 feet. By the theory of evolution the more time the cards are in the air falling, the more time they have to organize and spell out the person's name when they finally land on the ground. According to the law of entropy, and common sense, giving the cards more time to fall to the ground only increases the disorder. The evolutionist, however, contrary to the laws of science and common sense, would have you believe that the more time the cards have to fall to the ground, the more orderly they will become.

The theory of evolution is the seed that germinated into communism and socialism. Hitler, Lenin, Stalin, and Trotsky, were all converts to the theory of evolution. Evolution was the foundational philosophy for their political actions and their justification for their maniacal brutality. Once one becomes a believer in evolution, it is a small step beyond that to being a believer in a communist revolution. If there is no life giver, there is no law giver, no one made me, no one owns me, and, therefore, there is no right and wrong. Thus, there is nothing intrinsically wrong with theft, assault, torture, murder, even murdering millions of people. The Learned Elders of Zion explain that the theory of evolution serves the same destructive purpose as communism and socialism. Paragraphs two and three of Protocol 2 states:

> The intellectuals of the goyim will puff themselves up with their knowledges and without any logical verification of them will put into effect all the information available from science, which our agentur specialists have cunningly pieced together for the purpose of educating their minds in the direction we want. Do not suppose for a moment that these statements are empty words: think carefully of the successes we arranged for Darwinism (Evolution), Marxism (Communism), Nietzsche-ism (Socialism). To us Jews, at any rate, it should be plain to see what a disintegrating importance these directives have had upon the minds of the goyim.[772]

The theory of evolution is founded upon racism. In order to understand this evolutionary racism we must examine what is meant by the term race. Race is simply defined as a group of persons who have a common lineage.[773] Evolutionists, however, limit the concept of race to differences in physical appearance. Such categorization of people is contrary to biblical concepts. God in the bible does not once categorize different people according to physical appearance. He distinguishes different people by their tongues, families, nations, and countries. *See* Genesis 10:5, 20, 31; Revelation 10:11.

Prior to the 1800's, races of people were generally categorized according to their nationality (the German race, the English race, etc.).[774] With the popularity of Charles Darwin's theory of evolution, which was first published in 1859, it eventually became the widespread practice to define race according to physical appearance.

Darwin was a racist who believed that Blacks were closer to apes in the evolutionary process. In fact, the liberal humanists don't want the general public to know that the full title of Darwin's seminal 1859 book on evolution was: "THE ORIGIN OF SPECIES BY MEANS OF NATURAL SELECTION OR THE PRESERVATION OF FAVORED RACES IN THE STRUGGLE FOR LIFE." Darwin elaborated on his racist views as follows:

> At some future period, not very distant as measured by centuries, the civilized races of man will almost certainly exterminate and replace the savage races throughout the world. At the same time the anthromorphous apes will no doubt be exterminated. The break between man and his nearest allies will then be wider, for it will intervene between man in a more civilized state, as we may hope, even than the Caucasian and some ape as low as a baboon instead of as now between the Negro or

Australian and the gorilla.⁷⁷⁵

The Elders of Zion have claimed that the theory of evolution flowed from them, it is therefore not surprising to find that racist theory upon which it is based endemic within Judaism. The most revered and authoritative rabbi in Judaism, Moses ben Maimon (a/k/a Maimonide) (1135-1204 A.D.), states that Blacks are not men but are animals in a category just above an ape.⁷⁷⁶ Maimonide stated:

> [T]he Negroes found in the remote South, and those who resemble them from among them that are with us in these climes. The status of those is like that of irrational animals. To my mind they do not have the rank of men, but have among the beings a rank lower than the rank of man but higher than the rank of apes. For they have the external shape and lineaments of a man and a faculty of discernment that is superior to that of the apes.⁷⁷⁷

Maimonide's categorization of Blacks as animals just above the rank of apes should not be a surprise to most Jews, because, according to Baba Mezia 114b, the orthodox Jewish view is that only Jews are men, gentiles ("heathen") are not men.

It seems that Darwin's theory is based more upon the racist Jewish religious beliefs than it is based upon science. Darwin's racist theory of evolution, however, is refuted by real science. Many scientists hold that because the physical variations that are used to categorize people into different races (skin color, eye shape, etc.) are trivial (only .012 percent of human biological variation) and that genetically all humans are fundamentally the same, racial distinctions based upon physical appearance are not founded on biological reality but are in fact a social construct.[778]

Professor of Epidemiology Raj Bhopal, who is the head of the Department of Epidemiology and Public Health at the University of Newcastle, stated in *The British Medical Journal*: "Humans are one species: races are not biologically distinct, there's little variation in genetic composition between geographically separate groups, and the physical characteristics distinguishing races result from a small number of genes that do not relate closely to either behaviors or disease."[779]

In addition, a panel of "scientists, including geneticists and anthropologists meeting at the American Association for the Advancement of Science convention, said that the whole notion of race, based on skin color and hair type, is a social construction that has nothing to do with the genetic makeup of humans. . . . So while society busily tries to classify and reclassify races, the researchers say, it should remember that race is an artificial way to organize and categorize and has nothing to do with humans' fundamental makeup."[780]

Those scientists maintain that it is a misnomer, therefore, to label people with different physical characteristics as being of different races. Because racial distinctions are somewhat arbitrary, there is no standardization of racial categories; in fact, the labels for the various races have changed with some frequency. There has been a recent trend in the United States to categorize races of people according to their perceived national or regional origin, such as African-American, Mexican-American, etc.

God "hath made of one blood all nations of men for to dwell on all the face of the earth." Acts 17:26. Racial distinctions are contrary to the commands of God: "**Judge not according to the appearance**, but judge righteous judgement." John 7:24. See also 1 Samuel 16:7 "But the LORD said unto Samuel, Look not on his countenance, or on the height of his stature; because I have refused him: for the LORD seeth not as man seeth; for **man looketh on the outward appearance, but the LORD looketh on the heart.**"

Christians should understand that our war is not a carnal war where distinctions are made between races of people as defined by the pagan world system. Christians are in a spiritual war against unseen "spiritual wickedness in high places." Ephesians 6:12. **"For though we walk in the flesh, we do not war after the flesh: (For the weapons of our warfare *are* not carnal,** but mighty through God to the pulling down of strong holds;) Casting down imaginations, and every high thing that exalteth itself against the knowledge of God, and bringing into captivity every thought to the obedience of Christ; And having in a readiness to revenge all disobedience, when your obedience is fulfilled. **Do ye look on things after the outward appearance?** If any man trust to himself that he is Christ's, let him of himself think this again, that, as he *is* Christ's, even so *are* we Christ's." (2 Corinthians 10:3-7)

It is a natural heathen view of the world that judges men after their outward appearance. A Christian, on the other hand, is imbued with the Holy Spirit and does not judge a person based upon his skin color or outward physical appearance. A Christian instead has "the mind of Christ."

> **But the natural man receiveth not the things of the Spirit of God: for they are foolishness unto him: neither can he know *them*, because they are spiritually discerned.** But he that is spiritual judgeth all things, yet he himself is judged of no man. For who hath known the mind of the Lord, that he may instruct him? **But we have the mind of Christ.** (1 Corinthians 2:14-16)

The racist carnal mind is enmity against God.

For they that are after the flesh do mind the things of the flesh; but they that are after the Spirit the things of the Spirit. For to be carnally minded *is* death; but to be spiritually minded *is* life and peace. Because **the carnal mind *is* enmity against God**: for it is not subject to the law of God, neither indeed can be. **So then they that are in the flesh cannot please God.** But ye are not in the flesh, but in the Spirit, if so be that the Spirit of God dwell in you. Now if any man have not the Spirit of Christ, he is none of his. (Romans 8:5-9)

The racism of Judaic/evolution tends to bleed into "Christian" Zionist churches. One example is former pastor and bible teacher Steve Van Nattan. Van Nattan is a "Christian" Zionist, who vociferously criticizes evolution. With the same zeal, however, he preaches a racist gospel. His racist gospel flows directly from the same fount as does evolution, Judaic Zionism.

Van Nattan posted on his internet website the following statement: "I believe that God does not want the races confounded, but if a man and woman do marry outside of this ideal, it is no longer any of my business-- 'One flesh' is higher law than racial bounds of habitation."[781]

On Van Nattan's resume page, where he advertised himself and presented his supposed qualifications to be a pastor, he proudly proclaimed his racism: "I will not do interracial marriages because they break 'the bounds of habitation' set by God- Acts 17:26."[782]

It is preposterous for Van Nattan to suggest that Acts 17:26 supports his racist view. That passage reads: "And hath made of one blood all nations of men for to dwell on all the face of the earth, and hath determined the times before appointed, and the bounds of their habitation" Acts 17:26. That passage expressly states that all nations are made of "one blood" and that God has provided for them to dwell on "all the face of the earth."

It is the height of depravity for Van Nattan to twist God's word to say that because God sets the boundaries for the habitation of nations that he somehow prohibits interracial marriage. It takes a special reprobate mind to use a passage that states that all men are of one blood to support a claim that men should maintain separate blood identities.

The Gospel is clear. In God's kingdom there is no distinction between Jew or Gentile, black or white skin, or any other difference based upon one's physical traits or lineage. John 1:13; Galatians 3:16, 26, 29; Romans 10:11-13; 9:6-8. All who are saved are chosen by the grace of God through faith in Jesus Christ. Van Nattan, however, calls this gospel truth "mongrel teaching" and those who preach it heretics. Van Nattan states: "I do appreciate it when an heretic responds so abundantly, for in it the man reveals many new and interesting aspects of his mongrel teaching."[783] "Mongrel" when applied to men is a term used by racists to describe a person who is the result of interbreeding between two people who are perceived to be of different supposed races. There is no place for such racism in Christ's church. Van Nattan is not in Christ's church; Van Nattan's theology is Judaic and Babylonian.

That same Van Nattan falsely accuses others of being racist antisemites for revealing the truth about the antichrist theology of Zionist Jews and revealing that God's plan of salvation is by God's grace and includes Jews and Gentiles without regard to their lineage. As we have seen, Van Nattan is himself a racist; he is a particular kind of racist; he is a lying, hypocritical racist. That is not surprising, "Christian" Zionism has a tendency to turn men into brute beasts who rail against the true gospel of Jesus Christ. God explains this fact in chapter one of Jude:

> But these speak evil of those things which they know not: but what they know naturally, as brute beasts, in those things they corrupt themselves. (Jude 1:10)

God prophesied that lying hypocrites such as Steve Van Nattan would arise.

> Now the Spirit speaketh expressly, that in the latter times some shall depart from the faith, giving heed to seducing spirits, and doctrines of devils; **Speaking lies in hypocrisy**; having their conscience seared with a hot iron. (1 Timothy 4:1-2)

What does it mean to speak lies in hypocrisy? It is to falsely accuse another of the very sin of which the accuser is guilty. Steve Van Nattan is an example of one who speaks lies in hypocrisy.

Most do not know that the theory of evolution was popularized through a fraud. In 1913 Piltdown Man was announced to the world as clear evidence of a transition between man and ape. For 40 years it was touted as evidence in support of evolution, until in 1953 it was exposed as a forgery. It was determined that the skull of Piltdown Man was from a modern man and that the jawbone and teeth were from an orangutan. The teeth in the jaw had been filed down to make them look human. The bones and teeth had been chemically treated to give them the appearance of being prehistoric. The bones were then planted at the burial site in which they were found.

There is a strong belief among those who have investigated the matter that the noted Jesuit Priest Pierre

Teilhard de Chardin, was instrumental in perpetrating that hoax. The scientist who helped unmask the forgery, Dr. Kenneth Oakley, formerly of the British Museum, said that a letter written to him by Teilhard in 1954 had given him "strong indications that Teilhard was in collusion with Charles Dawson," in committing the Piltdown Man hoax.

The atheistic political and scientific theories of heliocentrism, evolution, and communism are for the purpose of corrupting our youth, generation after generation. If people can be convinced that there is no God, it is easy to convince them that there is no rule-giver and hence are no moral absolutes. Morals become subjective. The standard is whatever serves the interest of the individual. Paragraph 10 of Protocol 9 states:

> We have fooled, bemused and corrupted the youth of the "goyim" by rearing them in principles and theories which are known to us to be false although it is that they have been inculcated.[784]

Some have developed a code of conduct that as long as what they do does not cause direct harm to anyone else it is okay. They do not realize that conduct that violates God's laws causes unperceived harm to many others. After the sin has degenerated the person and the harm is caused to the sinner and victims, the lie of their satanic code of conduct is revealed.

An example of the subversion of the morals of our youth and the Christian morals of our society is found in the pornography industry, which is almost completely under the control of Jews. While many Jews gravitate to pornography because of the immense profits, many Jews view pornography as a means to vent their hatred of Christ by subverting Christian culture. Jewish Professor of American History Nathan Abrams researched the pornography industry and concluded that

"Jewish involvement in the X-rated industry can be seen as a proverbial two fingers to the entire WASP establishment in America. . . . Jewish involvement in porn, by this argument, is the result of an atavistic hatred of Christian authority: they are trying to weaken the dominant culture in America by moral subversion."[785] Al Goldstein, the publisher of the pornographic *Screw* magazine, stated: "The only reason that Jews are in pornography is that we think that Christ sucks. Catholicism sucks. We don't believe in authoritarianism."[786]

There is a goal to the Jewish strategy in promoting pornography and all manner of concupiscence. It helps the Zionists control Gentiles by putting them in a hedonistic stupor. Henry Makow quotes Sociologist Erica Carle who states that "Sex is the ultimate weapon in people-taming and people control"[787] Carle opines that when sex can be established as a constant and dominant idea in the mind, the mind can be incapacitated. She states that a fixation on sex destroys emotions, personal identity, individuality, family life, maternal and paternal feelings. "All else can be forgotten or regarded as unimportant, when the mind is captured by the dominant idea of sex."[788]

Henry Makow explains the point of the destruction of Christian principles through a statement a Zionist speaker made during a secret 1936 *B'nai B'rith* meeting:

> As long as there remains among the Gentiles any moral conception of the social order, and until all faith, patriotism and dignity are uprooted, our reign over the world shall not come.[789]

25 Jewish Media Control

The control of the media is one of the principal sources of Jewish power. It is through their dominance of major media outlets that Jews have command over the general population to steer their thoughts and passions. Paragraph five of Protocol 2 states:

> In the hands of the States of today there is a great force that creates the movement of thought in the people, and that is the Press. The part played by the Press is to keep pointing out requirements supposed to be indispensable, to give voice to the complaints of the people, to express and to create discontent. It is in the Press that the triumph of freedom of speech finds its incarnation. But the goyim States have not known how to make use of this force; and it has fallen into our hands. Through the Press we have gained the power to influence while remaining ourselves in the shade; thanks to the Press we have got the gold in our hands, notwithstanding that we have had to gather it out of the oceans of blood and tears. But it has paid us, though we have

sacrificed many of our people. Each victim on our side is worth in the sight of God a thousand goyim.[790]

The Zionists refer to this power of the press as "the great power." Paragraph five of Protocol 7 states:

We must compel the governments of the goyim to take action in the direction favored by our widely conceived plan, already approaching the desired consummation, by what we shall represent as public opinion, secretly promoted by us through the means of that so-called "great power" - the press, which, with a few exceptions that may be disregarded, is already entirely in our hands.[791]

Who can question the authenticity of the Protocols of the Learned Elders of Zion when Protocol after Protocol is being fulfilled before our very eyes? Protocol 7 states that the press is in Jewish hands; that Protocol is confirmed when one sees the major media outlets under Jewish control. John Whitley reported in 2003 that "seven Jewish Americans run the vast majority of US television networks, the printed press, the Hollywood movie industry, the book publishing industry, and the recording industry."[792] He explained that "[m]ost of these industries are bundled into huge media conglomerates." He listed the Jewish men and stated that "[t]hose seven Jewish men collectively control ABC, NBC, CBS, the Turner Broadcasting System, CNN, MTV, Universal Studios, MCA Records, Geffen Records, DGC Records, GRP Records, Rising Tide Records, Curb/Universal Records, and Interscope Records."[793] Whitley's research revealed:

Most of the larger independent newspapers are owned by Jewish interests as well. An example is media mogul Samuel I. 'Si' Newhouse, who owns two dozen daily newspapers from Staten Island to Oregon, plus the Sunday supplement Parade; the Conde Nast collection of magazines, including Vogue, The New Yorker, Vanity Fair, Allure, GQ, and Self; the publishing firms of Random House, Knopf, Crown, and Ballantine, among other imprints; and cable franchises with over one million subscribers.[794]

Whitley's conclusions are as valid today as they were in 2003. Whitley explains why: "I could add that Michael Eisner could depart Disney tomorrow but the company will remain in the hands of Shamrock Holdings, whose principal office is now located in Israel."[795]

Former Vice President of the United States, Spiro Agnew, stridently discussed the Jewish control of the major media outlets in a 1976 Newsweek article:

> The people who own and manage national impact media are Jewish and, with other influential Jews, helped create a disastrous U.S. Mideast policy. All you have to do is check the real policy makers and owners and you find a much higher concentration of Jewish people than you're going to find in the population.
>
> By national impact media I am referring to the major news wire services, pollsters, Time and Newsweek Magazines, the New York Times, Washington Post, and the International Herald Tribune. For example, CBS' Mr. (William) Paley's Jewish. Mr. Julian Goodman, who runs NBC, and there's a Leonard Goldenson at ABC. Mrs. Katherine Graham owns the

Washington Post and Mr. Sulzberger the New York Times. They are all Jews!

You go down the line in that fashion. . . . not just with ownership but go down to the managing posts and discretionary posts. . . . and you'll find that through their aggressiveness and their inventiveness, they now dominate the news media. Not only in the media, but in academic communities, the financial communities, in the foundations, in all sorts of highly visible and influential services that involve the public, they now have a tremendous voice.

Our policy in the Middle East in my judgment is disastrous, because it's not even handed. I see no reason why nearly half the foreign aid this nation has to give goes to Israel, except for the influence of this Zionist lobby. I think the power of the news media is in the hands of a few people. . . . it's not subject to control of the voters, it's subject only to the whim of the board of directors.[796]

How did the major media outlets become completely controlled by Zionist Jews and their fellow travelers? J.P. Morgan was an agent of international Jewish (Rothschild) banking interests. On February 17, 1917, Congressman Oscar Callaway presented the following facts before the United States Congress which explained the successful efforts of J.P. Morgan and his cabal to control public opinion in order to involve the United States in World War I.

Mr. CALLAWAY. Mr. Chairman, under unanimous consent, I insert in the record at this point a statement showing the newspaper combination, which explains their activity in this war matter, just discussed by the gentleman from Pennsylvania, [Mr. Moore]:

"In March, 1915, the J.P. Morgan interests, the steel, shipbuilding, and powder interests, and their subsidiary organizations, got together 12 men high up in the newspaper world and employed them to select the most influential newspapers in the United States and sufficient number of them to control generally the policy of the daily press of the United States.

"These 12 men worked the problem out by selecting 170 newspapers, and then began, by an elimination process, to retain only those necessary for the purpose of controlling the general policy of the daily press throughout the country. They found it was only necessary to purchase the control of 25 of the greatest newspapers.

"The 25 papers were agreed upon; emissaries were sent to purchase the policy, national and international, of these papers; an agreement was reached; the policy of the papers was bought, to be paid for by the month; an editor was furnished for each paper to properly supervise and edit information regarding the questions of preparedness, militarism, financial policies, and other things of national and international nature considered vital to the interest of the purchasers.

"This contract is in existence at the present time, and it accounts for the news columns of the daily press of the country being filled with all sorts of preparedness argument and misrepresentations as to the present condition of the United States Army and Navy and the possibility and probability of the United States being attacked by foreign foes.

"This policy also included the suppression of everything in opposition to the wishes of the interests served. The effectiveness of this scheme has been conclusively demonstrated by the character of stuff carried in the daily press throughout the country since March, 1915. They have resorted to anything necessary to commercialize public sentiment and sandbag the national congress into making extravagant and wasteful appropriations for the Army and Navy under the false pretense that it was necessary. Their stock argument is that it is 'patriotism.' They are playing on every prejudice and passion of the American people."[797]

How successful have the Jews and their fellow conspirators been in controlling public knowledge and opinion? Read and weep over the sad truth as John Swinton, the former Chief of Staff for the New York Times, explains the state of the supposed free press in the United States in a speech before the New York Press Club in 1953.

There is no such thing, at this date of the world's history, in America, as independent press. You know it and I know it. There is not one of you who dares to write your honest opinions, and if you did, you know beforehand that it would never appear in print. I am paid weekly for keeping my honest opinion out of the paper I am connected with. Others of you are paid similar salaries for similar things, and any of you who would be so foolish as to write honest opinions would be out on the streets looking for another job. If I allowed my honest opinions to appear in one issue of my paper, before twenty-four hours my occupation would be gone. The business of the journalists is to destroy the truth; to lie outright; to pervert; to vilify; to fawn at the feet of mammon, and to sell his country and his race for his daily bread. You know it and I know it and what folly is this toasting an independent press? We are the tools and vassals of rich men behind the scenes. We are the jumping jacks, they pull the strings and we dance. Our talents, our possibilities and our lives are all the property of other men. We are intellectual prostitutes.[798]

The Zionists have succeeded in controlling the press through the so-called press services like the Associated Press (AP) and United Press International (UPI). Those press services act as choke points to censor news. This method is explained in paragraphs 4 and 15 of Protocol 12.

> Not a single announcement will reach the public without our control. Even now this is already being attained by us inasmuch as all news items are received by a few agencies, in whose offices they are focused from all parts of the world. These agencies will then be already entirely ours and will give publicity only to what we dictate to them.

* * *

We shal have a sure triumph over our opponents since they will not have at their disposition organs of the press in which they can give full and final expression to their views owing to the aforesaid methods of dealing with the press.[799]

The news coverage (or rather lack thereof) of the infamous leaked Downing Street Memo illustrates how the Zionist warmongers use their news services to censor inconvenient news. The memo and the media censoring of it is explained in detail in this author's book, *9/11 - Enemies Foreign and Domestic*.

The highly classified British memo, leaked in the midst of Britain's May 2005 election campaign, indicated that President Bush decided to overthrow Iraqi President Saddam Hussein by summer 2002 and was determined to falsify U.S. intelligence data to support his policy.[800] The memo revealed that plans for invading Iraq by the Bush administration were well under way while Bush was lying to the American public by telling them that no decision had been made to go to war.

The secret Downing Street memo[801] also revealed that on July 23, 2002 British Prime Minister Tony Blair and members of his cabinet were going along with Bush and devising a plan for a joint U.S./British military invasion of Iraq.[802] However, two days later Blair dissembled to the House of Commons by stating that "we have not got to the stage of military action . . . we have not yet reached the point of decision."[803]

Without question, the Downing Street memo was one of the most significant news events of the year. The memo presents clear evidence that the Bush Administration lied the U.S. into the Iraq War. Yet, media analysts at *Editor and Publisher* reported: "The liberal Web site Media Matters for America found that editorials in four of the five largest U.S. newspapers -- USA Today, The Wall Street Journal, The New

York Times, and the Los Angeles Times - 'remained conspicuously silent about the controversy surrounding the document.'"[804]

Several editors blamed their own lack of coverage of the memo on the Associated Press' (AP) lack of coverage.[805] "The Associated Press is a not-for-profit cooperative, which means it is owned by its 1,500 U.S. daily newspaper members. They elect a board of directors that directs the cooperative."[806] Most U.S. Newspapers rely heavily on the reporting by the AP, especially regarding international news.

The Associated Press filters the news through its control bureaus; the Downing Street memo seems to have been one of many worthy news stories that never made it passed the censors in the control bureau. AP's Middle East control bureau, which is located in Israel, demonstrates that the AP is controlled by Zionist Jews. Alison Weir explains that the AP Middle East control bureau "is staffed largely by Jewish and Israeli journalists, many with close family ties to the Israeli military. Their reporting invariably contains pro-Israel spin and context. Quite often, they don't even send out reports on newsworthy items that reveal negative facts about Israel."[807]

"Deborah Seward, Associated Press international editor, has told Eric Boehlert of Salon magazine that the AP 'dropped the ball' in failing to pick up the Downing Street memo story earlier. AP's deputy international editor, Nick Tatro, told Boehlert 'It was our intent to do a story, and it just didn't happen,' for a variety of reasons."[808] The AP is recognized for their unparalleled reach, with news sources throughout the world. It is astounding that their explanation for not reporting on this blockbuster story is that they "dropped the ball" and "it just didn't happen!" That does not pass the smell test.

Why can't the International Editor and the Deputy

International Editor for the AP offer any explanation for not reporting the news of the memo other than to state that they just didn't do it? Obviously, the story was deliberately spiked by the AP, and they don't want to admit it. It is not difficult to perceive at work the hidden hand of the Zionists who control the AP. How many other stories have never seen the light of day because the AP deliberately "dropped the ball" or the reporting purposely "just didn't happen?" Former CIA Analyst, Ray McGovern, has labeled the major media outlets as "the domesticated press," for their purposeful efforts in avoiding any meaningful coverage of the Downing Street memo.[809]

These powerful Zionists not only censor the news, they also provide endless "circuses" and amusements to distract the people from being aware that their liberties have been stolen from them. Paragraph three of Protocol 13 states:

> We further distract them with amusements, games, pastimes, passions, people's palaces ... soon we shall begin through the press to propose competitions in art, in sport in all kinds: these interests will finally distract their minds from questions in which we should find ourselves compelled to oppose them. Growing more and more unaccustomed to reflect and form any opinions of their own, people will begin to talk in the same tone as we because we alone shall be offering them new directions for thought . . . of course through such persons as will not be suspected of solidarity with us.[810]

26 The Real Reason Politicians Support Israel

Samuel Untermeyer, who introduced Cyrus Scofield to the Zionist leaders who financed Scofield's research trips to Oxford and arranged the publication and distribution of Scofield's reference bible,[811] was also the Zionist agent who directly controlled President Woodrow Wilson.

The political rulers who rise to high office and other influential religious and opinion leaders are picked in advance for their positions by the Zionist Jews. The criteria for their selection is their political naivete and servile obedience to Zionist interests. Paragraph two of Protocol 2 states:

> The administrators, whom we shall choose from among the public, with strict regard to their capacities for servile obedience, will not be persons trained in the arts of government, and will therefore easily become pawns in our game in the hands of men of learning and genius who will be their advisers, specialists bred and reared from early childhood to rule

the affairs of the whole world.[812]

That explains how we end up with misfits like Woodrow Wilson, Franklin Roosevelt, and Harry Truman (not to mention George Bush and Barack Obama) as our presidents. They were picked in advance based upon their blind obedience to the Zionist cause. "The love of money is the root of all evil." 1 Timothy 6:10. Zionists often use the tried-and-true method of bribery to compromise a President.

Texe Marrs reveals how in 1948 Zionist power-broker, Abraham Feinberg, delivered a two-million-dollar bribe in $100 bills packed in suitcases to Truman; in return Truman was to recognize Israel as a sovereign state. Marrs explains:

> This bribe to Truman, confirmed by recently released FBI archives, means that Israel is today and always has been an illegitimate state established on the basis of a criminal act.
>
> The Truman White House was overflowing with Jewish bureaucrats, treacherous Communists, and Israel firsters with little allegiance to the U.S.A. In the Truman White House also was Harry Hopkins, a secret Soviet agent who arranged for Stalin and Russia to be given America's nuclear blueprints and materials. The fledgling nation of Israel was also given atomic bomb materials and plans.
>
> Two dedicated American patriots, Secretary of Defense James Forrestal and General George Patton, refused to go along with the Jewish treachery and takeover of the White House. Both were cruelly assassinated. Forrestal was "suicided," being thrown out of a sixteenth floor window.

***

While President Truman, for the most part, meticulously followed the marching orders dictated to him by his Zionist overlords, he privately chafed about his subordinate status. He despised the Jews' smug, superior attitudes and resented the fact that they had bribed him to recognize Israel.

Interestingly, Truman finally rebelled in what appears to have been a small but was actually a very significant way. When the declaration to recognize Israel was brought to him for his signature, it first read: ". . . the new Jewish State of Israel." Truman took his pen and lined through the words "new Jewish." This meant that the U. S. recognized not a "new Jewish State"—a religious and racial designation—but instead simply a "State."

To this day, the Zionists insist theirs is a "Jewish" State. In other words, a Jewish religious theocracy. But this is not so. Israel was recognized by President Truman and the U.S. as a secular State, not as a Jewish religious theocracy. This has tremendous significance for the Palestinians. Today, the Palestinians are unfairly treated as non-citizens in Israel. They are allowed neither to vote or to own property, as the Jews spout the fiction that Israel was founded as a Jewish State and those of other races and religions do not belong.

[N]o one can accurately say that President Harry Truman did not fully understand the unpatriotic sentiments and attitudes of the Jews who reside in America. After his retirement, in 1956, Truman confided in an interview his knowledge that American Jews were disloyal to the U.S. He stated: "When a Jew born and living in America talks to his Jewish companions about 'our government,' he means the government of Israel."[813]

As stated in paragraph two of Protocol 2, the Zionists put their servile Presidents "in the hands of men of learning and genius who will be their advisers."[814] That ensures that the Presidential pawn follows their dictates and acts in their interests. An example of that is found in the Obama administration, where his chief of staff for the first two years of Obama's Presidency was Rahm Emanuel. Rahm Emanuel is a dual citizen of Israel. His father was a member of the Irgun, a Zionist terror gang. Emanuel's father took part in the successful plot to assassinate Count Bernadotte, a Swedish diplomat and United Nations envoy who tried to broker peace in Palestine.[815] What are Emanuel's loyalties? During the 1991 Gulf War, Rahm Emanuel served, not in the U.S. miliary, but instead in the Israeli Defense Forces (IDF).[816]

Texe Marrs states that Barrack Obama was groomed to be President of the United States by his Zionist handlers. The Zionist philosophy was so ingrained in Obama that Abner Mikva, who was the Jewish former White House Counsel in the Clinton Administration, told the Chicago Tribune on December 12, 2008 that "Barack Obama will go down in history as America's first Jewish President."[817] Interestingly, on September 18, 2011, *New York Magazine* depicted on its cover the back of President Obama's head wearing a yarmulke with a title calling him "America's First Jewish President."[818] The exoteric point of the cover was not to reveal that Obama is Jewish but to reveal, as was expressed in the subtitle: "Barack Obama is the best friend Israel has right now."

Judson Miner gave Obama his first job in Chicago. Miner, who is a Jewish lawyer, stated "I used to tease Barack that he had Jewish blood."[819] On April 16, 2008, the Los Angeles Times reported that Barack Obama claimed that he had Jewish kinship after he told an audience that "My links to the Jewish community are not political. They preceded my entry into politics."[820] Victor Thorn reported for the *American Free Press*:

> Rabbi Arnold Wolf (who died in 2008), a Democratic Socialist. "We had a party for [Obama] at our house when he was just starting back in the 1990s. I said right away: '[H]ere's a guy who could sell our product, and sell it with splendor.'"
>
> From the research done on Barack Obama during the past few years, it's clear that his rise to power can be unequivocally mapped as follows. At the top exist extremely wealthy Jewish financiers such as the Rothschilds and George Soros, who've set his course in motion. To carry out this plan are mid-level Jewish operatives (Rahm Emanuel, Axelrod, Summers, Katz etc), along with hard-line Marxist sympathizers.
>
> Lastly, at the street level are a host of black nationalists such as Van Jones and Rev. Jeremiah Wright, whose rhetoric is aggressively anti-white. Toss in a very pro-Obama unabashedly Jewish-controlled media, and it's ultimately clear how he reached the Oval Office.[821]

Thorn's point that Obama would never have reached the office of President unless he was approved in advance by powerful Zionists is supported by the evidence. Texe Marrs explains Barrack Obama's socialist leanings are part and parcel of his Zionist training, during which he was groomed to be an obedient servant to the Zionist agenda:

> Barack Obama is America's first Jewish President. No, not by DNA, not according to the flesh, but regardless, a Zionist Jew; and the Jew part is so ingrained in his nature that the world's most influential billionaire Jewish Illuminati honor him as a devout Zionist who can be trusted. Obama, the Jews say, "has a Jewish soul." Obama is Jewish "in his gut," says one top Jewish politico.

* * *

> As I show in my new video [*Rothschild's Choice*], Barack Obama's white mother was a Communist, his white grandparents were Communists, and the black man who mentored him from youth, Frank Marshall Davis, was also a Communist. Davis was, moreover, a perverted, bisexual dope-head and a bigoted racist.

* * *

> Obama's most intimate Chicago associates were, and are today, Communists. Virtually all are Jews, and most are gay. Indeed, Barack Obama's whole life has been a sordid cesspool and saga of Communist instruction, Zionist philosophy, intensely perverted homosexual buggery, fervent anti-Americanism and a "Hate Whitey" form of black racism. What we have here is a President whose agenda is alien

to our Constitution, a man committed to Marxist aims and a Zionist Police State.[822]

George W. Bush, in like manner, was under the complete control of Zionist Jews. When Israeli spies were arrested celebrating the explosions in the World Trade Center towers on 9/11/2001, the political influence of Israel over the U.S. government was immediately brought o bear to secure their release back to Israel. Witnesses saw the group filming the smoking New York skyline. The men seemed quite happy with the spectacle of the burning towers. A neighbor witnessed the men shouting cries of joy and mockery. They all had prior knowledge of the 9/11 attacks and were set up in advance to film the World Trade Center explosions. The fact that the group was set up in advance to film the explosions in the WTC Towers was confirmed by CIA Field Agent Robert Baer.[823] At least two of the arrested Israelis were determined to be Mossad agents. They all worked for a moving company, Urban Moving, which was later determined to be a Mossad front operation. All had prior knowledge of the attacks and were prime suspects; however, they were eventually released and allowed to return to Israel.

Who was behind the release of the Israeli spies? Michael Chertoff, as head of the Criminal Division of the Department of Justice, had control over the entire investigation (read: cover-up) of 9-11. Chertoff obstructed justice by ordering the return of the spies to Israel. Why would Chertoff do such a thing? He is a dual citizen of Israel. His real loyalties are with Israel.

In 2005, Christopher Bollyn exposed the fact that Michael Chertoff was an Israeli national. Chertoff was the Assistant Attorney General responsible for the Criminal Division of the U.S. Department of Justice during and after the 9-11-2001 attacks.[824] Israel made certain it had key people in place to ensure that there would be no blowback on Israel.

Chertoff was one of those key men.

Bollyn was able to substantiate his allegation that Chertoff is an Israeli national; Bollyn obtained a flight manifest that showed that Chertoff spent part of his childhood in Israel.[825] The flight manifest from El Al flight LY207/17 from Israel to New York on 18 August 1955 indicates passenger #28 was Michael Chertoff. Chertoff would have been approximately three years old at that time. Chertoff travelled with his father, Gershon Baruch Chertoff, an orthodox rabbi, who sat in seat #26 and his Israeli mother Livia Eisen Chertoff, who sat in seat #27.

Assistant Attorney General Chertoff remained at his post until 2003. Chertoff was appointed to the position of the Director of the U.S. Department of Homeland Security in 2005. Bollyn explained that the Chertoff family involvement in Israeli intelligence affairs has deep roots. Chertoff's mother was the first hostess on El Al and was involved in secret Mossad missions. In fact, her obituary in the December 21, 1998, (Newark, N.J.) Star-Ledger specifically mentions her involvement in Operation Magic Carpet.[826]

Michael Chertoff has resurfaced. Mitt Romney named Michael Chertoff co-chair of his counterterrorism and intelligence advisory committee in October 2011.[827] Mitt Romney, who as of this writing is the Republican candidate for President of the United States is also under Zionist control. It matters not to the Zionists who wins the election, both Obama and Romney are under their wing.

Mitt Romney was the cofounder and former CEO of Bain Capital. At that time, in 1992, the managing director of Bain Capital was Orit Gadiesh. She was also the chairman of the subsidiary, Bain & Company.[828] Bain Capital owns Clear Channel, which is the largest chain of radio stations in the United States. Clear Channel owns the networks that air The

Glenn Beck Program, The Rush Limbaugh Show, America Now with Andy Dean, The Sean Hannity Show, Coast to Coast AM, The Savage Nation, The Mark Levin Show, and The Dave Ramsey Show.[829]

Orit Gadiesh was born in Israel in 1951. Gadiesh served in Israeli military intelligence and was once the war room assistant to Ezer Weizman and Moshe Dayan. At the time Ezer Weizman was the Deputy Chief of Staff for the Israeli Defense Forces and later became president of Israel.[830] Gadiesh is the daughter of Israeli Brigadier General Falk Gadiesh (born Falk Gruenfeld, Berlin, 1921). She has had close ties with Mitt Romney since 1991. When Romney was elected Governor of Massachusetts in 2002, he appointed Gadiesh to his transition team.[831]

Orit Gadiesh is currently on the board of directors of the Peres Center for Peace. That organization is headed by a former chief of staff of the Israeli military, Lt. General Amnon Lipkin-Shahak.[832] A high-level member of the Mossad and managing director of the Marc Rich Foundation, Avner Azulay, is on the executive board of the Peres Center.[833]

Mitt Romney had been schooled in the needs of the Zionists before he was recruited as their pick as the Republican candidate for President. In 2007, Romney attended the Mossad's Herzliya Conference on Israeli Security.[834] Romney reportedly also worked together with Israeli prime minister Benjamin Netanyahu as consultants at the Boston Consulting Group early in their careers.[835]

Whether Zionist Mitt Romney wins or Zionist Barrack Obama wins matters not to the Zionists Jews, because they control both the Democratic and Republican parties. It does not matter to them whether it's Heckle or Jeckle as President, the Zionists will win either way. Zionist Jew Harold Wallace Rosenthal explains how issues are framed by the Jews who control both sides of the debate. The gullible Gentiles do not see that the debate is being limited to only the narrow issue allowed by the Jews.

> We Jews have put issue upon issue to the American people. Then we promote both sides of the issue as confusion reigns. With their eye's fixed on the issues, they fail to see who is behind every scene. We Jews toy with the American public as a cat toys with a mouse.[836]

Political campaigns are the best examples of this principle in action. In 1968, Alabama Governor George Wallace stated the truth that "there is not a dime's worth of difference between the Democrat and Republican Parties!" It was true then, and it is true now. The Zionists care not if the Republican candidate or the Democratic candidate wins the election. Heads they win; tails they win. Political campaigns are not unlike professional wrestling matches. They are exhibitions for the mindless masses who mistakenly think that the outcome of an election will make a difference.

Zionist Jews usually groom their candidates for President well in advance of their selection. The Zionists then use the advisors who surround the President to control his every move. However, that does not ensure the obedience of their chosen front-man. How can the Zionists be sure that their hand-picked politician will be obedient? They compromise them through some hidden embarrassment that the Jews hold over the politician's head. It would be so much easier to just put their own Jews in place, but that would tend to reveal the Jewish nature of the conspiracy, so they use Gentile front-men. This is explained in paragraph three of Protocol 8:

> For a time, until there will no longer be any risk in entrusting responsible posts in our State

> to our brother-Jews, we shall put them in the hands of persons whose past and reputation are such that between them and the people lies an abyss, persons who, in case of disobedience to our instructions, must face criminal charges or disappear - this in order to make them defend our interests to their last gasp.[837]

What is the abyss that is mentioned in Protocol 8? Paragraph 13 of Protocol 10 explains that it is some embarrassing skeleton in the closet that the Zionists hold over the head of the Politician.

> In order that our scheme may produce this result we shall arrange elections in favor of such presidents as have in their past some dark, undiscovered stain, some "Panama" or other - then they will be trustworthy agents for the accomplishment of our plans out of fear of revelations and from the natural desire of everyone who has attained power, namely, the retention of the privileges, advantages and honor connected with the office of president.[838]

President Barrack Obama is the latest example of a compromised politician with a secret "stain" that the Zionist Jews hold over his head to keep him in line. Jerome Corsi (Harvard, Ph.D.), a reporter for WorldNet Daily, reported: "Former radical activist John Drew has said that when he met Obama when Obama was a student at Occidental College, he thought Obama and his then-Pakistani roommate were 'gay' lovers."[839] Corsi further states:

> A prominent member of Chicago's homosexual community claims Obama's participation in the "gay" bar and bathhouse scene was so well known that many who were

aware of his lifestyle were shocked when he ran for president and finally won the White House.[840]

Corsi interviewed Kevin DuJan, who revealed the secret life of Obama:

> DuJan, founder and editor of the Hillary Clinton-supporting website HillBuzz.org, told WND he has first-hand information from two different sources that "Obama was personally involved in the gay bar scene."
>
> "If you just hang out at these bars, the older guys who have been frequenting these gay bars for 25 years will tell you these stories," DuJan said. "Obama used to go to the gay bars during the week, most often on Wednesday, and they said he was very much into older white guys."
>
> Obama, DuJan said, is "not heterosexual and he's not bisexual. He's homosexual."
>
> Investigative journalist Wayne Madsen, who worked with the National Security Agency from 1984 to 1988 as a Navy intelligence analyst, confirmed DuJan's claims.
>
> "It is common knowledge in the Chicago gay community that Obama actively visited the gay bars and bathhouses in Chicago while he was an Illinois state senator," Madsen told WND.[841]

There are eye-witness accounts of Obama's sodomite activities. Larry Sinclair, a sodomite, claimed that he had sex and used cocaine twice with Obama while Obama was an

Illinois state senator.[842] Furthermore, Sinclair reveals that in October 2007, Donald Young told him that he was intimately involved with then-Senator Barrack Obama.[843] Obama's Zionist handlers simply could not allow Young to compromise Obama's chances to win the Presidency. Corsi interviewed a worker at Obama's Chicago church, Trinity United Church of Christ, whose pastor is the infamous racist, Jeremiah Wright. Corsi discovered from her that the Zionists have been working overtime keeping a lid on Obama's sexual proclivities.

> "At Trinity, if you even hint at talking about Obama being gay, you are reminded of our dear departed choir director," she said. "He was killed, and it wasn't a robbery. The Christmas presents weren't touched. The TV was not taken, nothing in the apartment was missing."
>
> Carolyn's reference was to Donald Young, the 47-year-old homosexual choirmaster at Trinity who died of multiple gunshot wounds in his Chicago apartment Dec. 24, 2007.
>
> Young's murder was preceded Nov. 17, 2007, with the execution-style murder of 25-year-old Larry Bland, another black gay member of Trinity United. He also was murdered in his home, dying of multiple gunshot wounds, according to his death certificate.
>
> Just two days after the murder of Young, a third openly "gay" member of Wright's church, Nate Spencer, reportedly died of septicemia, pneumonia and AIDS. . . . The murders of Donald Young and Larry Bland remain today open cases of unsolved homicide.[844]

On May 21, 2012, Newsweek ran a cover story with a picture of President Obama with a rainbow halo and a title: "The First Gay President."[845] The exoteric point of the cover was to simply reveal Obama as the strongest supporter of gay rights ever to become President. However, in view of what we know about Obama's sodomite character, could there be an esoteric meaning behind the cover, intended to express the secret knowledge of the insiders that Obama is a sodomite?

President Woodrow Wilson is another example of a compromised politician. We see Protocols 8 and 10 in action in President Wilson's career. Immediately upon being elected U.S. President, Wilson was faced with perfectly timed breach of promise lawsuit from a married woman with whom he had an affair when he was President of Princeton University. She was the wife of one of his professors. President Wilson did not have the necessary $40,000 demanded by the woman. This was going to become a public scandal that would have ruined Wilson's marriage and political career.

Mr. Samuel Untermeyer, a wealthy Zionist Jew, arranged to pay the $40,000 on behalf of President Wilson. President Wilson was relieved when Mr. Untermeyer showed President Wilson a stack of love letters written by Wilson that were delivered to him by the woman in return for the $40,000 payment. Untermeyer assured President Wilson that he would retain the love letters he wrote to the woman to ensure that he would be protected from any further attempt to extract money from him in the future.[846]

Wilson clearly understood that in those love letters Untermeyer held his future in his hands. From that moment on, President Wilson was under the complete control of the Zionists. Soon after, President Wilson was doing Untermeyer's bidding. At the behest of Untermeyer, President Wilson appointed the first Talmudic Jew, Louis Dembitz Brandeis, to the U.S. Supreme Court. That was followed by Wilson's signing the Federal Reserve act into law and petitioning congress for a declaration of War against Germany, which brought the United States into World War I. Who wrote the legal opinion that convinced Wilson of the case for declaring war on Germany? None other than Justice Brandeis.

The ultimate goal of the Zionist Jews is to bring about world government under Jewish control. They use conflict and war as a means of establishing world government. Paragraph four of Protocol 9 states:

> [A]ll states are in torture; they exhort to tranquility, are ready to sacrifice everything for peace: but we will not give them peace until they openly acknowledge our international super-government, and with submissiveness.[847]

We see the principle in Protocol 9 coming to bear after World War I. The League of Nations was established. Woodrow Wilson failed in his effort to get the United States to join the League of Nations. Without the United States, the League of Nations had no power and lost legitimacy.

What did the Zionists do after their failed attempt to establish a world government through the League of Nations? They started World War II. After World War II, the Zionists succeeded in establishing a world body of nations called the United Nations. The United States joined the United Nations, and its headquarters is in New York city. While it does not yet have the full powers envisioned by its Zionist/Socialist founders, each decade sees it gaining more and more power. The United Nations seems to be the precursor to a true world government envisioned in Protocol 9.

The key to convincing the world of the need for a world government is to incite wars between nations. The best way to do that is to have a single person who can declare war. The founding fathers of the United States clearly understood how the war-making power has been much abused throughout history and so gave the power to declare war to Congress and not to the President. Article One, Section Eight of the Constitution states that "Congress shall have power to . . . declare War." The Zionists don't much like that as it is an impediment to starting wars. They simply arrange to invest the President with the power to declare war. They explain this in Paragraph 13 of Protocol 10.

> Independently of this we shall invest the president with the right of declaring a state of war. We shall justify this last right on the ground that the president as chief of the whole army of the country must have it at his disposal, in case of need for the defense of the new republican constitution, the right to defend which will belong to him as the responsible representative of this constitution.[848]

The Zionists seem to have accomplished their goal. On September 14, 2001, the United States Congress passed a joint resolution titled: "The Authorization for Use of Military Force." That resolution gave President George Bush the almost unlimited war powers to attack any country he, in his sole discretion, deemed to have aided or harbored organizations or persons who planned, authorized, or committed the September 11, 2001, attacks on the United States. The declaration states in pertinent part:

> That the President is authorized to use all necessary and appropriate force against those nations, organizations, or persons he determines planned, authorized, committed, or aided the terrorist attacks that occurred on

September 11, 2001, or harbored such organizations or persons, in order to prevent any future acts of international terrorism against the United States by such nations, organizations or persons.[849]

The "Authorization for Military Force" Joint Resolution gave President Bush complete discretion to invade any country in the world with no prior declaration of war by Congress. President Bush wasted no time in sending the United States Armed Forces to invade Afghanistan. As explained in this author's book, *9/11 - Enemies Foreign and Domestic*, Afghanistan had nothing to do with the September 11, 2001, attacks. *9/11 - Enemies Foreign and Domestic* sets forth irrefutable evidence that proves the September 11, 2001 attacks were false-flag attacks perpetrated by Israel, aided and abetted by treasonous high officials in the U.S. government.

The "Authorization for Military Force" Joint Resolution is just one of many future acts planned by the Zionists to undermine the constitutional protections against tyranny. Ultimately, they would like to abolish all of the restrictions in the constitution that infringe on their efforts to enslave us all. They seem hellbent on centralizing all power in the office of President. They explain how they seek to accomplish this in Paragraphs 16, 17, and 18 of Protocol 10.

> The president will, at our discretion, interpret the sense of such of the existing laws as admit of various interpretation; he will further annul them when we indicate to him the necessity to do so, besides this, he will have the right to propose temporary laws, and even new departures in the government constitutional working, the pretext both for the one and the other being the requirements for the supreme welfare of the State.

By such measure we shall obtain the power of destroying little by little, step by step, all that at the outset when we enter on our rights, we are compelled to introduce into the constitutions of States to prepare for the transition to an imperceptible abolition of every kind of constitution, and then the time is come to turn every form of government into our despotism.

The recognition of our despot may also come before the destruction of the constitution; the moment for this recognition will come when the peoples, utterly wearied by the irregularities and incompetence - a matter which we shall arrange for - of their rulers, will clamor: "Away with them and give us one king over all the earth who will unite us and annihilate the causes of disorders - frontiers, nationalities, religions, State debts - who will give us peace and quiet which we cannot find under our rulers and representatives."[850]

Conclusion

The Protocols of the Learned Elders of Zion are a blueprint for world domination by Zionist Jews. "Christian" Zionists are a crucial part of their plans to bring about their world kingdom headquartered in Israel. "Christian" Zionists do not know that the Jewish Zionists hate them and consider them "useful idiots" to be disposed of once they achieve their satanic kingdom.

"Christian" Zionism is just the latest in Jewish corruptions of biblical doctrines. During the Babylonian captivity, an occult society of Jews replaced God's commands with Babylonian dogma. Their new religion became Judaism. Jesus explained the corrupt Judaic religion: "Howbeit in vain do they worship me, teaching for doctrines the commandments of men." (Mark 7:7) Jesus revealed the heart of Judaism: "Ye are of your father the devil, and the lusts of your father ye will do." John 8:44.

The Judaic variant of Babylonianism was cloaked in Christian language, while keeping its Babylonian substance, to become the apostate Roman Catholic Church. The Babylonian religion thus flowed through the Jews to the Roman Catholic Church. The modern-day Jews are seeking to infect nominal "Christian" denominations with a supposed philosemitic variant of that Babylonian religion. This has given rise to the "Christian" Zionist movement, which is neither Christian nor

Zionist in the biblical sense.

God's Zion is in a heavenly Jerusalem. Revelation 21:10. Jesus made clear that "My kingdom is not of this world." John 18:36. All Christians are the body of Christ without regard to their ethnic background. The chosen believers in Christ are Christ's body. "Now ye are the body of Christ, and members in particular." (1 Corinthians 12:27) Jesus is in believers and believers are in Jesus. John 14:20; 17:20-23. There is one spiritual body of Christ, with Jesus the head. Colossians 1:18.

The leading "Christian" Zionist preachers are wolves in sheep's clothing. Jesus warned about such ravening spiritual wolves. The devilish, worldly Zionism is the evil fruit springing of the pulpits of the "Christian" Zionist churches.

> Beware of false prophets, which come to you in sheep's clothing, but inwardly they are ravening wolves. Ye shall know them by their fruits. Do men gather grapes of thorns, or figs of thistles? Even so every good tree bringeth forth good fruit; but a corrupt tree bringeth forth evil fruit. A good tree cannot bring forth evil fruit, neither *can* a corrupt tree bring forth good fruit. Every tree that bringeth not forth good fruit is hewn down, and cast into the fire. Wherefore by their fruits ye shall know them. (Matthew 7:15-20)

Just as the Jews did, so also the "Christian" Zionists teach man-made doctrine, as though it is God's word. For example, God commanded his disciples to "[g]o ye into all the world, and preach the gospel to every creature." (Mark 16:15) A significant segment of "Christian" Zionists expressly violate Jesus' command and instead consider it a waste of time to preach the gospel to Jews.

The supposed philosemitism of "Christian" Zionists is in reality an esoteric form of antisemitism. The gospel is the means of salvation. "So then faith cometh by hearing, and hearing by the word of God." (Romans 10:17) Purposely refusing to preach the gospel to Jews, because they are Jews, is the epitome of antisemitism.

Steven Paas concluded that the philosemitism of "Christian" Zionism and antisemitism share some of the same prejudicial assumptions about Jews. Paas opines that antisemitism is a possible consequence of "Christian" Zionism. Paas stated:

> [S]ections of philosemitic "Christian" Zionism could easily turn to the opposite. It should not be forgotten that in the last analysis antisemitism in its narrow focus on the Jews and Israel shares some assumptions with philosemitism. The extremes touch.[851]

What Paas views as only a possibility is in fact a reality. The refusal of "Christian" Zionists to evangelize the Jews because they are Jews is not the possibility of antisemitism, it is the purest form of antisemitism. The public expression of love for the Jews in words spoken by the "Christian" Zionists is in reality an esoteric hatred for Jews. When we judge the "Christian" Zionist tree by its fruit, we find that it bares the bitter fruit of hatred.

The refusal to evangelize the Jews is evidence of a current of antisemitism flowing through the "Christian" Zionist camp. For example, Max Blumenthal has alleged that arch-Zionist John Hagee is an antisemite. Blumenthal states: "For nearly two years, a handful of independent journalists and I have raised the alarm about Hagee's long record of anti-Semitic statements."[852] The allegations of antisemitism were enough for presidential candidate John McCain to cut ties with Hagee.[853]

That bitter fruit of hatred is born of the common Babylonian theology shared between "Christian" Zionists and Jews. The Jewish religion is born of a Babylonian chauvinism, where all Gentiles are hated by the Jews. It is not surprising to find that the "Christian" Zionists return that hatred, only in a more subtle and esoteric way. "[T]he serpent was more subtil than any beast of the field which the LORD God had made."(Genesis 3:1)

Paul warned that after he departed grievous wolves would enter in among the disciples and that "of your own selves shall men arise, speaking perverse things, to draw away disciples after them." Acts 20:29-31. Furthermore, God prophesied that "some shall depart from the faith, giving heed to seducing spirits, and doctrines of devils." 1 Tim 4:1. The attempt to corrupt the gospel to comport with this Judaic/Babylonian mysticism was immediately detected by the early Christian disciples.

> For there are certain men crept in unawares, who were before of old ordained to this condemnation, ungodly men, turning the grace of our God into lasciviousness, and denying the only Lord God, and our Lord Jesus Christ. Jude 1:4.

The Devil's disciples succeeded in perverting the gospel and creating a Judaic/Babylonian form of ersatz "Christianity," which grew to become the Roman Catholic Church. That church has a facade of piety, but it is the habitation of devils, and its doom is sealed by God.

> And he cried mightily with a strong voice, saying, Babylon the great is fallen, is fallen, and is become the habitation of devils, and the

hold of every foul spirit, and a cage of every unclean and hateful bird. (Revelation 18:2)

There are many other corrupt children of Babylon the Great; she is "the mother of harlots and abominations of the earth." Revelation 17:5. "Christian" Zionism is one of those harlot children. God warns the children of the harlot to come out of her to avoid the judgement of God:

> And I heard another voice from heaven, saying, **Come out of her, my people**, that ye be not partakers of her sins, and that ye receive not of her plagues. For her sins have reached unto heaven, and God hath remembered her iniquities. Reward her even as she rewarded you, and double unto her double according to her works: in the cup which she hath filled fill to her double. (Revelation 18:4-6)

God's warning to come out of Babylon the Great is to "my people." The consequences of not being one of God's people are dire. "The Son of man shall send forth his angels, and they shall gather out of his kingdom all things that offend, and them which do iniquity; And shall cast them into a furnace of fire: there shall be wailing and gnashing of teeth." Matthew 13:41-42. Jesus will say to them: "Depart from me, ye cursed, into everlasting fire, prepared for the devil and his angels . . . And these shall go away into everlasting punishment: but the righteous into life eternal." Matthew 25:41,46.

There are only two types of religions in the world. They are diametrically opposed to each other, as though separated by a great gulf. On the one side of that gulf are the many varieties of the religion of salvation by personal merit, whether it be works or blood descent. God has made clear that salvation cannot be obtained by one's lineage, works, or even the force of one's own will; salvation is a gift by the sovereign will of God. In fact, because Jesus made it clear that salvation is not exclusive to the Jews and indeed was completely by the will of God, the Jews received him not.

> He came unto his own, and his own received him not. But as many as received him, to them gave he power to become the sons of God, even to them that believe on his name: Which were born, not of blood, nor of the will of the flesh, nor of the will of man, but of God. (John 1:11-13)

On the other side of the great gulf is the one and only religion of the free grace of God, found in the Holy Bible. The premise of the bible is that man is spiritually dead in sins and trespasses, and his will is enslaved to sin. Man must be made spiritually alive again by a new birth that can only come from God through his sovereign election. The religion of God's grace boldly proclaims that the sovereign God planned salvation for helpless sinners and that he furnishes them with the ability and the desire to receive it. God states in his Holy Bible:

> But God, who is rich in mercy, for his great love wherewith he loved us, Even when we were dead in sins, hath quickened us together with Christ, (by grace ye are saved;) And hath raised us up together, and made us sit together in heavenly places in Christ Jesus: That in the ages to come he might shew the exceeding riches of his grace in his kindness toward us through Christ Jesus. For by grace are ye saved through faith; and that not of yourselves: it is the gift of God: Not of works, lest any man should boast. For we are his workmanship, created in Christ Jesus unto good works, which God hath before ordained

that we should walk in them. Ephesians 2:4-10.

God has provided salvation for his elect. It is a free gift from God, without regard to blood descent. The "Christian" Zionists replaces the sovereign grace of God and instead adheres to an alternative salvation for the Jews, based upon the fact that they are Jews.

Jews have a zeal for God, but it is not according to knowledge. Jews try to establish their own righteousness, rather than rest in the imputed righteousness of Christ.

> For I bear them record that they have a zeal of God, but not according to knowledge. For they being ignorant of God's righteousness, and going about to establish their own righteousness, have not submitted themselves unto the righteousness of God. For Christ is the end of the law for righteousness to every one that believeth. Romans 10:2-4.

The gospel of Jesus Christ is that our sins are remitted once and for all by the sacrifice of Jesus on the cross. If you are one of God's people, and you are presently a "Christian" Zionist, a Catholic, a Jew, or practice a religion that is based upon Babylonian dogma and liturgy, you are commanded by God to come out of that religion. How do you know if you are one of God's people? First, you will be born again. "Except a man be born again, he cannot see the kingdom of God." John 3:3.

How is one born again? One is spiritually born again by the grace of God alone, through faith in Jesus Christ alone. You cannot work your way to heaven. Salvation is a gift of God, by his grace through faith in Jesus Christ. Ephesians 2:8-10.

What about the commandments of God? They were intended to act as a schoolmaster, the purpose of which was to bring men to faith in Christ. Galatians 3:24-25. Jesus makes clear that all the law and the prophets are summarized in just two commandments. "Thou shalt love the Lord thy God with all thy heart, and with all thy soul, and with all thy mind." and "Thou shalt love thy neighbour as thyself." Matthew 22:35-40. God states that in order to gain entrance into heaven one must obey and keep all of God's law. *See* Leviticus 18:5; Luke 10:25-28. "For whosoever shall keep the whole law, and yet offend in one point, he is guilty of all." James 2:10.

All who do not keep every one of God's commands are under a curse. "Cursed is every one that continueth not in all things which are written in the book of the law to do them." Galatians 3:10. If we sin by transgressing God's law, we must be punished, because God is just. The cursed punishment for violating God's law is eternal darkness where there is weeping and gnashing of teeth. *See* John 5:29; Matthew 25:1-46, 13:41-43; Romans 2:5-8; 2 Thessalonians 1:7-9.

One cannot enter heaven with any sin. "Know ye not that the unrighteous shall not inherit the kingdom of God?" 1 Corinthians 6:9. "For thou art not a God that hath pleasure in wickedness: neither shall evil dwell with thee. The foolish shall not stand in thy sight: thou hatest all workers of iniquity." Psalms 5:4-5. *See also* Galatians 5:19-21. The punishment for one's sins is to be cast into the lake of fire and brimstone. Revelation 21:7-8. No one is capable of keeping God's law through their own effort; none is righteous, not one single person.

> As it is written, There is **none** righteous, **no, not one**: There is **none** that understandeth, there is **none** that seeketh after God. They are all gone out of the way, they are together become unprofitable; there is **none** that doeth

good, **no, not one**. Romans 3:10-12.

How can anyone inherit the kingdom of God, if no one is righteous or does any good, but God requires perfect righteousness? God's very character holds the answer.

> The LORD, The LORD God, merciful and gracious, longsuffering, and abundant in goodness and truth, Keeping mercy for thousands, forgiving iniquity and transgression and sin, and that will by no means clear the guilty. Exodus 34:6-7.

God is perfectly righteous. He is both perfectly just and perfectly merciful. If God is perfectly just and must therefore punish sin, how can he allow his children into heaven without them being punished for their sins? If God punished the sinner, then no one could enter heaven, since the due punishment for sin is eternal torment in fire. If God simply forgives the sin, without punishment, that would be unjust.

God resolved the dilemma of punishing sin and at the same time forgiving the sinner by coming to earth and living a perfect life and allowing himself to be punished in our place for our sins. "For he hath made him to be sin for us, who knew no sin; that we might be made the righteousness of God in him." 2 Corinthians 5:21. The Jesus of the Holy Scriptures is the sovereign potentate over all of creation; he is Lord of Lords and King of Kings who created heaven and earth. 1 Titus 6:15; Revelation 17:4; 19:6. He came to earth and paid the price for sin, so that if you believe in him, all of your sins will be forgiven. He punished himself for our sins (being perfectly just) and forgives us who committed the sins (showing perfect mercy).

If you believe in the Lord Jesus Christ, his perfect life will be imputed to you, and in the eyes of God you are sinless and righteous. Galatians 3:6-9. You are justified not because you are good, but because Christ is good and paid the price for your sins. He took the complete punishment for your sin, which was required by God's perfect justice, so that he could forgive you completely, according to his perfect mercy. "Come now, and let us reason together, saith the LORD: though your sins be as scarlet, they shall be as white as snow; though they be red like crimson, they shall be as wool." (Isa 1:18)

Jesus is the only way to heaven. "Jesus saith unto him, I am the way, the truth, and the life: no man cometh unto the Father, but by me." John 14:6. Jesus makes it clear that it is all or nothing: "He that is not with me is against me." Matthew 12:30. If you do not believe in Jesus, then you will have to pay the eternal price for your own sin in the lake of fire, because the perfect justice of God requires that sin be punished. Revelation 20:11-15. The only way to avoid being punished for your sins is by having Jesus pay the price in your stead. It is through faith in the work of Jesus Christ and not by one's own works that one is saved. Romans 3:21-28; 4:1-8. Jesus has redeemed us from the curse of the law by being cursed in our stead. He, who knew no sin was punished for our sins. Galatians 3:11-14.

None seek after God. Romans 3:10-18. The bible makes it clear that all men are born dead in trespasses and sin and must be spiritually reborn to be saved from their sins. "And you hath he quickened, who were dead in trespasses and sins." Ephesians 2:1. Salvation can only be by the spiritual faith that is a gift from Jesus. Romans 5:15-18. A man who is spiritually dead cannot make himself spiritually alive again; that is a rebirth that only God can accomplish. God must supply the faith, because man in his fallen state is incapable of believing in Jesus.

Jesus is "the author and finisher of our faith." Hebrews 12:2. That means that Jesus is the source of saving faith, and Jesus sees that faith to its completion. One cannot have faith <u>in</u>

Jesus Christ without God giving one the faith of Jesus Christ. "[T]he scripture hath concluded all under sin, that the promise by **faith of Jesus Christ** might be **given to them that believe.**" Galatians 3:22. *See also* Romans 3:22; Galatians 2:16; Revelation 14:12; Ephesians 3:12; Philippians 3:9.

If one tries to add works to faith as a means of salvation, that is evidence that one does not have saving faith. Galatians 2:16. Certainly, true faith will bring repentance and bear the fruit of good works. James 2:17; Acts 3:19; Matthew 3:8. However, that does not mean that salvation is merited by good works. In fact, all of your self-righteous works are as filthy rags to God. Isaiah 64:6. Salvation is a free gift, given by a loving Jesus, not a reward earned by the sinner. Once we are freed from the bondage of sin, we can bear the fruit of righteousness. "But now being made free from sin, and become servants to God, ye have your fruit unto holiness, and the end everlasting life." (Romans 6:22) *See also* Romans 5:16-19; 7:1-8:17.

The bible explains that God the Father must draw one to believe in Jesus. "No man can come to me, except the Father which hath sent me draw him: and I will raise him up at the last day." (John 6:44) No one can come to Jesus unless the Father draws him. "All" those that are chosen for salvation "shall" come to Jesus. Jesus stated: "**All that the Father giveth me shall come to me; and him that cometh to me I will in no wise cast out.**" John 6:37. Furthermore, Jesus assures us that he will lose none of those whom God the Father has given him. "**[O]f all which he hath given me I should lose nothing, but should raise it up again at the last day.**" John 6:39.

Learn from the example of the man who knew he lacked saving faith. "Lord, I believe; help thou mine unbelief." (Mark 9:24) One needs to pray to Jesus to "help thou mine unbelief." Praying to Jesus for saving faith is the best evidence that one is being drawn by the Father to Jesus. Jesus guarantees the pull of the Father will be effectual. All who are drawn to Jesus by the Father will believe in Jesus and be saved, and Jesus will raise them up on the last day.

Those who believe in Jesus are adopted children of God. They are chosen by God for adoption before the world was created.

> **According as he hath chosen us in him before the foundation of the world, that we should be holy and without blame before him in love: Having predestinated us unto the adoption of children by Jesus Christ to himself, according to the good pleasure of his will.** (Ephesians 1:4-5)

To be glorified with Christ as an adopted son of God is too wonderful a thought to even comprehend. "But as it is written, Eye hath not seen, nor ear heard, neither have entered into the heart of man, the things which God hath prepared for them that love him." 1 Corinthians 2:9. We shall be called sons of God, because we are his children and are imbued with eternal life.

> Behold, what manner of love the Father hath bestowed upon us, that we should be called the sons of God: therefore the world knoweth us not, because it knew him not. Beloved, now are we the sons of God, and it doth not yet appear what we shall be: but we know that, when he shall appear, we shall be like him; for we shall see him as he is. 1 John 3:1-2.

Endnotes

1. Henry Makow, Illuminati: The Cult That Hijacked the World, at 163 (2011).

2. Cornerstone Church, 18755 Stone Oak Parkway, San Antonio, Texas 78258, http://www.sacornerstone.org (last visited on May 15, 2012).

3. Outreach Magazine, 2008-The Outreach 100, The Tope 100 Largest Churches, http://www.sermoncentral.com/articleb.asp?article=Top-100-Largest-Churches3 (last visited on May 15, 2012).

4. Cornerstone Church, Beliefs, http://www.sacornerstone.org/about-beliefs (last visited on May 15, 2012). John Hagee Ministries, Beliefs, http://www.jhm.org/Home/About/Beliefs (last visited on May 15, 2012).

5. G. Richard Fisher, The Other Gospel Of John Hagee: Christian Zionism And Ethnic Salvation, *Personal Freedom Outreach*, http://www.pfo.org/jonhagee.htm (last visited on May 15, 2012).

6. John Hagee Ministries, http://www.jhm.org (last visited on May 15, 2012).

7. Robert B. Bluey, John Hagee: Iran Poses Grave Threat to Western Civilization, *Human Events*, March 16, 2006, http://www.humanevents.com/article.php?id=13250 (last visited on May 16, 2012).

8. Robert B. Bluey, John Hagee: Iran Poses Grave Threat to Western Civilization, *Human Events*, March 16, 2006, http://www.humanevents.com/article.php?id=13250 (last visited on May 16, 2012).

9. Christians United For Israel, http://www.cufi.org/site/PageServer (last visited on May 15, 2012).

10. Nicole Balnius, Rapture Ready, Who's Who of Prophecy, http://www.raptureready.com/who/John_Hagee.html (last visited on May 15, 2012).

11. Nicole Balnius, Rapture Ready, Who's Who of Prophecy, http://www.raptureready.com/who/John_Hagee.html (last visited on May 15, 2012).

12. Nicole Balnius, Rapture Ready, Who's Who of Prophecy, http://www.raptureready.com/who/John_Hagee.html (last visited on May 15, 2012).

13. Sarah Posner, Lobbying for Armageddon, August 3, 2006, http://www.alternet.org/story/39748/ (last visited on May 15, 2012).

14. Max Blumenthal, Birth Pangs of a New Christian Zionism, The Nation, August 8, 2006, http://www.thenation.com/issue/august-14-2006.

15. Werther, Rev. John Hagee's War, The Manchurian Clergyman, Counterpunch, Weekend Edition, July 29-31, 2006, http://www.counterpunch.org/2006/07/29/the-manc

hurian-clergyman/.

16. Sarah Posner, Lobbying for Armageddon, August 3, 2006, http://www.alternet.org/story/39748/ (last visited on May 15, 2012).

17. Thomas L. McFadden, *PASTOR JOHN HAGEE: Is the Devil in Him?*, American Free Press May 7, 2010, http://www.americanfreepress.net/html/john_hagee_devil_221.html.

18. G. Richard Fisher, The Other Gospel Of John Hagee: Christian Zionism And Ethnic Salvation, *Personal Freedom Outreach*, http://www.pfo.org/jonhagee.htm (last visited on May 15, 2012).

19. G. Richard Fisher, The Other Gospel Of John Hagee: Christian Zionism And Ethnic Salvation, *Personal Freedom Outreach*, http://www.pfo.org/jonhagee.htm (last visited on May 15, 2012), citing "San Antonio fundamentalist battles anti-Semitism," *Houston Chronicle*, April 30, 1988, sec. 6, pg. 1, available at *Houston Chronicle Archives*, http://www.chron.com/CDA/archives/archive.mpl/1988_540301/san-antonio-fundamentalist-battles-anti-semitism.html (last visited on May 17, 2012).

20. G. Richard Fisher, The Other Gospel Of John Hagee: Christian Zionism And Ethnic Salvation, *Personal Freedom Outreach*, http://www.pfo.org/jonhagee.htm (last visited on May 15, 2012), citing "San Antonio fundamentalist battles anti-Semitism," *Houston Chronicle*, April

30, 1988, sec. 6, pg. 1, available at *Houston Chronicle Archives*, http://www.chron.com/CDA/archives/archive.mpl/1988_540301/san-antonio-fundamentalist-battles-anti-semitism.html (last visited on May 17, 2012).

21. G. Richard Fisher, The Other Gospel Of John Hagee: Christian Zionism And Ethnic Salvation, *Personal Freedom Outreach*, http://www.pfo.org/jonhagee.htm (last visited on May 15, 2012), citing "San Antonio fundamentalist battles anti-Semitism," *Houston Chronicle*, April 30, 1988, sec. 6, pg. 1, available at *Houston Chronicle Archives*, http://www.chron.com/CDA/archives/archive.mpl/1988_540301/san-antonio-fundamentalist-battles-anti-semitism.html (last visited on May 17, 2012).

22. G. Richard Fisher, The Other Gospel Of John Hagee: Christian Zionism And Ethnic Salvation, *Personal Freedom Outreach*, http://www.pfo.org/jonhagee.htm (last visited on May 15, 2012).

23. John Hagee, In Defense of Israel, at 136, quoted by John Hagee's Visit to Fresno, Bet Shalom Messianic Congregation, http://betshalomfresno.org/?page_id=409 (last visited on May 26, 2012).

24. John Hagee and Dual Covenant Theology, Telling The Jews They Don't Need Jesus, http://www.nowtheendbegins.com/pages/deception/john-hagee-and-dual-covenant-theology.htm (last visited on May 26, 2012).

25. Steven Paas, Christian Zionism Examined, A Review of Ideas on Israel, the Church, and the Kingdom, at 28 (2012).

26. Steven Paas, Christian Zionism Examined, A Review of Ideas on Israel, the Church, and the Kingdom, at 98 (2012).

27. Steven Paas, Christian Zionism Examined, A Review of Ideas on Israel, the Church, and the Kingdom, at 102 (2012).

28. Babylonian Talmud: *Tractate Sanhedrin, Folio 90a*, Sanhedrin Translated into English with Notes, Glossary and Indices Chapters I - VI by Jacob Shachter, Chapters VII - XI by H. Freedman, B.A., Ph.D., Under the Editorship of Rabbi Dr I. Epstein B.A., Ph.D., D. Lit. (1961), *available at* http://www.come-and-hear.com/sanhedrin/sanhedrin_90.html.

29. Babylonian Talmud: *Tractate Sanhedrin, Folio 90a*, Sanhedrin Translated into English with Notes, Glossary and Indices Chapters I - VI by Jacob Shachter, Chapters VII - XI by H. Freedman, B.A., Ph.D., Under the Editorship of Rabbi Dr I. Epstein B.A., Ph.D., D. Lit. (1961), *available at* http://www.come-and-hear.com/sanhedrin/sanhedrin_90.html.

30. Michael Hoffman, *Judaism Discovered*, at 534 (2008).

31. Elizabeth Dilling, *The Jewish Religion, Its Influence Today* (1963), *at*

http://www.come-and-hear.com/dilling/chapt03.html#The_18_Benedictions.

32. Steven Paas, Christian Zionism Examined, A Review of Ideas on Israel , the Church, and the Kingdom, at 105 (2012).

33. Steven Paas, Christian Zionism Examined, A Review of Ideas on Israel , the Church, and the Kingdom, at 113 (2012).

34. Steven Paas, Christian Zionism Examined, A Review of Ideas on Israel , the Church, and the Kingdom, at 106 (2012).

35. Steven Paas, Christian Zionism Examined, A Review of Ideas on Israel , the Church, and the Kingdom, at 111 (2012).

36. Steven Paas, Christian Zionism Examined, A Review of Ideas on Israel , the Church, and the Kingdom, at 107 (2012).

37. Steven Paas, Christian Zionism Examined, A Review of Ideas on Israel , the Church, and the Kingdom, at 108 (2012).

38. Steven Paas, Christian Zionism Examined, A Review of Ideas on Israel , the Church, and the Kingdom, at 109 (2012).

39. John Hagee Minstries, Beliefs, http://www.jhm.org/Home/About/Beliefs (last visited on May 15, 2012).

40. John Hagee Ministries, Why Christians Should Support Israel, The Apple of HIS Eye, http://www.jhm.org/Home/About/WhySupportIsrae

l (last visited on May 15, 2012).

41.http://www.blessedquietness.com/journal/prophecy/zionism.htm (web page current as of 10-1-03).

42.G. Richard Fisher, The Other Gospel Of John Hagee: Christian Zionism And Ethnic Salvation, *Personal Freedom Outreach*, http://www.pfo.org/jonhagee.htm (last visited on May 15, 2012), citing David Becker, "John Hagee Warns of Martin Luther's Theology," Religion & Politics Digest, RPD 3207, 07/22/98, pp. 3-4. Available on RPD's web site: http://www.erols.com/rpdigest/03207.htm.

43.G. Richard Fisher, The Other Gospel Of John Hagee: Christian Zionism And Ethnic Salvation, *Personal Freedom Outreach*, http://www.pfo.org/jonhagee.htm (last visited on May 15, 2012).

44.Steven Paas, Christian Zionism Examined, A Review of Ideas on Israel , the Church, and the Kingdom, at 92 (2012).

45.William Varner, The Promises to Israel, http://www.ankerberg.com/Articles/biblical-prophecy/BP0899W4.htm (last visited on May 19, 2012).

46.R.B. YERBY, THE ONCE AND FUTURE ISRAEL, p. 73-75 (1977).

47.See R.B. YERBY, THE ONCE AND FUTURE ISRAEL, p. 47 (1977).

48.E.g., The Heart of God for the Jewish People, http://www.threemacs.org/themes/jewish/godsheart.htm (last visited on October 10, 2012).

49. John F. Walvoord, The Rapture Question (Grand Rapids, Michigan, Zondervan, 1979), p. 25.

50. Keith A. Mathison, Dispensationalism, Rightly Dividing the People of God? (Phillipsburg, New Jersey, Presbyterian & Reformed, 1995), back cover.

51. Stephen Sizer, Christian Zionism: Dispensationalism And The Roots Of Sectarian Theology, A History of Dispensational Approaches, Information Clearing House, http://www.informationclearinghouse.info/article45 31.htm (last visited on May 19, 2012), quoting Michael Horton, 'The Church and Israel' Modern Reformation May/June (1994), p. 1.

52. Lewis Sperry Chafer, Dispensationalism (Dallas, Seminary Press, 1936), p. 107, quoted by Stephen Sizer, Christian Zionism: Dispensationalism And The Roots Of Sectarian Theology, A History of Dispensational Approaches, Information Clearing House, http://www.informationclearinghouse.info/article45 31.htm (last visited on May 19, 2012).

53. Darby, Collected Writings., Vol. 11, p. 363.

54. C.I. Scofield, Scofield Bible Correspondence Course (Chicago, Moody Bible Institute, 1907), pp. 45-46.

55. Ryrie, Dispensationalism., p. 40. Emphasis added.

56. Stephen Sizer, Christian Zionism: Dispensationalism And The Roots Of Sectarian Theology, A History of Dispensational

Approaches, Information Clearing House, http://www.informationclearinghouse.info/article4531.htm (last visited on May 19, 2012), quoting Dwight Pentecost, Things to Come (Findlay, Ohio, Dunham, 1958), p. 529.

57. Foreword to John Gerstner, Wrongly Dividing the Word of Truth (Brentwood, Tennessee, Wolgemuth & Hyatt, 1991), p. ix.

58. Stephen Sizer, Christian Zionism: Dispensationalism And The Roots Of Sectarian Theology, A History of Dispensational Approaches, Information Clearing House, http://www.informationclearinghouse.info/article4531.htm (last visited on May 19, 2012).

59. Stephen Sizer, Christian Zionism: Dispensationalism And The Roots Of Sectarian Theology, A History of Dispensational Approaches, Information Clearing House, http://www.informationclearinghouse.info/article4531.htm (last visited on May 19, 2012), quoting Wagner, Anxious for Armageddon (Scotdale, Ontario, Herald, 1995), p. 89.

60. James Barr, Escaping from Fundamentalism (London, SCM, 1984), p. 6, quoted by Stephen Sizer, Christian Zionism: Dispensationalism And The Roots Of Sectarian Theology, A History of Dispensational Approaches, Information Clearing House, http://www.informationclearinghouse.info/article4531.htm (last visited on May 19, 2012).

61. WILLIAM R. KIMBALL, THE RAPTURE, A Question of Timing, p. 35 (1985); JOHN L. BRAY,

MILLENNIUM - THE BIG QUESTION, P. 34 (1984).

62. JOHN L. BRAY, THE ORIGIN OF THE PRETRIBULATION RAPTURE TEACHING, p. 17, 24 (1982); JOHN L. BRAY, MILLENNIUM - THE BIG QUESTION, P. 34 (1984).

63. Clifton A. Emahiser, *Old Jerusalem Shall Never Rise Again*, at 3, at http://www.israelect.com/reference/CliftonAEmahiser/studies/Old%20Jerusalem%20Shall%20Never%20Rise%20Again.pdf (last visited on March 15, 2010) (quoting John Bray, *Israel in Bible Prophecy*, at 30).

64. Stephen Sizer, Christian Zionism: Dispensationalism And The Roots Of Sectarian Theology, A History of Dispensational Approaches, Information Clearing House, http://www.informationclearinghouse.info/article4531.htm (last visited on May 19, 2012).

65. Stephen Sizer, Christian Zionism: Dispensationalism And The Roots Of Sectarian Theology, A History of Dispensational Approaches, Information Clearing House, http://www.informationclearinghouse.info/article4531.htm (last visited on May 19, 2012).

66. Clarence Bass, Backgrounds to Dispensationalism. (Grand Rapids, Eerdmans), quoted by Stephen Sizer, Christian Zionism: Dispensationalism And The Roots Of Sectarian Theology, A History of Dispensational Approaches, Information Clearing House, http://www.informationclearinghouse.info/article45

31.htm (last visited on May 19, 2012).

67. Clarence Bass, Backgrounds to Dispensationalism. (Grand Rapids, Eerdmans), quoted by Stephen Sizer, Christian Zionism: Dispensationalism And The Roots Of Sectarian Theology, A History of Dispensational Approaches, Information Clearing House, http://www.informationclearinghouse.info/article4531.htm (last visited on May 19, 2012).

68. Charles Samples, The Greatest Hoax, http://www.sweetliberty.org/issues/hoax/greatesthoax.htm (last visited on October 1, 2012).

69. James J. Drummey, The Real McCarthy Record, The New American, May 11, 1987, http://www.knology.net/~bilrum/mccarthy.htm.

70. James J. Drummey, The Real McCarthy Record, The New American, May 11, 1987, http://www.knology.net/~bilrum/mccarthy.htm.

71. Medford Evans, Assassination of Joe McCarthy (1970), ISBN: 978-0882792170. See also Dave Martin, James Forrestal And Joe McCarthy, September 29, 2011, http://rense.com/general94/frr.htm.

72. M. Stanton Evans, Blacklisted by History: The Untold Story of Senator Joe McCarthy and His Fight Against America's Enemies (2007), ISBN: 978-1400081066.

73. Thomas R. Eddlem, Glenn Beck: History Vindicated Joe McCarthy, June 25, 2010, http://www.thenewamerican.com/component/k2/item/4778-glenn-beck-history-vindicated-joe-mccarth

y?Itemid=651.

74. Scott Speidel, Florida State University, How the Jewish Marxists in America Destroyed Joe McCarthy, http://reactor-core.org/secret/how-the-marxists-destroyed-joe-mccarthy.html (web address current as of October 20, 2003).

75. Scott Speidel, Florida State University, How the Jewish Marxists in America Destroyed Joe McCarthy, http://reactor-core.org/secret/how-the-marxists-destroyed-joe-mccarthy.html (web address current as of October 20, 2003).

76. Scott Speidel, Florida State University, How the Jewish Marxists in America Destroyed Joe McCarthy, http://reactor-core.org/secret/how-the-marxists-destroyed-joe-mccarthy.html (web address current as of October 20, 2003).

77. Scott Speidel, Florida State University, How the Jewish Marxists in America Destroyed Joe McCarthy, http://reactor-core.org/secret/how-the-marxists-destroyed-joe-mccarthy.html (web address current as of October 20, 2003).

78. Scott Speidel, Florida State University, How the Jewish Marxists in America Destroyed Joe McCarthy, http://reactor-core.org/secret/how-the-marxists-destroyed-joe-mccarthy.html (web address current as of October 20, 2003).

79. Scott Speidel, Florida State University, How the Jewish Marxists in America Destroyed Joe McCarthy, http://reactor-core.org/secret/how-the-marxists-destroyed-joe-mccarthy.html (web address current as of October 20, 2003).

80. Scott Speidel, Florida State University, How the Jewish Marxists in America Destroyed Joe McCarthy, http://reactor-core.org/secret/how-the-marxists-destroyed-joe-mccarthy.html (web address current as of October 20, 2003).

81. Scott Speidel, Florida State University, How the Jewish Marxists in America Destroyed Joe McCarthy, http://reactor-core.org/secret/how-the-marxists-destroyed-joe-mccarthy.html (web address current as of October 20, 2003).

82. Henry Makow, Judaized Christianity: Front for New World Order, January 13, 2010, http://www.thetruthseeker.co.uk/oldsite/article.asp?ID=11973.

83. Clarence Bass, Backgrounds to Dispensationalism. (Grand Rapids, Eerdmans), quoted by Stephen Sizer, Christian Zionism: Dispensationalism And The Roots Of Sectarian Theology, A History of Dispensational Approaches, Information Clearing House, http://www.informationclearinghouse.info/article4531.htm (last visited on May 19, 2012).

84. *Id.* at p. 50.

85.JOHN L. BRAY, MILLENNIUM - THE BIG QUESTION, P. 58 (1984).

86.WILLIAM R. KIMBALL, THE RAPTURE, A Question of Timing, p. 51 (1985).

87.Craig A. Blaising 'Dispensationalism, The Search for Definition' in Dispensationalism, Israel and the Church, The Search for Definition ed. Craig A. Blaising & Darrell L. Bock (Grand Rapids, Michigan, Zondervan, 1992) p. 21, quoted by Stephen Sizer, Christian Zionism: Dispensationalism And The Roots Of Sectarian Theology, A History of Dispensational Approaches, Information Clearing House, http://www.informationclearinghouse.info/article4531.htm (last visited on May 19, 2012).

88.C.E. Carlson, The Zionist Created Scofield "bible," http://christianparty.net/scofield.htm (website address current as of August 9, 2003).

89.C.E. Carlson, The Zionist Created Scofield "bible," http://christianparty.net/scofield.htm (website address current as of August 9, 2003).

90.Charles E. Carlson, The Messianic Movement Smuggles Zionism into the Mainline Church, April 5, 2012, http://whtt.org/newwhtt/main.php?nid=10189&ncateid=1.

91.C.E. Carlson, The Zionist Created Scofield "bible," http://christianparty.net/scofield.htm (website address current as of August 9, 2003).

92.C.E. Carlson, The Zionist Created Scofield "bible," http://christianparty.net/scofield.htm

(website address current as of August 9, 2003).

93. CYRUS SCOFIELD -- WHO WAS HE?
Excerpt from "The Unified Conspiracy Theory,"
http://www.sweetliberty.org/issues/hoax/scofield.htm (website address current as of August 9, 2003).

94. CYRUS SCOFIELD -- WHO WAS HE?
Excerpt from "The Unified Conspiracy Theory,"
http://www.sweetliberty.org/issues/hoax/scofield.htm (website address current as of August 9, 2003).

95. C.E. Carlson, The Zionist Created Scofield "bible," http://christianparty.net/scofield.htm (website address current as of August 9, 2003).

96. CYRUS SCOFIELD -- WHO WAS HE?
Excerpt from "The Unified Conspiracy Theory,"
http://www.sweetliberty.org/issues/hoax/scofield.htm (website address current as of August 9, 2003).

97. CYRUS SCOFIELD -- WHO WAS HE?
Excerpt from "The Unified Conspiracy Theory,"
http://www.sweetliberty.org/issues/hoax/scofield.htm (website address current as of August 9, 2003).

98. CYRUS SCOFIELD -- WHO WAS HE?
Excerpt from "The Unified Conspiracy Theory,"
http://www.sweetliberty.org/issues/hoax/scofield.htm (website address current as of August 9, 2003).
Scofield: The Christian Leader With Feet of Clay, http://www.virginiawater.co.uk/christchurch/articles/scofield1.html (website address current as of August 9, 2003).

99. CYRUS SCOFIELD -- WHO WAS HE?
Excerpt from "The Unified Conspiracy Theory,"
http://www.sweetliberty.org/issues/hoax/scofield.ht

m (website address current as of August 9, 2003).

100. CYRUS SCOFIELD -- WHO WAS HE? Excerpt from "The Unified Conspiracy Theory," http://www.sweetliberty.org/issues/hoax/scofield.htm (website address current as of August 9, 2003).

101. Scofield: The Christian Leader With Feet of Clay, http://www.virginiawater.co.uk/christchurch/articles/scofield1.html (website address current as of August 9, 2003).

102. Scofield: The Christian Leader With Feet of Clay, http://www.virginiawater.co.uk/christchurch/articles/scofield1.html (website address current as of August 9, 2003).

103. Luisa Kroll, Megachurches, Megabusinesses, Forbes, September 17, 2003.

104. Luisa Kroll, Megachurches, Megabusinesses, Forbes, September 17, 2003.

105. Rick Meisel, Chuck Smith, General Teachings/Activities, *Biblical Discernment Ministries*, January 2002, http://www.rapidnet.com/~jbeard/bdm/exposes/smith/general.htm (web address current as of September 24, 2005), quoting Chuck Smith, Answers for Today, p. 157 (1993).

106. Luisa Kroll, Megachurches, Megabusinesses, Forbes, September 17, 2003.

107. Edward Hendrie, *The Anti-Gospel, The Perversion of Christ's Grace Gospel*.

108. Temple Mount Fanatics Foment a New Thirty Years' War, *Executive Intelligence Review*, November 3, 2000, http://www.larouchepub.com/other/2000/temple_mount_2743.html (web address current as of November 11, 2005).

109. Temple Mount Fanatics Foment a New Thirty Years' War, *Executive Intelligence Review*, November 3, 2000, http://www.larouchepub.com/other/2000/temple_mount_2743.html (web address current as of November 11, 2005).

110. Temple Mount Fanatics Foment a New Thirty Years' War, *Executive Intelligence Review*, November 3, 2000, http://www.larouchepub.com/other/2000/temple_mount_2743.html (web address current as of November 11, 2005).

111. Temple Mount Fanatics Foment a New Thirty Years' War, *Executive Intelligence Review*, November 3, 2000, http://www.larouchepub.com/other/2000/temple_mount_2743.html (web address current as of November 11, 2005).

112. Arno Weinstein, In the Shadow of Stern: The Inside Story of a LEHI Intelligence Officer, B'tzedek, http://www.btzedek.com/focus/focus01.html (web address current as of November 11, 2005).

113. Arno Weinstein, In the Shadow of Stern: The Inside Story of a LEHI Intelligence Officer, B'tzedek,

http://www.btzedek.com/focus/focus01.html (web address current as of November 11, 2005).

114.Evangelical Christians and the Building of the Temple, The Hebrew University of Jerusalem, http://sicsa.huji.ac.il/20Ariel.html (web address current as of November 11, 2005).

115.Evangelical Christians and the Building of the Temple, The Hebrew University of Jerusalem, http://sicsa.huji.ac.il/20Ariel.html (web address current as of November 11, 2005).

116.Evangelical Christians and the Building of the Temple, The Hebrew University of Jerusalem, http://sicsa.huji.ac.il/20Ariel.html (web address current as of November 11, 2005).

117.Christian Zionism, http://www.theocracywatch.org/christian_zionism.htm (last visited on January 2, 2011).

118.Christian Zionism, http://www.theocracywatch.org/christian_zionism.htm (last visited on January 2, 2011).

119.Sean McBride, *On a Learjet to Hell*, 16 May 2007, http://www.mail-archive.com/political-research@yahoogroups.com/msg07361.html.

120.Steven Paas, Christian Zionism Examined, A Review of Ideas on Israel , the Church, and the Kingdom, at 94, n.17 (2012).

121.Steven Paas, Christian Zionism Examined, A Review of Ideas on Israel , the Church, and the Kingdom, at 95 (2012).

122. Hal Lindsey, The 1980's: Countdown to Armageddon (New York, Bantam, 1981), p. 179, cited by Stephen Sizer, Christian Zionism: Dispensationalism And The Roots Of Sectarian Theology, A History of Dispensational Approaches, Information Clearing House, http://www.informationclearinghouse.info/article4531.htm (last visited on May 19, 2012).

123. Hal Lindsey, The Late Great Planet Earth (New York, Bantam, 1970), back cover, cited by Stephen Sizer, Christian Zionism: Dispensationalism And The Roots Of Sectarian Theology, A History of Dispensational Approaches, Information Clearing House, http://www.informationclearinghouse.info/article4531.htm (last visited on May 19, 2012).

124. Hal Lindsey, The Road to Holocaust (New York, Bantam, 1989), p. 195. For other statistics see George Marsden, Understanding Fundamentalism and Evangelicalism (Grand Rapids, Eerdmans, 1991) p. 77, and Michael Lienesch, Redeeming America: Piety and Politics in the New Christian Right (Chapel Hill, North Carolina, North Carolina Press, 1993), p. 311, cited by Stephen Sizer, Christian Zionism: Dispensationalism And The Roots Of Sectarian Theology, A History of Dispensational Approaches, Information Clearing House, http://www.informationclearinghouse.info/article4531.htm (last visited on May 19, 2012).

125. Stephen Sizer, Christian Zionism: Dispensationalism And The Roots Of Sectarian Theology, A History of Dispensational Approaches, Information Clearing House,

http://www.informationclearinghouse.info/article45 31.htm (last visited on May 19, 2012).

126. Hal Lindsey, International Intelligence Briefing (Palos Verdes, California, HLM), cited by Stephen Sizer, Christian Zionism: Dispensationalism And The Roots Of Sectarian Theology, A History of Dispensational Approaches, Information Clearing House, http://www.informationclearinghouse.info/article45 31.htm (last visited on May 19, 2012).

127. Wagner, Anxious for Armageddon (Scotdale, Ontario, Herald, 1995), p. 25, cited by Stephen Sizer, Christian Zionism: Dispensationalism And The Roots Of Sectarian Theology, A History of Dispensational Approaches, Information Clearing House, http://www.informationclearinghouse.info/article45 31.htm (last visited on May 19, 2012).

128. Stephen Sizer, Christian Zionism: Dispensationalism And The Roots Of Sectarian Theology, A History of Dispensational Approaches, Information Clearing House, http://www.informationclearinghouse.info/article45 31.htm (last visited on May 19, 2012).

129. Stan Moody, The Pathology of Christian Zionism, An Address to the 10th International Conference of Holy Land Christian Ecumenical Foundation, HCEF, October 25, 2008, http://www.christianzionism.org/Article/MoodyS03 .pdf.

130. Stan Moody, The Pathology of Christian Zionism, An Address to the 10th International

Conference of Holy Land Christian Ecumenical Foundation, HCEF, October 25, 2008, http://www.christianzionism.org/Article/MoodyS03.pdf.

131. Stan Moody, The Pathology of Christian Zionism, An Address to the 10th International Conference of Holy Land Christian Ecumenical Foundation, HCEF, October 25, 2008, http://www.christianzionism.org/Article/MoodyS03.pdf.

132. Stan Moody, The Pathology of Christian Zionism, An Address to the 10th International Conference of Holy Land Christian Ecumenical Foundation, HCEF, October 25, 2008, http://www.christianzionism.org/Article/MoodyS03.pdf.

133. February 22, 2001. Proclamation of the Fourth International Christian Congress on Biblical Zionism. Available at http://christianactionforisrael.org/4thcongress3_pf.html(12/13/03), quoted by John Hubers, Palestinians, Christian Zionists and the Good News Gospel, Journal of Lutheran Ethics.

134. John Hubers, Palestinians, Christian Zionists and the Good News Gospel, Journal of Lutheran Ethics, http://www.elca.org/What-We-Believe/Social-Issues/Journal-of-Lutheran-Ethics/Issues/May-2007/Palestinians-Christian-Zionists-and-the-Good-News-Gospel.aspx#_ednref9 (last visited on June 2, 2012).

135. John Hubers, Palestinians, Christian Zionists and the Good News Gospel, Journal of Lutheran

Ethics.

136. February 22, 2001. Proclamation of the Fourth International Christian Congress on Biblical Zionism. Available at http://christianactionforisrael.org/4thcongress3_pf.html(12/13/03), quoted by John Hubers, Palestinians, Christian Zionists and the Good News Gospel, Journal of Lutheran Ethics.

137. Stephen Sizer, Christian Zionism: Dispensationalism And The Roots Of Sectarian Theology, A History of Dispensational Approaches, Information Clearing House, http://www.informationclearinghouse.info/article4531.htm (last visited on May 19, 2012).

138. Stephen Sizer, Christian Zionism: Dispensationalism And The Roots Of Sectarian Theology, A History of Dispensational Approaches, Information Clearing House, http://www.informationclearinghouse.info/article4531.htm (last visited on May 19, 2012).

139. Stephen Sizer, Christian Zionism: Dispensationalism And The Roots Of Sectarian Theology, A History of Dispensational Approaches, Information Clearing House, http://www.informationclearinghouse.info/article4531.htm (last visited on May 19, 2012).

140. International Christian Embassy Jerusalem (Jerusalem, ICEJ, 1993), p. 9, cited by Stephen Sizer, Christian Zionism: Dispensationalism And The Roots Of Sectarian Theology, A History of Dispensational Approaches, Information Clearing House,

http://www.informationclearinghouse.info/article45 31.htm (last visited on May 19, 2012).

141. Stephen Sizer, Christian Zionism: Dispensationalism And The Roots Of Sectarian Theology, A History of Dispensational Approaches, Information Clearing House, http://www.informationclearinghouse.info/article45 31.htm (last visited on August 21, 2012), quoting International Christian Embassy Jerusalem (Jerusalem, ICEJ, 1993), p. 9.

142. John Hubers, Palestinians, Christian Zionists and the Good News Gospel, Journal of Lutheran Ethics.

143. Sam Storms, The Dispensational Premillennial View of the Kingdom of God, Enjoying God Ministries, November 6, 2006, http://www.enjoyinggodministries.com/article/the-dispensational-premillennial-view-of-the-kingdom-of-god/ (last visited on May 19, 2012).

144. http://www.blessedquietness.com/journal/believe.htm (web address current as of 9-24-03).

145. Steve Van Nattan, Blessed Quietness Journal, http://www.blessedquietness.com/journal/believe.htm (last visited on October 20, 2012).

146. http://www.blessedquietness.com/journal/prophecy/zionism.htm (web page current as of 10-1-03).

147. Dillard Thurman, Zionists Dream of Millennial Reign!, http://www.preteristcentral.com/Zionists%20Dream%20of%20a%20Millennial%20Kingdom.html (last visited on May 19, 2012).

148.WILLIAM R. KIMBALL, THE RAPTURE, A Question of Timing, p. 32 (1985).

149.*Id.*

150.*Id.*

151.Anti-Zion, Jews on the Jewish Question, http://www.diac.com/~bkennedy/az/A-E.html (current as of September 10, 2001).

152.Ivan Fraser, Protocols of the Learned Elders of Zion, Proofs of an Ancient Conspiracy, http://www.vegan.swinternet.co.uk/articles/conspiracies/protocols_proof.html (current as of September 10, 2001).

153.Robert Maryks, *Jesuits of Jewish Ancestry. A Biographical Dictionary* (2008), at http://sites.google.com/a/jewishjesuits.com/www/.

154.JOHN L. BRAY, MILLENNIUM - THE BIG QUESTION, P. 34 (1984).

155.Moses ben Nahman Gerondi, Jewish Encyclopedia, http://www.jewishencyclopedia.com/articles/11129-moses-ben-nahman-gerondi (last visited on May 26, 2012).

156.Moses ben Nahman Gerondi, Jewish Encyclopedia, http://www.jewishencyclopedia.com/articles/11129-moses-ben-nahman-gerondi (last visited on May 26, 2012), quoted by Marshal Hall, Dispensationalism & Millennialism: Their Origin and Their Future, http://www.fixedearth.com/dandmotf.html (last visited on May 26, 2012).

157. Moses ben Nahman Gerondi, Jewish Encyclopedia, http://www.jewishencyclopedia.com/articles/11129-moses-ben-nahman-gerondi (last visited on May 26, 2012).

158. Moses ben Nahman Gerondi, Jewish Encyclopedia, http://www.jewishencyclopedia.com/articles/11129-moses-ben-nahman-gerondi (last visited on May 26, 2012).

159. Moses ben Nahman Gerondi, Jewish Encyclopedia, http://www.jewishencyclopedia.com/articles/11129-moses-ben-nahman-gerondi (last visited on May 26, 2012).

160. Sahnedrin, Chapter 11, Translated into English by H. Freedman, B.A., Ph.D., under the editorship of Rabbi Dr. I. Epstein B.A., Ph.D., D. Lit., located at http://www.come-and-hear.com/sanhedrin/sanhedrin_90.html#chapter_xi (last visited on May 26, 2012).

161. Sahnedrin, Chapter 11, Translated into English by H. Freedman, B.A., Ph.D., under the editorship of Rabbi Dr. I. Epstein B.A., Ph.D., D. Lit., located at http://www.come-and-hear.com/sanhedrin/sanhedrin_90.html#chapter_xi (last visited on May 26, 2012).

162. Dispensationalism & Millennialism: Their Origin and Their Future, http://www.fixedearth.com/the_bible/dandmotf.html (last visited on February 16, 2013).

163. The Temple Mount and Fort Antonia, http://askelm.com/temple/t980504.htm (web address current as of October 30, 2003).

164. The Secret Key to the Dome of the Rock, http://askelm.com/temple/t991001.htm (web address current as of October 30, 2003).

165. The Left Behind Series, *at* http://www.rapidnet.com/~jbeard/bdm/BookReviews/left.htm (last visited on March 14, 2010).

166. David D. Kirkpatrick, "The 2004 Campaign: The Conservatives: Club of the Most Powerful Gathers in Strictest Privacy", *The New York Times*, August 28, 2004, http://www.nytimes.com/2004/08/28/politics/campaign/28conserve.html?ex=1146110400&en=f173712f417dcad1&ei=5070 (last visited on May 27, 2010).

167. David D. Kirkpatrick, "The 2004 Campaign: The Conservatives: Club of the Most Powerful Gathers in Strictest Privacy", New York Times, August 28, 2004, http://www.nytimes.com/2004/08/28/politics/campaign/28conserve.html?ex=1146110400&en=f173712f417dcad1&ei=5070 (last visited on May 27, 2010).

168. David D. Kirkpatrick, "The 2004 Campaign: The Conservatives: Club of the Most Powerful

Gathers in Strictest Privacy", New York Times, August 28, 2004, http://www.nytimes.com/2004/08/28/politics/campaign/28conserve.html?ex=1146110400&en=f173712f417dcad1&ei=5070 (last visited on May 27, 2010).

169.David D. Kirkpatrick, "The 2004 Campaign: The Conservatives: Club of the Most Powerful Gathers in Strictest Privacy", New York Times, August 28, 2004, http://www.nytimes.com/2004/08/28/politics/campaign/28conserve.html?ex=1146110400&en=f173712f417dcad1&ei=5070 (last visited on May 27, 2010).

170.ANTHONY C. SUTTON, AMERICA'S SECRET ESTABLISHMENT, AN INTRODUCTION TO THE ORDER OF SKULL & BONES, at p. 212 (1986).

171.ANTHONY C. SUTTON, AMERICA'S SECRET ESTABLISHMENT, AN INTRODUCTION TO THE ORDER OF SKULL & BONES, at p. 212 (1986).

172.ANTHONY C. SUTTON, AMERICA'S SECRET ESTABLISHMENT, AN INTRODUCTION TO THE ORDER OF SKULL & BONES, at p. 7 (1986).

173.ANTHONY C. SUTTON, AMERICA'S SECRET ESTABLISHMENT, AN INTRODUCTION TO THE ORDER OF SKULL & BONES, at p. 200 (1986).

174. David Bay, Secret Societies Killed Jesus Christ, www.cuttingedge.org http://home.talkcity.com/InspirationAv/jforjesus/secret_societies.html (current as of October 1, 2001).

175. David D. Kirkpatrick, "The 2004 Campaign: The Conservatives: Club of the Most Powerful Gathers in Strictest Privacy", New York Times, August 28, 2004, http://www.nytimes.com/2004/08/28/politics/campaign/28conserve.html?ex=1146110400&en=f173712f417dcad1&ei=5070 (last visited on May 27, 2010).

176. David D. Kirkpatrick, "The 2004 Campaign: The Conservatives: Club of the Most Powerful Gathers in Strictest Privacy", New York Times, August 28, 2004, http://www.nytimes.com/2004/08/28/politics/campaign/28conserve.html?ex=1146110400&en=f173712f417dcad1&ei=5070 (last visited on May 27, 2010).

177. John F. Kennedy, http://en.wikiquote.org/wiki/John_F._Kennedy (last visited on May 27, 2012).

178. John F. Kennedy, http://en.wikiquote.org/wiki/John_F._Kennedy (last visited on May 27, 2012).

179. Mary Louise, Operation Mockingbird, CIA Media Manipulation, August 3, 2007, http://www.bibliotecapleyades.net/sociopolitica/sociopol_mediacontrol05.htm (last visited on September 29, 2012). See also "CIA: Marker of

Policy or Tool? Survey Finds Widely Feared Agency Is Tightly Controlled" New York Times. April 25, 1966.

180. Eric Jewell, The Unholy Alliance, Christianity and the NWO, Part III, March 22, 2002, http://www.rense.com/general21/unholy3.htm.

181. Eric Jewell, The Unholy Alliance, Christianity and the NWO, Part I, February 25, 2002, http://www.rense.com/general20/unholy.htm.

182. Eric Jewell, The Unholy Alliance, Christianity and the NWO, Part I, February 25, 2002, http://www.rense.com/general20/unholy.htm.

183. Eric Jewell, The Unholy Alliance, Christianity and the NWO, Part II, March 6, 2002, http://www.rense.com/general20/unholy2.htm.

184. Eric Jewell, The Unholy Alliance, Christianity and the NWO, Part II, March 6, 2002, http://www.rense.com/general20/unholy2.htm.

185. Barbara Aho, The Council for National Policy, http://watch.pair.com/cnp.html (last visited on May 29, 2012).

186. Barbara Aho, The Council for National Policy, http://watch.pair.com/cnp.html (last visited on May 29, 2012), citing Council for National Policy Index: http://watch.pair.com/cnpdbase.html.

187. Eric Jewell, The Unholy Alliance, Christianity and the NWO, Part II, March 6, 2002, http://www.rense.com/general20/unholy2.htm.

188. Eric Jewell, The Unholy Alliance, Christianity and the NWO, Part II, March 6, 2002, http://www.rense.com/general20/unholy2.htm.

189. Eric Jewell, The Unholy Alliance, Christianity and the NWO, Part II, March 6, 2002, http://www.rense.com/general20/unholy2.htm.

190. William F. Jasper, *The Power Behind the Presidency*, New American, August 13, 2001.

191. William Norman Grigg, *An Internationalist Primer*, New American, September 13, 1996. See also William F. Jasper, *The Power Behind the Presidency*, New American, August 13, 2001.

192. William F. Jasper, *The Power Behind the Presidency*, New American, August 13, 2001.

193. David Rockefeller, Honorary Chairman, Council on Foreign Relations, http://www.cfr.org/experts/world/david-rockefeller/b987 (last visited on May 27, 2012).

194. David Rockefeller: Memoirs, pg. 405 (2002).

195. Henry Makow, The Protocols of Zion Updated, http://www.savethemales.ca/000334.html (last visited on September 10, 2012).

196. The Harold Wallace Rosenthal Interview 1976, The Hidden Tyranny, http://www.macquirelatory.com/Wallace%20Interview%201967.htm (last visited on September 10, 2012).

197. The Harold Wallace Rosenthal Interview 1976, The Hidden Tyranny,

http://www.macquirelatory.com/Wallace%20Interview%201967.htm (last visited on September 10, 2012).

198. The Harold Wallace Rosenthal Interview 1976, The Hidden Tyranny, http://www.macquirelatory.com/Wallace%20Interview%201967.htm (last visited on September 10, 2012).

199. The Harold Wallace Rosenthal Interview 1976, The Hidden Tyranny, http://www.macquirelatory.com/Wallace%20Interview%201967.htm (last visited on September 10, 2012).

200. The Harold Wallace Rosenthal Interview 1976, The Hidden Tyranny, http://www.macquirelatory.com/Wallace%20Interview%201967.htm (last visited on September 10, 2012).

201. Carol A. Valentine, The Traitors Among Us, January 2002, http://www.public-action.com/911/chrzion.html (quoted passages from the Talmud appear in link at that point in the article).

202. Carol A. Valentine, The Traitors Among Us, January 2002, http://www.public-action.com/911/chrzion.html.

203. Fifth Column, http://dictionary.reference.com/browse/fifth+column.

204. Fifth Column, http://dictionary.reference.com/browse/fifth+colum

n.

205.Christopher Jon Bjerknes, Will Israel's Fifth Column of "Christian" Zionists Genocide 1.5 Billion Moslems for the Sake of 5 Million Israeli Jews—Jews Who Are in No Danger?, November 06, 2007, http://jewishracism.blogspot.com/2007/11/will-israels-fifth-column-of-christian.html.

206.

207.NewsMax, July 31, 2002, http://www.newsmax.com/showinsidecover.shtml?a=2002/7/31/101825 (website address current as of 1 June 2003).

208.Richard Evans, Zionists Represent a Fifth Column in America, January 12, 2012, http://beforeitsnews.com/alternative/2012/01/zionists-represent-a-fifth-column-in-america-1624505.html.

209.Richard Evans, Zionists Represent a Fifth Column in America, January 12, 2012, http://beforeitsnews.com/alternative/2012/01/zionists-represent-a-fifth-column-in-america-1624505.html.

210.Richard Evans, Zionists Represent a Fifth Column in America, January 12, 2012, http://beforeitsnews.com/alternative/2012/01/zionists-represent-a-fifth-column-in-america-1624505.html.

211.Richard Evans, Zionists Represent a Fifth Column in America, January 12, 2012, http://beforeitsnews.com/alternative/2012/01/zionis

ts-represent-a-fifth-column-in-america-1624505.html.

212. Richard Evans, Zionists Represent a Fifth Column in America, January 12, 2012, http://beforeitsnews.com/alternative/2012/01/zionists-represent-a-fifth-column-in-america-1624505.html.

213. Richard Evans, Zionists Represent a Fifth Column in America, January 12, 2012, http://beforeitsnews.com/alternative/2012/01/zionists-represent-a-fifth-column-in-america-1624505.html.

214. Texe Marrs, Sayanim Everywhere, http://www.texemarrs.com/082012/sayanim_everywhere.htm (last visited on September 17, 2012).

215. Texe Marrs, Sayanim Everywhere, http://www.texemarrs.com/082012/sayanim_everywhere.htm (last visited on September 17, 2012).

216. USA Patriot Act of 2001, Case Studies, http://readthebill.org/cases/civilliberties/ (last visited on September 14, 2012).

217. USA Patriot Act of 2001, Case Studies, http://readthebill.org/cases/civilliberties/ (last visited on September 14, 2012).

218. Ginger Gibson, Ron Paul: 'Glee' in administration after 9/11, Politico, December 8, 2011, http://www.politico.com/news/stories/1211/70156.html.

219. US 'planned attack on Taleban', BBC, 18 September 2001, http://news.bbc.co.uk/2/hi/south_asia/1550366.stm.

220. US 'planned attack on Taleban', BBC, 18 September 2001, http://news.bbc.co.uk/2/hi/south_asia/1550366.stm.

221. O'Neill: Bush planned Iraq invasion before 9/11, CNN, January 14, 2004, http://www.cnn.com/2004/ALLPOLITICS/01/10/oneill.bush/.

222. New Documents Show Bush Administration Planned War in Iraq Well Before 9/11/2001, September 24, 2010, http://crooksandliars.com/karoli/new-documents-show-bush-administration-plan.

223. G. Edward Griffin, The Creature From Jeckyl Island, A Second Look at the Federal Reserve, Third Edition, at 518 (1998).

224. G. Edward Griffin, The Creature From Jeckyl Island, A Second Look at the Federal Reserve, Third Edition, at 516-17 (1998), quoting Leonard Lewin, ed., *Report from Iron Mountain on the Possibility and Desirability of Peace* (New York; Dell Publishing, 1967), pp. 13-14.

225. G. Edward Griffin, The Creature From Jeckyl Island, A Second Look at the Federal Reserve, Third Edition, at 522 (1998), quoting Leonard Lewin, ed., *Report from Iron Mountain on the Possibility and Desirability of Peace* (New York; Dell Publishing, 1967), pp. 66.

226. G. Edward Griffin, The Creature From Jeckyl Island, A Second Look at the Federal Reserve, Third Edition, at 522 (1998), quoting Leonard Lewin, ed., *Report from Iron Mountain on the Possibility and Desirability of Peace* (New York; Dell Publishing, 1967), pp. 66.

227. G. Edward Griffin, The Creature From Jeckyl Island, A Second Look at the Federal Reserve, Third Edition, at 523 (1998), quoting Leonard Lewin, ed., *Report from Iron Mountain on the Possibility and Desirability of Peace* (New York; Dell Publishing, 1967), pp. 70-71.

228. G. Edward Griffin, The Creature From Jeckyl Island, A Second Look at the Federal Reserve, Third Edition, at 523 (1998).

229. Donn deGrand Pre, Barbarians Inside the Gates, Book Two, The Vipers Venom, at 204 (2002).

230. Donn deGrand Pre, Barbarians Inside the Gates, Book Two, The Vipers Venom, at 203 (2002).

231. Letters and Other Writings of James Madison, http://archive.org/stream/lettersandotherw04madiiala#page/490/mode/2up.

232. James Madison, The Most Dreaded Enemy of Liberty, http://www.informationclearinghouse.info/article18562.htm (circa 1793).

233. Christopher Bollyn, *Solving 9/11 - The Deception That Changed The World*, May 17,

2010, http://www.bollyn.com/solving-9-11-the-book#article_12159, also available at: http://www.bollyn.com/public/Solving_9-11_-_The_Deception_That_Changed_The_World.pdf.

234. Christopher Bollyn, *Solving 9/11 - The Deception That Changed The World*, May 17, 2010, http://www.bollyn.com/solving-9-11-the-book#article_12159, also available at: http://www.bollyn.com/public/Solving_9-11_-_The_Deception_That_Changed_The_World.pdf.

235. Christopher Bollyn, *Solving 9/11 - The Deception That Changed The World*, May 17, 2010, http://www.bollyn.com/solving-9-11-the-book#article_12159, also available at: http://www.bollyn.com/public/Solving_9-11_-_The_Deception_That_Changed_The_World.pdf.

236. The Israeli Spy Ring Scandal, http://www.whatreallyhappened.com/spyring.html (web page current as of May 9, 2002).

237. Henry Makow, Illuminati: The Cult That Hijacked the World, at 151 (2011).

238. Confessions of an Ex-Mossad Agent, Excerpt from Victor Ostrovsky's, "By way of deception", What Really Happened, http://whatreallyhappened.com/WRHARTICLES/deception.html (last visited on September 29, 2012).

239. Confessions of an Ex-Mossad Agent, Excerpt from Victor Ostrovsky's, "By way of deception",

What Really Happened, http://whatreallyhappened.com/WRHARTICLES/deception.html (last visited on September 29, 2012).

240. Henry Makow, Illuminati: The Cult That Hijacked the World, at 151 (2011).

241. James Bennet, A DAY OF TERROR: THE ISRAELIS; Spilled Blood Is Seen as Bond That Draws 2 Nations Closer, New York Times, September 12, 2001, http://www.nytimes.com/2001/09/12/us/day-terror-israelis-spilled-blood-seen-bond-that-draws-2-nations-closer.html .

242. James Bennet, A DAY OF TERROR: THE ISRAELIS; Spilled Blood Is Seen as Bond That Draws 2 Nations Closer, New York Times, September 12, 2001, http://www.nytimes.com/2001/09/12/us/day-terror-israelis-spilled-blood-seen-bond-that-draws-2-nations-closer.html .

243. Report: Netanyahu says 9/11 terror attacks good for Israel, Haaretz Service and Reuters, Apr.16, 2008, http://www.haaretz.com/news/report-netanyahu-says-9-11-terror-attacks-good-for-israel-1.244044.

244. Christopher Bollyn, *Solving 9/11 - The Deception That Changed The World*, May 17, 2010, http://www.bollyn.com/solving-9-11-the-book#article_12159, also available at: http://www.bollyn.com/public/Solving_9-11_-_The_Deception_That_Changed_The_World.pdf.

245.Christopher Bollyn, *Solving 9/11 - The Deception That Changed The World*, May 17, 2010, http://www.bollyn.com/solving-9-11-the-book#article_12159, also available at: http://www.bollyn.com/public/Solving_9-11_-_The_Deception_That_Changed_The_World.pdf.

246.Christopher Bollyn, *Solving 9/11 - The Deception That Changed The World*, May 17, 2010, http://www.bollyn.com/solving-9-11-the-book#article_12159, also available at: http://www.bollyn.com/public/Solving_9-11_-_The_Deception_That_Changed_The_World.pdf.

247.Christopher Bollyn, *Solving 9/11 - The Deception That Changed The World*, May 17, 2010, http://www.bollyn.com/solving-9-11-the-book#article_12159, also available at: http://www.bollyn.com/public/Solving_9-11_-_The_Deception_That_Changed_The_World.pdf.

248.Christopher Bollyn, *Solving 9/11 - The Deception That Changed The World*, May 17, 2010, http://www.bollyn.com/solving-9-11-the-book#article_12159, also available at: http://www.bollyn.com/public/Solving_9-11_-_The_Deception_That_Changed_The_World.pdf.

249.Christopher Bollyn, *Solving 9/11 - The Deception That Changed The World*, May 17, 2010, http://www.bollyn.com/solving-9-11-the-book#article_12159, also available at:

http://www.bollyn.com/public/Solving_9-11_-_The_Deception_That_Changed_The_World.pdf.

250. Transcript of Interview by Mark Glenn with Dr. Alan Sabroski and Phil Tourney, March 15, 2010, http://www.bibliotecapleyades.net/sociopolitica/sociopol_911zion_02.htm.

251. Alan Sabrosky, Zionism Unmasked: The Dark Face Of Jewish Nationalism, 11 March 2010, http://www.bigeye.com/sabrosky.htm.

252. Military Now Know Israel Did 911, http://www.youtube.com/watch?v=C9O5vQep-nM (last visited on December 12, 2010).

253. Transcript of Interview by Mark Glenn with Dr. Alan Sabroski and Phil Tourney, March 15, 2010, http://www.bibliotecapleyades.net/sociopolitica/sociopol_911zion_02.htm.

254. How 911 Was Done, http://how911wasdone.blogspot.com/, quoting the Washington Times, September 10, 2001.

255. DONN DE GRAND PRE, BARBARIANS INSIDE THE GATES, THE BLACK BOOK OF BOLSHEVISM, p. 314-15 (2000) (citing JACK BERNSTEIN, THE LIFE OF AN AMERICAN JEW IN RACIST MARXIST ISRAEL (1984)).

256. http://64.39.19.39/ (current as of November 1, 2001). See also http://www.halcyon.com/jim/ussliberty/.

257.http://64.39.19.39/lewis.txt (current as of November 1, 2001). See also http://www.halcyon.com/jim/ussliberty/.

258.Salvador Astucia, Opium Lords, http://www.jfkmontreal.com/johnson's_hidden_loyalties.htm#Secret%20Ethnicity (website current as of March 26, 2003).

259.William Kunstler, My Life as a Radical Lawyer, p. 158 (1994), quoted in Texe Marrs, Conspiracy of the Six Pointed Star, at 232 (2011).

260.William Kunstler, My Life as a Radical Lawyer, p. 158 (1994), quoted in Texe Marrs, Conspiracy of the Six Pointed Star, at 232 (2011).

261.Arieh O'Sullivan, *Vanunu: Israel behind JFK Assassination*, Jerusalem Post, Jul. 25, 2004.

262.Protocols of the Learned Elders of Zion, Protocol 17, http://www.biblebelievers.org.au/przion6.htm#protocol%20No.%2017 (last visited on August 25, 2012).

263.Protocols of the Learned Elders of Zion, Introduction, http://www.biblebelievers.org.au/przion1.htm#INTRODUCTION (last visited on August 22, 2012).

264.Ivan Fraser, The Protocols of the Learned Elders of Zion: Proofs of an Ancient Conspiracy, History of the Origins of the Protocols, http://www.bibliotecapleyades.net/sociopolitica/esp_sociopol_zion03.htm (last visited on October 17, 2012) quoting L. Fry, Waters Flowing Eastward, available at http://zioncrimefactory.com/wp-content/uploads/2011/09/WatersFlowingEastward.pdf.

265. Ivan Fraser, The Protocols of the Learned Elders of Zion: Proofs of an Ancient Conspiracy, History of the Origins of the Protocols, http://www.bibliotecapleyades.net/sociopolitica/esp_sociopol_zion03.htm (last visited on October 17, 2012) quoting L. Fry, Waters Flowing Eastward, available at http://zioncrimefactory.com/wp-content/uploads/2011/09/WatersFlowingEastward.pdf.

266. Ivan Fraser, The Protocols of the Learned Elders of Zion: Proofs of an Ancient Conspiracy, History of the Origins of the Protocols, http://www.bibliotecapleyades.net/sociopolitica/esp_sociopol_zion03.htm (last visited on October 17, 2012) quoting L. Fry, Waters Flowing Eastward, available at http://zioncrimefactory.com/wp-content/uploads/2011/09/WatersFlowingEastward.pdf.

267. L. Fry, Waters Flowing Eastward (1931), available at http://zioncrimefactory.com/wp-content/uploads/2011/09/WatersFlowingEastward.pdf.

268. Rose Cohen, *Bali, Australia & The Mossad* (October 17, 2002), *at* http://www.rense.com/general30/balias.htm.

269. The International Jew, the World's Foremost Problem, Compiled from articles published by the Ford Motor Company in the Dearborn Independent from 1920-1922, available at http://www.biblebelievers.org.au/intern_jew.htm

(last visited on November 29, 2010).

270. Speech by Prime Minister Mahathir Mohamad, October 16, 2003, http://www.adl.org/anti_semitism/malaysian.asp.

271. Speech by Prime Minister Mahathir Mohamad, October 16, 2003, http://www.adl.org/anti_semitism/malaysian.asp.

272. *See* Jack Mohr, *Satan's Kids*, http://www.christianbiblestudy.org/OPS/JM/JM0018c.htm (current as of September 9, 2001).

273. Protocols of the Learned Elders of Zion, Protocol 1, http://www.biblebelievers.org.au/przion2.htm#PROTOCOL%20No.%201 (last visited on August 22, 2012).

274. Protocols of the Learned Elders of Zion, Protocol 17, http://www.biblebelievers.org.au/przion6.htm#protocol%20No.%2017 (last visited on August 25, 2012).

275. Protocols of the Learned Elders of Zion, Protocol 17, http://www.biblebelievers.org.au/przion6.htm#protocol%20No.%2017 (last visited on August 25, 2012).

276. Eric Jewell, The Unholy Alliance, Christianity and the NWO, Part II, March 6, 2002, http://www.rense.com/general20/unholy2.htm.

277. Eric Jewell, The Unholy Alliance, Christianity and the NWO, Part II, March 6, 2002,

http://www.rense.com/general20/unholy2.htm.

278. Cathy Burns, Billy Graham and His Friends.

279. Dave Hunt, The Gospel that Saves, http://www.reachingcatholics.org/gospels.html (last visited on May 29, 2012). See also, Wolves in Sheep's Clothing, http://www.sweetliberty.org/issues/wolves/graham.htm (last visited on May 29, 2012).

280. Doug Groothuis, Unmasking the New Age, (Downers Grove: InterVarsity Press, 1986), p. 120, cited by Lucis Trust (Lucifer Publishing Co.) A Satanic Leader for a One World Religion, Part of the United Nations, June 22, 2008, http://cantontruth.blogspot.com/2008/06/lucis-trust-lucifer-trust-satanic.html. See also, Wolves in Sheep's Clothing, http://www.sweetliberty.org/issues/wolves/graham.htm (last visited on May 29, 2012).

281. Lucis Trust (Lucifer Publishing Co.) A Satanic Leader for a One World Religion, Part of the United Nations, June 22, 2008, http://cantontruth.blogspot.com/2008/06/lucis-trust-lucifer-trust-satanic.html.

282. Lucis Trust (Lucifer Publishing Co.) A Satanic Leader for a One World Religion, Part of the United Nations, June 22, 2008, http://cantontruth.blogspot.com/2008/06/lucis-trust-lucifer-trust-satanic.html.

283. Randall E. King, When Worlds Collide: Politics, Religion, and Media at the 1970 East Tennessee Billy Graham Crusade, (March 22,

1997), http://www.highbeam.com/doc/1G1-19592304.html.

284. Randall E. King, When Worlds Collide: Politics, Religion, and Media at the 1970 East Tennessee Billy Graham Crusade, (March 22, 1997), http://www.highbeam.com/doc/1G1-19592304.html.

285. William Randolph Hearst, http://foundsf.org/index.php?title=William_Randolph_Hearst (last visited on October 6, 2012).

286. William Randolph Hearst, http://foundsf.org/index.php?title=William_Randolph_Hearst (last visited on October 6, 2012).

287. Hearst News Bans Rense, December 9, 2008, http://rense.com/general84/hearst.htm.

288. Texe Marrs, The Illuminati Builds Tower of Infamy, http://www.texemarrs.com/012005/illuminati_builds_tower_of_infamy.htm (last visited on October 7, 2012).

289. Donn deGrand Pre, Barbarians Inside the Gates, Book Two, The Vipers Venom, at 187 (2002), quoting Zbigniew Brzezinski, Between Two Ages: America's Role in the Technetronic Era (1970).

290. Zbigniew Brzezinski, Between Two Ages: America's Role in the Technetronic Era, at 72, quoted by Alan Stang, Your New President, Zbig Brother, News With Views, October 29, 2008,

http://www.newswithviews.com/Stang/alan170.htm.

291. Zbigniew Brzezinski, Between Two Ages: America's Role in the Technetronic Era, at 123, quoted by Alan Stang, Your New President, Zbig Brother, News With Views, October 29, 2008, http://www.newswithviews.com/Stang/alan170.htm.

292. Texe Marrs, The Illuminati Builds Tower of Infamy, http://www.texemarrs.com/012005/illuminati_builds_tower_of_infamy.htm (last visited on October 7, 2012).

293. Nixon, Billy Graham Target Jews on Tape, *St. Petersburg Times*, March 2, 2002, http://www.sptimes.com/2002/03/02/news_pf/Worldandnation/Nixon__Billy_Graham_t.shtml.

294. Nixon, Billy Graham Target Jews on Tape, *St. Petersburg Times*, March 2, 2002, http://www.sptimes.com/2002/03/02/news_pf/Worldandnation/Nixon__Billy_Graham_t.shtml.

295. WHITE HOUSE TAPES: Billy Graham Apologizes over Nixon Conversation and Says He Does Not 'Recall Having Those Feelings about Any Group, Especially the Jews', Western Mail (UK), March 18, 2002.

296. Texe Marrs, The Nixon White House Tapes and the Urgent Warnings of President Richard Nixon and Evangelist Billy Graham on the Dangers of the Synagogue of Satan, Power of Prophecy, http://www.texemarrs.com/082011/stranglehold_art

icle.htm (last visited on May 29, 2012).

297. Texe Marrs, The Nixon White House Tapes and the Urgent Warnings of President Richard Nixon and Evangelist Billy Graham on the Dangers of the Synagogue of Satan, Power of Prophecy, http://www.texemarrs.com/082011/stranglehold_article.htm (last visited on May 29, 2012).

298. Billy Graham's Sad Disobedience, at 7 (1997), available at http://www.wayoflife.org/free_ebooks/downloads/Billy_Grahams_Sad_Disobedience.pdf.

299. http://www.cuttingedge.org/n1082.html (site active as of July 17, 2001).

300. Martin L. Wagner, Freemasonry: An Interpretation, at 104-105 (1912), available at http://www.mindserpent.com/American_History/organization/mason/freemasonry/freemasonry.html.

301. Wagner, at 84-85.

302. Wagner, at 85-86.

303. Wagner, at 152-53.

304. Wagner, at 271.

305. Wagner, at 310-11.

306. Wagner, at 310.

307. Wagner, at 29-300.

308. Wagner, at 338.

309. Stephen Knight, The Brotherhood, at 236 (1986).

310. Wagner, at 338.

311. Knight, at 236.

312. Wagner, at 338.

313. Knight, at 236.

314. Knight, at 237.

315. ALBERT PIKE, MORALS AND DOGMA OF THE ANCIENT AND ACCEPTED SCOTTISH RITE OF FREEMASONRY, p. 205 (1871).

316. DES GRIFFIN, THE FOURTH REICH OF THE RICH, p. 70 (1993).

317. ALBERT PIKE, MORALS AND DOGMA OF THE ANCIENT AND ACCEPTED SCOTTISH RITE OF FREEMASONRY, p. 566 (1871).

318. Id. at p. 567.

319. Id.

320. Id.

321. Id. at 566.

322. Martin L. Wagner, Freemasonry: An Interpretation, at 182 (1912) available at http://www.mindserpent.com/American_History/organization/mason/freemasonry/freemasonry.html.

323. Protocols of the Learned Elders of Zion, Protocol 4, http://www.biblebelievers.org.au/przion3.htm#PROTOCOL%20No.%204 (last visited on August 31, 2012). See also Des Griffin, Fourth Reich of the Rich, p. 216 (1993).

324. Texe Marrs, Masonic Jews Plot to Control World, Power of Prophecy, April 2003, http://www.texemarrs.com/masonic_jews_plot_world_control.htm (website address current as of April 4, 2003).

325. Texe Marrs, Masonic Jews Plot to Control World, Power of Prophecy, April 2003, http://www.texemarrs.com/masonic_jews_plot_world_control.htm (website address current as of April 4, 2003).

326. Protocols of the Learned Elders of Zion, Protocol 15, http://www.biblebelievers.org.au/przion5.htm#protocol%20No.%2015 (last visited on August 25, 2012).

327. Protocols of the Learned Elders of Zion, Protocol 11, http://www.biblebelievers.org.au/przion4.htm#protocol%20No.%2011 (last visited on August 25, 2012).

328. Martin L. Wagner, Freemasonry: An Interpretation, at 113 (1912), quoting Mystic Masonry, pp. 119, 130, 138, 139, 140, available at http://www.mindserpent.com/American_History/organization/mason/freemasonry/freemasonry.html.

329. Martin L. Wagner, Freemasonry: An Interpretation, at 182 (1912), available at http://www.mindserpent.com/American_History/organization/mason/freemasonry/freemasonry.html.

330. Texe Marrs, Masonic Jews Plot to Control World, Power of Prophecy, April 2003, http://www.texemarrs.com/masonic_jews_plot_world_control.htm (website address current as of April 4, 2003).

331. Texe Marrs, Masonic Jews Plot to Control World, Power of Prophecy, April 2003, http://www.texemarrs.com/masonic_jews_plot_world_control.htm (website address current as of April 4, 2003).

332. Michael Hoffman, *Judaism Discovered,* at 768 (2008) (citing "The Place of Kabbalah in the Doctrine of Russian Freemasons," in Aries: Journal for the Study Western Esotericism, vol. 4, no. 1 (Brill Academic 2004) and Heimbichner, *Blood on the Alter*).

333. Henry Makow, Illuminati 2, Deceit and Seduction, at 10 (2010).

334. Henry Makow, Illuminati 2, Deceit and Seduction, at 10 (2010).

335. ALBERT PIKE, MORALS AND DOGMA OF THE ANCIENT AND ACCEPTED SCOTTISH RITE OF FREEMASONRY, p. 741 (1871).

336. Martin L. Wagner, Freemasonry: An Interpretation, at 210 (1912), available at http://www.mindserpent.com/American_History/organization/mason/freemasonry/freemasonry.html.

337.Martin L. Wagner, Freemasonry: An Interpretation, at 212 (1912), available at http://www.mindserpent.com/American_History/organization/mason/freemasonry/freemasonry.html.

338.Wagner, at 206.

339.Martin L. Wagner, Freemasonry: An Interpretation, at 212 (1912), available at http://www.mindserpent.com/American_History/organization/mason/freemasonry/freemasonry.html.

340.Athol Bloomer, *The Eucharist and The Jewish Mystical Tradition • Part 1*, Association of Hebrew Catholics, *at* http://hebrewcatholic.org/PrayerandSpirituality/eucharistjewishm.html (originally published in The Hebrew Catholic #77, pp 15-18 (Summer-Fall 2002)).

341.Athol Bloomer, *The Eucharist and The Jewish Mystical Tradition • Part 1*, Association of Hebrew Catholics, *at* http://hebrewcatholic.org/PrayerandSpirituality/eucharistjewishm.html (originally published in The Hebrew Catholic #77, pp 15-18 (Summer-Fall 2002)).

342.Rabbi Geoffrey W. Dennis, *The Encyclopedia of Jewish Myth, Magic, and Mysticism*, at 199 (2007), quoted by Michael Hoffman in *Judaism Discovered*, at 239-40 (2008).

343.Dennis, at 199.

344.Dan Cohn-Sherbok and Lavinia Cohn-Sherbok, Jewish and Christian Mysticism: An Introduction, at 167 (1994).

345.Michael Hoffman, *Judaism Discovered*, at 239 (2008).

346.Michael Hoffman, *Judaism Discovered*, at 240 (2008).

347.Michael Hoffman, *Judaism Discovered*, at 240 (2008).

348.Martin L. Wagner, Freemasonry: An Interpretation, at 183 (1912), available at http://www.mindserpent.com/American_History/organization/mason/freemasonry/freemasonry.html.

349.Martin L. Wagner, Freemasonry: An Interpretation, at 183 (1912), available at http://www.mindserpent.com/American_History/organization/mason/freemasonry/freemasonry.html.

350.Martin L. Wagner, Freemasonry: An Interpretation, at 464-65 (1912), available at http://www.mindserpent.com/American_History/organization/mason/freemasonry/freemasonry.html.

351.Martin L. Wagner, Freemasonry: An Interpretation, at 423 (1912), available at http://www.mindserpent.com/American_History/organization/mason/freemasonry/freemasonry.html.

352.Martin L. Wagner, Freemasonry: An Interpretation, at 226 (1912), available at http://www.mindserpent.com/American_History/organization/mason/freemasonry/freemasonry.html.

353.Martin L. Wagner, Freemasonry: An Interpretation, at 223 (1912), available at http://www.mindserpent.com/American_History/organization/mason/freemasonry/freemasonry.html.

354. Wagner, at 254, quoting Buck at 257.

355. Wagner, at 254-55.

356. Wagner, at 247.

357. Wagner, at 220.

358. Wagner, at 221-22

359. Wagner, at 258-59, quoting Weiss, Obelisk and Freemasonry, p. 40.

360. Wagner, at 262.

361. Wagner, at 239.

362. Wagner, at 245.

363. Wagner, 239-40.

364. Wagner, at 251.

365. Wagner, at 279-80.

366. DONN DE GRAND PRE, BARBARIANS INSIDE THE GATES, THE BLACK BOOK OF BOLSHEVISM, p. 248 (2000).

367. DONN DE GRAND PRE, BARBARIANS INSIDE THE GATES, THE BLACK BOOK OF BOLSHEVISM, p. 204 (2000).

368. Michael Hoffman, *Judaism Discovered,* at 770 (2008).

369. Babylonian Talmud: *Tractate Sanhedrin, Folio 65b,* at n.24, Sanhedrin Translated into English

with Notes, Glossary and Indices Chapters I - VI by Jacob Shachter, Chapters VII - XI by H. Freedman, B.A., Ph.D., Under the Editorship of Rabbi Dr I. Epstein B.A., Ph.D., D. Lit. (1961), *available at* http://www.come-and-hear.com/sanhedrin/sanhedrin_65.html.

370. Martin L. Wagner, Freemasonry: An Interpretation, at 142 (1912) available at http://www.mindserpent.com/American_History/organization/mason/freemasonry/freemasonry.html.

371. Martin L. Wagner, Freemasonry: An Interpretation, at 142 (1912) available at http://www.mindserpent.com/American_History/organization/mason/freemasonry/freemasonry.html.

372. Martin L. Wagner, Freemasonry: An Interpretation, at 140-141 (1912) available at http://www.mindserpent.com/American_History/organization/mason/freemasonry/freemasonry.html, citing Mystic Masonry, pp. XXXV, XXXVI, XXXVII, 87, 242, 255, 266.

373. Martin L. Wagner, Freemasonry: An Interpretation, at 105 (1912), available at http://www.mindserpent.com/American_History/organization/mason/freemasonry/freemasonry.html

374. Martin L. Wagner, Freemasonry: An Interpretation, at 117 (1912).

375. Henry Makow, Judaized Christianity: Front for New World Order, January 13, 2010, http://www.thetruthseeker.co.uk/oldsite/article.asp?ID=11973.

376. Henry Makow, Judaized Christianity: Front for New World Order, January 13, 2010, http://www.thetruthseeker.co.uk/oldsite/article.asp?ID=11973.

377. Martin L. Wagner, Freemasonry: An Interpretation, at 10 (1912).

378. Henry Makow, Judaized Christianity: Front for New World Order, January 13, 2010, http://www.thetruthseeker.co.uk/oldsite/article.asp?ID=11973.

379. Martin L. Wagner, Freemasonry: An Interpretation, at 11 (1912).

380. Henry Makow, Judaized Christianity: Front for New World Order, January 13, 2010, http://www.thetruthseeker.co.uk/oldsite/article.asp?ID=11973.

381. Henry Makow, Judaized Christianity: Front for New World Order, January 13, 2010, http://www.thetruthseeker.co.uk/oldsite/article.asp?ID=11973.

382. JOHN ROBISON, PROOFS OF A CONSPIRACY at pg. 7 (1798).

383. Library of Congress: George Washington Warns of Illuminati, http://consciouslifenews.com/library-congress-confirms-george-washington-aware-nefarious-illuminati/1122149/# (last visited on February 3, 2013).

384. JOHN ROBISON, at pg. 4.

385. JOHN ROBISON, at pgs. 12,17.

386.John S. Torell, European-American Evangelical Association, July 1999, http://www.eaec.org/NL99jul.htm (current as of October 2, 2001).

387.John S. Torell, supra.

388.John S. Torell, supra.

389.John S. Torell, supra.

390.John S. Torell, supra.

391.COLLIER'S ENCYCLOPEDIA, volume 13, p. 550 (1991).

392.EDMOND PARIS, THE SECRET HISTORY OF THE JESUITS, p. 69 (1975).

393.COLLIER'S ENCYCLOPEDIA, volume 13, p. 550 (1991).

394.EDMOND PARIS, at p. 70.

395.COLLIER'S ENCYCLOPEDIA, volume 13, p. 550 (1991); *see also,* EDMOND PARIS, supra at 70.

396.EDMOND PARIS, at p. 73.

397.EDMOND PARIS, at p. 70.

398.*Id.* at 70-71.

399.*Id.* at 71.

400.John S. Torell, supra.

401.John S. Torell, supra.

402.John S. Torell, supra.

403.Eric Jon Phelps, VATICAN ASSASSINS: "WOUNDED IN THE HOUSE OF MY FRIENDS," p. 206 (2001) (citing G.B. Nicolini, History of the Jesuits, Their Progress, Doctrines, and Designs, at 356-57 (1854)).

404.Eric Jon Phelps, supra at 206.

405.John S. Torell, supra.

406.Eric Jon Phelps, VATICAN ASSASSINS: "WOUNDED IN THE HOUSE OF MY FRIENDS," p. 213-15 (2001) (quoting Nesta Webster, Secret Societies and Subversive Movements, at 139 (1924) and Lady Queenborough, Occult Theocracy, at 313 (1933)).

407.Evil People, Adam Weishaupt S.J., http://one-evil.org/content/people_18c_weishaupt.html (last visited on February 5, 2013).

408.Robison at 58, supra.

409.Robison at 59, supra.

410.COLLIER'S ENCYCLOPEDIA, volume 13, p. 550 (1991).

411.EDMOND PARIS, THE SECRET HISTORY OF THE JESUITS, p. 75 (1975).

412.*Id.*

413. Protocols of the Learned Elders of Zion, Protocol 15, http://www.biblebelievers.org.au/przion5.htm#protocol%20No.%2015 (last visited on August 25, 2012).

414. Protocol 15, supra.

415. Protocol 15, supra.

416. Michael Hoffman II, Secret Societies an Psychological Warfare, pp. 57-58, 2001.

417. WILLIAM STILL, NEW WORLD ORDER, The Ancient Plan of Secret Societies, p. 123 (1990).

418. *Id.* at p. 108.

419. *Id.*

420. David Allen Rivera, The Illuminati Leadership Changes, Final Warning: A History of the New World Order, http://www.the7thfire.com/new_world_order/final_warning/illuminati_leadership_changes.htm (web address current as of April 17, 2004).

421. Herbert G. Dorsey III, The Historical Influence of International Banking, http://www.illuminati-news.com/international-banking.htm (web address current as of April 17, 2004).

422. Protocol 15, supra.

423. Stephen Knight, The Brotherhood, The Secret World of the Freemasons, at 283 (1986).

424. Stephen Knight, supra at 269-296.

425. Stephen Knight, supra at 281.

426. Stephen Knight, supra at 274.

427. Stephen Knight, supra at 273.

428. Stephen Knight, supra at 274.

429. Stephen Knight, supra at 273.

430. Stephen Knight, supra at 294-295.

431. Protocols of the Learned Elders of Zion, Protocol 1, http://www.biblebelievers.org.au/przion2.htm#PROTOCOL%20No.%201 (last visited on August 22, 2012).

432. DONN DE GRAND PRE, BARBARIANS INSIDE THE GATES, THE BLACK BOOK OF BOLSHEVISM, p. 250 (2000) (quoting Representative Louis McFadden, radio address, May 2, 1934).

433. 75 Congressional Record 12595-12603.

434. See EDWARD GRIFFIN, THE CREATURE FROM JEKYLL ISLAND: A SECOND LOOK AT THE FEDERAL RESERVE (3RD Edition 1998).

435. CONG. REC. 12595-96 (1932) (speech of Rep. McFadden), *at* http://iresist.com/cbg/mcfadden_speech_1932.html (current as of September 30, 2001).

436. CONG. REC. 12595-96 (1932) (speech of Rep. McFadden), *at* http://iresist.com/cbg/mcfadden_speech_1932.html (current as of September 30, 2001).

437. Israel Shahak, Jewish History, Jewish Religion: The Weight of Three Thousand Years (1994), *available at* http//www.biblebelievers.org.au/jewhis3.htm#Orthodoxy%20and%20Interpretation.

438. Israel Shahak, Jewish History, Jewish Religion: The Weight of Three Thousand Years (1994), *available at* http//www.biblebelievers.org.au/jewhis3.htm#Orthodoxy%20and%20Interpretation.

439. Israel Shahak, Jewish History, Jewish Religion: The Weight of Three Thousand Years (1994), *available at* http//www.biblebelievers.org.au/jewhis3.htm#Orthodoxy%20and%20Interpretation.

440. Israel Shamir, Seven Lean Kine, November 28, 2008, *available at* http://www.thetruthseeker.co.uk/article.asp?ID=9743.

441. Protocols of the Learned Elders of Zion, Protocol 2, http://www.biblebelievers.org.au/przion2.htm#PROTOCOL%20No.%202 (Last visited on August 22, 2012).

442. Ivan Fraser, The Protocols of the Learned Elders of Zion: Proofs of an Ancient Conspiracy, quoting The American Bulletin, May 5, 1935,

http://www.bibliotecapleyades.net/sociopolitica/esp_sociopol_zion04.htm (last visited on October 17, 2012).

443. Ivan Fraser, The Protocols of the Learned Elders of Zion: Proofs of an Ancient Conspiracy, quoting The American Bulletin, May 5, 1935, http://www.bibliotecapleyades.net/sociopolitica/esp_sociopol_zion04.htm (last visited on October 17, 2012).

444. MICHAEL A. HOFFMAN II, JEWISH COMMUNISTS: THE DOCUMENTARY RECORD, http://www.hoffman-info.com/communist.html (website current as of March 5, 2003) (citing N.Y. Times, Oct. 7, 1999 and Newsweek, Oct. 18, 1999, p. 30).

445. New World Encyclopedia, http://www.newworldencyclopedia.org/entry/Comintern#cite_note-0 (last visited on September 19, 2012) (citing MI-5, History, The Inter-War Period. Retrieved December 19, 2007).

446. Henry Makow, Illuminati: The Cult That Hijacked the World, at 56 (2011).

447. MICHAEL A. HOFFMAN II, JEWISH COMMUNISTS: THE DOCUMENTARY RECORD, http://www.hoffman-info.com/communist.html (website current as of March 5, 2003).

448. MICHAEL A. HOFFMAN II, JEWISH COMMUNISTS: THE DOCUMENTARY RECORD,

http://www.hoffman-info.com/communist.html (website current as of March 5, 2003) (quoting Dmitri Volkogonov, *Lenin: A New Biography,* p. 112).

449.MICHAEL A. HOFFMAN II, JEWISH COMMUNISTS: THE DOCUMENTARY RECORD, http://www.hoffman-info.com/communist.html (website current as of March 5, 2003).

450.ROBERT WILTON, THE LAST DAYS OF THE ROMANOVS (1920).

451.Gordon "Jack" Mohr, The Talmudic Effect on Judeo-Christianity, http://www.christianbiblestudy.org/OPS/JM/jm0027c.htm (current as of September 19, 2001).

452.ROBERT WILTON, THE LAST DAYS OF THE ROMANOVS, p. 148 (1920).

453.COLONEL GORDON "JACK" MOHR, THE TALMUDIC EFFECT ON JUDEO-CHRISTIANITY, http://www.christianbiblestudy.org/OPS/JM/jm0027e.htm (current as of September 17, 2001).

454.*Izvestia,* July 27, 1918.

455.HENRY FORD, THE INTERNATIONAL JEW, vol. 1, p. 225 (1920).

456.HENRY FORD, THE INTERNATIONAL JEW, vol. 1, p. 225 (1920).

457.MICHAEL A. HOFFMAN II, JEWISH COMMUNISTS: THE DOCUMENTARY

RECORD, http://www.hoffman-info.com/communist.html (website current as of March 5, 2003) (quoting The Christian News, Jan. 8, 1996, p. 2).

458. MICHAEL A. HOFFMAN II, JEWISH COMMUNISTS: THE DOCUMENTARY RECORD, http://www.hoffman-info.com/communist.html (website current as of March 5, 2003).

459. Henry Makow, Communism - A Ruse for Illuminati Jewish Theft & Murder, April 28, 2008, http://www.savethemales.ca/communism_disguises_illuminati.html.

460. Slava Katamidze, Loyal Comrades, Ruthless Killers -The Secret Services of the USSR 1917-1991, at 25, quoted by Henry Makow, Communism - A Ruse for Illuminati Jewish Theft & Murder, April 28, 2008, http://www.savethemales.ca/communism_disguises_illuminati.html.

461. Henry Makow, Communism - A Ruse for Illuminati Jewish Theft & Murder, April 28, 2008, http://www.savethemales.ca/communism_disguises_illuminati.html.

462. Henry Makow, Communism - A Ruse for Illuminati Jewish Theft & Murder, April 28, 2008, http://www.savethemales.ca/communism_disguises_illuminati.html.

463. Sever Plocker, Stalin's Jews, December 26, 2006, http://www.ynetnews.com/articles/0,7340,L-33429

99,00.html.

464. DES GRIFFIN, FOURTH REICH OF THE RICH, p. 62 (1976).

465. *Id.*

466. Protocols of the Learned Elders of Zion, Protocol 3, http://www.biblebelievers.org.au/przion2.htm#PROTOCOL%20No.%203 (last visited on October 17, 2012).

467. DONN DE GRAND PRE, BARBARIANS INSIDE THE GATES, THE BLACK BOOK OF BOLSHEVISM, p. 209 (2000) (quoting BEJAMIN FREEDMAN, FACTS ARE FACTS (1954)).

468. Baruch Levy, Letter to Karl Marx, `La Revue de Paris', p. 574, June 1, 1928. http://www4.stormfront.org/posterity/ci/tjg.html (current as of September 9, 2001). *See also* DON DE GRAND PRE, BARBARIANS INSIDE THE GATES, p. 64 (2000).

469. DONN DE GRAND PRE, BARBARIANS INSIDE THE GATES, THE BLACK BOOK OF BOLSHEVISM, p. 313-14 (2000) (citing JACK BERNSTEIN, THE LIFE OF AN AMERICAN JEW IN RACIST MARXIST ISRAEL (1984)).

470. DONN DE GRAND PRE, BARBARIANS INSIDE THE GATES, THE BLACK BOOK OF BOLSHEVISM, p. 313-14 (2000) (citing JACK BERNSTEIN, THE LIFE OF AN AMERICAN JEW IN RACIST MARXIST ISRAEL (1984)).

471. DONN DE GRAND PRE, BARBARIANS INSIDE THE GATES, THE BLACK BOOK OF BOLSHEVISM, p. 313-14 (2000) (citing JACK BERNSTEIN, THE LIFE OF AN AMERICAN JEW IN RACIST MARXIST ISRAEL (1984)).

472. JACK BERNSTEIN, MY FAREWELL TO ISRAEL THE THORN IN THE MIDEAST.

473. Protocols of the Learned Elders of Zion, Protocol 14, http://www.biblebelievers.org.au/przion5.htm#protocol%20No.%2014 (last visited on August 25, 2012).

474. See John S. Torell, Showdown in Jerusalem, The Dove, winter 1995.

475. Walter White, Jr., The Hidden Tyranny, http://www.fourwinds10.com/corner/J224-ch4.pdf, http://www.antichristconspiracy.com/HTML%20Pages/Harold_Wallace_Rosenthal_Interview_1976.htm (web address current as of April 21, 2002).

476. RABBI DAVID A. COOPER, GOD IS A VERB, KABBALAH AND THE PRACTICE OF MYSTICAL JUDAISM, at 156 (1997) (emphasis added).

477. *Id.* at 160 (emphasis added).

478. Henry Makow, Illuminati 2, Deceit and Seduction, at 13 (2010).

479. Henry Makow, Illuminati 2, Deceit and Seduction, at 207 (2010).

480. See John S. Torell, Showdown in Jerusalem, The Dove, winter 1995.

481. MICHAEL A. HOFFMAN, JUDAISM'S STRANGE GODS, at p. 92, (2000).

482. Steven Paas, Christian Zionism Examined, A Review of Ideas on Israel, the Church, and the Kingdom, at 111 (2012).

483. Steven Paas, Christian Zionism Examined, A Review of Ideas on Israel, the Church, and the Kingdom, at 77 (2012).

484. Steven Paas, Christian Zionism Examined, A Review of Ideas on Israel, the Church, and the Kingdom, at 77 (2012).

485. Henry Makow, Illuminati, the Cult that Hijacked the World (2011), http://antimatrix.org/Convert/Books/Henry_Makow/Henry_Makow_Illuminati_The_Cult_that_Hijacked_the_World.html.

486. Henry Makow, Illuminati: The Cult That Hijacked the World, at 59 (2011).

487. Henry Makow, Illuminati: The Cult That Hijacked the World, at 59 (2011).

488. Philip Gardiner, Watchers, Elohim, and Egregors, Abridged from 'Forbidden Knowledge: Secret Societies,' http://www.bibliotecapleyades.net/vida_alien/alien_watchers18.htm (last visited on September 19, 2012). See also John Kominski, The Egregore, April 7, 2008, http://www.johnkaminski.info/pages/articles/the_eg

regore.htm

489. John Kominski, The Egregore, April 7, 2008, http://www.johnkaminski.info/pages/articles/the_egregore.htm.

490. Texe Marrs, The Holy Serpent of the Jews, http://www.texemarrs.com/092012/holy_serpent_of_jews.htm (last visited on September 18, 2012).

491. Texe Marrs, The Holy Serpent of the Jews, http://www.texemarrs.com/092012/holy_serpent_of_jews.htm (last visited on September 18, 2012).

492. Chika Flint, Examining Judaism and the Origin of the Six Pointed Star, December 18, 2011.

493. Chika Flint, Examining Judaism and the Origin of the Six Pointed Star, December 18, 2011.

494. Chika Flint, Examining Judaism and the Origin of the Six Pointed Star, December 18, 2011.

495. Chika Flint, Examining Judaism and the Origin of the Six Pointed Star, December 18, 2011.

496. Chika Flint, Examining Judaism and the Origin of the Six Pointed Star, December 18, 2011.

497. Leviathan and Behemoth, Jewish Encyclopedia, http://www.jewishencyclopedia.com/articles/9841-leviathan-and-behemoth (last visited on September 20, 2012).

498. Chika Flint, Examining Judaism and the Origin of the Six Pointed Star, December 18, 2011.

499. Chika Flint, Examining Judaism and the Origin of the Six Pointed Star, December 18, 2011.

500. Joel David Bakst, Journey To the Center of the Torah: The Secret In the Serpent's Belly (2007) (citing *Leshem Shevo VeAchlama Sefer Dayah* p.179 and *Sifra DiZtenuta* Chapter 1), http://www.chazonhatorah.org/journey-to-the-center-of-the-torah-the-secret-in-the-serpent-s-belly.htm#_ftnref5.

501. Protocols of the Learned Elders of Zion, Preface, http://www.biblebelievers.org.au/przion1.htm#PREFACE (last visited on October 17, 2012).

502. See John S. Torell, Showdown in Jerusalem, The Dove, winter 1995.

503. Baruch Levy, Letter to Karl Marx, `La Revue de Paris', p. 574, June 1, 1928. http://www4.stormfront.org/posterity/ci/tjg.html (current as of September 9, 2001). *See also* DON DE GRAND PRE, BARBARIANS INSIDE THE GATES, p. 64 (2000).

504. Babylonian Talmud: *Tractate Sanhedrin, Folio 58b*, Sanhedrin Translated into English with Notes, Glossary and Indices Chapters I - VI by Jacob Shachter, Chapters VII - XI
by H. Freedman, B.A., Ph.D., Under the Editorship of Rabbi Dr I. Epstein B.A., Ph.D., D. Lit. (1961), *available at* http://www.come-and-hear.com/sanhedrin/sahedrin_58.html.

505.Michael Hoffman, *Judaism Discovered*, at 196 (2008) (quoting *Zohar Hadash, Bereshit* 18d-19a).

506.Henry Makow, Illuminati: The Cult That Hijacked the World, at 60-61 (2011).

507.The Kibbutz, Jewish Virtual Library, http://www.jewishvirtuallibrary.org/jsource/Society_&_Culture/kibbutz.html (last visited on September 19, 2012).

508.The Kibbutz, Jewish Virtual Library, http://www.jewishvirtuallibrary.org/jsource/Society_&_Culture/kibbutz.html (last visited on September 19, 2012).

509.Karl Marx, Critique of the Gotha Programme, http://www.marxists.org/archive/marx/works/1875/gotha/ch01.htm (last visited on September 19, 2012).

510.Henry Makow, Illuminati: The Cult That Hijacked the World, at 60-61 (2011).

511.Henry Makow, Illuminati: The Cult That Hijacked the World, at 60-61 (2011).

512.Harmony Daws, Why Evangelicals Want to be Jews and Not Christians, EVANGELICALS: IN THE IMITATION OF JEWS, April 28, 2010, http://mysteryworshipers.wordpress.com/2011/05/04/why-evangelicals-want-to-be-jews-and-not-christians/.

513.Edith Starr Miller, Occult Theocrasy, pp. 77 (1933) (quoting Flavien Brenier. Source: Lt. Gen. A. Netchvolodow, Nicolas II et les Juifs, p. 139.).

514. Edith Starr Miller, Occult Theocrasy, pp. 78-79 (1933) (quoting Flavien Brenier. Source: Lt. Gen. A. Netchvolodow, Nicolas II et les Juifs, p. 139.).

515. Edith Starr Miller, Occult Theocrasy, p. 80 (1933).

516. Edith Starr Miller, Occult Theocrasy, p. 81 (1933).

517. Babylonian Talmud: *Tractate Sanhedrin, Folio 58b*, Sanhedrin Translated into English with Notes, Glossary and Indices Chapters I - VI by Jacob Shachter, Chapters VII - XI
by H. Freedman, B.A., Ph.D., Under the Editorship of Rabbi Dr I. Epstein B.A., Ph.D., D. Lit. (1961), *available at* http://www.come-and-hear.com/sanhedrin/sahedrin_58.html.

518. *Sanhedrin, Folio 58b.*

519. Babylonian Talmud: *Tractate Yebamoth, Folio 98a,* Yebamoth Translated into English with Notes Glossary and Indices by Rev. Dr. Israel W. Slotki, M.A., Litt.D., Under the Editorship of Rabbi Dr I. Epstein B.A., Ph.D., D. Lit. (1961), *available at* http://www.come-and-hear.com/yebamoth/yebamoth_98.html .

520. The Curse Against Christians at Jamnia About 90 AD, http://www.defendingthebride.com/bb/curse.html#end (last visited on August 20, 2012).

521. The Curse Against Christians at Jamnia About 90 AD, http://www.defendingthebride.com/bb/curse.html#e

nd (last visited on August 20, 2012).

522. Steven Paas, Christian Zionism Examined, A Review of Ideas on Israel , the Church, and the Kingdom, at 13 (2012).

523. Ariel Toaff, *Blood Passover, The Jews of Europe and Ritual Murder*, translated into English by Gian Marco Lucchese and Pietro Gianetti, 24 August 2007, English version available in HTML at http://www.bloodpassover.com/, English version available in PDF at http://www.israelshamir.net/BLOODPASSOVER.pdf, original Italian version available in PDF at http://www.laboratorio99.com/upload/Pasque%20di%20Sangue.pdf.

524. Bar Ilan University, Ramat-Gan, 52900 Israel, *at* http://www1.biu.ac.il/indexE.php (last visited on April 7, 2010).

525. Adi Schwartz, *The Wayward Son*, Haaretz, February 22, 2007, cited by Michael Hoffman in *Judaism Discovered*, at 581 (2008).

526. Ariel Toaff, *Blood Passover*, at 10-11.

527. Ariel Toaff, *Blood Passover*, at 167.

528. Ariel Toaff, *Blood Passover*, at 167.

529. Ariel Toaff, *Blood Passover*, at 170.

530. Michael A. Hoffman II, *Judaism's Strange God's*, at 364 (2000) (quoting *Romemut Yisrael Ufarashat Hagalut*).

531. Michael A. Hoffman II, *Judaism's Strange God's*, at 364 (2000) (quoting *Romemut Yisrael Ufarashat Hagalut*).

532. Michael Hoffman, *Judaism Discovered*, at 529 (2008) (quoting Roman A. Foxbrunner, *Habad: The Hasidism of Shneur of Lyady*, at 108-09 (1993) (quoting Rabbi Shneur Zalman)).

533. Babylonian Talmud: Tractate 'Abodah Zarah, Folio 17a.

534. Babylonian Talmud: Tractate Sanhedrin Folio 106a.

535. Babylonian Talmud: Tractate Gittin Folio 57a.

536. Michael Hoffman, *Judaism Discovered*, at 357 (2008).

537. Chagigah 27a (a/k/a Hagigah 27a), *A Translation of the Treatise Chagigah from the Babylonian Talmud*, With Introduction, Notes, Glossary, and Indices by the Rev. A. W. Strean, M.A. Fellow, and Divinity and Hebrew Lecturer, of Corpus Christi College, Cambridge, and Formerly Tyrwhitt's Hebrew Scholar, at 145 (1891), *available at* http://www.archive.org/details/chagigahbabyloni00unknuoft.

538. Tractate Baba Bathra Folio 75a at footnote 15.

539. Michael Hoffman, *Judaism Discovered*, at 196 (2008) (quoting *Zohar Hadash, Bereshit* 18d-19a).

540. Michael Hoffman, *Judaism Discovered*, at 196 (2008).

541. Michael Hoffman, *Judaism Discovered*, at 203 (2008).

542. William Wotton, *Miscellaneous Discourses Relating to the Traditions and Usages of the Scribes and Pharisees in Our Blessed Saviour Jesus Christ's Time* (London 1718) (quoted by Michael Hoffman, *Judaism Discovered*, at 193 (2008)).

543. Michael Hoffman, *Judaism Discovered*, at 192 n.156 (2008).

544. Judaism vs. Christianity: The War The Lamb Wins, http://www.fixedearth.com/talmud.html (current as of September 11, 2001).

545. DONN DE GRAND PRE, BARBARIANS INSIDE THE GATES, THE BLACK BOOK OF BOLSHEVISM, p. 209 (2000) (quoting BEJAMIN FREEDMAN, FACTS ARE FACTS (1954)).

546. Michael Hoffman, *Judaism Discovered*, at 785 (2008).

547. Lawrence Fine, Chapter on Kabbalistic Texts, From: *Back to the Sources: Reading the Classic Jewish Texts* ("The First Complete Modern Guide to the Great Books of the Jewish Tradition: What They Are and How to Read Them"), at p. 337 (2006) (bold emphasis added, italics in original).

548. Lawrence Fine, Chapter on Kabbalistic Texts, From: *Back to the Sources: Reading the Classic Jewish Texts* ("The First Complete Modern Guide to the Great Books of the Jewish Tradition: What They Are and How to Read Them"), at p. 337 (2006) (quoting Zohar III, 152a).

549.Blavatsky, Theosophical Glossary, p. 168 (quoted by Barbara Aho, Mystery, Babylon the Great Catholic or Jewish?, at http://watch.pair.com/mystery-babylon.html#cabala (last visited on April 17, 2010)).

550.MICHAEL A. HOFFMAN, JUDAISM'S STRANGE GODS, at p. 88, (2000).

551.MICHAEL A. HOFFMAN, JUDAISM'S STRANGE GODS, at p. 88, (2000). See also Michael Hoffman, *Judaism Discovered*, at 779 (2008) (quoting Gershom Scholem, *Kabbalah* pp.183-84).

552.MICHAEL A. HOFFMAN, JUDAISM'S STRANGE GODS, at p. 91, (2000).

553.Michael Hoffman, *Judaism Discovered*, at 780 (2008) (quoting Helen Jacaobus, *Eye Jinx*, Jewish Chronicle, May 7, 1999).

554.Chika Flint, Examining Judaism and the Origin of the Six Pointed Star, December 18, 2011.

555.Protocols of the Learned Elders of Zion, Protocol 3, http://www.biblebelievers.org.au/przion2.htm#PROTOCOL%20No.%203 (Last visited on August 23, 2012).

556.Protocols of the Learned Elders of Zion, Protocol 23, http://www.biblebelievers.org.au/przion7.htm#PROTOCOL%20No.%2023 (last visited on August 25, 2012).

557.Protocols of the Learned Elders of Zion, Protocol 3, http://www.biblebelievers.org.au/przion2.htm#PROTOCOL%20No.%203 (last visited on October 18, 2012).

558.Protocols of the Learned Elders of Zion, Protocol 17, http://www.biblebelievers.org.au/przion6.htm#protocol%20No.%2017 (last visited on August 25, 2012).

559.Barry Chamish, *The Vatican's Plot Against Israel*, January 27, 2001, http://us.altnews.com.au/article.php?sid=41 (current as of September 26, 2001).

560.Barry Chamish, You Thought It Was Too Fantastic To Be True, July 29, 2003, http://rense.com/general39/fanta.htm.

561.Barry Chamish, You Thought It Was Too Fantastic To Be True, July 29, 2003, http://rense.com/general39/fanta.htm.

562.Barry Chamish, You Thought It Was Too Fantastic To Be True, July 29, 2003, http://rense.com/general39/fanta.htm.

563.Barry Chamish, You Thought It Was Too Fantastic To Be True, July 29, 2003, http://rense.com/general39/fanta.htm.

564.NESTA WEBSTER, SECRET SOCIETIES AND SUBVERSIVE MOVEMENTS, http://web.archive.org/web/20021005055527/http://www.plausiblefutures.com/text/SS.html (website address current as of 2-28-05) (citing Lexicon of

Freemasonry, p. 323).

565. ALBERTO RIVERA, DOUBLE CROSS, Chick publications, p. 27, 1981(quoting THE GREAT ENCYCLICAL LETTERS OF POPE LEO XIII, p. 304, Benziger Brothers (1903).

566. AVRO MANAHATTAN, THE VATICAN BILLIONS, Chick Publications, p.183 (1983).

567. AVRO MANAHATTAN, THE VATICAN BILLIONS, Chick Publications, p.41 (1983).

568. ALBERTO RIVERA, THE GODFATHERS, Chick Publications, p. 32, 1982 (quoting The Registers of Boniface VIII, The Vatican Archives, L. Fol. 387 and THE CATHOLIC ENCYCLOPEDIA, Encyclopedia Press (1913)).

569. RALPH E. WOODROW, BABYLON MYSTERY RELIGION, p. 72, 1966.

570. COLLIER'S ENCYCLOPEDIA, volume 19, p. 239 (1991).

571. ALBERTO RIVERA, THE GODFATHERS, Chick Publications, p. 32, 1982 (quoting The Registers of Boniface VIII, The Vatican Archives, L. Fol. 387 and THE CATHOLIC ENCYCLOPEDIA, Encyclopedia Press (1913)).

572. Maurice Pinay, *The Plot Against the Church*, http://www.catholicvoice.co.uk/pinay/ (last visited February 10, 2010).

573. Maurice Pinay, *The Plot Against the Church, Part 4, The Jewish "Fifth Column" in the Clergy, Chapter 4, Jewry - The Father of the Gnostics*,

http://www.catholicvoice.co.uk/pinay/part4a.htm (last visited on February 10, 2010).

574. Stephan A. Hoeller, *Valentinus- A Gnostic For All Seasons*, http://www.gnosis.org/valentinus.htm (last visited on February 10, 2010).

575. Edward Hendrie, *The Anti-Gospel, The Perversion of Christ's Grace Gospel*, available at www.antichristconspiracy.com and www.lulu.com.

576. Philip Schaff, *History of the Christian Church, Volume II, Ante Nicene Christianity, A.D. 100-325*, http://www.ccel.org/ccel/schaff/hcc2.v.xi.ii.html (last visited on February 10, 2010).

577. Irenaeus, Against Heresies, Book I, Ch. XXIV.

578. Irenaeus, *Against Heresies*, Book III, Chapter XXI, *available at* http://www.ccel.org/ccel/schaff/anf01.ix.iv.xxii.html (last visited March 24, 2010).

579. Irenaeus, *Against Heresies*, Book I, Chapter XXVI, *available at* http://www.ccel.org/ccel/schaff/anf01.ix.ii.xxvii.html (last visited March 24, 2010).

580. Irenaeus, *Against Heresies*, Book I, Chapter XXV, *available at* http://www.ccel.org/ccel/schaff/anf01.ix.ii.xxvi.html. (last visited March 24, 2010).

581. Irenaeus, *Against Heresies*, Book I, Chapter XXVI, *available at* http://www.ccel.org/ccel/schaff/anf01.ix.ii.xxvii.html (last visited March 24, 2010).

582. Irenaeus, *Against Heresies*, Book I, Chapter XXV, *available at* http://www.ccel.org/ccel/schaff/anf01.ix.ii.xxvi.html. (last visited March 24, 2010).

583. Irenaeus, *Against Heresies*, Book III, Chapter XXI, *available at* http://www.ccel.org/ccel/schaff/anf01.ix.iv.xxii.html (last visited March 24, 2010).

584. Rabbi Tovia Singer, Does the Hebrew Word Alma Really Mean "Virgin"?, *available at* http://www.outreachjudaism.org/alma.htm (last visited on April 17, 2010). See also Rabbi Shraga Simmons, Ask Rabbi Simmons, Jesus as the Messiah, *at* http://judaism.about.com/library/3_askrabbi_o/bl_simmons_messiah3.htm (last visited on April 17, 2010).

585. G.A. RIPLINGER, BLIND GUIDES, p. 19.

586. G.A. RIPLINGER, BLIND GUIDES, p. 19.

587. G.A. RIPLINGER, BLIND GUIDES, p. 19.

588. Edward Hendrie, *Antichrist Conspiracy Inside the Devil's Lair*, at Chapter 7 (2010), *available at* www.antichristconspiracy.com and www.lulu.com.

589. Noah Webster, AMERICAN DICTIONARY OF THE ENGLISH LANGUAGE, *Cardinal* (1828). See also Online Etymology Dictionary, *Cardinal, at* http://www.etymonline.com/index.php?term=cardinal (last visited on March 16, 2010).

590. Jewish Encyclopedia, High Priest, *available at* http://www.jewishencyclopedia.com/view.jsp?artid

=721&letter=H&search=high%20priest (last visited on March 16, 2010).

591. Jewish Encyclopeidia, Sanhedrin, *available at* http://www.jewishencyclopedia.com/view.jsp?artid=229&letter=S&search=sanhedrin (last visited on March 16, 2010).

592. Sägmüller, J.B. (1908). Cardinal. In The Catholic Encyclopedia. New York: Robert Appleton Company. Retrieved March 16, 2010 from New Advent: http://www.newadvent.org/cathen/03333b.htm.

593. The High Priest and His Garments, http://www.domini.org/tabern/highprst.htm (last visited on March 16, 2010).

594. CATECHISM OF THE CATHOLIC CHURCH, § 830-831, 1994.

595. CATECHISM OF THE CATHOLIC CHURCH, § 2034-2035, 1994.

596. ALBERTO RIVERA, FOUR HORSEMEN, Chick Publications, p. 25, 1985 (quoting AVRO MANHATTAN, VATICAN IMPERIALISM IN THE 20th CENTURY, p. 76.). *See also*, JOHN W. ROBBINS, ECCLESIASTICAL MEGALOMANIA, at p. 132 (1999).

597. ALBERTO RIVERA, THE GODFATHERS, Chick Publications, p. 32, 1982 (quoting The Registers of Boniface VIII, The Vatican Archives, L. Fol. 387 and THE CATHOLIC ENCYCLOPEDIA, Encyclopedia Press (1913)).

598.ALBERTO RIVERA, DOUBLE CROSS, Chick publications, p. 27, 1981(quoting THE GREAT ENCYCLICAL LETTERS OF POPE LEO XIII, p. 304, Benziger Brothers (1903).

599.G.A. RIPLER, NEW AGE BIBLE VERSIONS, p. 134 (1993).

600.*Id.*

601.NOAH WEBSTER, AMERICAN DICTIONARY OF THE ENGLISH LANGUAGE (1st ed. 1828) republished by Foundation for American Christian Education, San Francisco, California.

602.Oxford University Press (1979).

603.JOHN PAUL II, CROSSING THE THRESHOLD OF HOPE, p. 12, 1994.

604.*Id.* at p. 6.

605.*E.g.,* W. GRINTON BERRY, FOXE'S BOOK OF MARTYRS, p. 357.

606.Athol Bloomer, *The Eucharist and The Jewish Mystical Tradition • Part 3*, Association of Hebrew Catholics, *at* http://hebrewcatholic.org/HCLives/Bloomer-Athol/eucharistandjewi.html, (originally published in The Hebrew Catholic #80 (Spring/Summer 2004)).

607.Kabbalah, Jewish Virtual Library, http://www.jewishvirtuallibrary.org/jsource/judaica/ejud_0002_0011_0_10514.html (last visited on March 3, 2010).

608.Athol Bloomer, *The Eucharist and The Jewish Mystical Tradition* • *Part 3*, Association of Hebrew Catholics, *at* http://hebrewcatholic.org/HCLives/Bloomer-Athol/ eucharistandjewi.html, (originally published in The Hebrew Catholic #80 (Spring/Summer 2004)).

609.Daniel Chanan Matt, *Zohar, The Book of Enlightenment*, at 132 (1983), *at* http://books.google.com/.

610.J.P. Stehelin, F.R.S., editor of *The Tradition of the Jews*, at 301 (1748), based upon Johann Andreas Eisenmenger's *Entdecktes Judenthum* (Judaism Revealed), at 137 of the section titled The Traditions of the Jews with the Expositions and Doctrines of the Rabbins (1700) (Stehelin's 1748 English translation was reprinted with Introduction and Annotated Bibliography by Michael A. Hoffman II (2006)).

611.THE RANDOM HOUSE DICTIONARY OF THE ENGLISH LANGUAGE, unabridged edition, 1973.

612.Salvation is Obtained From . . . Mary?, http://www.aloha.net/~mikesch/mary.htm (web address current as of April 3, 2005), quoting Arthur Burton Calkins, TOTUS TUUS, pp.21, 27, Academy of the Immaculate, New Bedford, Massachusetts, ISBN 0-9635345-0-5, Nihil Obstat and Imprimatur of the Catholic Church.

613.Salvation is Obtained From . . . Mary?, http://www.aloha.net/~mikesch/mary.htm (web address current as of April 3, 2005), quoting Arthur Burton Calkins, TOTUS TUUS, pp.21, 27,

Academy of the Immaculate, New Bedford, Massachusetts, ISBN 0-9635345-0-5, Nihil Obstat and Imprimatur of the Catholic Church.

614.The Rosary, Roses of Prayer for The Queen of Heaven, Daniel A. Lord, S.J., Nihil Obstat Athur J. Scanlan S.T.D: Censor Liborum, Imprimatur + Francis J. Spellman, D.D. Archbishop, New York, http://www.truecatholic.org/rosary.htm (web address current as of March 20, 2005).

615.COLLIER'S ENCYCLOPEDIA, volume 20, p. 169 (1991).

616.*E.g., CATECHISM OF THE CATHOLIC CHURCH*, §§ 105, 1141,1163, 1203, 1249, 1667 (1997), http://www.scborromeo.org/index2.htm (web address current as of March 22, 2005).

617.The Rosary, Roses of Prayer for The Queen of Heaven, Daniel A. Lord, S.J., Nihil Obstat Athur J. Scanlan S.T.D: Censor Liborum, Imprimatur + Francis J. Spellman, D.D. Archbishop, New York, http://www.truecatholic.org/rosary.htm (web address current as of March 20, 2005).

618.Rosary Meditations, http://www.cfalive.org/ReadRosary.htm (web address current as of March 20, 2005).

619.Prayer to Mary, Queen of Heaven, http://www.catholic-forum.com/saints/pray0421.htm (web address current as of March 20, 2005).

620.J.NEUNER, S.J & J. DUPUIS, S.J., THE CHRISTIAN FAITH IN THE DOCTRINAL DOCUMENTS OF THE CATHOLIC CHURCH, PIUS X, ENCYCLICAL LETTER *AD DIEM* § 712

(6th ed. 1996).

621.J.NEUNER, S.J & J. DUPUIS, S.J., THE CHRISTIAN FAITH IN THE DOCTRINAL DOCUMENTS OF THE CATHOLIC CHURCH, THE SECOND VATICAL COUNCIL, DOGMATIC CONSTITUTION *LUMEN GENTIUM,* § 716a (6th ed. 1996).

622.CATECHISM OF THE CATHOLIC CHURCH, § 2679, 1994.

623.J.NEUNER, S.J & J. DUPUIS, S.J., THE CHRISTIAN FAITH IN THE DOCTRINAL DOCUMENTS OF THE CATHOLIC CHURCH, THE SECOND VATICAL COUNCIL, DOGMATIC CONSTITUTION *LUMEN GENTIUM,* § 718a (6th ed. 1996).

624.*Id.* at § 718b.

625.CATECHISM OF THE CATHOLIC CHURCH, § 2677, 1994.

626.J.NEUNER, S.J & J. DUPUIS, S.J., THE CHRISTIAN FAITH IN THE DOCTRINAL DOCUMENTS OF THE CATHOLIC CHURCH, THE SECOND VATICAL COUNCIL, DOGMATIC CONSTITUTION *LUMEN GENTIUM,* § 716a (6th ed. 1996).

627.J.NEUNER, S.J & J. DUPUIS, S.J., THE CHRISTIAN FAITH IN THE DOCTRINAL DOCUMENTS OF THE CATHOLIC CHURCH, § 713, PIUS XII, APOSTOLIC CONSTITUTION, *MUNIFICENTISSIMUS DEUS* (6th ed. 1996).

628. J.NEUNER, S.J & J. DUPUIS, S.J., THE CHRISTIAN FAITH IN THE DOCTRINAL DOCUMENTS OF THE CATHOLIC CHURCH, § 716a (6th ed. 1996).

629. Mary Co-redemptrix, Coredemptrix Mediatrix Advocate, A Response to 7 Common Objections, Imprimatur: Ernesto Cardinal Corripio Ahumada, Mexico City, May 1, 2001, Vox Populi Mariae Mediatrici, http://www.voxpopuli.org/response_to_7_common_objections_part1.php.

630. Mark Miravalle, Are You Afraid of Mary "Co-redemptrix"?, July 15, 2011, http://www.fifthmariandogma.com/articles/are-you-afraid-of-mary-co-redemptrix/.

631. THE PROTOCOLS OF THE LEARNED ELDERS OF ZION, Paragraph 3, Protocol 17, http://www.thewinds.org/library/protocols_of_zion.html (current as of September 9, 2001).

632. Clare Kolewski, Communist infiltration into the Catholic Church, June 21, 2009, http://www.examiner.com/article/communist-infiltration-into-the-catholic-church.

633. Clare Kolewski, Communist infiltration into the Catholic Church, June 21, 2009, http://www.examiner.com/article/communist-infiltration-into-the-catholic-church.

634. Mystery, Babylon the Great, Catholic or Jewish?, Part IV, http://watch.pair.com/mystery-babylon-4.html (last visited on October 13, 2012).

635.*McCalls Magazine*, January 1978.

636.DAVID O'BEALE, IN PURSUIT OF PURITY, p. 264 (1986). David W. Cloud, Way of Life Literature, Bible Baptist Church, 1701 Harns Rd., Oak Harbor, WA 98277; http://wayoflife.org/~dcloud/fbns/falwellandrome.htm.

637.*See generally,* ERROLL HULSE, BILLY GRAHAM - THE PASTOR'S DILEMMA (1966).

638.http://www.rapidnet.com/~jbeard/bdm/exposes/graham/general.htm (site active as of July 17, 2001).

639.*O Timothy*, Vol. 10, Issue 9, 1993, pp. 16-17.

640.Athol Bloomer, *The Eucharist and The Jewish Mystical Tradition • Part 3*, Association of Hebrew Catholics, *at* http://hebrewcatholic.org/HCLives/Bloomer-Athol/eucharistandjewi.html, (originally published in The Hebrew Catholic #80 (Spring/Summer 2004)).

641.Athol Bloomer, *The Eucharist and The Jewish Mystical Tradition • Part 1*, Association of Hebrew Catholics, *at* http://hebrewcatholic.org/PrayerandSpirituality/eucharistjewishm.html, (last visited on February 12, 2010) (originally published in The Hebrew Catholic #77, pp 15-18 (Summer-Fall 2002)).

642.Athol Bloomer, *The Eucharist and The Jewish Mystical Tradition • Part 1*, Association of Hebrew Catholics, *at* http://hebrewcatholic.org/PrayerandSpirituality/eucharistjewishm.html, (last visited on February 12,

2010) (originally published in The Hebrew Catholic #77, pp 15-18 (Summer-Fall 2002)).

643. Fortescue, A. (1910). Liturgy. In The Catholic Encyclopedia. New York: Robert Appleton Company. Retrieved February 19, 2010 from New Advent: http://www.newadvent.org/cathen/09306a.htm.

644. Joseph Cardinal Ratzinger, The Reservation of the Blessed Sacrament, Institute for Sacred Architecture, Volume 12, Fall/Winter 2006, *available at* http://www.sacredarchitecture.org/articles/reservation_of_the_blessed_sacrament/.

645. Joseph Cardinal Ratzinger, The Reservation of the Blessed Sacrament, Institute for Sacred Architecture, Volume 12, Fall/Winter 2006, *available at* http://www.sacredarchitecture.org/articles/reservation_of_the_blessed_sacrament/.

646. Michael Hoffman, *Judaism Discovered* (2008).

647. Yesod, Jewish Virtual Library, *at* http://www.jewishvirtuallibrary.org/jsource/Judaism/Yesod.html (last visited on March 2, 2010).

648. Alexander Hislop, *The Two Babylons*, at 164 (1959).

649. Ryan Erlenbush, What does IHS stand for? The meaning of the Holy Name of Jesus, January 3, 2012, http://newtheologicalmovement.blogspot.com/2012/01/what-does-ihs-stand-for-meaning-of-holy.html.

650.Maere, R. (1910). IHS. In The Catholic Encyclopedia. New York: Robert Appleton Company. Retrieved October 26, 2012 from New Advent: http://www.newadvent.org/cathen/07649a.htm. Ecclesiastical approbation. Nihil Obstat. June 1, 1910. Remy Lafort, S.T.D., Censor. Imprimatur. +John Cardinal Farley, Archbishop of New York.

651.Maere, R. (1910). IHS. In The Catholic Encyclopedia. New York: Robert Appleton Company. Retrieved October 26, 2012 from New Advent: http://www.newadvent.org/cathen/07649a.htm. Ecclesiastical approbation. Nihil Obstat. June 1, 1910. Remy Lafort, S.T.D., Censor. Imprimatur. +John Cardinal Farley, Archbishop of New York.

652.Maere, R. (1910). IHS. In The Catholic Encyclopedia. New York: Robert Appleton Company. Retrieved October 26, 2012 from New Advent: http://www.newadvent.org/cathen/07649a.htm. Ecclesiastical approbation. Nihil Obstat. June 1, 1910. Remy Lafort, S.T.D., Censor. Imprimatur. +John Cardinal Farley, Archbishop of New York.

653. Holweck, F. (1910). Holy Name of Jesus. In The Catholic Encyclopedia. New York: Robert Appleton Company. Retrieved October 26, 2012 from New Advent: http://www.newadvent.org/cathen/07421a.htm. Ecclesiastical approbation. Nihil Obstat. June 1, 1910. Remy Lafort, S.T.D., Censor. Imprimatur. +John Cardinal Farley, Archbishop of New York.

654.Maere, R. (1910). IHS. In The Catholic Encyclopedia. New York: Robert Appleton Company. Retrieved October 26, 2012 from New Advent: http://www.newadvent.org/cathen/07649a.htm. Ecclesiastical approbation. Nihil Obstat. June 1, 1910. Remy Lafort, S.T.D., Censor. Imprimatur. +John Cardinal Farley, Archbishop of New York.

655.Ryan Erlenbush, What does IHS stand for? The meaning of the Holy Name of Jesus, January 3, 2012, http://newtheologicalmovement.blogspot.com/2012/01/what-does-ihs-stand-for-meaning-of-holy.html.

656.Ron Byerly, IHS, http://www.eyeoftheneedle.net/Church%20Traditions/ihs.htm (last visited on October 26, 2012).

657.The New American, Dark Dealings in the Vatican?, at p. 24, March 3, 1997.

658.The New American, Dark Dealings in the Vatican?, at p. 24, March 3, 1997.

659.The New American, The Catholic Church in Crisis, p. 39, June 9, 1997.

660.*Id.*

661.Roman Catholic cardinal endorses Zionism, Washington Post, Mar. 31 2005, http://www.cardinalrating.com/cardinal_97_article_873.htm.

662.Shlomo Shamir, Catholic Church equates anti-Zionism with anti-Semitism, Haaretz, October 13, 2012, http://www.haaretz.com/news/catholic-church-equates-anti-zionism-with-anti-semitism-1.128020.

663.Shulamit Aloni: "It's a Trick We Always Use," http://wideeyecinema.com/?p=3804 (last visited on December 12, 2010).

664.Shlomo Shamir, Catholic Church equates anti-Zionism with anti-Semitism, Haaretz, October 13, 2012, http://www.haaretz.com/news/catholic-church-equates-anti-zionism-with-anti-semitism-1.128020.

665.Melinda Henneberger, *Vatican Says Jews' Wait for Messiah Is Validated by the Old Testament,* New York Times, January 18, 2002, http://www.hughhewitt.com/past_news_links_01.02/01.18.02.Vatican_Says_Wait_for_Messiah.html (Current as of February 10, 2002).

666.Michael Hoffman II, Secret Societies and Psychological Warfare, at p. 75 (2001).

667.Michael Hoffman II, Secret Societies and Psychological Warfare, at p. 75 (2001).

668.Ted Pike, ADL's Foxman: New Testament Is Anti-Semitic, February 15, 2006, http://truthtellers.org/alerts/ntantisemitic.html, quoting Abraham Foxman, Never Again? The Threat of the New Anti-Semitism, at 47-48.

669.*Israeli Youths Burn New Testaments*, USA Today, May 21, 2008, *at* http://www.usatoday.com/news/religion/2008-05-21-jewish-new-testament_N.htm.

670.*Israeli Youths Burn New Testaments*, USA Today, May 21, 2008, *at* http://www.usatoday.com/news/religion/2008-05-21-jewish-new-testament_N.htm.

671.Contemporary Global Anti-Semitism: A Report Provided to the United States Congress, Released by the Special Envoy to Monitor and Combat Anti-Semitism, Gregg J. Rickman, United States Department of State, March 13, 2008, http://www.state.gov/j/drl/rls/102406.htm.

672.Report on Global Anti-Semitism, U.S. Department of State, Released by the Bureau of Democracy, Human Rights, and Labor, January 5, 2005, http://www.state.gov/j/drl/rls/40258.htm.

673.Report on Global Anti-Semitism, U.S. Department of State, Released by the Bureau of Democracy, Human Rights, and Labor, January 5, 2005, http://www.state.gov/j/drl/rls/40258.htm.

674.Ted Pike, ADL's Foxman: New Testament Is Anti-Semitic, February 15, 2006, http://truthtellers.org/alerts/ntantisemitic.html, quoting Abraham Foxman, Never Again? The Threat of the New Anti-Semitism, at 47.

675.Ted Pike, ADL's Foxman: New Testament Is Anti-Semitic, February 15, 2006, http://truthtellers.org/alerts/ntantisemitic.html.

676.Ted Pike, ADL's Foxman: New Testament Is Anti-Semitic, February 15, 2006, http://truthtellers.org/alerts/ntantisemitic.html, quoting Abraham Foxman, Never Again? The Threat of the New Anti-Semitism, at 47-48.

677.CONG. REC. 12595-96 (1932) (speech of Rep. McFadden), *at* http://iresist.com/cbg/mcfadden_speech_1932.html (current as of September 30, 2001).

678.Protocols of the Learned Elders of Zion, Protocol 9, http://www.biblebelievers.org.au/przion3.htm#PROTOCOL%20No.%209 (Last visited on September 9, 2012).

679.Henry Makow, Illuminati: The Cult That Hijacked the World, at 146 (2011).

680.Henry Makow, Illuminati: The Cult That Hijacked the World, at 146 (2011).

681.Henry Makow, Illuminati: The Cult That Hijacked the World, at 146 (2011).

682.Christopher Jon Bjerknes, Adolf Eichmann Was a Crypto-Jewish Zionist Nazi, Jewish Racism, November 28, 2007, http://jewishracism.blogspot.com/2007/11/adolf-eichmann-was-crypto-jewish.html.

683.Christopher Jon Bjerknes, Adolf Eichmann Was a Crypto-Jewish Zionist Nazi, Jewish Racism, November 28, 2007, http://jewishracism.blogspot.com/2007/11/adolf-eichmann-was-crypto-jewish.html.

684.Christopher Jon Bjerknes, Adolf Eichmann Was a Crypto-Jewish Zionist Nazi, Jewish Racism, November 28, 2007, http://jewishracism.blogspot.com/2007/11/adolf-eichmann-was-crypto-jewish.html.

685. K. Polkehn, "The Secret Contacts: Zionism and Nazi Germany, 1933-1941", Journal of Palestine Studies, Volume 5, Number 3/4, (Spring-Summer, 1976), pp. 54-82, at 74; citing "RFSS film roll 411" (quoted by Christopher Jon Bjerknes, Adolf Eichmann Was a Crypto-Jewish Zionist Nazi, Jewish Racism, November 28, 2007, http://jewishracism.blogspot.com/2007/11/adolf-eichmann-was-crypto-jewish.html).

686. M. Steinglass, "Emil Ludwig before the Judge", American Jewish Times, (April, 1936), p. 35; as quoted in: L. Brenner, Zionism in the Age of the Dictators, Chapter 6, Croom Helm, London, L. Hill, Westport, Connecticut, (1983), p. 59 (quoted by Christopher Jon Bjerknes, Adolf Eichmann Was a Crypto-Jewish Zionist Nazi, Jewish Racism, November 28, 2007, http://jewishracism.blogspot.com/2007/11/adolf-eichmann-was-crypto-jewish.html).

687. DONN DE GRAND PRE, BARBARIANS INSIDE THE GATES, THE BLACK BOOK OF BOLSHEVISM, p. 149 (2000) (citing DIETRICH BRONDER, BEFORE HITLER CAME; HENNEKE KARDEL, ADOLPH HITLER, FOUNDER OF ISRAEL).

688. Bryan Mark Rigg, Hitler's Jewish Soldiers, (2004), University Press of Kansas, http://just-another-inside-job.blogspot.com/2007/04/150-000-jews-in-hitlers-army.html.

689. Bryan Mark Rigg, Hitler's Jewish Soldiers (2004), University Press of Kansas, http://www.kansaspress.ku.edu/righit.html.

690.Bryan Mark Rigg, Hitler's Jewish Soldiers (2004), University Press of Kansas, http://www.kansaspress.ku.edu/righit.html.

691.DONN DE GRAND PRE, BARBARIANS INSIDE THE GATES, THE BLACK BOOK OF BOLSHEVISM, p. 149 (2000) (quoting HENNEKE KARDEL, ADOLPH HITLER: FOUNDER OF ISRAEL (1997)).

692.Edwin Black, The Transfer Agreement (2001).

693.Edwin Black, The Transfer Agreement, at 380-81 (2001).

694.Henry Makow, Illuminati: The Cult That Hijacked the World, at 155 (2011).

695.Henry Makow, Illuminati: The Cult That Hijacked the World, at 155 (2011).

696.Henry Makow, Illuminati: The Cult That Hijacked the World, at 162 (2011).

697.Henry Makow, Illuminati: The Cult That Hijacked the World, at 154 (2011).

698.Henry Makow, Illuminati: The Cult That Hijacked the World, at 154 (2011).

699.DONN DE GRAND PRE, BARBARIANS INSIDE THE GATES, THE BLACK BOOK OF BOLSHEVISM, p. 154 (2000) (quoting ISRAEL SHAHAK AND NORTON MEZVINSKY, JEWISH FUNDAMENTALISM IN ISRAEL, p. 125 (1999)).

700. ERIC JON PHELPS, VATICAN ASSASSINS: "WOUNDED IN THE HOUSE OF MY FRIENDS," p. 535-36 (2001).

701. Benjamin Freedman, A Jewish Defector Warns America: Benjamin Freedman Speaks on Zionism, http://www.sweetliberty.org/issues/israel/freedman.htm (last visited on September 7, 2012), audio at Benjamin H. Freedman Warns America, http://www.youtube.com/watch?v=puECgVo-GqE&feature=related (last visited on September 7, 2012).

702. Benjamin Freedman, A Jewish Defector Warns America: Benjamin Freedman Speaks on Zionism, http://www.sweetliberty.org/issues/israel/freedman.htm (last visited on September 7, 2012), audio at Benjamin H. Freedman Warns America, http://www.youtube.com/watch?v=puECgVo-GqE&feature=related (last visited on September 7, 2012).

703. Carroll Quigley, Tragedy and Hope: A History of the World in Our Time (1966), http://www.carrollquigley.net/pdf/Tragedy_and_Hope.pdf.

704. 1974 Interview with Rudy Maxa of the Washington Post, Interview Transcript - Part 3, http://www.carrollquigley.net/Interviews/Carroll_Quigley_1974_Interview_Transcript_Part3.htm (last visited on May 11, 2022).

705. Fritz Springmeier, Bloodlines of the Illuminati (1995), https://docs.google.com/viewer?a=v&pid=sites&srcid=ZGVmYXVsdGRvbWFpbnx0ZXNsYXNlY3Jld

HMyfGd4OjNiMDZhMWZiMzdhNTFiNGQ (last visited on May 11, 2022).

706. Stephen S. Wise (1874–1949), United States Holocaust Memorial Museum, https://encyclopedia.ushmm.org/content/en/article/stephen-s-wise-18741949 (last visited on May 11, 2022).

707. Id.

708. Douglas Reed, The Controversy of Zion, at 166-67 (1956), https://modernhistoryproject.org/mhp?Article=ContRoZion&C=29.0#America.

709. Id.

710. Id.

711. 1974 Interview with Rudy Maxa of the Washington Post, Interview Transcript - Part 1, http://www.carrollquigley.net/Interviews/Carroll_Quigley_1974_Interview_Transcript_Part1.htm (last visited on May 11, 2022).

712. 1974 Interview with Rudy Maxa of the Washington Post Interview Transcript - Part 5, http://www.carrollquigley.net/Interviews/Carroll_Quigley_1974_Interview_Transcript_Part5.htm (last visited on May 11, 2022).

713. Rare interview with Professor Carroll Quigley (1974), https://www.youtube.com/watch?v=pKClR0qCv4I (last visited on May 11, 2022).

714. A Jewish Defector Warns America:Benjamin Freedman Speaks on Zionism, http://www.sweetliberty.org/issues/israel/freedman.htm (last visited on May 11, 2022).

715. Tragedy and Hope, at 255.

716. Walter Rothschild and the Balfour Declaration, https://www.rothschildarchive.org/collections/rothschild_faqs/walter_rothschild_and_the_balfour_declaration (last visited on May 11, 2022).

717. Balfour Declaration: Text of the Declaration, (November 2, 1917), https://www.jewishvirtuallibrary.org/text-of-the-balfour-declaration.

718. Carroll Quigley, Tragedy and Hope: A History of the World in Our Time (1966), http://www.carrollquigley.net/pdf/Tragedy_and_Hope.pdf.

719. Tragedy and Hope, at 950.

720. Tragedy and Hope, at 324.

721. Rare interview with Professor Carroll Quigley (1974), https://www.youtube.com/watch?v=pKClR0qCv4I (last visited on May 11, 2022).

722. 1974 Interview with Rudy Maxa of the Washington Post Interview Transcript - Part 4, http://www.carrollquigley.net/Interviews/Carroll_Quigley_1974_Interview_Transcript_Part4.htm (last visited on May 11, 2022).

723. 1974 Interview with Rudy Maxa of the Washington Post Interview Transcript - Part 5, http://www.carrollquigley.net/Interviews/Carroll_Quigley_1974_Interview_Transcript_Part5.htm (last visited on May 11, 2022).

724. Id.

725. Id.

726. A Jewish Defector Warns America:Benjamin Freedman Speaks on Zionism, http://www.sweetliberty.org/issues/israel/freedman.htm (last visited on May 11, 2022).

727. Protocols of the Learned Elders of Zion, Protocol 1, http://www.biblebelievers.org.au/przion2.htm#PROTOCOL%20No.%201 (last visited on August 22, 2012).

728. Protocols of the Learned Elders of Zion, Protocol 1, http://www.biblebelievers.org.au/przion2.htm#PROTOCOL%20No.%201 (last visited on August 22, 2012).

729. Protocols of the Learned Elders of Zion, Protocol 1, http://www.biblebelievers.org.au/przion2.htm#PROTOCOL%20No.%201 (last visited on August 22, 2012).

730. Michael Hoffman, *Judaism Revealed*, at 775 (2008) (quoting Yesaiah Tishbi, *Torat ha-Rave-Kelippah b-Kabbalat ha-Ari* ("The Theory of Evil and the Satanic Sphere in Kabbalah"), pp. 139-142 [1942; reprinted 1982]).

731. Michael Hoffman, *Judaism Revealed*, at 775 (2008) (quoting Yesaiah Tishbi, *Torat ha-Rave-Kelippah b-Kabbalat ha-Ari* ("The Theory of Evil and the Satanic Sphere in Kabbalah"), [1942; reprinted 1982]).

732. Jonathan Cook, *Why There Are No 'Israelis' in the Jewish State - Citizens Classed as Jewish or Arab Nationals*, Media Monitors, April 6, 2010, *at* http://usa.mediamonitors.net/content/view/full/73038.

733. Jonathan Cook, *Why There Are No 'Israelis' in the Jewish State - Citizens Classed as Jewish or Arab Nationals*, Media Monitors, April 6, 2010, *at* http://usa.mediamonitors.net/content/view/full/73038.

734. Jonathan Cook, *Why There Are No 'Israelis' in the Jewish State - Citizens Classed as Jewish or Arab Nationals*, Media Monitors, April 6, 2010, *at* http://usa.mediamonitors.net/content/view/full/73038.

735. Jonathan Cook, *Why There Are No 'Israelis' in the Jewish State - Citizens Classed as Jewish or Arab Nationals*, Media Monitors, April 6, 2010, *at* http://usa.mediamonitors.net/content/view/full/73038.

736. Jonathan Cook, *Why There Are No 'Israelis' in the Jewish State - Citizens Classed as Jewish or Arab Nationals*, Media Monitors, April 6, 2010, *at* http://usa.mediamonitors.net/content/view/full/73038.

737.Israel Shahak, Jewish History, Jewish Religion: The Weight of Three Thousand Years (1997), *available at* http://www.biblebelievers.org.au/jewhis1.htm.

738.Israel Shahak, Jewish History, Jewish Religion: The Weight of Three Thousand Years (1997), *available at* http://www.biblebelievers.org.au/jewhis1.htm.

739.Israel Shahak, Jewish History, Jewish Religion: The Weight of Three Thousand Years (1997), *available at* http://www.biblebelievers.org.au/jewhis1.htm.

740.Israel Shahak, Jewish History, Jewish Religion: The Weight of Three Thousand Years (1997), *available at* http://www.biblebelievers.org.au/jewhis1.htm.

741.Israel Shahak, Jewish History, Jewish Religion: The Weight of Three Thousand Years (1997), *available at* http://www.biblebelievers.org.au/jewhis1.htm.

742.Protocols of the Learned Elders of Zion, Protocol 9, http://www.biblebelievers.org.au/przion3.htm#PROTOCOL%20No.%209 (Last visited on September 9, 2012).

743.Henry Makow, Illuminati: The Cult That Hijacked the World, at 152 (2011).

744.*Zionism Promotes Anti-Semitism*, Jews Against Zionism, *at* http://www.jewsagainstzionism.com/antisemitism/zionismpromotes.cfm (last visited on March 26,

2010).

745. *Zionism and Anti-Semitism*, Jews Against Anti-Semitism, *at* http://www.jewsagainstzionism.com/zionism/zanda.cfm (last visited on March 26, 2010).

746. Shulamit Aloni: "It's a Trick We Always Use," http://wideeyecinema.com/?p=3804 (last visited on December 12, 2010).

747. Shulamit Aloni, Jewish Virtual Library, http://www.jewishvirtuallibrary.org/jsource/biography/aloni.html (last visited on December 12, 2010).

748. Leader of Nazis Has Jewish Father, Lakeland Ledger, AP, July 24, 1977, *available at* http://news.google.com/newspapers?nid=1346&dat=19770724&id=KXosAAAAIBAJ&sjid=vPoDAAAAIBAJ&pg=4602,6288087. See also R. D. Flavin, *Frank Collin: From neo-Nazi to Hyper-Diffusionist and Witch* (previously published in The Greenwich Village Gazette, Feb. 21, 1997, as "The Many Faces of Frank Collin").

749. Homo-Facism After Hitler, The Pink Swastika, at 278, *at* http://www.defendthefamily.com/pfrc/books/pinkswastika/html/Chapter8.htm (last visited on March 26, 2010).

750. Hassane Zerouky, Hamas is a Creation of Mossad (23 March 2004) (the article originally appeared in French in L'Humanité), *available at* http://www.globalresearch.ca/articles/ZER403A.html.

751. Henry Makow, Illuminati: The Cult That Hijacked the World, at 151 (2011).

752. Henry Makow, Illuminati: The Cult That Hijacked the World, at 151 (2011).

753. Confessions of an Ex-Mossad Agent, Excerpt from Victor Ostrovsky's, "By way of deception", What Really Happened, http://whatreallyhappened.com/WRHARTICLES/deception.html (last visited on September 29, 2012).

754. Michael Hoffman, *Judaism Discovered* (2008) at 907.

755. Charles E. Carlson, Judeo-Christians and Messianic Churches Speak a New Language, Apr 26, 2012, http://mysteryworshipers.wordpress.com/2012/04/27/judeo-christians-and-messianic-churches-speak-a-new-language/.

756. Charles E. Carlson, Judeo-Christians and Messianic Churches Speak a New Language, Apr 26, 2012, http://mysteryworshipers.wordpress.com/2012/04/27/judeo-christians-and-messianic-churches-speak-a-new-language/.

757. Chris McGreal, Rachel Corrie Verdict Exposes Israeli Military Mindset, *The Guardian*, 28 August 2012, http://www.guardian.co.uk/commentisfree/2012/aug/28/rachel-corrie-verdict-exposes-israeli-military-mindset.

758. Chris McGreal, Rachel Corrie Verdict Exposes Israeli Military Mindset, *The Guardian*, 28 August

2012, http://www.guardian.co.uk/commentisfree/2012/aug/28/rachel-corrie-verdict-exposes-israeli-military-mindset.

759.Chris McGreal, Rachel Corrie Verdict Exposes Israeli Military Mindset, *The Guardian*, 28 August 2012, http://www.guardian.co.uk/commentisfree/2012/aug/28/rachel-corrie-verdict-exposes-israeli-military-mindset.

760.Chris McGreal, Rachel Corrie Verdict Exposes Israeli Military Mindset, *The Guardian*, 28 August 2012, http://www.guardian.co.uk/commentisfree/2012/aug/28/rachel-corrie-verdict-exposes-israeli-military-mindset.

761.Chris McGreal, Rachel Corrie Verdict Exposes Israeli Military Mindset, *The Guardian*, 28 August 2012, http://www.guardian.co.uk/commentisfree/2012/aug/28/rachel-corrie-verdict-exposes-israeli-military-mindset.

762.Chris McGreal, Rachel Corrie Verdict Exposes Israeli Military Mindset, *The Guardian*, 28 August 2012, http://www.guardian.co.uk/commentisfree/2012/aug/28/rachel-corrie-verdict-exposes-israeli-military-mindset.

763.Chris McGreal, Rachel Corrie Verdict Exposes Israeli Military Mindset, *The Guardian*, 28 August 2012, http://www.guardian.co.uk/commentisfree/2012/au

g/28/rachel-corrie-verdict-exposes-israeli-military-mindset.

764.Harriet Sherwood, Rachel Corrie Ruling 'Deeply Troubling', Says Her Family, *The Guardian*, 28 August 2012, http://www.guardian.co.uk/world/2012/aug/28/rachel-corrie-ruling-deeply-troubling?intcmp=239.

765.Chris McGreal, Rachel Corrie Verdict Exposes Israeli Military Mindset, *The Guardian*, 28 August 2012, http://www.guardian.co.uk/commentisfree/2012/aug/28/rachel-corrie-verdict-exposes-israeli-military-mindset.

766.Protocols of the Learned Elders of Zion, Protocol 16, http://www.biblebelievers.org.au/przion5.htm#protocol%20No.%2016 (last visited on October 9, 2012).

767.Protocols of the Learned Elders of Zion, Protocol 4, http://www.biblebelievers.org.au/przion3.htm#PROTOCOL%20No.%204 (Last visited on August 23, 2012).

768.MARSHAL HALL, THE EARTH IS NOT MOVING, p. 97 (1991)

769.GERARDUS BOUW, GEOCENTRICITY, p. 254-56 (1992).

770.Dr. Neville Thomas Jones, Ph.D., Airy's Experiment, http://www.geocentricuniverse.com/Airy.htm (last visited on August 24, 2012).

771.GERARDUS BOUW, GEOCENTRICITY, p. 303 (1992).

772.Protocols of the Learned Elders of Zion, Protocol 2, http://www.biblebelievers.org.au/przion2.htm#PROTOCOL%20No.%202 (Last visited on August 22, 2012).

773.*See* Noah Webster, THE AMERICAN DICTIONARY OF THE ENGLISH LANGUAGE (1828); THE COMPACT EDITION OF THE OXFORD ENGLISH DICTIONARY, Oxford University Press, at 2400 (1979). *See also,* THE AMERICAN HERITAGE ILLUSTRATED ENCYCLOPEDIC DICTIONARY (1987).

774.CREATION, June-Aug. 1999, Vol. 21, No. 3, at 22.

775.Bobby O'Connor, *The Racism of Evolution Theory,* CHARLESTON GAZETTE, June 25, 1998 at P18. (Quoting CHARLES DARWIN, THE DESCENT OF MAN (1874)). *See also* Benno C. Schmidt, *Principle and Prejudice: The Supreme Court and Race in the Progressive Era. Part 1: The Heyday of Jim Crow,* 82 COLUM. L. REV. 444, 453 (1982).

776.Israel Shahak, Jewish History, Jewish Religion: The Weight of Two Thousand Years (1994), *available at* http://www.biblebelievers.org.au/jewhis2.htm#Prejudice%20and%20Prevarication.

777.Moses Maiminodes, The Guide of the Perplexed [*Moreh Nevuk'him*], translated by

Schlomo Pines [Chicago: University of Chicago Press, 1963], vol. 2, pp 618-19 (quoted by Michael Hoffman in Judaism's Strange Gods, at 65 (2002).

778.*Id.*

779.Raj Bhopal, *Is Research Into Ethnicity and Health Racist, Unsound, or Important to Science?*, BRITISH MEDICAL JOURNAL, June 14, 1997.

780.Jim Dawson, *'Race' is Social Notion With No Base in Biology, Genetics, Scientists Say*, STAR TRIBUNE (Minneapolis, MN), February 20, 1995, at 6A.

781.Steve Van Nattan, Answer to your question: "What do you believe?", Blessed Quietness Journal, http://www.blessedquietness.com/journal/believe.htm (web address current as of October 21, 2012).

782.http://www.blessedquietness.com/journal/resume.htm (web page current as of September 30, 2003). Steve Van Nattan's resume web page has been deleted by Van Nattan. However, it downloaded before it was deleted and saved by this author at: http://www.antichristconspiracy.com/HTML%20Pages/Resume%20of%20Steve%20Van%20Nattan.htm.

783.http://www.blessedquietness.com/journal/prophecy/hendrie.htm (web address current as of October 28, 2003).

784.Protocols of the Learned Elders of Zion, Protocol 9, http://www.biblebelievers.org.au/przion3.htm#PROTOCOL%20No.%209 (Last visited on August 23,

548

2012).

785. Nathan Abrams, *Triple Ethics, Jews in the American Porn Industry*, Jewish Quarterly (Winter 2004), *available at* http://www.fpp.co.uk/BoD/origins/porn_industry.html.

786. Ted Pike, Jews Behind *'The Ten'*, August 8, 2007, at http://www.truthtellers.org/alerts/jewsbehindtheten.htm.

787. Henry Makow, Illuminati 2, Deceit and Seduction, at 20 (2010).

788. Henry Makow, Illuminati 2, Deceit and Seduction, at 20 (2010).

789. Henry Makow, Illuminati 2, Deceit and Seduction, at 10 (2010).

790. Protocols of the Learned Elders of Zion, Protocol 2, http://www.biblebelievers.org.au/przion2.htm#PROTOCOL%20No.%202 (Last visited on August 22, 2012).

791. Protocols of the Learned Elders of Zion, Protocol 7, http://www.biblebelievers.org.au/przion3.htm#PROTOCOL%20No.%207 (Last visited on August 23, 2012).

792. John Whitley, *Seven Jewish American Control Most US Media*, Real News 24/7 (November 21, 2003), *available at* http://www.realnews247.com/seven_jewish_americ

ans_control_media_rense.htm.

793.Id.

794.Id.

795.Id.

796.Texe Marrs, Conspiracy of the Six Pointed Star, at 108 (2011), quoting Newsweek, Vol. 87, 1976).

797.CONG. REC. 2947-2948 (February 9, 1917) (speech of Rep. Callaway), http://www.iahf.com/media.html (current as of October 3, 2001).

798.ERIC JON PHELPS, VATICAN ASSASSINS: "WOUNDED IN THE HOUSE OF MY FRIENDS," p. 465 (2001) (quoting A U.S. Police Action: Operation Vampire Killer, pp. 18-19 (1992)).

799.Protocols of the Learned Elders of Zion, Protocol 12, http://www.biblebelievers.org.au/przion4.htm#protocol%20No.%2012 (last visited on August 25, 2012).

800.Warren P. Strobel and John Walcott, Bush Made Intel Fit Iraq Policy, *Kansas City Star*, May 6, 2005, http://www.kansascity.com/mld/kansascity/news/politics/11574258.htm (web address current as of May 7, 2005).

801.The Secret Downing Street Memo, http://www.timesonline.co.uk/article/0,,2087-15936

07,00.html (web address current as of May 9, 2005).

802.Michael Smith, Blair Planned Iraq War From Start, *Times Online*, May 1, 2005, http://www.timesonline.co.uk/article/0,,2087-1592724,00.html (web address current as of May 9, 2005).

803.Michael Smith, Blair Planned Iraq War From Start, *Times Online*, May 1, 2005, http://www.timesonline.co.uk/article/0,,2087-1592724,00.html (web address current as of May 9, 2005).

804.Editor and Publisher, Survey Finds Editorial Treatment of 'Downing Street Memo' Mixed, June 15, 2005, http://www.editorandpublisher.com/eandp/news/article_display.jsp?vnu_content_id=1000962804 (web address current as of June 18, 2005).

805.Editor and Publisher, Survey Finds Editorial Treatment of 'Downing Street Memo' Mixed, June 15, 2005, http://www.editorandpublisher.com/eandp/news/article_display.jsp?vnu_content_id=1000962804 (web address current as of June 18, 2005).

806.Associated Press, http://www.ap.org/pages/about/faq.html#2, (web address current as of June 18, 2005).

807.Kourosh Ziabari, Criticize Israel and lose your career, Opinion Maker, July 7, 2011, http://www.opinion-maker.org/2011/07/criticize-israel-and-lose-your-career/.

808. Editor and Publisher, Survey Finds Editorial Treatment of 'Downing Street Memo' Mixed, June 15, 2005, http://www.editorandpublisher.com/eandp/news/article_display.jsp?vnu_content_id=1000962804 (web address current as of June 18, 2005).

809. Jan Herman, The Domesticated Press, http://blogcritics.org/straightup/2005/06/15/113743.php, (web address current as of June 18, 2005).

810. Protocols of the Learned Elders of Zion, Protocol 13, http://www.biblebelievers.org.au/przion5.htm#protocol%20No.%2013 (last visited on August 25, 2012).

811. Cyrus Schofield, Who Was He?, Excerpted from the Unified Conspiracy Theory, http://www.sweetliberty.org/issues/hoax/scofield.htm (last visited on August 23, 2012).

812. Protocols of the Learned Elders of Zion, Protocol 2, http://www.biblebelievers.org.au/przion2.htm#PROTOCOL%20No.%202 (Last visited on August 22, 2012).

813. Texe Marrs, President Harry S. Truman and the Jews, http://www.texemarrs.com/092011/truman_and_the_jews_article.htm (last visited on September 8, 2012).

814. Protocols of the Learned Elders of Zion, Protocol 2,

http://www.biblebelievers.org.au/przion2.htm#PROTOCOL%20No.%202 (Last visited on August 22, 2012).

815. Victor Thorn, *RAHM EMANUEL: Ardent Zionist called Obama's 'Svengali'*, American Free Press, http://www.americanfreepress.net/html/rahm_emanuel_157.html (last visited on November 13, 2010).

816. Rahm Emanuel, Obama's Pick for Chief of Staff, Is Tough, Direct and Wedded to His Jewish Roots, Jewish Journal, November 6, 2008, http://www.jewishjournal.com/nation/article/rahm_emanuel_obamas_pick_for_chief_of_staff_is_tough_direct_and_wedded_to_h/.

817. Victor Thorn, American Free Press, http://www.americanfreepress.net/html/obama_jewish_195.html (last visited on September 26, 2012).

818. John Heilemann, The Tsuris, September 18, 2011, http://nymag.com/news/politics/israel-2011-9/.

819. Victor Thorn, American Free Press, http://www.americanfreepress.net/html/obama_jewish_195.html (last visited on September 26, 2012).

820. Victor Thorn, American Free Press, http://www.americanfreepress.net/html/obama_jewish_195.html (last visited on September 26, 2012).

821. Victor Thorn, American Free Press, http://www.americanfreepress.net/html/obama_jewish_195.html (last visited on September 26, 2012).

822. Texe Marrs, Rothschild's Choice, Power of Prophecy, http://www.texemarrs.com/rothschilds_choice_article.htm (last visited on September 26, 2012).

823. 9/11: Core of Corruption - In the Shadows FULL HD, http://www.youtube.com/watch?v=ANMKiUwcEWo (last visited on April 26, 2011).

824. Christopher Bollyn, *Michael Chertoff's Childhood in Israel*, October 26, 2007, http://www.bollyn.com/michael-chertoffs-childhood-in-israel.

825. Christopher Bollyn, *Michael Chertoff's Childhood in Israel*, October 26, 2007, http://www.bollyn.com/michael-chertoffs-childhood-in-israel.

826. Christopher Bollyn, *Michael Chertoff's Childhood in Israel*, October 26, 2007, http://www.bollyn.com/michael-chertoffs-childhood-in-israel.

827. Christopher Bollyn, Mitt Romney An Agent of the State of Israel, June 13, 2012, http://rense.com/general95/mittagnt.html.

828. Christopher Bollyn, Mitt Romney An Agent of the State of Israel, June 13, 2012, http://rense.com/general95/mittagnt.html.

829. Christopher Bollyn, Mitt Romney An Agent of the State of Israel, June 13, 2012, http://rense.com/general95/mittagnt.html.

830.Christopher Bollyn, Mitt Romney An Agent of the State of Israel, June 13, 2012, http://rense.com/general95/mittagnt.html.

831.Christopher Bollyn, Mitt Romney An Agent of the State of Israel, June 13, 2012, http://rense.com/general95/mittagnt.html.

832.Christopher Bollyn, Mitt Romney An Agent of the State of Israel, June 13, 2012, http://rense.com/general95/mittagnt.html.

833.Christopher Bollyn, Mitt Romney An Agent of the State of Israel, June 13, 2012, http://rense.com/general95/mittagnt.html.

834.Christopher Bollyn, Mitt Romney An Agent of the State of Israel, June 13, 2012, http://rense.com/general95/mittagnt.html.

835.Christopher Bollyn, Mitt Romney An Agent of the State of Israel, June 13, 2012, http://rense.com/general95/mittagnt.html.

836.The Harold Wallace Rosenthal Interview 1976, The Hidden Tyranny, http://www.macquirelatory.com/Wallace%20Interview%201967.htm (last visited on September 10, 2012).

837.Protocols of the Learned Elders of Zion, Protocol 8, http://www.biblebelievers.org.au/przion3.htm#PROTOCOL%20No.%208 (Last visited on August 22, 2012).

838.Protocols of the Learned Elders of Zion, Protocol 10,

http://www.biblebelievers.org.au/przion4.htm#protocol%20No.%2010 (last visited on August 25, 2012).

839.Jerome R. Corsi, Trinity Church Members Reveal Obama Shocker!, WorldNet Daily, http://www.wnd.com/2012/10/trinity-church-members-reveal-obama-shocker/ (last visited on October 4, 2012).

840.Jerome R. Corsi, Trinity Church Members Reveal Obama Shocker!, WorldNet Daily, http://www.wnd.com/2012/10/trinity-church-members-reveal-obama-shocker/ (last visited on October 4, 2012).

841.Jerome R. Corsi, Claim: Obama Hid 'Gay Life' to Become President, WorldNet Daily, http://www.wnd.com/2012/09/claim-obama-hid-gay-life-to-become-president/ (last visited on October 4, 2012).

842.Jerome R. Corsi, Trinity Church Members Reveal Obama Shocker!, WorldNet Daily, http://www.wnd.com/2012/10/trinity-church-members-reveal-obama-shocker/ (last visited on October 4, 2012).

843.Jerome R. Corsi, Trinity Church Members Reveal Obama Shocker!, WorldNet Daily, http://www.wnd.com/2012/10/trinity-church-members-reveal-obama-shocker/ (last visited on October 4, 2012).

844.Jerome R. Corsi, Trinity Church Members Reveal Obama Shocker!, WorldNet Daily, supra.

845. Eric Randall, Barack Obama: Our First Gay-Female-Hispanic-Asian-Jewish President, The Atlantac, May 14, 2012, http://www.theatlanticwire.com/politics/2012/05/obama-our-first-gay-female-black-hispanic-asian-jewish-president/52299/.

846. Benjamin H. Freedman, The Hidden Tyranny (excerpt), http://www.sweetliberty.org/issues/hoax/unt.htm (last visited on August 23, 2012).

847. Protocols of the Learned Elders of Zion, Protocol 9, http://www.biblebelievers.org.au/przion3.htm#PROTOCOL%20No.%209 (Last visited on August 23, 2012).

848. Protocols of the Learned Elders of Zion, Protocol 10, http://www.biblebelievers.org.au/przion4.htm#protocol%20No.%2010 (last visited on August 25, 2012).

849. PUBLIC LAW 107–40—SEPT. 18, 2001, 115 STAT. 224, http://www.gpo.gov/fdsys/pkg/PLAW-107publ40/pdf/PLAW-107publ40.pdf (passed by Congress on September 14, 2001, published on September 18, 2001) (last visited on August 25, 2012).

850. Protocols of the Learned Elders of Zion, Protocol 10.

851. Steven Paas, Christian Zionism Examined, A Review of Ideas on Israel, the Church, and the Kingdom, at 115 (2012).

852.Max Blumenthal, Hagee: Pro-Israel, Anti-Semitic?, May 28, 2008, http://www.cbsnews.com/2100-215_162-4122421.html.

853.Max Blumenthal, Hagee: Pro-Israel, supra.

Other books available from Great Mountain Publishing®

The Damnable Heresy of Salvation by Dead Faith (Expanded Edition)
Edward Hendrie
ISBN: 978-1-943056-11-8

Good works follow salvation; they do not earn salvation. Good works do not save us. The works of faith are those works ordained and performed by God through the believer. They are the result of faith. It is that perfect faith that justifies the believer."For by grace are ye saved through faith; and that not of yourselves: it is the gift of God: Not of works, lest any man should boast. For we are his workmanship, created in Christ Jesus unto good works, which God hath before ordained that we should walk in them. For we are his workmanship, created in Christ Jesus unto good works, which God hath before ordained that we should walk in them." Ephesians 2:8-10.In Romans, chapters 6 and 8, Paul explains faith without good works cannot save. Paul says that God's elect "walk not after the flesh, but after the Spirit." Romans 8:1. He states that those who do not walk in the Spirit but instead walk in the flesh "shall not inherit the kingdom of God." Galatians 5:15-25.John explains: "If we say that we have fellowship with him, and walk in darkness, we lie, and do not the truth: But if we walk in the light, as he is in the light, we have fellowship one with another, and the blood of Jesus Christ his Son cleanseth us from all sin." 1 John 1:6-7.James asks a rhetorical question: "What doth it profit, my brethren, though a man say he hath faith, and have not works? can faith save him?" James 2:14. James succinctly explains that "faith without works is dead." James 2:20. The pronouncement in James that true faith bears the fruit of good works is a theme found in the gospel. But some perniciously preach that God saves a person by faith that has no good works. That is one of the "damnable heresies" about which Peter warned. See 2 Peter 2:1-22.

The Sphere of Influence: The Heliocentric Perversion of the Gospel
Edward Hendrie
ISBN: 978-1-943056-06-4

This book is a sequel to *The Greatest Lie on Earth (Expanded Edition): Proof That Our World Is Not a Moving Globe.* It will primarily focus on the infiltration into the church of the superstitious myth of heliocentrism and how that infiltration has served to undermine the gospel. The gospel is the entire Holy Bible, not just some of it. Matthew 4:4. Christian belief is an all or nothing proposition. "All scripture is given by inspiration of God, and is profitable for doctrine, for reproof, for correction, for instruction in righteousness." 2 Timothy

3:16. God's account of his creation is part and parcel of the gospel. A person with genuine faith believes what Jesus said about both heavenly and earthly things. "If I have told you earthly things, and ye believe not, how shall ye believe, if I tell you of heavenly things?" John 3:12. Jesus is God. Jesus created all things in heaven and on earth. See Colossians 1:16-18. God has revealed himself through his creation. "[T]hat which may be known of God is manifest in them; for God hath shewed it unto them. For the invisible things of him from the creation of the world are clearly seen, being understood by the things that are made, even his eternal power and Godhead; so that they are without excuse." Romans 1:19-20. If men have a misunderstanding of God's creation, they will also have a misunderstanding of who God is. If people believe in a creation that does not exist, they consequently also believe in a creator that does not exist. It is essential, therefore, to have an accurate understanding of God's creation. God did not make a movable, spherical earth. If men believe in a heliocentric creation, they will necessarily believe in a heliocentric creator. A heliocentric creation does not exist. So also, a heliocentric creator does not exist. A heliocentric creator is a false god. We have been warned to avoid the preaching of a false gospel, which presents a false Jesus. "For if he that cometh preacheth another Jesus, whom we have not preached, or if ye receive another spirit, which ye have not received, or another gospel, which ye have not accepted, ye might well bear with him." 2 Corinthians 11:4.

The Greatest Lie on Earth
Proof That Our World Is Not a Moving Globe
Edward Hendrie
ISBN-13: 978-1-943056-01-9

This book reveals the mother of all conspiracies. It sets forth biblical proof and irrefutable evidence that will cause the scales to fall from your eyes and reveal that the world you thought existed is a myth. The most universally accepted scientific belief today is that the earth is a globe, spinning on its axis at a speed of approximately 1,000 miles per hour at the equator, while at the same time it is orbiting the sun at approximately 66,600 miles per hour. All of this is happening as the sun, in turn, is supposed to be hurtling through the Milky Way galaxy at approximately 500,000 miles per hour. The Milky Way galaxy, itself, is alleged to be racing through space at a speed ranging from 300,000 to 1,340,000 miles per hour. What most people are not told is that the purported spinning, orbiting, and speeding through space has never been proven. In fact, every scientific experiment that has ever been performed to determine the motion of the earth has proven that the earth is stationary. Yet, textbooks ignore the scientific proof that contradicts the myth of a spinning and orbiting globe. Christian schools have been hoodwinked into teaching heliocentrism, despite the clear teaching in the Bible that the earth is not a sphere and does not move. This book reveals the evil forces behind the heliocentric deception, and why scientists and the Christian churches have gone along with it.

**The Greatest Lie on Earth (Expanded Edition)
Proof That Our World Is Not a Moving Globe**
Edward Hendrie
ISBN-13: 978-1943056-03-3

This book is an expanded edition of *The Greatest Lie on Earth*. It contains more than 1,000 pages of authoritative evidence with more than 1,300 endnotes that document proof beyond any doubt that the earth is flat and stationary. The book reveals the mother of all conspiracies. It sets forth biblical proof and irrefutable evidence that will cause the scales to fall from your eyes and reveal that the world you thought existed is a myth. The most universally accepted scientific belief today is that the earth is a globe, spinning on its axis at a speed of approximately 1,000 miles per hour at the equator, while at the same time it is orbiting the sun at approximately 66,600 miles per hour. All of this is happening as the sun, in turn, is supposed to be hurtling through the Milky Way galaxy at approximately 500,000 miles per hour. The Milky Way galaxy, itself, is alleged to be racing through space at a speed ranging from 300,000 to 1,340,000 miles per hour. What most people are not told is that the purported spinning, orbiting, and speeding through space has never been proven. In fact, every scientific experiment that has ever been performed to determine the motion of the earth has proven that the earth is stationary. Yet, textbooks ignore the scientific proof that contradicts the myth of a spinning and orbiting globe. Christian schools have been hoodwinked into teaching heliocentrism, despite the clear teaching in the Bible that the earth is not a sphere and does not move. This book reveals the evil forces behind the heliocentric deception, and why scientists and the Christian churches have gone along with it.

Antichrist: The Beast Revealed
Edward Hendrie
ISBN-13: 978-0-9832627-8-7

The antichrist is among us, here and now. This book proves it by comparing the biblical prophecies about the antichrist with the evidence that those prophecies have been fulfilled. This book documents the man of sin's esoteric confession that he is the antichrist. You will learn how the antichrist has changed times and laws as prophesied by Daniel, and how he is today sitting in the temple of God, "shewing himself that he is God," in fulfillment of Paul's prophecy in 2 Thessalonians 2:4. The beast of Revelation has come into the world, "after the working of Satan with all power and signs and lying wonders, and with all deceivableness of unrighteousness," as prophesied in 2 Thessalonians 2:10. The antichrist's adeptness as a hypocrite is the reason for his evil success. Indeed, to be the antichrist, his evil character must be concealed beneath a facade of piety. "And no marvel; for Satan himself is transformed into an angel of light. Therefore it is no great thing if his ministers also be transformed as the ministers of righteousness; whose end shall be according to their works." 2 Corinthians 11:14-15. The key to revealing the identity of the antichrist is to uncover his hypocrisy. Because the hypocrisy of the antichrist is so extreme, those who have been hoodwinked by his religious doctrines will be shocked to learn of it. This book exposes the concealed iniquity of the antichrist and juxtaposes it against his publicly proclaimed false persona of righteousness, thus bringing into clear relief that man of sin, the son of perdition, who is truly a ravening wolf in sheep's clothing, speaking lies in hypocrisy. See Matthew 7:15 and 1 Timothy 4:1-3.

9/11-Enemies Foreign and Domestic
Edward Hendrie
ISBN-13: 978-0983262732

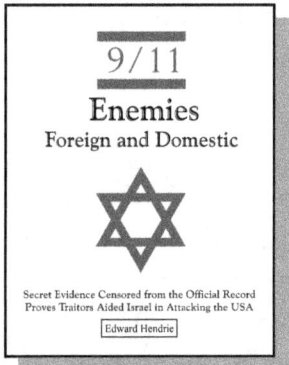

9/11-Enemies Foreign and Domestic proves beyond a reasonable doubt that the U.S. Government's conspiracy theory of the attacks on September 11, 2001, is a preposterous cover story. The evidence in 9/11-Enemies Foreign and Domestic has been suppressed from the official government reports and censored from the mass media. The evidence proves that powerful Zionists ordered the 9/11 attacks, which were perpetrated by Israel's Mossad, aided and abetted by treacherous high officials in the U.S. Government. 9/11-Enemies Foreign and Domestic identifies the traitors by name and details their subversive crimes. There is sufficient evidence in 9/11-Enemies Foreign and Domestic to indict important officials of the U.S. Government for high treason. The reader will understand how the U.S. Government really works and what Sir John Harrington (1561-1612) meant when he said: "Treason doth never prosper: what's the reason? Why if it prosper, none dare call it treason." There are millions of Americans who have taken an oath to defend the U.S. Constitution against all enemies foreign and domestic. The mass media, which is under the control of a disloyal cabal, keeps those patriotic Americans ignorant of the traitors among them. J. Edgar Hoover, former Director of the FBI, explained: "The individual is handicapped by coming face-to-face with a conspiracy so monstrous-he simply cannot believe it exists." 9/11-Enemies Foreign and Domestic erases any doubt about the existence of the monstrous conspiracy described by Hoover and arms the reader with the knowledge required to save our great nation. "My people are destroyed for lack of knowledge." Hosea 4:6.

Solving the Mystery of BABYLON THE GREAT
Edward Hendrie
ISBN-13: 978-0983262701

"Attorney and Christian researcher Edward Hendrie investigates and reveals one of the greatest exposés of all time. . . . a book you don't want to miss. Solving the Mystery of Babylon the Great is packed with documentation. Never before have the crypto-Jews who seized the reins of power in Rome been put under such intense scrutiny." Texe Marrs, Power of Prophecy. The evidence presented in this book leads to the ineluctable conclusion that the Roman Catholic Church was established by crypto-Jews as a false "Christian" front for a Judaic/Babylonian religion. That religion is the core of a world conspiracy against man and God. That is not a conspiracy theory based upon speculation, but rather the hard truth based upon authoritative evidence, which is documented in this book. Texe Marrs explains in his foreword to the book: "Who is Mystery Babylon? What is the meaning of the sinister symbols found in these passages? Which city is being described as the 'great city' so full of sin and decadence, and who are its citizens? Why do the woman and beast of Revelation seek the destruction of the holy people, the saints and martyrs of Jesus? What does it all mean for you and me today? Solving the Mystery of Babylon the Great answers these questions and more. Edward Hendrie's discoveries are not based on prejudice but on solid evidence aligned forthrightly with the 'whole counsel of God.' He does not condone nor will he be a part of any project in which Bible verses are taken out of context, or in which scriptures are twisted to mean what they do not say. Again and again you will find that Mr. Hendrie documents his assertions, backing up what he says with historical facts and proofs. Most important is that he buttresses his findings with scriptural understanding. The foundation for his research is sturdy because it is based on the bedrock of God's unshakeable Word."

The Anti-Gospel
Edward Hendrie
ISBN-13: 978-0983262749

Edward Hendrie uses God's word to strip the sheep's clothing from false Christian ministers and expose them as ravening wolves preaching an anti-gospel. The anti-gospel is based on a myth that all men have a will that is free from the bondage of sin to choose whether to believe in Jesus. The Holy Bible, however, states that all men are spiritually dead and cannot believe in Jesus unless they are born again of the Holy Spirit. Ephesians 2:1-7; John 3:3-8. God has chosen his elect to be saved by his grace through faith in Jesus Christ. Ephesians 1:3-9; 2:8-10. God imbues his elect with the faith needed to believe in Jesus. Hebrews 12:2; John 1:12-13. The devil's false gospel contradicts the word of God and reverses the order of things. Under the anti-gospel, instead of a sovereign God choosing his elect, sovereign man decides whether to choose God. The calling of the Lord Jesus Christ is effectual; all who are chosen for salvation will believe in Jesus. John 6:37-44. The anti-gospel has a false Jesus, who only offers the possibility of salvation, with no assurance. The anti-gospel blasphemously makes God out to be a liar by denying the total depravity of man and the sovereign election of God. All who preach that false gospel are under a curse from God. Galatians 1:6-9.

Murder, Rape, and Torture in a Catholic Nunnery
Edward Hendrie
ISBN-13: 978-1-943056-00-2

There has probably not been a person more maligned by the powerful forces of the Roman Catholic Church than Maria Monk. In 1836 she published the famous book, *Awful Disclosures of the Hotel Dieu Nunnery of Montreal*. In that book, she told of murder, rape, and torture behind the walls of the cloistered nunnery. Because the evidence was verifiably true, the Catholic hierarchy found it necessary to fabricate evidence and suborn perjury in an attempt to destroy the credibility of Maria Monk. The Catholic Church has kept up the character assassination of Maria Monk now for over 175 years. Even today, there can be found on the internet websites devoted to libeling Maria Monk. Edward Hendrie has examined the evidence and set it forth for the readers to decide for themselves whether Maria Monk was an impostor, as claimed by the Roman Catholic Church, or whether she was a brave victim. An objective view of the evidence leads to the ineluctable conclusion that Maria Monk told the truth about what happened behind the walls of the Hotel Dieu Nunnery of Montreal. The Roman Catholic Church, which is the most powerful religious and political organization in the world, has engaged in an unceasing campaign of vilification against Maria Monk. Their crusade against Maria Monk, however, can only affect the opinion of the uninformed. It cannot change the evidence. The evidence speaks clearly to those who will look at the case objectively. The evidence reveals that the much maligned Maria Monk was a reliable witness who made awful but accurate disclosures about life in a cloistered nunnery.

What Shall I Do to Inherit Eternal Life?
Edward Hendrie
ISBN-13: 978-0983262770

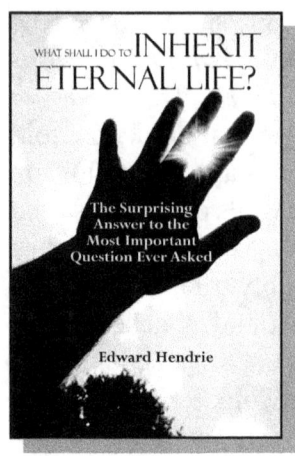

A certain ruler posed to Jesus the most important question ever asked: "Good Master, what shall I do to inherit eternal life?" (Luke 18:18) The man came to the right person. Jesus is God, and therefore his answer to that question is authoritative. This book examines Jesus' surprising answer and definitively explains how one inherits eternal life. This is a book about God's revelation to man. Except for the Holy Bible, this is the most important book you will ever read.

Rome's Responsibility for the Assassination of Abraham Lincoln, With an Appendix Containing Conversations Between Abraham Lincoln and Charles Chiniquy

Thomas M. Harris
ISBN-13: 978-0983262794

The author of this book, General Thomas Maley Harris, was a medical doctor, who recruited and served as commander of the Tenth West Virginia Volunteers during the Civil War. He rose in rank through meritorious service to become a brigadier general in the Union Army. General Harris established a reputation for faithfulness, industriousness, intelligence, and efficiency. He was noted for his leadership in preparing his troops and leading them in battle. He was brevetted a major general for "gallant conduct in the assault on Petersburg." After the Civil War, General Harris served one term as a representative in the West Virginia legislature, and was West Virginia's Adjutant General from 1869 to 1870. General Harris was a member of the Military Commission that tried and convicted the conspirators who assassinated President Abraham Lincoln. He had first hand knowledge of the sworn testimony of the witnesses in that trial. This book summarizes the salient evidence brought out during the military trial and adds information from other sources to present before the public the ineluctable conclusion that the assassination of Abraham Lincoln was the work of the Roman Catholic Church. The Roman Catholic Church has been largely successful in suppressing the circulation of this book. This book has never been given a place on bookstore shelves, as it exposed too much for the Roman Catholic hierarchy to tolerate. Any display of this book would bring an instant boycott of the bookstore. It is only now, in the age of the internet, where the marketplace of ideas has been opened wide, that this book can be found by those searching for the truth of who was behind the assassination of Abraham Lincoln.

The above books can be ordered from bookstores and from internet sites, including, but not limited to:

www.antichristconspiracy.com
www.911enemies.com
www.mysterybabylonthegreat.net
www.antigospel.com
https://play.google.com
www.barnesandnoble.com

Edward Hendrie
edwardhendrie@gmail.com